FEDERAL INTERVENTION IN AMERICAN POLICE DEPARTMENTS

For much of American history, the federal government has played a limited role in local police regulation. That all changed in 1994, when Congress passed a little-known statute that permitted the US Attorney General to reform troubled police departments. Since then, many of the nation's largest police departments – including those in Los Angeles, Washington, DC, Seattle, New Orleans, Pittsburgh, Cincinnati, Cleveland, and Albuquerque – have been subject to federal oversight. But until recently, we've known little about how this federal process works. Drawing on original interviews, court documents, statistical data, and media reports, this book provides the first comprehensive account of federal intervention in American police departments. It shows that, under the right circumstances, federal intervention is uniquely effective at combating misconduct in police departments. However, federal intervention is far from perfect. This book concludes by arguing that Congress should expand and improve federal oversight of policing.

STEPHEN RUSHIN is an assistant professor at the University of Alabama School of Law. He specializes in police regulation, criminal law, criminal procedure, and privacy law. He holds a JD and PhD from Berkeley. His research has appeared in top academic journals like the *California Law Review*, the *Cornell Law Review*, the *Duke Law Journal*, and the *Minnesota Law Review*. Numerous national media outlets have featured his research and expertise, including the *Wall Street Journal, Washington Post, Chicago Tribune, Los Angeles Times, Philadelphia Inquirer, NPR, PBS Frontline, Time Magazine, Al Jazeera America*, and *BBC America*.

FEDERAL INTERVENTION IN AMERICAN POLICE DEPARTMENTS

STEPHEN RUSHIN
University of Alabama

CAMBRIDGE
UNIVERSITY PRESS

CAMBRIDGE
UNIVERSITY PRESS

University Printing House, Cambridge CB2 8BS, United Kingdom

One Liberty Plaza, 20th Floor, New York, NY 10006, USA

477 Williamstown Road, Port Melbourne, VIC 3207, Australia

4843/24, 2nd Floor, Ansari Road, Daryaganj, Delhi – 110002, India

79 Anson Road, #06–04/06, Singapore 079906

Cambridge University Press is part of the University of Cambridge.

It furthers the University's mission by disseminating knowledge in the pursuit of education, learning, and research at the highest international levels of excellence.

www.cambridge.org
Information on this title: www.cambridge.org/9781107105737
10.1017/9781316226476

First published 2017

Printed in the United States of America by Sheridan Books, Inc.

A catalogue record for this publication is available from the British Library.

Library of Congress Cataloging-in-Publication Data
Names: Rushin, Stephen.
Title: Federal intervention in American police departments / Stephen Rushin, University of Alabama
Description: Cambridge, United Kingdom ; New York, NY, USA : Cambridge University Press, 2017. | Based on author's thesis (doctoral – University of California, Berkeley, 2015) issued under title: Structural reform litigation in American police departments. | Includes bibliographical references and index.
Identifiers: LCCN 2016054000 | ISBN 9781107105737 (hardback)
Subjects: LCSH: Police – United States. | Police misconduct – Law and legislation – United States. | Federal-city relations – United States. | Intervention (Federal government) – United States. | Civil rights – United States. | BISAC: LAW / General.
Classification: LCC KF5399 .R87 2017 | DDC 353.3/60973–dc23
LC record available at https://lccn.loc.gov/2016054000

ISBN 978-1-107-10573-7 Hardback
ISBN 978-1-107-51356-3 Paperback

CONTENTS

FIGURES

TABLES

ACKNOWLEDGMENTS

Thank you to everyone who made this book possible. I owe a debt of gratitude to all of the interview participants who spoke with me over the last several years. Special thanks to all of my friends and colleagues at the University of Alabama, University of California, Berkeley, and the University of Illinois who provided helpful comments. This book benefited from funding provided in part by all three universities. This book also benefited from helpful comments from Franklin E. Zimring, Malcolm Feeley, Calvin Morrill, Sean Farhang, Robert Lawless, Paul Heald, Arden Rowell, Suja Thomas, Pamela Foohey, Summer Kim, Samuel Walker, Kenworthy Bilz, Gabriel Chin, Andrea Roth, Melissa Wasserman, David Hyman, Catherine Albiston, Jonathan Simon, Jamelle Sharpe, Robin Fretwell Wilson, Seth Stoughton, Jason Mazzone, Andrew Leipold, Margareth Etienne, Jacqueline Ross, Eric Johnson, Rebecca Sandefur, Luke Milligan, Jenny Carroll, Pamela Pierson, and Richard Leo.

I also benefited from conversations with Rachel Harmon, Kami Chavis Simmons, and Joshua Chanin. Thank you to the schools that allowed me to present parts of this book at various colloquia, workshops, and roundtables, including the University of Alabama, the University of Illinois, University of California, Berkeley, Notre Dame University, Arizona State University, DePaul University, Indiana University, Illinois Institute of Technology, and Northern Illinois University. Some of the material in this book has previously appeared in prior law review articles: Stephen Rushin, *Federal Enforcement of Police Reform*, 82 FORDHAM L. REV. 3189 (2014), Stephen Rushin, *Structural Reform Litigation in American Police Departments*, 99 MINN. L. REV. 1343 (2015), and Stephen Rushin, *Using Data to Reduce Police Violence*, 57 B.C. L. REV. 117 (2016).

Introduction

On the afternoon of August 9, 2014, a white police officer named Darren Wilson shot an unarmed eighteen-year-old black man named Michael Brown in Ferguson, Missouri.[1] Almost immediately after the shooting, civil unrest erupted in the St. Louis suburb.[2] As darkness fell that evening, residents erected a makeshift memorial "in the middle of the street where [Michael Brown had] been sprawled in plain view for more than four hours."[3] Mr. Brown's mother was among the mourners to lay flowers in this memorial, spelling out Mr. Brown's initials in rose petals over the bloodstains on the street.[4] The community was simmering with anger and distrust. But things got worse when police officers appeared on the scene with dogs.[5] What happened next was emblematic of the strained relationship between police and the city's residents.[6] City residents watched as one of the officers on the scene allegedly allowed his dog to urinate on the memorial.[7] To the dismay of protesters, a police vehicle later drove over the memorial, smashing the flowers and candles.[8]

While these alleged acts of callous indifference angered Ferguson residents, they merely escalated tensions that had been growing in the community for several years. Most of us know the rest of this story. For several days thereafter, Ferguson resembled a war zone. Looters and rioters joined peaceful protesters. Buildings and cars burned. Ten members of the public

[1] Andrew Hart, *Ferguson, Missouri Community Furious After Male Shot Dead by Police*, Huffington Post, August 10, 2014 (describing the aftermath on August 9 and 10 after Michael Brown's shooting).

[2] Mark Follman, *Michael Brown's Mom Laid Flowers Where He Was Shot – and Police Crushed Them*, Mother Jones, August 27, 2014, *available at* www.motherjones.com/politics/2014/08/ferguson-st-louis-police-tactics-dogs-michael-brown.

[3] *Id.* [4] *Id.* [5] *Id.*

[6] *Id.* (explaining that what happened next "was emblematic of what has inflamed the city of Ferguson").

[7] *Id.*

[8] *Id.* ("soon the candles and flowers had been smashed, after police drove over them").

and six police officers suffered injuries.[9] Police made numerous arrests.[10] Within a few weeks of the Michael Brown shooting, the US Department of Justice (hereinafter "DOJ") announced that it had begun an investigation into the conduct of the Ferguson Police Department.[11] Thereafter, the DOJ spent around one hundred days in Ferguson, interviewing city leaders, participating in ride-alongs with on-duty police officers, analyzing 35,000 pages of internal records, meeting with community groups, and reviewing thousands of internal emails.[12]

The findings of this investigation were troubling, to say the least. The DOJ documented numerous examples of egregious misconduct – behavior that demonstrated a disregard for basic constitutional protections. Take the example of a thirty-two-year-old black man who was sitting in his parked car one afternoon after playing basketball in a public park[13] when a Ferguson Police Department officer demanded to see his identification[14] and subjected him to an unlawful pat down.[15] When the man objected to the officer searching his car without a warrant, the officer pulled out his gun and arrested him.[16] Prosecutors eventually charged this man with making a false declaration, for identifying himself as "Mike" rather than "Michael," and failing to wear a seatbelt in a parked car.[17] Because of these charges, the man eventually lost his job as a contractor for the federal government.[18] In another unsettling case, Ferguson police issued a routine parking ticket to a black woman in 2007 for $151.[19] When the woman failed to pay the ticket, she was charged with seven additional offenses – each new offense imposing new fines and fees.[20] From 2007 until 2014, the woman paid $550, was

9 Los Angeles Times Staff, *Ferguson Grand Jury Decision Recap: Mayhem as Police Cars, Businesses Burn*, LA Times, November 24, 2014, *available at* www.latimes.com /nation/nationnow/la-na-nn-ferguson-grand-jury-day-1-htmlstory.html.

10 More Than Fifty Arrested at Ferguson Police Station on "Moral Monday," Other Events Elsewhere, St. Louis Post-Dispatch, October 13, 2014, *available at* http://m.stltoday.com/news/local/crime-and-courts/more-than-arrested-at-ferguson-police-station-on-moral-monday/article_c1752132-9731-542e-8525-1885fae7fd10.html (describing how forty-three protesters were arrested outside the police station and more were arrested elsewhere in the city).

11 Devlin Barrett, *Justice Department to Investigate Police Force*, Wall Street Journal, September 5, 2014, *available at* www.wsj.com/articles/ferguson-police-chief-welcomes-justice-department-probe-1409849928 (stating that the DOJ opened its investigation of Ferguson on September 5, 2014 – less than a month after the Brown shooting).

12 United States Dep't of Justice, Investigation of the Ferguson Police Department, March 4, 2015, *available at*: www.justice.gov/sites/default/files/opa/press-releases/attachments/2015/03/04/ferguson_police_department_report.pdf.

13 *Id.* at 3. 14 *Id.* 15 *Id.* 16 *Id.* 17 *Id.* 18 *Id.* 19 *Id.* at 4. 20 *Id.*

arrested twice, and spent six days in jail because of this single parking offense.[21] As of the date that the DOJ released its investigative findings, the woman still owed the municipality $541.[22]

At this point, you may wonder what would motivate Ferguson officials to treat their constituents this way. Part of the problem in Ferguson was a city culture that pressured the police department to do everything in its power to generate revenue. Because of this, the DOJ found that the Ferguson Police Department viewed black residents "less as constituents to be protected than as potential offenders and sources of revenue."[23] Supervisors and leadership perpetuated this culture. These departmental leaders did little "to ensure that officers act[ed] in accordance with law and policy and rarely respond[ed] meaningfully to civilian complaints of officer misconduct."[24]

In many ways, Ferguson is a microcosm of the police misconduct problem that the United States faces today. Ferguson should have focused on protecting its constituents. Instead, it routinely violated their civil rights. And the Ferguson municipal government that should have responded to citizen complaints instead did nothing. But Ferguson is not all doom and gloom. The events in Ferguson should also give us hope. When the Ferguson Police Department abdicated its responsibility to its citizens, the federal government stepped in to protect the Constitution. Only a couple decades earlier, such a federal investigation of a local police department would have been unimaginable. For most of American history, the federal government had played a minimal role in overseeing local police departments. However, over the last twenty years American policing law has undergone a transformation. This transformation started in 1994 when Congress passed a little-known statute – 42 USC § 14141 (hereinafter "§ 14141") – that gave the US attorney general the authority to investigate and overhaul local police departments engaged in a "pattern or practice" of unconstitutional misconduct.

Ultimately, the federal investigation in Ferguson concluded that the police officers routinely "violate the Fourth Amendment in stopping people without reasonable suspicion, arresting them without probable cause, and using unreasonable force" against them.[25] Ferguson recently agreed to a negotiated settlement with the DOJ, meaning that in the coming years, the Ferguson Police Department agreed to implement significant policy and procedural changes aimed at curbing future misconduct. It won't be easy. If history is any guide, the process will take many

[21] *Id.* [22] *Id.* [23] *Id.* at 2. [24] *Id.* [25] *Id.* at 27.

years to complete and cost local taxpayers millions of dollars. But in the end, this process should provide Ferguson residents with an improved police force that no longer systemically violates civil rights.

Ferguson isn't the only city to be subject to this sort of federal intervention via § 14141. In the twenty years since Congress authorized federal interventions into local police departments, the DOJ has investigated or overhauled dozens of police departments across the country, including those in New York, Los Angeles, Chicago, Washington, DC, Seattle, Albuquerque, Baltimore, New Orleans, Pittsburgh, Cincinnati, Newark, Cleveland, Miami, Portland, and, of course, Ferguson.[26] These federal interventions represent the new frontier in American police regulation. In recent decades, the federal government has slowly reshaped the field of American policing law using this regulatory tool. Thus far, though, little research has examined how this sort of federal intervention works. This book fills that gap in the available literature. It provides a comprehensive analysis of federal interventions in American police departments. It delves into the history of American police regulation and the emergence of § 14141 as a tool for unprecedented federal intervention into local police departments. It explores the benefits and limitations of federal intervention as a regulatory tool.

Ultimately, though, this book takes a normative position. It argues that § 14141 represents a first step in addressing the problem of police misconduct in the United States. In order to address the structural, organizational, and political causes of police misconduct, this book argues that the Congress should further expand federal oversight of local police departments.

I Defining the Problem of Police Misconduct

Before delving into the book, it may be useful to present some basic facts about policing in the United States. First, policing in the United States is highly decentralized, both in literal terms and in terms of regulation. Literally, the term "police" describes a field of roughly 18,000 separate law enforcement agencies employing around 700,000 sworn officers who

[26] *See* Stephen Rushin, *Federal Enforcement of Police Reform*, 82 Fordham L. Rev. 3189, 3244–3247 (showing all investigations and settlements under § 14141 between 1994 and 2013); *see also* Kimbriell Kelly, Sarah Childress, & Steven Rich, *Forced Reform, Mixed Results*, Wash. Post, November 13, 2015, *available at* www.washingtonpost.com/sf/investigative/2015/11/13/forced-reforms-mixed-results (listing additional settlements that have happened from 2013 until present).

serve predominantly at the local level.[27] We are not a nation of one police force. We are a nation of thousands of decentralized police departments. From a regulatory perspective, there is no single governmental body that truly oversees or regulates American police. Traditionally, local departments have been generally free to develop their own policing strategies and priorities, without significant state or federal government regulation. This is not to say that local police departments are without oversight. In most cases, local police departments are directly accountable to local political leaders, like a mayor, city council, or city manager. So when critics allege that the United States suffers from a police misconduct problem, this is a significant claim. It suggests that misconduct is present in a substantial number of the local police departments in the United States. It also suggests that local political leaders have been unwilling or unable to prevent this misconduct.

This realization is even more powerful when you understand a second basic fact about police misconduct. Law enforcement leaders and academics generally understand what kinds of policies and procedures can effectively combat misconduct. Over the last several decades, police departments have teamed up with social scientists to verify the effectiveness of numerous misconduct prevention tools. These studies have produced reputable findings about the prevention of police misconduct. For example, experts know that mechanisms like body cameras, dash cameras, and early intervention systems can reduce the occurrence of police misconduct. This is not to say that we have identified the "secret recipe" for ending police misconduct as we know it. Police departments, like any organization, will always have some misconduct. In the future, policing experts will discover new tactics that may further reduce misconduct. However, law enforcement experts today have identified a package of widely accepted policies and procedures that can demonstrably reduce the likelihood of misconduct in police departments. Professional organizations like the International Association of Chiefs of Police (IACP), the Commission on Law Enforcement Accreditation (CALEA), and the Police Assessment Resource Center (PARC) have attempted to expand the knowledge of these ideal policies and procedures. The failure by some police departments to combat police misconduct is not necessarily due to a lack of available information, but rather a lack of commitment. This leads to an

[27] Brian A. Reaves, U.S. Dep't of Justice, Census of State and Local Law Enforcement Agencies 2 (2011), *available at* www.bjs.gov/content/pub/pdf/csllea08.pdf (putting the number of state and local law enforcement agencies at 17,985).

obvious question. If many in the law enforcement community know how to reduce misconduct in local police departments, why haven't all police departments simply adopted these measures?

The answer leads us to the third basic fact about police misconduct. It is often expensive and unpopular for local political leaders to invest in oversight designed to reduce police misconduct. Many fail to consider the real cost of addressing police misconduct. This book discusses many major police departments that have undergone sustained, federally mandated reform efforts aimed at curbing wrongdoing. In each case, the cost of these efforts was substantial – often totaling in the tens or hundreds of millions of dollars over several years.[28] In most departments, correcting a pattern of police misconduct is not as simple as changing an internal policy. It requires oversight. It requires additional manpower. It requires technological tools. This leads to an uncomfortable realization. Fighting police misconduct is expensive. Municipal budgets, on the other hand, are finite. Communities undergoing significant police reforms have to make tough choices. In some cases, communities have been forced to raise taxes to pay for the cost of police reform.[29] In other cases, communities have had to reallocate scarce municipal resources that could have otherwise gone to fund schools, roads, or parks.

The strength of police unions and civil service protections also complicate the implementation of police reform efforts. The majority of American law enforcement officers are part of unions. Many of those who are not part of a union are organized into associations that wield considerable political influence. Time and time again, police unions and associations have pushed back against efforts to improve the oversight of local police departments. These groups commonly contend that efforts to

[28] Rich Exner, *How Much Cleveland Will Pay to Reform Its Police Department Under Consent Decree*, Cleveland Plain Dealer, June 2, 2015, *available at* www.cleveland.com/datacentral/index.ssf/2015/06/how_much_it_will_cost_clevelan.html (estimating that the consent decree should cost at least $30 million and that the New Orleans decree should cost around $55 million); *see also* Kelly, Childress, & Rich *supra* note 26 (describing how the Los Angeles consent decree cost anywhere between $100 and $300 million depending on whom you ask).

[29] New Orleans is an example of this phenomenon. Richard Rainey, *Mitch Landrieu Requests a Doubling of Tax Rates for New Orleans Police and Fire*, Times-Picayune, May 1, 2014, *available at* www.nola.com/politics/index.ssf/2014/05/mitch_landrieus_tax_hike_plan.html; Tyler Bridges, *Legislature Approves Property Tax Hike for New Orleans Police and Fire; Now Heads to Voters*, Lens, May 29, 2014, *available at* http://thelensnola.org/2014/05/29/legislature-approves-property-tax-hike-for-new-orleans-police-now-heads-to-voters.

limit discretion or improve oversight will reduce officer aggressiveness, thereby increasing crime.

Once more, a fourth basic fact about police misconduct makes the situation even more challenging for reform advocates. Police misconduct disproportionately affects politically marginalized minorities. The fact that minority groups sometimes lack the same political power as the majority makes it difficult for minorities to combat police misconduct through the democratic system. The minority groups most disadvantaged by police wrongdoing are often unable to achieve reform through the democratic process. It has become common knowledge today that blacks and Latinos make up a disproportionate number of individuals killed by law enforcement every year.[30] Evidence from some major cities suggests that blacks and Latinos are also overrepresented in unjustified stops, searches, and seizures.[31] Additionally, police misconduct disproportionately affects another, very different kind of minority group – criminals and criminal suspects. Police predictably use their discretionary power against people they suspect of criminal activity. Criminals and criminal suspects are among the most politically marginalized minority groups in the United States. In some states, felons are ineligible to vote while serving their sentences.[32] Others permanently

[30] Oliver Laughland, Jon Swaine, & Jamiles Lartey, *US Police Killings Headed for 1,100 This Year, With Black Americans Twice as Likely to Die*, THE GUARDIAN, July 1, 2015, *available at* www.theguardian.com/us-news/2015/jul/01/us-police-killings-this-year-black-americans (describing the overrepresentation of black individuals in police killings in the United States); Nicole Santa Cruz, Ruben Vives, & Marisa Gerber, *Why the Deaths of Latinos at the Hands of Police Haven't Drawn as Much Attention*, LA TIMES, July 18, 2015, *available at* www.latimes.com/local/crime/la-me-0718-latino-police-20150718-story.html (describing how in Los Angeles County in 2015, Latinos made up over half of all deaths caused by law enforcement at the time of the story and also explaining how black victims made up a disproportionate number of those killed by law enforcement in Los Angeles County).

[31] *See, e.g.*, Joseph Goldstein, *Judge Rejects New York's Stop-and-Frisk Policy*, NY TIMES, August 12, 2013, at A1 (describing how black and Latino young men made up a disproportionate number of the individuals stopped and frisked by the NYPD in recent years).

[32] According to the National Conference of State Legislatures, states vary tremendously on the voting rights of felons. Only two states allow felons to vote while incarcerated – Maine and Vermont. All others at least temporarily limit voting rights while behind bars. Another thirty-eight states and the District of Columbia allow felons to automatically gain most voting rights after they complete their sentences. In some states, ex-felons must wait a period of time before having their voting rights restored. And in other states, ex-felons must apply to have their voting rights restored. *See Felon Voting Rights*, NATIONAL CONFERENCE OF STATES LEGISLATURES, *available at* www.ncsl.org/research/elections-and-campaigns/felon-voting-rights.aspx.

disenfranchise convicted felons.[33] Given all of these conditions, locally elected political leaders have often been unwilling or unable to address police misconduct.

This is not to say that locally supported, bottom-up police reform is impossible. Several recent, high profile incidents of alleged law enforcement misconduct have sparked a national conversation about policing. In the wake of riots in Ferguson in 2014, the Black Lives Matter movement has galvanized renewed support for greater oversight of local police departments. Politicians, academics, and community advocates have also chimed in on how we can better address police misconduct. But much of this ongoing national conversation tends to miss the mark. At its core, the fight against police misconduct boils down to a single difficult question. How do we get thousands of local police departments to adopt costly and sometimes politically unpopular reforms aimed at preventing misconduct that primarily affects a politically marginalized minority of the population?

II The Need for Improved Federal Oversight of Local Police Departments

This book argues that in order to fight police misconduct effectively, we as a country must improve federal oversight of local police departments. To do this, we must increase the power of the federal government to document and respond to misconduct in local police departments. This sort of expanded federal oversight of local police departments would require an act of Congress. Such an act of Congress is sure to be contentious. Given the current dysfunction in Washington, such an act of Congress may even seem impossible. Feasibility aside, the goal of this book is to imagine the most effective and constitutionally permissible response to local police wrongdoing.

Some may claim that federal oversight of local police departments constitutes an unprecedented expansion of federal power. In reality, though, this book's proposal would represent a continuation of a nearly century-long trend of the federal government gradually expanding local police oversight. Through the first 150 years of our nation's history – an era this book describes as the Hands-Off Era – the federal government left police regulation entirely to the states and municipalities. That changed

[33] *Id.* (stating that in Virginia, Florida, and Iowa, felons permanently lose their voting rights).

in the mid-twentieth century when the federal government came to recognize that local police misconduct was prevalent throughout the nation. In the decades thereafter, the federal government gradually pushed back against this perceived national epidemic of police misconduct by installing mechanisms that increased the cost of local police wrongdoing. During this Buildup Era the federal government did not force localities to fight police misconduct. Instead, the federal government carved out mechanisms for victims of police misconduct to punish misbehaving police departments through lawsuits or evidentiary exclusion.

During the late twentieth century, though, Congress came to realize that its Buildup Era responses were inadequate. When Congress passed § 14141, it gave the federal government the authority to intervene into problematic local police departments. This marked the beginning of the Intervention Era in local police regulation. This book focuses primarily on the history of the Intervention Era in American policing. While this interventionary power has brought about meaningful reform in a handful of targeted agencies, it too has proven ineffective at stimulating widespread reform across the thousands of American police departments, in part because of resource and informational constraints. Thus, today we are a nation at a crossroads. We must decide whether we are going to fully embrace the federal government as a legitimate and necessary overseer of local police conduct. This book argues that the best way to reduce local police misconduct is for Congress to expand federal oversight of local police departments.

A *The Hands-Off and Buildup Eras*

For most of American history, we have conceptualized policing as an entirely local institution. The responsibility of regulating police misconduct during this Hands-Off Era fell almost entirely on the states and localities. Federal regulators did not come to view police misconduct as a pervasive national epidemic until the early twentieth century. Many point to the release of the *Report on Lawlessness in Law Enforcement* by the National Commission on Law Observance and Enforcement (NCLOE) in 1931 as the first major recognition of police misconduct as a pervasive national epidemic.[34] President Herbert Hoover had appointed the NCLOE

[34] Samuel Walker, *Records of the Committee on Official Lawlessness*, in RECORDS OF THE WICKERSHAM COMMISSION ON LAW OBSERVANCE AND ENFORCEMENT, at v–vi (1997),

to investigate the administration of justice in the United States.[35] George W. Wickersham, who had previously served as the US attorney general under President Howard Taft, chaired the commission.[36] Other members of the commission included Harvard Law School dean Roscoe Pound and several other prominent reform advocates.[37] Ultimately, the reports that followed by the NCLOE came to be known as the Wickersham Commission Reports.

The Wickersham Commission produced fourteen separate reports on a range of topics including prohibition, prisons, probation, juvenile justice, prosecution, and the causes of crime. Most of these reports had little immediate impact on national policy, with one notable exception: the *Report on Lawlessness in Law Enforcement*.[38] This report vividly described the use of abusive interrogation tactics known as the "third degree – that is, the use of physical brutality, or other forms of cruelty to obtain involuntary confessions or admissions" by law enforcement agencies across the country.[39] The report described how police across the country commonly resorted to physical violence, intimidation, and isolation to get suspects to confess to criminal acts.[40] In total, the report showed the presence of this interrogation tactic in fifteen different cities spread out geographically across the country. Although police leaders across the country denounced the *Report on Lawlessness in Law Enforcement*, the issue of local police misconduct was now part of the national conversation. It would be years, though, before the federal government intervened in any significant way into local police affairs.

In the years since the Wickersham Commission, the federal government has gradually expanded oversight of local police departments. It has done so by purposefully trying to raise the cost of police misconduct. In some cases, the federal government increased the financial cost of police misconduct by allowing individuals to file civil suits to collect monetary damages in the event of wrongdoing. Not every cost-raising mechanism was financial. Federal courts also made police misconduct expensive by refusing to consider at trial evidence obtained by police in violation of the Constitution. According to this logic, if police misconduct is sufficiently expensive – either in monetary terms or otherwise – then rational municipalities should take steps to limit this cost by implementing police reform measures. Thus began

available at www.lexisnexis.com/documents/academic/upa_cis/1965_wickersham commpt1.pdf.

[35] *Id.* at v. [36] *Id.* [37] *Id.* [38] *Id.* at vii. [39] *Id.* at ix. [40] *Id.*

the Buildup Era. There are two primary examples of how the federal government increased the cost of police misconduct during this Buildup Era.

First, federal courts increased the cost of misconduct by developing the exclusionary rule. The first major step in this direction happened in the US Supreme Court case of *Mapp* v. *Ohio*. Years before *Mapp*, the Court had attempted to remove the incentive for law enforcement officers to engage in misconduct by excluding from criminal court any evidence obtained by officers in violation of the Constitution.[41] But this earlier decision applied only to police officers employed by the federal government. It did not apply to the vast majority of police officers who worked at the local and state levels. These local police officers were still free to violate the Constitution during their investigations with relative impunity. In *Mapp*, the Court finally changed this.[42] The *Mapp* decision extended this so-called exclusionary rule to cover the behavior of local police officers.[43] Today, because of the *Mapp* decision and its progeny, police officers have a somewhat reduced incentive to engage in misconduct.

After *Mapp*, the exclusionary rule became the primary weapon for fighting local police misconduct. In the decades that followed, the Court turned to the exclusionary rule to discourage a range of police behaviors. Most famously, in the *Miranda* v. *Arizona* decision from 1966, the Supreme Court held that police must read criminal suspects a list of prophylactic warnings before initiating an interrogation.[44] The Supreme Court used the exclusionary rule established in *Mapp* as the enforcement mechanism for this new *Miranda* protocol. If a police officer failed to read a criminal suspect his or her *Miranda* rights, any incriminating statement obtained in that interrogation is generally deemed inadmissible in court. The Court has also used the exclusionary rule to enforce a number of other limitations on police behavior,

[41] *Weeks* v. *United States*, 232 US 383 (1914).

[42] *See generally Mapp* v. *Ohio*, 367 US 643 (1961) (mandating the exclusion of evidence obtained in violation of the Fourth Amendment by a state law enforcement officer).

[43] *Id.* at 655–661.

[44] The justices in the *Miranda* decision cited the Wickersham Commission Report multiple times in explaining the long, documented history of police brutality and misconduct during interrogations. *Miranda* v. *Arizona*, 384 US 436, 445 n.5, 447–448 (1966) (citing the Wickersham Commission Report as part of the evidence for abusive interrogation styles used at the time).

including limitations on searches of cars,[45] searches of homes,[46] and stops-and-frisks.[47]

Second, Congress and federal courts carved out avenues for civilians to file federal civil rights lawsuits against local police officers and police departments during the Buildup Era. During the same year as the *Mapp* decision, the Court also handed down another pivotal decision that would allow for additional federal oversight of local police departments. In *Monroe* v. *Pape*, the Court concluded that individuals who were victimized by police misconduct could file suits against police officers under the Civil Rights Act of 1871 (now codified as 42 USC § 1983).[48] Congress originally wrote the Civil Rights Act of 1871, otherwise known as the Ku Klux Klan Act, to give newly freed slaves a legal remedy against state government officials who deprived them of their constitutional rights. But the language of the act was broad. It established that "any citizen of the United States or other person within the jurisdiction thereof" has a right of action in federal court against any state actor that deprives them of "any rights, privileges, or immunities secured by the Constitution and the laws."[49]

Despite the sweeping language of this act, courts generally prevented its use as a legal basis to sue police officers for the first ninety years of its existence. That changed in *Monroe*. There, the Supreme Court finally concluded that this broad language allowed civilians to file federal lawsuits against police officers who violated their constitutional rights.[50] Nearly two decades later in *Monell* v. *Department of Social Services of the City of New York*, the Court further expanded federal oversight of local police departments. In that case, the Court held that civilians could use § 1983 to sue both individual police officers *and* their employers, in certain limited

[45] *See, e.g., Arizona* v. *Gant*, 556 US 332 (2009) (limiting the ability of a police officer to search a vehicle incident to an arrest and using the exclusionary rule as a mechanism to enforce this new judicial mandate).

[46] *See, e.g., Kyllo* v. *United States*, 533 US 27 (2001) (limiting the ability of police officers to use heat sensors to gain an extrasensory look into a person's house and enforcing this new judicial mandate through the exclusionary rule).

[47] *See, e.g., Terry* v. *Ohio*, 392 US 1 (1968) (providing police with a limited ability to execute stops-and-frisks, but providing that failure to abide by the limitations of the court's ruling in this case would lead to evidentiary exclusion).

[48] 365 US 367 (1961). [49] 42 USC § 1983 (2000).

[50] At first glance, this power to file federal lawsuits against local police officers seems as if it would significantly deter wrongdoing. But a legal doctrine known as "qualified immunity" prevents individuals from winning such a suit against a police officer unless they can show that the police officer's conduct violated "clearly established law." For more on this legal doctrine, see the detailed discussion of qualified immunity in Chapter 2.

situations.[51] In *Monroe* and *Monell* the federal government armed civilians with two new, valuable litigation options to hold police accountable for wrongdoing.

In addition to evidentiary exclusion and civil liability, the federal government has also taken on a greater role in overseeing local police misconduct by prosecuting the most egregious instances of police misconduct under 18 USC § 242. In sum, by the late 1990s the federal government was positioned to engage in some sort of meaningful oversight of local police behavior. No doubt, this type of federal intervention into local police behavior motivated some police departments to take steps towards professionalization. But despite the increased cost of police misconduct, many problematic police departments still seemed unwilling or unable to address these problems on their own.

So, in 1994, in response to the release of the George Holliday video showing Los Angeles Police Department (LAPD) officers beating Rodney King on a Southern California highway, Congress took the most significant step to date in expanding federal oversight of local police departments. This began the next era in the federal regulation of local police conduct: the Intervention Era.

B The Intervention Era

Most of us know the story of the Rodney King beating. In March 1991, two police squad cars pursued a suspected drunk driver speeding on a Los Angeles highway.[52] At first, the incident seemed routine – the kind of

[51] *See Monell* v. *Dep't of Soc. Servs.*, 436 US 658, 694–701 (1978) (holding that a claimant under § 1983 could recover from a police department based on the actions of an officer if the department was deliberately indifferent in failing to train or supervise the officer).

[52] The pursuit started around 12:30 AM when California Highway Patrol (CHP) officers first observed King's Hyundai speeding in the northeastern San Fernando Valley in Los Angeles. Seth Mydans, *Seven Minutes in Los Angeles – A Special Report: Videotaped Beating by Officers Puts Full Glare on Brutality Issue*, NY Times, March 18, 1991, *available at* www.nytimes.com/1991/03/18/us/seven-minutes-los-angeles-special-report-videotaped-beating-officers-puts-full.html. When the CHP officers put on their emergency lights and sirens, King slowed but did not stop. Indep. Comm'n on the L.A. Police Dep't, Report of the Independent Commission on the Los Angeles Police Department 4 (1991) [hereinafter Christopher Commission Report]. An LAPD squad car – assigned to Officers Laurence Powell and Timothy Ward – then joined the pursuit. *Id.*

incident that police handle on a regular basis.[53] Only minutes later, a video taken by a nearby onlooker showed three LAPD officers brutally beating one of the car's occupants – a man named Rodney King – while another eleven officers stood by watching.[54] The images shocked and disgusted the nation.[55] This is the story that most of us know.

What many people don't know is how the Rodney King incident radically transformed the regulation of police misconduct in the United States. Within weeks of this event, the US House Subcommittee on Civil and Constitutional Rights convened a hearing to examine how the federal government could combat local police wrongdoing.[56] "[T]here is no excuse for the type of behavior recorded on video tape in Los Angeles," declared Representative Don Edwards, chairman of the subcommittee.[57] "We want to know how widespread is police misconduct in Los Angeles and nationwide. We want to know how effective the Federal Government's response has been ... [and] [w]e want to look at ... whether [federal laws] need to be strengthened."[58]

[53] At around 12:50 AM, Powell and Ward radioed in a "Code 6," which signifies that a chase had come to a close. Christopher Commission Report, *supra* note 52, at 4. The LAPD radio transmission operator then broadcast a "Code 4," a notification to all officers that no additional assistance is needed at the scene of the pursuit. *Id.* at 5. Despite these transmissions, 11 additional LAPD units with 21 officers and a helicopter appeared at the scene; at least 12 of the officers arrived after the radio transmission operator had sent out the Code 4 broadcast. *Id.* The Christopher Commission also found that "a number of these officers had no convincing explanation for why they went to the scene after the Code 4 broadcast." *Id.*

[54] Amateur camera work by George Holliday caught a glimpse of the LAPD ruthlessly kicking and striking King "with 56 baton strokes." *Id.* at 3. King required 20 stitches and suffered a broken cheekbone and right ankle. Within days, video of the beating made headlines across the country, sparking public protests and outcry. *An Aberration or Police Business as Usual?* NY Times, March 10, 1994, at 47. Chief Gates called the incident as "an aberration." David Parrish, *Police "Street Justice" Called Normal Conduct*, Daily News, March 10, 1991, at N1. In the aftermath of these events, the City of Los Angeles formed an independent commission to formally investigate the conditions that precipitated the Rodney King incident, headed by Warren Christopher. *See generally* Christopher Commission Report, *supra* note 52. The Christopher Commission Report found a wide range of systematic problems affecting the LAPD including problems with use of force, complaint procedures, training policies, and structural organization. *See generally id.*

[55] President George H. W. Bush called the events "shocking" and ordered an investigation by the Department of Justice. *See* Seth Mydans, *Videotaped Beating by Officers Puts Full Glare on Brutality Issue*, NY Times, March 18, 1991, at A1.

[56] *Police Brutality: Hearing Before the H. Subcomm. on Civil and Const. Rights of the Comm. on the Judiciary*, 102d Cong. 172 (1991).

[57] *Id.* at 1. [58] *Id.*

The subcommittee attempted to do just that. The Rodney King incident was a wakeup call for federal policymakers. For one thing, the event illustrated the organizational causes of local police misconduct. Subsequent investigations by both Congress and local officials in Los Angeles concluded that the Rodney King beating was not the result of a few rogue officers. It was indicative of a diseased organizational culture within the LAPD that condoned violence, tolerated racism, and failed to respond to misconduct.[59] The Rodney King incident was no aberration. It was part of a pattern and practice of misconduct that had afflicted the LAPD for years.[60] This was no surprise to policing scholars. In the years leading up to the Rodney King incident, there was a growing recognition that police misconduct often stemmed from a lack of adequate organizational oversight. Calls for reform, though, had been largely ignored until that fateful evening in March 1991.

The Rodney King incident also painfully demonstrated how the existing federal law had failed to reign in local police misconduct. Admittedly,

[59] Christopher Commission Report, *supra* note 52, at ix–x (explaining that after the city of Los Angeles investigated the use of force post-Rodney King incident, investigators discovered that in the years leading up to the King beating "183 officers had four or more allegations [of excessive force], 44 had six or more, 16 had eight or more, and one had 16 such allegations").

[60] Subsequent investigations into these incidents uncovered an organizational culture that permitted gross misconduct, patterns of excessive use of force, a failure by the LAPD to properly discipline officers, an inability to properly process citizen complaints, and a failure to adopt an early warning system to identify problematic police officers. In the investigation after the Rodney King incident, the Christopher Commission found that, among the officers who were subject to the most allegations of excessive use of force, "the performance evaluation reports for [these problematic officers] were very positive" as they "document[ed] every complimentary comment received and express[ed] optimism about the officer's progress in the Department." *Id.* at x. After the Rodney King incident, the Christopher Commission found that the LAPD's internal procedures for handling citizen complaints frequently led to public frustration. Out of 2,152 citizen allegations of excessive force, the LAPD sustained only 42. Once more, the commission determined that internal policies and procedures used by the Internal Affairs Division make it hard for citizens to file complaints. *Id.* at xix. Years later, investigators found that many of the basic problems remained. Merrick J. Bobb, Mark H. Epstein, Nicolas H. Miller, and Manuel A. Abascal, Five Years Later: A Report to the Los Angeles Police Commission on the Los Police Department's Implementation of Independent Commission Recommendations 34 (May 1996) (hereinafter Five Years Later Report on LAPD), *available at* www.parc.info/client_files/Special%20Reports/2%20-%20Five%20Years%20Later%20-%20Christopher%20Commission.pdf.

important Supreme Court decisions like *Mapp, Miranda, Monroe*, and *Monell* had gradually increased the available remedies in cases of police wrongdoing. And statutes like § 1983 and § 242 provided additional avenues for redress. Despite this progress, the federal government continued to play a limited role in regulating local police misconduct. As one high-ranking DOJ official testified during the Rodney King hearings, the federal government is "not the front line," but instead "more of a backstop" in combating police misconduct.[61]

After the Rodney King hearings, Congress passed the Violent Crime Control and Law Enforcement Act (VCCLEA) of 1994. Most people know the VCCLEA as the bill that attempted to reduce crime by ratcheting up sentences for criminal offenders. But hidden inside this largely punitive measure was a little-known statute – § 14141 – that has turned out to be a monumentally important shift in the federal regulation of local policing. In the event that a police department like the LAPD is engaged in "pattern or practice" of unconstitutional misconduct, § 14141 gives the US attorney general the authority to seek a federal court order forcing that police department to make policy changes aimed at deterring future misconduct.[62] Essentially, § 14141 gives the federal government the power to force reform in local police departments.

This was a transformative moment in policing and civil rights history. Three short years after the DOJ described itself as a mere "backstop" in combating police misconduct, Congress pushed the federal government onto the front lines. Because of § 14141, the DOJ found itself with a new and expansive authority to force reform in problematic local police departments. The impact of § 14141 has been significant. Over the last twenty years, the DOJ has used § 14141 to overhaul police departments in many of the nation's largest cities. In each of the documented cases, policing has measurably improved after the initiation of federal oversight.

This underscores the most valuable feature of § 14141: the federal government's ability to intervene into problematic police departments

61 *Police Brutality: Hearing Before the H. Subcomm. on Civil and Const. Rights of the Comm. on the Judiciary*, 102d Cong. 3 (1991) (statement of John R. Dunne, Assistant Attorney General, Civil Rights Division).

62 42 USC § 14141 (1994). Congress passed this statute as part of the VCCLEA of 1994. Pub. L. No. 103–322, 108 Stat. 1796. The statute makes it unlawful for a police agency to engage in a pattern or practice of unconstitutional misconduct, § 14141(a), and gives the attorney general the authority to seek injunctive or equitable relief to force police agencies to implement reforms aimed at curbing misconduct, § 14141(b).

and take action. During the Buildup Era, the federal government gradually expanded its oversight of local police departments through the invention of the exclusionary rule, the expansion of avenues for litigation against police departments, and increasing numbers of criminal prosecutions. While these Buildup Era reforms were significant, they often failed to stimulate widespread reform in local police departments. All of the regulatory developments in the Buildup Era were minimally invasive. Although each mechanism raised the cost of police misconduct, none of these mechanisms forced local police departments to make any changes aimed at proactively deterring future wrongdoing. Section 14141 represented the first major step in a new era of police regulation. For the first time, Congress gave the federal government the power to intervene into problematic local police departments and *force* them to implement proactive reforms aimed to curbing future misconduct. This signified the beginning of the Intervention Era in local police regulation.

Nevertheless, the Intervention Era has not yet solved the nation's police misconduct epidemic. Reactive intervention alone has not proven to be sufficient to bring about the kind of reform that many advocates desire. The underwhelming results of the Intervention Era can be traced back to a few remaining problems. For one thing, the federal government has only responded to local police misconduct during the Intervention Era via piecemeal litigation after it successfully identifies a problematic police department. By itself, this is not problematic. If the federal government had both ample data to identify problematic police departments and the financial resources to enforce § 14141 aggressively, then this sort of enforcement mechanism could work. Under these ideal conditions, police departments across the country would be effectively put on notice – if you fail to control your police officers, the DOJ will intervene quickly and forcefully.

Unfortunately, none of these optimal enforcement conditions exist. The federal government lacks virtually any data on local police behavior. In fact, national recordkeeping on local police conduct is so abysmal that, as FBI director James Comey has bluntly put it, "I can't tell you how many people were shot by the police last week, last month, [or] last year."[63] The federal government also lacks the necessary resources to intervene into many problematic police departments. Between 1994 and 2013, the

[63] Michael S. Schmidt, *F.B.I. Director Speaks Out on Race and Police Bias*, NY Times, February 12, 2015, at A1.

DOJ only investigated around three police agencies and intervened into around one police agency each year.[64]

Two potential problems emerge from this lack of data and lack of resources. First, the average police chief has little motivation to make proactive reforms aimed at curbing future wrongdoing. Between 1994 and 2013, the federal government investigated only 0.017 percent of police departments annually.[65] And the federal government intervened in only 0.006 percent of police departments annually.[66] Given these lottery-like odds, a rational police chief has little motivation to change his behavior because of the unlikely threat of federal intervention. Second, because of the lack of national data on police behavior, federal intervention has often appeared haphazard or procedurally unjust. As one city leader in Steubenville, Ohio, commented after his selection for federal intervention via § 14141, "You see all these problems that have come up at the police departments in Los Angeles and New York and New Orleans, and you've got to wonder, why us?"[67] This sort of skepticism is understandable, as the federal government has yet to develop a clear and transparent methodology for identifying which police departments are in need of federal reform.

Compounding these problems, the federal government has not developed a mechanism to ensure the sustainability of reforms brought about via federal intervention. The period of federal intervention into local police departments can be lengthy, sometimes lasting as long as a decade or more.[68] Further, once that process concludes, the federal government

[64] *See infra* Chapter 3 (describing the number of investigations conducted by the DOJ each year during this time period, based on data collected directly from the DOJ).

[65] Assuming the DOJ investigates around three agencies per year during this period and there are 18,000 police departments, as described *supra* note 26, then that would mean that the DOJ typically investigated 3/18,000 police departments on an annual basis, or 0.017 percent.

[66] Assuming the DOJ brings a § 14141 action against an average of one agency per year during this time period, and there are 18,000 police departments as described *supra* note 26, then that would mean the DOJ typically brought actions against 1/18,000 police departments on an annual basis, or 0.006 percent.

[67] Eric Lichtblau, *U.S. Low Profile in Big-City Police Probes Is Under Fire; Law: Critics Say Justice Dep't Boldly Pursues Misconduct Cases in Smaller Towns but Goes Slower on Larger Inquiries*, LA Times, March 17, 2000, at A1 (quoting Gary Dufour, former city manager of Steubenville, Ohio).

[68] Stephen Rushin, *Structural Reform Litigation in American Police Departments*, 99 Minn. L. Rev. 1343, 1392 (showing in figure 5 the length of selected cases involving federal intervention via § 14141, with each taking between five and twelve years to complete).

must ultimately leave. The available evidence suggests that some cities may revert back to problematic practices after federal regulators leave town. For example, some have accused departments like the Pittsburgh Bureau of Police of sliding back into patterns of unconstitutional misconduct after federal overseers left the city.[69] Without any formal mechanism in place, the sustainability of reforms after federal intervention remains uncertain.

C *The Path Forward: Expanded Oversight of Local Police*

So where do we go from here? The Intervention Era has given us a glimpse of how federal regulation can improve American policing. Nevertheless, the Intervention Era has failed to bring about widespread reform. This book argues that the limitations of the Intervention Era do not represent fundamental problems with federal oversight. They represent commitment problems. We as a country have not yet bought into the idea of the federal government as a legitimate regulator of local police conduct. In passing § 14141, Congress gave the federal government expansive legal authority to intervene into local police departments. However, it failed to give the federal government the tools needed to use this expansive legal authority. You might say that in passing § 14141, Congress gave the DOJ a powerful weapon without adequate ammunition. This book argues that the federal government must finish the job. Congress must provide the federal government with the necessary resources to regulate local police misconduct effectively.

This book proposes a threefold package of reforms to improve federal oversight of local police departments. First, the federal government should collect better data on local police behavior. We currently have federal statistics how many civilians die at the hands of law enforcement every year in the United States. We have no data on the number of officer-involved shootings each year. We do not keep track of the number of injuries caused by police annually. Nor do we keep any national

[69] Laura Maggi, *Pittsburgh Bureau of Police Was First in Nation With Official Federal Intervention*, TIMES-PICAYUNE, October 16, 2011, *available at* www.nola.com/crime/index.ssf/2011/10/pittsburgh_bureau_of_police_wa.html (describing the Pittsburgh experience with federal intervention); Jeffrey Benzing, *Pittsburgh Police Could Face Second Federal Consent Decree, Peduto Says*, PUBLICSOURCE, July 1, 2014, *available at* http://publicsource.org/from-the-source/pittsburgh-police-could-face-second-federal-consent-decree-peduto-says (describing how Pittsburgh may have fallen back into a pattern or practice of misconduct).

statistics on citizen complaints against local police officers. Congress did recently pass the Deaths in Custody Reporting Act, which will require local police departments to report the number of individuals killed in police custody each year.[70] Similar laws handed down by Congress, though, have previously gone unenforced.[71] Requiring police departments to report more data on officer behavior to the federal government is both feasible and cost-effective. The federal government already requires local police departments to report data on the number of crimes that occur in each jurisdiction.[72] Congress could easily require local police departments to report additional data on anything from the number of officer-involved shootings, to the number of civilian complaints, to the number of civil rights lawsuits. This list is by no means exhaustive. The federal government already has a useful enforcement mechanism to ensure that localities meet such reporting requirements. The bottom line is that these additional reporting requirements would not be financially burdensome for local police departments and would shed important light on the behavior of local police departments. This book considers several ways the DOJ could harness these additional databases to incentivize reform in local police departments.

Second, it is time for the federal government to move from reactive to proactive regulation of local police departments. One way to accomplish this would be for the federal government to tie federal funding to local police departments to the enactment of reforms aimed at curbing police misconduct. The federal government currently provides upwards of $500 million in grant money to local and state police departments every year. But the overwhelming majority of these grants go to the promotion of public safety, the encouragement of agency coordination, and the purchase of new policing equipment. The federal government

[70] Death in Custody Reporting Act, Pub. L. No. 113–242 (codified as 42 USC § 13727 (2015)).

[71] Technically, this law is simply a reauthorization of an earlier measure passed in 2000. It took several years for law enforcement agencies to report data via the original version of this law. And the original version expired shortly thereafter in 2006. As a result, the DOJ did not release any comprehensive statistics from the first attempt at this sort of database. Allie Gross, *Congress Is Finally Going to Make Local Law Enforcement Report How Many People They Kill*, Mother Jones, December 17, 2014, *available at* www.motherjones.com/politics/2014/12/death-custody-reporting-act-police-shootings-ferguson-garner.

[72] U.S. Dep't of Justice, Bureau of Justice Statistics, Uniform Crime Reports (UCR): Crime in the United States (2000–2012), Law Enforcement Officers Killed and Assaulted (hereinafter UCR Reports Police Deaths and Assaults Data), www.fbi.gov/about-us/cjis/ucr/ucr-publications.

almost never ties this funding to the promotion of "lawfulness, accountability, or fairness in policing."[73] By changing this, Congress could inspire proactive reform. In addition to this proposal, this book lays out several additional, ambitious models of proactive federal regulation of local police departments.

Third, the federal government should look for ways to increase the frequency of federal interventions via § 14141 or other similar top-down reform efforts. Congress could conceivably accomplish this by providing the DOJ with substantially more funding to investigate and intervene into more police departments via § 14141. This book also considers a number of other, less costly ways for the federal government to increase the frequency of these sorts of top-down reform efforts. This book concludes by arguing that this package of reforms would represent the next step in the evolution of police regulation. While some of these reforms may be contentious, they would likely contribute to substantial reductions in local police misconduct.

III Roadmap of the Book

The first chapter of this book describes the problem of police misconduct in the United States. This chapter complicates the typical narrative surrounding police misconduct. It argues that police misconduct is not evenly spread across the country. Instead, the United States has historically suffered from a small handful of corrupt police departments that systemically violate civil rights with virtual impunity. This realization raises a simple question – why have a handful of communities abdicated their responsibility for fighting police wrongdoing? The answer is at the heart of the regulatory challenge we face today. This chapter evaluates unique conditions that have led to the presence of systemic misconduct in a handful of police departments in the United States. It also chronicles the historical rise and fall of the Hands-Off and Buildup Eras in American police regulation. Ultimately, Chapter 1 concludes that while cost-raising mechanisms made police misconduct more expensive during the Buildup Era, they did not consistently inspire proactive change in police departments. Thus, the failure of the Buildup Era motivated Congress to eventually pass § 14141 in 1994, thereby beginning the Intervention Era.

[73] Rachel Harmon, *Federal Programs and the Real Cost of Policing*, 90 NYU L. Rev. 870, 890 (2015).

It seems fitting, then, that Chapters 2–4 use § 14141 and the modern Intervention Era as a case study to examine the feasibility of expanded federal oversight of local policing. Since its passage in 1994, the DOJ has used § 14141 to intervene into dozens of police departments across the country. The successes and failures of § 14141 are instructive as we examine whether the federal government should take on a more proactive role in the regulation of local police departments. Section 14141 is a sort of experiment in the federal oversight of local police departments. Since § 14141 represents the first time that the federal government has had the legal authority to overhaul a local police department, it provides useful information on how local police departments will respond to external, top-down reform efforts. And § 14141 provides the only empirical data on how the federal government might manage the complex task of overseeing the nation's 18,000 police departments.

Chapter 2 describes legislative history that led to the passage of § 14141 and the beginning of the Intervention Era. At the time of its passage, virtually no news outlets discussed the importance of § 14141. Congress buried the measure in a complex, omnibus crime bill. Despite this lack of media attention, § 14141 has grown in importance over the last several years. Chapter 3 examines how the DOJ has gone about enforcing and implementing § 14141. There has been little academic research on § 14141 in the past. Despite the general agreement among scholars that § 14141 represented one of the most transformational statutes in American policing history, we have generally known little about this statute – little about how the DOJ enforced this statute, how many police departments had become targets of DOJ intervention pursuant to this statute, and how effective the DOJ had been in using this statute to bring about sustainable reform. To fill this gap in the available literature, this chapter relies on in-depth interviews with stakeholders involved in federal interventions into local police departments.[74] These stakeholders

[74] I conducted these interviews between 2012 and 2013. Qualitative studies commonly use semistructured interviews. For some examples, *see, e.g.*, Avlana Eisenberg, *Expressive Enforcement*, 61 UCLA L. Rev. 855, 919 (2014); Keith Guzik, *The Agencies of Abuse: Intimate Abusers' Experience of Presumptive Arrest and Prosecution*, 42 Law & Soc'y Rev. 111, 115 (2008); Helen B. Marrow, *Immigrant Bureaucratic Incorporation: The Dual Roles of Professional Missions and Government Policies*, 74 Am. Soc. Rev. 756, 759 (2009); David Orzechowicz, *Privileged Emotion Managers: The Case of Actors*, 71 Soc. Psychol. Q. 143, 145 (2008). During semistructured interviews, a researcher commonly asks a participant a set of preplanned questions. The researcher also commonly asks unplanned follow-up questions that help the researcher gain a more detailed understanding of the participant's responses. *See* Eisenberg, *supra*, at 919. The field of

fall into three different categories: DOJ officials tasked with enforcing § 14141, external monitors assigned to oversee federal reform efforts in local police departments, and police officials in agencies targeted by the DOJ via § 14141.[75] The overwhelming majority of these stakeholders have requested anonymity, given their continued work in this field. The purpose of these interviews was to create a qualitative understanding of how the DOJ has utilized the relatively expansive power afforded to it in § 14141.[76] This chapter quotes from these stakeholder interviews. The evidence drawn from these stakeholder interviews paints a complex image of federally initiated reform in local police departments. The goal of Chapter 3 is to provide a detailed quantitative and qualitative picture of the DOJ's use of § 14141.

Chapter 4 then provides a vivid example of how federal intervention has brought about meaningful reform in one of the nation's largest police departments – the LAPD. For decades, the LAPD was a national symbol of police corruption. In 1991, the LAPD came under intense scrutiny after

individuals involved in the federal intervention process is surprisingly small. Few departments have undergone full-scale federal intervention. Only a small number of litigators have actually handled § 14141 cases at the DOJ. And only a handful of companies have served as external monitors in the existent § 14141 cases.

75 In total, eight of the interview participants had significant experience at the DOJ handling § 14141 cases, fifteen had experience as law enforcement officials in affected municipalities, and fourteen had experience as monitors in previous or ongoing federal intervention cases.

76 To identify relevant stakeholders, I used court documents, monitor reports, and other public information to identify the name and contact information for a population of individuals who have played a substantial role in federal interventions into police departments since the passage of § 14141. These stakeholders fall into three different categories: DOJ litigators, external monitors, and police officials. I developed these interview scripts by conducting a preliminary, exploratory interview with one monitor, one DOJ litigator, and one law enforcement executive. I also reviewed court documents, monitor reports, and the existing literature to develop this interview script. This study did not attempt to interview frontline police officers, since past studies have already surveyed these officers about their impressions of federal intervention via § 14141. To facilitate each interview, I used three interview scripts – one for monitors, one for DOJ litigators, and one for law enforcement professionals. These scripts asked questions about each participant's role in § 14141 cases. These scripts also asked participants to describe each step in the federal intervention process to the best of their ability. And these scripts inquired about specific tensions that arise during this sort of federal intervention. I used these scripts to guide semistructured interviews. When participants had experience in two or more of these categories – for example, when an interview participant had both been a DOJ litigator handling § 14141 cases and worked on an external monitoring team – I asked the participant questions from both scripts. I recorded and transcribed all interviews when possible. I then analyzed these transcripts to identify common themes in the participants' responses.

the Rodney King incident. Subsequent investigations found that officers in the LAPD were engaged in systemic misconduct. Although such evidence of systemic misconduct existed, the city of Los Angeles did little to fix the apparent problems. In 1998, the LAPD again found itself in the national spotlight because of the so-called Rampart Scandal, which implicated dozens of police officers in egregious misconduct. Despite multiple, highly publicized instances of misconduct, the city of Los Angeles had failed to reform its own police department. In May 2000, the DOJ concluded that the LAPD was in violation of § 14141. So began a period of federal intervention that lasted over a decade. By the end of this process, the federal government had achieved something remarkable. It transformed the LAPD from a national symbol of corruption to a model police department. Of course, not every instance of federal intervention has proven as effective. Chapter 4 also discusses cases like Alamance County, North Carolina, where the DOJ has faced significant roadblocks.

Chapter 4 also uses an array of examples to theorize on some of the benefits and drawbacks of § 14141 – and federal intervention more broadly – as a regulatory mechanism in the local policing context. It highlights how § 14141 has seemingly improved a number of police departments through forcing municipalities to allocate scarce resources, instigating a change in leadership in problematic police agencies, and providing legal cover for top-down reforms. Even so, the current model of federal intervention also appears flawed, as there are few mechanisms to ensure the sustainability of federal intervention. The current case selection process remains shrouded in secrecy. The DOJ lacks the resources for optimal enforcement. And the current piecemeal interventionary approach does little to incentivize widespread reform.

Based on these observations about the benefits and limitations of the Intervention Era, Chapter 5 reimagines how the federal government could reform local police departments through engaging in truly federalized oversight of local police departments. On this point, it may also be useful to outline the limitations of this book's argument at the outset. This book does not purport to claim that expanding federal oversight of local police departments will effectively end all misconduct. This book makes a narrower claim. It argues that expanded federal oversight of local police misconduct represents a desirable option *compared to the alternatives*. The question we should be asking is not whether federal oversight of local policing will eliminate all misconduct. It won't. The question we should be asking is whether expanded federal oversight of local police misconduct will more effectively reduce misconduct than the alternative – namely, the Buildup Era and Intervention Era reforms. When viewed in this light, Chapter 5 concludes that expanded federal oversight of local police departments represents the closest thing we may ever have to an answer to police misconduct.

1

The Problem of Police Misconduct

Introduction

No academic research has ever thoroughly examined the historical underpinnings of the Intervention Era. The few academics who have previously studied this subject have told a simple story – that the Rodney King incident made apparent the inadequacies of the federal approach to police regulation and motivated Congress to take action. Under this view, the Intervention Era was a response to a single, traumatizing incident of police wrongdoing that scarred the American psyche and demanded federal action. In some respects, this account is correct. The Rodney King beating instantly elevated the issue of police misconduct to the national stage and put pressure on some congressional representatives to take decisive action. You might say that § 14141 is the law that Rodney King wrote. But this traditional narrative is also incomplete. Congress did not pass § 14141 and begin the Intervention Era in a vacuum. Rather, the Intervention Era must be understood as a continuation of a century-long effort to combat structural, political, and organizational conditions that promote systemic wrongdoing within local police departments. Although many police agencies have made impressive strides in professionalizing their forces over the last several decades, patterns of misconduct continue to thrive in a relatively small number of police agencies. In these troubled agencies, a lack of external oversight and permissive organizational cultures facilitate widespread abuse. Wrongdoing is not only tolerated but sometimes applauded. These agencies demonstrate a systemic unwillingness or inability to control misconduct. This chapter argues that the emergence of these sorts of problematic police agencies should not come as a surprise. Given the unique American approach to law enforcement, their existence is inevitable.

The confluence of three major factors results in a systemic failure to control misconduct in a handful of police agencies. First, despite the quasi-militaristic organization of most police agencies, the very nature of police work puts considerable authority in the hands of frontline workers. As frontline workers, police officers necessarily wield considerable discretion. Frontline officers must also interact with individuals in intimate and vulnerable situations. This opens opportunities for constitutional violations. This is an unavoidable part of policing. No matter how well regulated the agency is, some officers will misuse this discretion and engage in misconduct. Beginning with the Wickersham Commission Report in 1931, national policymakers came to view the misconduct by frontline police officers as a pervasive national problem. In the decades that followed, numerous federal commissions reiterated these findings.

Second, policing in the United States is highly decentralized. This is because of a "conscious design choice rather than coincidence."[1] States have constitutional authority to control policing within their borders. States also have plenary power to control the creation of local governments. Over the last century, states have used this power to permit the incorporation of rural and suburban areas into autonomous municipalities with their own police forces. The result has been what some scholars describe as metropolitan fragmentation[2] and political decentralization[3] – that is, the existence of several independent governments within a state or metropolitan area, each controlling significant delegated authority over everything from education to policing. In the United States, this has resulted in the creation of around 18,000 local and autonomous police agencies. On the one hand, decentralization may make local governments more democratically accountable and efficient. On the other hand, decentralization and permissive state policies on incorporation have facilitated the creation of racially and economically disparate jurisdictions. When evidence of misconduct arises in a local municipality, these racial and economic disparities play a critical role in the local political response. In poorer communities, political leaders may not view unconstitutional misconduct as a pressing local concern. Such a municipality may not choose to allocate scarce resources to costly police reform, when doing so may take away resources from other worthy causes like local schools or parks. Similarly, in racially divided localities, the public may not see police misconduct that only affects a marginalized minority group

[1] Erika K. Wilson, *Towards a Theory of Equitable Federated Regionalism in Public Education*, 61 UCLA L. Rev. 1416, 1425 (2014).

[2] Professor Wilson uses this term to describe "the existence of several overlapping and independent local governments across metropolitan regions." *Id.* at 1425 n.35.

[3] Wilson further defines this term as the "delegation of political power to a subordinate unit of government." *Id.* at 1425 n.36.

as a major problem warranting significant attention. In such jurisdictions, the political process may even openly approve of police behavior that violates the rights of politically marginalized groups. Thus, decentralization facilitates the existence of some local police agencies that harbor patterns of wrongdoing.

Third, despite the evidence of such widespread misconduct, the federal government has historically played a minimal role in directly regulating the thousands of decentralized law enforcement agencies in the country. As one DOJ representative explained to the House Subcommittee on Civil and Constitutional Rights, federal officials have historically not been seen as "the front line troops in combating ... police abuse."[4] That responsibility falls to "the internal affairs bureaus of law enforcement agencies and with State and local prosecutors."[5] This combination of localization, discretion, and the lack of a national regulatory mechanism facilitated widespread wrongdoing in the early- to mid-twentieth century. Around this time, the law slowly began fighting back against local police misconduct through a host of regulatory tools. Courts placed limits on police behavior. When police conduct exceeded these limits, judges began excluding unlawfully obtained evidence from criminal trials. Courts hoped that this so-called exclusionary rule would motivate police officers to respect the constitutional limitations on their authority. Prosecutors both at the state and local levels began more vigorously levying criminal penalties against police officers who violated the law. And a series of US Supreme Court opinions opened up opportunities for victims of police misconduct to file civil suits in federal court. This chapter describes this rise in regulations as the Buildup Era.

During the Buildup Era, many police departments made impressive strides in professionalization. In fact, "[i]f one were to walk into a typical American police agency [today] ... one could not help but be struck by how much things have changed from what a similar visit would have revealed" decades earlier.[6] But despite this encouraging progress, many departments exhibited a continuing unwillingness to adopt proactive reforms to combat misconduct. So why do some police departments continue to infringe upon individual rights, despite the costs associated

[4] *Police Brutality: Hearing before the H. Subcomm. on Civil and Const. Rights of the Comm. on the Judiciary*, 102d Cong. 3 (1991) (statement of John R. Dunne, assistant attorney general, Civil Rights Division).

[5] *Id.*

[6] Michael C. Scott, *Progress in American Policing? Reviewing the National Reviews*, 34 L. & Soc'y Rev. 171, 175 (2008).

with such violations? This chapter argues that a number of departments continued to engage in systemic misconduct because of two fundamental flaws in the regulatory approach taken during the Buildup Era. The first major flaw is that mechanisms implemented during the Buildup Era do not actually force local police agencies to adopt any specific ameliorative policies. These Buildup Era mechanisms merely increased the cost of police wrongdoing. To borrow from the vocabulary of law and economics, the traditional federal approach to the regulation of local law enforcement permitted "efficient breaches." While these Buildup Era mechanisms can make police misconduct expensive, they cannot force police departments to adopt ameliorative reforms. Departments can choose not to adopt proactive reforms so long as they are prepared to pay the costs of such a breach. Historically, many departments have done just that.

A second limitation of the Buildup Era mechanism is that it implicitly views police wrongdoing as an officer problem, and not an organizational problem. Over the last several decades, policing scholars have come to view police misconduct as a "rotten barrel," rather than a "bad apple" problem.[7] That is to say, scholars have increasingly tied misconduct back to lax internal oversight and a departmental culture that permitted misconduct. In the absence of mandatory regulations, often with the implicit support of local political leaders, misconduct in many departments became routinized. It became common. It became an accepted part of day-to-day life, often ingrained into the organizational culture. Mere cost-raising reforms could not change that. This unique problem demanded a more invasive response.

I Why Some Police Agencies Fail to Control Misconduct

Why do some police departments in the United States fail to control misconduct within their ranks? This part develops a theory about the preconditions that lead to the existence of these problematic agencies. Several inherent characteristics of American policing – local political accountability, decentralization, significant frontline discretion, and the general lack of federal oversight – allow a handful of police departments to violate individual rights with virtual impunity.

[7] *See* Barbara Armacost, *Organizational Culture and Police Misconduct*, 72 Geo. Wash. L. Rev. 453, 457 (2004) (using the terms "bad apple" and "rotten barrel").

A Police Discretion: Necessary but Problematic

American police departments necessarily give frontline officers a significant amount of discretion.[8] The academic literature has long observed that, as frontline workers, police officers need discretion to complete their jobs.[9] If police did not have the ability to exercise discretion, and instead had to strictly enforce every rule of law, "the criminal law would be ordered but intolerable."[10] This has been well understood going back to the President's Commission on Law Enforcement and Administration of Justice, which recognized the importance of discretion. The authors of that report noted that police "are charged with performing [their jobs] where all eyes are upon them and where the going is always roughest – on the streets."[11] A police officer's job also requires interaction with individuals at their most vulnerable and desperate.[12] Much of the day-to-day work that police officers complete could be more accurately described as unstructured counseling; officers must calm everyday altercations, handle public nuisances, and offer assistance to "whoever needs help whether they

8 Charles D. Breitel, *Controls in Criminal Law Enforcement*, 27 U. Chi. L. Rev. 427 (1960) (explaining the necessity of discretion in police work and defining discretion as "the power to consider all circumstances and then determine whether any legal action is to be taken ... [a]nd if so taken, of what kind and degree, and to what conclusion").

9 The academic literature has generally observed two different types of discretion in police work – discretion about which laws to enforce and discretion about how to enforce those laws. For examples of discretion in how officers enforce the law, *see, e.g.*, Steven Maynard-Moody and Michael Musheno, Cops, Teachers, Counselors: Stories from the Front Lines of Public Service (2003) (describing how street-level bureaucrats like police officers have to deal with competing tensions of law abidance and cultural abidance); Michael Lipsky, Street-Level Bureaucracy: Dilemmas of the Individual in Public Services (1980) (recognizing in this hallmark book within socio-legal studies how police, as street-level bureaucrats, have the ability to exercise significant influence over how public policy is actually carried out). For examples of how police inevitably must decide which laws to enforce, *see, e.g.*, Herman Goldstein, *Police Discretion: The Ideal Versus the Real*, 23 Police Admin. Rev. 140 (1963) (describing how, as administrators of the law, police officers must invariably make decisions on which laws to rigidly enforce, and which laws to not enforce as consistently; in doing so police begin to actually influence the meaning of the law).

10 Breitel, *supra* note 8, at 427.

11 President's Commission on Law Enforcement and Administration of Justice, The Challenge of Crime in a Free Society 91 (1967) [hereinafter President's Commission on Law Enforcement], *available at* www.ncjrs.gov/pdffiles1/nij/42.pdf.

12 *Id.* (stating that "Policemen deal with people when they are both most threatening and most vulnerable, when they are angry, when they are frightened, when they are desperate, when they are drunk, when they are violent, and when they are ashamed").

want it or not."[13] While this kind of discretion is a necessary part of policing, a certain amount of officers granted such authority will invariably abuse it. The "supervision of subordinates with broad discretion and responsibilities" is especially tough, meaning that superiors cannot possibly "hold officers accountable for everything all the time."[14] Some misconduct is an unavoidable result of empowering frontline workers with considerable discretion. In the last century, the academic literature has recognized countless examples of how police discretion is invariably tied to some misconduct.

One of the first national recognitions of widespread misconduct among police officers came in 1931, when the National Commission on Law Observance and Enforcement, appointed by President Herbert Hoover, released the Wickersham Commission Report.[15] Perhaps the most famous portion of the Report was a section entitled the Report on Lawlessness in Law Enforcement. Some policing scholars have called this "one of the most important events in the history of American policing."[16]

[13] *Id.* at 91 and 92 (making this comparison to counseling and providing additional examples of the counseling-type role that police must adopt).

[14] Lipsky, *supra* note 9, at 164.

[15] Dwight C. Smith Jr., *Wickersham to Sutherland to Katzenbach: Evolving an "Official" Definition for Organized Crime*, 16 CRIME L. & SOC. CHANGE 135 (1991). George W. Wickersham, who served as the US attorney general under President William Howard Taft, chaired the commission. Samuel Walker, Records of the Committee on Official Lawlessness, *in* RECORDS OF THE WICKERSHAM COMMISSION ON LAW OBSERVANCE AND ENFORCEMENT, v (1997), *available at* www.lexisnexis.com/documents/academic/upa_cis/1965_WickershamCommPt1.pdf (last visited July 8, 2013). Prominent legal scholars and policymakers also sat on the commissions, including Harvard Law School dean Roscoe Pound and former US secretary of war Newton D. Baker. *Id.* In total, the Wickersham Commission issued fourteen total reports on a wide range of criminal justice issues. Richard A. Leo, *From Coercion to Deception: The Changing Nature of Police Interrogation in America*, 18 CRIME L. & SOC. CHANGE 35, 38 (1992). These reports were unique in part because they represented objective, technocratic approaches to understanding the problems plaguing the criminal justice system. Walker, *supra*, at v (explaining the detailed and objective approach used by the authors of the report).

[16] *Id.* While many of the commission's reports had little immediate effect on public policy, the Report on Lawlessness in Law Enforcement did motivate major changes in policing policy. *See Miranda* v. *Arizona*, 384 US 436, 446 (1966) (citing the Wickersham Report and the presence of the "third degree," a term used in the Report on Lawlessness in Law Enforcement, as a partial rationale for barring interrogations absent authorized warnings). It is also worth mentioning that it remains unclear why the commission chose to investigate policing, as there was "no political constituency with any strength at the national level demanding a federal investigation" into police misconduct. Walker, *supra* note 15, at viii. The American Civil Liberties Union (ACLU) and the National Association for the Advancement of Colored People (NAACP) were relatively small and weak interest

The report claimed "in uncompromising language" that police at the time regularly used physical brutality and cruelty during interrogations to obtain involuntary confession – something the authors of the report referred to as the "third degree."[17] The authors found that police agencies across the country utilized "third degree" tactics.[18] Police used physical brutality, threats, and illegal detentions to elicit confessions. They denied suspects the right to a lawyer during interrogations.[19] And they held suspects incommunicado for long periods of time in hopes of extorting a confession.[20] One of the root causes of this abuse was the fact that police officers necessarily need discretion to interrogate suspects, as it would be "impossible to lay down strict general rules covering all situations."[21]

Since the Report on Lawlessness in Law Enforcement, "no fewer than six national commissions [have] examined various dimensions" of police misconduct in the United States.[22] These reports, along with other academic research, have found certain categories of misconduct to be common across different policing agencies: racial profiling, excessive uses of force, unlawful searches and seizures, failures to cooperate with investigations involving fellow officers, dishonesty at trial, and the planting of evidence.[23] While the granting of discretion makes some amount of misconduct inevitable, empirical evidence over the last several decades has shown that certain departments had more apparent misconduct than others. Some of the first solid, empirical evidence for this proposition emerged around the end of the twentieth century when Congress asked the DOJ to compile records on the number of complaints filed at the national level against local police

groups at the time. *Id.* So the best historical evidence suggests that the *Report on Lawlessness* was not the result of "conventional interest group lobbying." *Id.* at viii. The three consultants who prepared the report were civil liberty advocates, which likely framed the tone of the report. *Id.*

17 *Id.* at ix; *see also* NATIONAL COMMISSION ON LAW OBSERVANCE AND ENFORCEMENT, REPORT ON LAWLESSNESS IN LAW ENFORCEMENT 3 (1931) (using the "third degree" terminology and explaining the commonality of this "secret" and "illegal" practice).

18 *Id.* at 4 (stating that the use of these tactics is "widespread" across departments in the United States).

19 *Id.* (identifying these categories).

20 *Id.* (further explaining how there was a "practice of holding the accused incommunicado, unable to get in touch with their family or friends or counsel" that is "so frequent that in places there are cells called 'incommunicado cells'").

21 *Id.* at 175. 22 Scott, *supra* note 6, at 172.

23 Kami Chavis Simmons, *New Governance and the "New Paradigm" of Police Accountability: A Democratic Approach to Police Reform*, 59, CATH. U. L. REV. 373, 380 (2010) (citing each of these as examples of common misconduct issues identified over the years).

agencies.[24] The results showed that certain police agencies – like those in New Orleans and Los Angeles – were the source of significantly more federal complaints for police wrongdoing than other major metropolitan areas.[25] This led policymakers to ask an obvious question: why do some police departments have more misconduct than others? What was different about Los Angeles or New Orleans that led to more apparent misconduct?

The answer, according to many policing scholars, is differences in organizational cultures and differences in internal policies to oversee and regulate the use of discretion. Policing scholars have increasingly recognized that "the roots of police misconduct rest within the organizational culture of policing."[26] That is to say, police departments that implicitly condone wrongdoing through using "lax supervision and inadequate investigation" techniques are more likely to see ongoing misconduct than departments that aggressively enforce internal regulations.[27] As explained in the next two subparts, the reason that departments can have such widely disparate internal policies, procedures, and cultures is because of the decentralization of American law enforcement, combined with the lack of mandatory federal oversight.

B Decentralization of American Law Enforcement

Policing in the United States has long been among the most decentralized institutions in the criminal justice system. In many countries, the central government regulates local police through a hierarchical,

24 *See Federal Response to Police Misconduct:* Hearing Before the H. Subcomm. on Civil and Const. Rights of the Comm. on the Judiciary, 103d Cong. 92–162 (1992) (showing the results from a DOJ study from 1985 to 1990 on the number of complaints sent to the federal government about police misconduct for each jurisdiction).

25 *Id.* at 152 (showing New Orleans and Los Angeles County as the top locations for misconduct).

26 Kami Chavis Simmons, *The Politics of Policing: Ensuring Stakeholder Collaboration in the Federal Reform of Local Police Departments*, 98 J. Crim. L. & Criminology 489, 505 (2008); *see also* Allyson Collins, Human Rights Watch, Shielded from Justice: Police Accountability in the United States 1, 33, 45 (1998) (detailing organizational contributors to police misconduct); Indep. Comm'n on the L.A. Police Dep't, Report on the Independent Commission of the L.A. Police Department (1991) [hereinafter Christopher Comm'n Report] (linking the LAPD's organizational mismanagement to misconduct); Barbara Armacost, *Organizational Culture and Police Misconduct*, 72 Geo. Wash. L. Rev. 453, 493–494 (2004) (explaining how organizational culture can facilitate police brutality).

27 Debra Livingston, *Police Reform and the Department of Justice: An Essay on Accountability*, 2 Buff. Crim. L. Rev. 815, 816 (1999).

top-down approach.[28] In these countries, a central headquarters exercises direct authority over local law enforcement agencies.[29] By contrast, the United States is among a handful of countries where state, municipal, or local governments deputize their own, largely independent police forces.[30] Decentralization has always been an accepted part of American law enforcement. But why has the United States taken such a radically different approach to policing than its global counterparts? The answer lays in part in the US Constitution. Since the federal government only has a handful of limited, enumerated powers, most governing responsibilities fall onto state governments. One of the most important responsibilities of the state government is to decide how to allocate the burden of governmental regulation. In virtually all cases, state governments have responded to this challenge by creating hundreds or thousands of smaller, local government units such as cities or municipalities.[31] The state then typically grants these smaller governmental units authority to handle a host of responsibilities like local education and law enforcement.

This creation of smaller, local-level governments happens through a process known as "incorporation."[32] For much of the twentieth century, many states were wary to grant localities the power to incorporate into their own local governments.[33] States instead encouraged large,

[28] LARRY E. SULLIVAN, MARIE SIMONETTI ROSEN, DORTHY MOSES SCHULZ, & M.R. HABERFELD, ENCYCLOPEDIA OF LAW ENFORCEMENT (2007), *available at* http://knowledge.sagepub.com/view/lawenforcement/n517.xml (stating that decentralized structures of law enforcement are less common, and citing various examples of centralized policing structures in France, Italy, Sweden, Finland, China, Vietnam, Cuba, and various other countries).

[29] *Id.* (describing, by contrast, how such centralization does not exist in the United States – and in the process describing the model for centralized police structure countries).

[30] *Id.* The US Constitution only affords the federal government with a small number of specific, enumerated powers. All other powers not specifically enumerated in the Constitution are, in theory, left to the state and localities. Since policing is not among the specific enumerated powers granted to the federal government, the power to hire and deputize police officers to enforce state laws has fallen outside the legitimate purview of the federal government.

[31] In *Hunter v. City of Pittsburgh*, the Supreme Court held that state governments have nearly complete authority over the creation of local municipalities within their borders. 207 US 161, 178–179 (1907) (holding that municipal governments exist and serve only with the blessing of the state government, which may "at its pleasure ... modify or withdraw all such powers").

[32] Wilson, *supra* note 1, at 1426–27 (using and defining the terms "incorporation" and "annexation").

[33] *Id.* (citing KENNETH T. JACKSON, CRABGRASS FRONTIER: THE SUBURBANIZATION OF THE UNITED STATES 144 (1985)).

existing cities to annex nearby unincorporated areas.[34] The prevailing belief was that, while decentralization was valuable, extensive decentralization would make government administration less efficient.[35] Around the mid-twentieth century, states started to implement more permissive standards for incorporation.[36] Historians trace back this increase in local municipality incorporation to "racial and ethnic changes in the demographics of central cities, particularly an influx of European immigrants and African American migrants from the South, [which] caused suburban residents to resist annexation."[37]

Once states began loosening incorporation requirements, these newly created municipalities wasted no time enacting land use, zoning, and tax policies that effectively excluded the economically disadvantaged and racial minorities.[38] Each of these newly created municipalities typically had a separate police force. One of the first times that decentralization was tied to misconduct regulation was in 1967, when the President's Commission on Law Enforcement and Administration of Justice issued a report entitled The Challenge of Crime in a Free Society.[39] In this report, the commission initially estimated there to be around 40,000 policing agencies in the United States.[40] The report also highlighted how these agencies varied widely from one part of the country to another.[41] Modern estimates suggest that the overwhelming majority of the nation's active, roughly 700,000, law enforcement officers serve in one of nearly 18,000 local or state police agencies.[42]

These permissive state regulations on incorporation inevitably facilitated the rise of tens of thousands of autonomous police agencies, each

34 *Id.*

35 *Id.* (stating that "[t]he preference for annexation during this time reflected an underlying normative belief that larger centralized governance structures were more efficient than smaller decentralized governance structures").

36 *Id.* ("As a result, states in relation to unincorporated suburbs began to shift their focus away from annexation and towards incorporation").

37 *Id.*

38 As Wilson explained in more detail, suburban communities adopted minimum lot-size requirements, or single-family home restrictions, in addition to zoning and other requirements to keep unwanted residents out of their town in a seemingly race-neutral way. *Id.* at 1428–1430.

39 President's Commission on Law Enforcement (1967). 40 *Id.*

41 For example, the commission noted that spending for urban departments was found to be around $27.31 per resident per year, while spending in smaller departments was only $8.74 per resident per year. *Id.*

42 Several decades ago, estimates wrongly put the number of policing agencies at around 40,000. *Id.* Subsequent studies have reduced this number substantially.

with limited jurisdiction over a demographically distinct area. It also resulted in wide variation from one department to another, even within a single metropolitan area. These permissive state regulations on incorporation have facilitated the creation of demographically varied municipalities, each with drastically different budgets and crime problems.

1 Local Variations in Police Practices

Each of these thousands of individual police departments must navigate the problems unique to their individual jurisdiction. Take, for example, a city like Camden, New Jersey, which has one of the highest crime rates in the nation.[43] During 2012, police in Camden had to respond to a staggering 86.3 murders per 100,000 residents – over eighteen times the national average.[44] Camden also drastically outpaced the national average in overall violent and property crime rates.[45] The average Camden resident only makes around $29,118 per year, resulting in over a third of all Camden residents living below the poverty line.[46] Less than an hour away in the state of New Jersey is the township of Brick, a community of approximately the same size as Camden.[47] Unlike Camden, Brick reported no murders in 2011 or 2012, and extremely low violent and property crime rates relative to the national average.[48] The median family income is between two and three times higher than Camden ($81,868), and only around 5 percent of the township's residents live under the poverty line.[49] It would be fair to say that law enforcement

[43] Camden had a violent crime rate of 2,566.1 crimes per 100,000 residents. This included an 86.3 murder rate, a 95.3 rape rate, a 1412.5 assault rate, and a 972.1 robbery rate – all among the top in the nation. US Dep't of Justice, Bureau of Justice Statistics, Uniform Crime Reports (UCR): Crime in the United States (2000–2012) [hereinafter UCR Reports], *available at* www.fbi.gov/about-us/cjis/ucr/ucr-publications (to access requisite data, click on desired year under "Crime in the United States," navigate to "Table 8," and find the crime data for Camden, New Jersey).

[44] *Id.* (using the murder rate found above from table 8 and comparing it to the murder rate in the United States, found in table 1).

[45] *Id.* (comparing in table 1 and table 8 the difference between Camden, New Jersey's crime rates, and those of the United States).

[46] United States Census Bureau, American Community Survey (2006–2010).

[47] *Id.* (navigating to table 8 and finding the data for Brick, New Jersey).

[48] The overall violent crime rate in Brick was 106.8 crimes per 100,000 residents, including a murder rate of 0, a rape rate of 7.9, an assault rate of 77.9, a robbery rate of 21.2, and a property crime rate of 1,642.3. *Id.* (to access requisite data, click on desired year under "Crime in the United States," navigate to "Table 8," and find the crime data for Brick, New Jersey).

[49] The median income in Brick is $81,868. *See id.*

officers in Camden are facing a categorically different problem than officers in Brick.

So it should come as no surprise that these two cities have adopted radically different approaches to policing. Camden has historically lacked the resources to hire enough police forces to man the streets. To compensate, Camden has been in the forefront in adopting highly efficient surveillance technologies.[50] Camden has also successfully consolidated its police department with the county-level agency to lower costs and avoid duplicative expenditures.[51] Brick, on the other hand, has not had to adopt such radical approaches to policing, as it has been able to maintain extremely low crime rates with relatively few officers per capita.[52]

The vast differences in local approaches to policing evident in Brick and Camden are not the exception; they are the rule. Federal surveys suggest that police departments across the country vary tremendously in size,[53] operating budget,[54] officer pay,[55] training requirements,[56] patrol methods,[57]

[50] *See generally* Conor Friedersdorf, *The Surveillance City of Camden, New Jersey*, THE ATLANTIC, December 12, 2013, *available at* www.theatlantic.com/national/archive/2013/12/the-surveillance-city-of-camden-new-jersey/282286/ (describing in detail how Camden has installed hundreds of surveillance cameras, license plate readers, and other devices to increase the efficiency of local law enforcement and help deter crime).

[51] *See generally* Heather Haddon, *Crime Dips in Camden as New County Police Force Replaces City Officers*, THE WALL STREET JOURNAL, August 5, 2013, *available at* http://online.wsj.com/news/articles/SB10001424127887323968704578650171849946106(detailing the so-called experiment whereby Camden has closed its city-wide police department and instead relied on the newly expanded county department).

[52] Brick deploys approximately 171.5 police officers per 100,000 residents, around half of what Camden deploys. *See* UCR Reports, *supra* note 43 (navigate to statistics on police employee data to find the number of police officers in Brick, New Jersey).

[53] BUREAU OF JUSTICE STATISTICS, U.S. DEP'T OF JUSTICE, LAW ENFORCEMENT MANAGEMENT AND ADMINISTRATIVE STATISTICS (LEMAS): 2007 SAMPLE SURVEYS OF LAW ENFORCEMENT AGENCIES 9 (2007) [hereinafter LEMAS] *available at* http://www.icpsr.umich.edu/icpsrweb/ICPSR/studies/31161. (table 1 showing that the average number of full-time police officers per 1,000 residents varies depending on the size of the population served).

[54] *Id.* at 10 (table 4 showing that the largest police departments spend around $385 per city resident, while the smallest departments spend only $209 per city resident).

[55] *Id.* (table 4 showing that the largest police departments spend around $121,900 per officer, while the smallest departments spend only $56,400 per officer).

[56] *See, e.g., id.* at 11 and 12 (table 5 showing that in larger departments, college degrees are more commonly required than in smaller departments; figure 6 showing that larger departments typically require more training hours than smaller departments).

[57] *See, e.g., id.* at 15 and 16 (table 12 showing the wide variation, largely by size, in the patrol method; table 13 showing that larger departments are typically more likely to have specific policies to deal with special populations and situations).

equipment,[58] and on-the-ground strategies.[59] Departments vary because of both jurisdictional challenges and the availability of local resources. The budgets of law enforcement agencies are almost always tied to the local municipal budget. These municipalities almost all rely on local property taxes and in some cases sales taxes. Thus, jurisdictions with a large concentration of poor residents, like Camden, often cannot afford to invest the same amount of money into their police departments as municipalities with a higher concentration of wealthy residents, like Brick. This is a particularly cruel realization, since the communities most adversely affected by resource disparities are also typically the agencies *most* in need of additional funds to fight crime. Once more, organizational research suggests that marginal or failing organizations – those failing to achieve their intended objective – are more likely to produce incidents of misconduct.[60] This theoretically suggests that departments struggling with higher crime rates and budgetary problems may have a greater proclivity towards misconduct while also lacking the resources to fight back.

Again the comparison between Brick and Camden is useful. Property values and incomes in Brick are significantly higher than those in Camden. Thus, a community like Brick is able to afford cutting-edge investments into policing. One of these investments that the Brick Township Police Department has been able to afford is accreditation through the Commission on Accreditation for Law Enforcement Agencies (CALEA). Departments with accreditation under CALEA are inspected periodically by a team of independent, CALEA-trained assessors to ensure that the departments are complying with procedural and operational standards.[61]

[58] *See, e.g., id.* at 17 and 18 (table 14 illustrating the disparate use of conducted energy devices in larger departments and table 15).

[59] *Id.* at 27 (describing in tables 30 and 31 the variation in strategies used by law enforcement, again varying by size of the force). A prime example of departmental variation in internal policies is the difference in how agencies respond to alleged misconduct. The Law Enforcement Management and Administration Statistics survey asks departments about the existence of internal checks to respond to misconduct. The results suggest that a department's likelihood of using independent oversight tools varies tremendously from department to department, depending in part on the size of the agency. The vast majority of departments serving population centers of more than a million people have a citizen review board (77 percent) and a substantial number give this citizen review board independent subpoena power (31 percent). *Id.* at 18 (reproducing the data from table 15, entitled "Use-of-force policies and procedures in local police departments, by size of population served, 2007"). Among smaller departments, these sorts of extensive oversight measures are virtually nonexistent. *Id.*

[60] Diane Vaughan, *The Dark Sides of Organizations: Mistakes, Misconduct, and Disaster*, 25 ANN. REV. SOC. 271, 288 (1999).

[61] JOHN DECARLO, AN ARGUMENT FOR LAW ENFORCEMENT ACCREDITATION AND OFFICER EDUCATION REQUIREMENTS (2010).

In 1984, only four agencies were CALEA accredited.[62] That number rose to 47 in 1987, 161 in 1990, 279 in 1993, and 985 by 2010.[63] But accreditation is still voluntary and expensive. Thus, the 985 agencies claiming CALEA accreditation in 2010 represent only 5.6 percent of all law enforcement agencies in the country.[64]

Camden, by contrast, has not undergone the costly CALEA accreditation. No doubt, the vast resource per capita disparity between Camden and Brick in part explains part of this difference. This is an important revelation, as it demonstrates how resource disparities can directly translate into misconduct disparities. Correcting and preventing misconduct can be expensive. As discussed more in Chapters 4 and 5, the reforms mandated via § 14141 can cost tens or hundreds of millions of dollars over several years.[65] Many of the reforms required for voluntary accreditation via CALEA may reduce civil liability exposure, presumably by decreasing the rate of wrongdoing. Evidence has also shown that the move towards accreditation and uniformity to national standards has made departments more receptive to shifting norms in policies and procedures.[66] But decentralization, which contributes to resource disparities, means that not all departments can even afford to invest in misconduct-deterring reforms like accreditation.

2 Local Democracy and Police Priorities

Given that political decentralization has created tens of thousands of local police agencies, the next obvious question is how do local police agencies develop strategies to police their unique municipalities? In such a decentralized environment, most agencies take their cues from local political preferences. This can have harmful effects on politically marginalized minorities in some jurisdictions. Historically, the influence of local preferences on police agencies has varied over time. The community

[62] The Commission on Accreditation for Law Enforcement Agencies, *Annual Report for 2010*, December 2, 2011, *available at* www.calea.org/content/calea-2010-annual-report, at 3.

[63] *Id.*

[64] There are approximately 17,985 state and local law enforcement agencies in the United States. *See* Brian A. Reaves, U.S. Dep't Of Justice, Census of State and Local Law Enforcement Agencies 2 (2011), *available at* www.bjs.gov/content/pub/pdf/csllea08.pdf. Thus, to calculate this percentage, I divided the 985 CALEA accredited agencies by the 17,985 total agencies in the country that could have been nationally accredited.

[65] *See infra* Chapters 5 and 6.

[66] Terry Gingerich & Gregory Russell, *Accreditation and Community Policing: Are They Neutral, Hostile, or Synergistic? An Empirical Test among Street Cops and Management Cops*, 2 Just. Pol'y J. 3 (1996).

policing movement has likely increased the sensitivity of local police departments to community preferences. In the early part of the twentieth century, the "degree of localism" in policing created a "decentralization … that often resembled fragmentation."[67] The lack of central regulation in policing contributed to local police departments that were "inward-looking" for policies and procedures, and "hermetically sealed" from outside influences.[68] Rather than coordinating with other police departments to develop best practices, police departments were most heavily influenced by local political leaders.[69] This turned many early police departments into mere adjuncts to political machines rather than neutral arbiters of the law, and led to substantial variation in policing styles.[70]

During the mid-twentieth century, policing went through a period of professionalization that increased cooperation and coordination between local agencies.[71] No longer were police departments rigidly sealed from other law enforcement agencies. By the 1940s and 1950s, "it had become clear that the only way to gain the public's trust and respect was to reduce the influence of politicians, train and educate police officers, and promote an image of professionalism in the eyes of the public."[72] This movement towards police professionalism reflected many beliefs of the time period: that police ought to focus on crime suppression, that police should be free from political influence, that police should feel free to act objectively and scientifically, and that departmental authority ought to be centralized and rationalized.[73] During this period, many police departments around

[67] Franklin E. Zimring, The City That Became Safe 103 (2011). [68] *Id.*

[69] Leonard A. Steverson, Policing in America: A Reference Handbook 16–18 (2008) (offering some examples about how the political patronage influence on policing led to exploitation); *see also* George L. Kelling & Mark H. Moore, The Evolving Strategy of Policing 3 (1988), *available at* https://ncjrs.gov/pdffiles1/nij/114213.pdf (last visited July 9, 2013) (stating that political influences were important during the Patronage Policing Era and explaining that police historically "lacked the powerful, central authority of their own to establish a legitimate, unifying mandate for their enterprise").

[70] *See generally* Robert M. Fogelson, Big-city Police 37 (1977) (describing big-city police as "adjuncts of the ward organizations").

[71] Kelling & Moore, *supra* note 69, at 4 (explaining how police leaders like August Vollmer "rallied police executives around the idea of reform during the 1920s and early 1930s" and galvanized a broader movement towards professionalization).

[72] Mitchel P. Roth, Crime and Punishment: A History of the Criminal Justice System: A History of the Criminal Justice System 259 (2010). Notable figures like William H. Parker, Orlando W. Wilson, and August Vollmer personified this gradual transformation.

[73] David A. Sklansky, The Persistent Pull of Police Professionalism 1 (2011), *available at* http://cms.hks.harvard.edu/var/ezp_site/storage/fckeditor/file/pdfs/

the country operated by a core set of beliefs and practices.[74] The ranks of police agencies were also increasingly unionized and protected by civil service laws – somewhat insulating these officers from political influences. In some cases, executives within police departments were also protected from political influence via civil service laws.[75] But by the 1980s, support for this so-called professional policing style waned. Empirical evidence suggested that some of the primary crime prevention tactics advocated by the professionalization movement were largely ineffective.[76] Many scholars believed that the professional policing

centers-programs/programs/criminal-justice/ExecSessionPolicing/NPIP-ThePersistentPullofPoliceProfessionalism-03-11.pdf.

74 Police saw their primary obligations as the investigation of crime, the enforcement of a wide variety of criminal laws, and the maintenance of order. *Id.* at 1 (explaining the focus of the professional policing era on crime control, law enforcement, and maintenance of order).

75 Los Angeles is a good example of a department that afforded executives within the LAPD with protection from firing or discipline at the hands of political officials. After the Rodney King beating, the City of Los Angeles passed City Charter Amendment F to give political officials authority to remove a police chief. *See* MERRICK BOBB, MARK EPSTEIN, NICOLAS H. MILLER, AND MANUAL A. ABASCAL, FIVE YEARS LATER: A REPORT TO THE LOS ANGELES COMMISSION ON THE LOS ANGELES POLICE DEPARTMENT'S IMPLEMENTATION OF INDEPENDENT COMMISSION RECOMMENDATIONS 67–68 (1996).

76 Common wisdom of the time suggested that police presence could deter crime, "and the most popular version of police crime prevention practice by the 1960s was what was called preventative patrol, usually the patrol activities of uniformed officers in marked cars conducting routine surveillance of designated geographic zones." ZIMRING, *supra* note 67, at 103. And despite the allegedly objective and scientific focus on professional policing, departments did virtually no research into the effectiveness of preventative patrols. *Id.* at 103 and 104 (describing the orthodox, albeit untested, conclusion around 1960 about how police could most effectively reduce crime and fight disorder – including through measures like preventative patrols). The first rigorous investigation of the effects of policing on crime came in 1974, when several social scientists teamed with large American police departments to empirically assess the effects of preventative patrols on criminal activity in Kansas City and Newark. *Id.* at 104–107 (summarizing the "revolutionary" uniqueness of the Kansas City study and also discussing the importance of the follow-up study in Newark). There, law enforcement purposefully altered the presence of preventative patrols in certain parts of the city to observe the effects on crime rates. *Id.* at 105 (summarizing the methodology of the Kansas City study). In both cases, the researchers found that the changes had little to no effect on crime. GEORGE L. KELLING & ANTHONY PATE, THE NEWARK FOOT PATROL EXPERIMENT (1981); GEORGE L. KELLING ET AL., THE KANSAS CITY PREVENTATIVE PATROL EXPERIMENT: A TECHNICAL REPORT (1974). Around this same time, several notable social scientists undertook the first significant empirical studies of policing behavior. *See, e.g.*, JEROME H. SKOLNICK & UNIVERSITY OF CALIFORNIA, BERKELEY CENTER FOR THE STUDY OF LAW AND SOCIETY, JUSTICE WITHOUT TRIAL: LAW ENFORCEMENT IN DEMOCRATIC SOCIETY (1966); EGON BITTNER, THE FUNCTIONS OF THE POLICE IN MODERN SOCIETY: A REVIEW OF BACKGROUND FACTORS, CURRENT PRACTICES, AND

model had become "thoroughly discredited" as many blamed the policing style "for making police departments insular, arrogant, resistant to outside criticism and feckless in responding to social ferment."[77] This motivated departments to seek new strategies – particularly those that sought input from the community.

Thus, in recent decades, there has been a growing push for police agencies to seek out community input and adopt policies that comport with local preferences. Known as community policing, this movement has sought to incorporate community sentiment into the decision-making process.[78] It was spurred in part because of the growing civil unrest and major urban riots against American law enforcement in the 1960s and 1970s.[79] These major riots struck cities across the country, including New York, Los Angeles, Newark, and Detroit.[80] The National Advisory Commission on Civil Disorders of 1970 later determined that police misconduct – including aggressive patrols and harassment in urban communities – contributed substantially to these events.[81] This demonstrated the apparent divide between law enforcement and the community it served[82] and further emphasized the need for a policing procedure that more closely sought the input of the community. In response, law enforcement moved away from a purely professional and technocratic approach and instead turned towards the community

Possible Role Models (1970); Albert J. Reiss, The Police and the Public (1971). Many of these early explorations of policing and crime control involved a technique called "embedded observation," where social scientists observed police officers in action. Zimring, *supra* note 67, at 104 (describing methodology used in many of the earliest empirical analyses of police behavior). But these studies had obvious methodological limits – while these studies could explore the everyday interactions of law enforcement with the public, they could not address bigger questions about the effectiveness of law enforcement in suppressing crime. *Id.* (concluding that while "[t]hese pioneering social scientists could impose their insights and judgments on the police behavior they observed, they could not alter the behavior . . . and they could not systemically test the impact of the behavior they observed on the communities being policed").

77 Sklansky, *supra* note 73, at 5; *see also* Herman Goldstein, Policing a Free Society (1977).

78 Sklansky, *supra* note 73, at 1 and 2 (categorizing as community policing the move towards selecting and pursuing goals in consultation with the public).

79 Michael Palmiotto, Community Policing: a Police-Citizen Partnership 13 (2011) (stating "police actions would precipitate a riot because of exaggerated rumors").

80 *Id.* (citing riots in Harlem [New York], Watts [Los Angeles], Newark [New Jersey], and Detroit [Michigan]).

81 *Id.* at 13 and 14 (citing aggressive patrols and harassment as major police precipitators of unrest).

82 *Id.* (discussing the emergence of various segmented opposition groups).

for assistance.[83] After all, "[c]ommunities with different problems and varied resources to bring to bear against them should try different things."[84] Thus, the community policing movement was about fundamentally changing the decision-making within departments.[85] The incorporation of citizen involvement in the organizational decision-making process means that policing can look very different from one decentralized police agency to another. Studies have found that while the use of community policing can increase the overall trust and confidence in law enforcement within a local jurisdiction, minority groups sometimes feel that their voices are not heard.[86] Minority residents also have

[83] *Id.* at 4 (distinguishing between bureaucratic/technocratic philosophies and more collaborative approaches).

[84] Wesley G. Skogan, *The Promise of Community Policing*, in POLICE INNOVATION: CONTRASTING PERSPECTIVES 27–44, 27 (David Weisburd & Anthony A. Braga eds., 2006).

[85] *Id.* at 27 (stating that community policing was about "changing decision-making processes and increasing new cultures within police departments"). Scholars have had trouble defining this community policing movement. Professor David Sklansky has argued that this movement reversed some of the important trends of the professionalism movement. Sklansky, *supra* note 73, at 2. During this time, police departments no longer focused narrowly on crime suppression, but instead broadened their goals. *Id.* at 1 (stating that "[p]olice departments broadened their focus on crime control to a range of other goals"). Departments started selecting these goals in consultation with the community. *Id.* at 1 and 2 (writing that police departments "selected and pursued those goals in consultation and cooperation with the public"). In order to make this process more feasible, departments decentralized authority. *Id.* at 2 (stating that "to facilitate that consultation and cooperation, authority within departments was decentralized"). Law enforcement moved away from a purely professional and technocratic approach to law enforcement and has instead turned towards the community for assistance. *Id.* at 4 (distinguishing between bureaucratic/technocratic philosophies and more collaborate approaches).

[86] For example, a study in Chicago found that "after eight years of citywide community policing, Chicagoans' views of their police improved by 10–15 percentage points on measures of their effectiveness, responsiveness, and demeanor." Skogan, *supra* note 84, at 31. But Chicagoans felt these benefits of community policing unevenly. Communities of color were less likely to participate in community policing efforts in part because of a fear of retaliation for working with police. *Id.; see also* Wesley G. Skogan & Lynn Steiner, *Community Policing in Chicago, Year Ten*, CRIM. JUST. INF. AUTH. (2004). A similar study in Houston found that white middle- and upper-class individuals reported satisfaction with community policing efforts. *See generally* WESLEY G. SKOGAN ET AL., ON THE BEAT: POLICE AND COMMUNITY PROBLEM SOLVING (1999). They also reported easy cooperation with police and, perhaps unsurprisingly, received much of the benefits. Conversely, black, Latino, blue-collar, and poor communities remained uninvolved and reported no changes in their opinions or experiences with law enforcement. *Id.* Thus, the benefits of community policing are not evenly distributed across an entire jurisdiction. Police also report a general disinterest in community policing efforts. Antony M. Pate & Penny Shtull, *Community Policing Grows in Brooklyn: An Inside View of the New York*

reported that, despite the fact that they are most commonly victims of crime and police brutality, they still have little say in the departmental policies or procedures. Instead, community policing transfers that power to whatever group is in the majority within the political constituency of a policing agency. Regardless of these concerns, the federal government has invested significant resources in encouraging local agencies to adopt community policing approaches. And it seems to be working, as most departments claim to utilize community policing strategies to decide how to allocate their resources and interact with the community.[87]

3 Why Minorities Lose

The structural decentralization of American law enforcement, combined with the recent emphasis on satisfying local community demands, has led to a remarkable variation in policies and procedures from one jurisdiction to the next. In some cases, though, the tactics that a local agency develops to deal with its own jurisdictional problems systemically violate the rights of certain segments of the population. Since decentralized law enforcement agencies take their cues from local political leaders, these systemic abuses are sometimes not just tolerated, but encouraged.

Take Maricopa County, Arizona, as an example. Joe Arpaio was elected sheriff of Maricopa County for six consecutive terms.[88] Sheriff Arpaio received international notoriety for his unconventional and legally questionable tactics.[89] One of the issues that Sheriff Arpaio emphasized heavily is the need for local law enforcement to help combat undocumented immigration into the United States. Before

City Police Department's Model Precinct, 40 CRIME & DELINQ. 384, 410 (1994) (explaining that many officers expressed resentment and could not fully understand or appreciate the reasons for community policing efforts). A survey of police officers found that 70 percent of police officers in one department were suspicious of community policing efforts because of a belief that it would burden police with unreasonable demands. *See generally* WESLEY G. SKOGAN & SUSAN M. HARTNETT, COMMUNITY POLICING, CHICAGO STYLE (1997), *available at* www.ncjrs.gov/App/abstractdb/AbstractDBDetails.aspx?id=175951 (last visited July 22, 2013).

87 The Violent Crime and Law Enforcement Act (1994) dedicated billions of dollars to training local officers in community policing efforts. Skogan, *supra* note 84, at 40. By 1999, approximately 88 percent of all new recruits and 85 percent of currently serving officers were trained in community policing. *Id.*

88 Phil Benson, *Sheriff Joe Arpaio Sworn in for 6th Term*, KPHO NEWS, January 6, 2013, *available at* www.kpho.com/story/20516330/sheriff-joe-arpaio-sworn-in-for-6th-term.

89 *See, e.g.*, *Justice Department to Question Sheriff Joe Arpaio for Civil Rights Lawsuit*, KTAR NEWS, February 7, 2014, *available at* http://ktar.com/22/1698793/Justice-Dept-to-question-Sheriff-Joe-Arpaio-for-civil-rights-lawsuit (describing how the DOJ is investigating Arpaio for civil rights violations).

2005, Sheriff Arpaio admitted that he personally did not view undocumented immigration as a "serious legal issue."[90] It was not until Maricopa County attorney Andrew Thomas won countywide election with the slogan "Stop Illegal Immigration" when Arpaio's office began emphasizing the need to crack down on undocumented immigrants.[91] By all accounts, Sheriff Arpaio responded to local community demands and altered his enforcement of the law to account for these prerogatives. His efforts, though, resulted in serious and ongoing allegations of racial profiling and a systemic unwillingness to investigate crimes against undocumented immigrants.[92] Maricopa County's location near the US border with Mexico, no doubt, has affected the tone of community policing demands. And even though around 30 percent of the population in Maricopa County is Latino,[93] the majority of voters continued to re-elect Sheriff Arpaio and thereby implicitly support his use of tactics that appear to disproportionately affect a significant minority group in the county.

No doubt, Maricopa County is one of many. When police are primarily accountable to local political leaders and majoritarian preferences, some agencies with particular demographic characteristics or local challenges will support the use of police procedures that disproportionately burden local minorities. Of course, this problem sounds similar to constitutional dilemmas in other institutional contexts like voting, schools, and housing. In these other contexts, the law has intervened to protect these minority interests. But, as discussed in the next part, our nation's legal response to police misconduct has traditionally been limited.

C *The Beginning of the Buildup Era*

The allocation of large amounts of discretion, combined with the decentralized nature of law enforcement, means that pockets of misconduct – often targeting politically marginalized minority groups – will inevitably emerge

[90] William Hermann & Edvard Pettersson, *Arizona's Arpaio Testifies Race Not Factor In Arrests*, BLOOMBERG NEWS, July 24, 2012, *available at* www.bloomberg.com/news/2012-07-24/-america-s-toughest-sheriff-to-answer-profiling-claims.html (quoting Arpaio as saying that before 2005, he never viewed illegal immigration as a "serious legal issue").

[91] E.J. Montini, *Still Doubting Thomas on Immigration*, ARIZONA REPUBLIC, July 18, 2010, *available at* www.azcentral.com/arizonarepublic/news/articles/2010/06/18/20100618Montini0618.html (quoting Thomas and describing his use of this slogan and issue during his campaign).

[92] *See Justice Department to Question Sheriff, supra* note 89.

[93] *See* UNITED STATES CENSUS BUREAU, *supra* note 46.

from time to time in the United States. Policymakers have not turned a blind eye to this problem. Instead, over the last century, there has been a growing recognition that police misconduct is a national problem demanding some federal responses. This led to the emergence of the Buildup Era. Three major regulatory mechanisms grew to prominence during the Buildup Era: the exclusionary rule, private civil litigation, and criminal culpability. All three of these mechanisms operate today as checks on police misconduct. The goal of each of these mechanisms is to increase the cost of wrongdoing in hopes of spurring reform. In many ways, the Buildup Era has achieved its goals. During the twentieth century, many police departments made impressive strides in professionalization. This broad trend towards reform is encouraging. But not all police departments responded to these limited oversight mechanisms. Some police departments have remained obstinate in the face of these regulations. This is because the very thing that made the Buildup Era effective has also made it problematic. The Buildup Era attempted to discourage police misconduct by making it expensive. The hope was that by making police misconduct costly, rational police departments would take steps to reduce misconduct. These cost-raising reforms cannot, by definition, *force* a police department to make specific policy or procedural changes. If a police department believes that unconstitutional behavior is worth the cost, it may continue to violate individual rights. While a number of police agencies have responded to Buildup Era reforms by implementing reform measures, some departments continued to engage in patterns of unconstitutional misconduct. The subparts that follow will evaluate each of the major regulatory mechanisms that emerged during the Buildup Era.

1 Exclusionary Rule

The first major mechanism that rose to prominence during the Buildup Era is the exclusionary rule established by the US Supreme Court case *Mapp* v. *Ohio*. Outside of the world of lawyers, most Americans have never heard of the *Mapp* case. Nevertheless, *Mapp* may be among the most well-known Supreme Court opinions in American history. Sure, *Mapp* lacks the name recognition of *Roe* v. *Wade* or *Bush* v. *Gore*. But the holding from the *Mapp* decisions is ingrained into the American consciousness. In *Mapp*, the Court held that "all evidence obtained in violation of the Constitution is … inadmissible in a state court."[94] In other words, if police break the law in obtaining evidence, that evidence generally cannot be used at trial. Today, we refer to this legal principle as the

[94] *Id.* at 655.

exclusionary rule. While this is a well-understood part of police regulation today, the exclusionary rule is a relatively newcomer to the world of criminal procedure.

It took several decades for the Court to develop the exclusionary rule and apply it to all American law enforcement actions. In the 1914 case of *Weeks* v. *United States*, the Court first established a version of the exclusionary rule.[95] There, police entered the home of Fremont Weeks and seized papers and personal belongings without a warrant.[96] The federal government used this illegally seized evidence to secure a conviction for transporting lottery tickets through the mail.[97] In a unanimous decision, the Court held that the seizure directly violated Weeks's Fourth Amendment constitutional right.[98] But the Court went a step further and ruled that the government could not use the illegally obtained evidence against him at trial.[99] Thus, *Weeks* represented the first application of the so-called exclusionary rule.[100] The ruling was limited, though. It only applied to actions taken by federal law enforcement.[101] Soon thereafter in 1920, the Supreme Court further expanded the exclusionary rule in *Silverthorne Lumber Co.* v. *United States*.[102] In that case, federal agents illegally seized tax books from Frederick Silverthorne, made copies of the records, and attempted to introduce those copies at trial.[103] The Supreme Court held that even the copies of the illegally obtained evidence were illegally tainted.[104] This precedent would be cited in the future as the

95 232 US 383 (1914).

96 *Id.* at 386 and 387 (explaining that the police had gone to the defendant's house and entered the house unlawfully before taking "possession of various papers and articles found there").

97 *Id.* at 389 and 390 (describing how the prosecutor used the papers at trial to show that the defendant had in his possession lottery tickets and statements in reference to a lottery).

98 *Id.* at 398 (holding that "the letters in question were taken from the house of the accused by an official of the United States acting under color of his office in direct violation of the constitutional rights of the defendant").

99 *Id.* (stating that "in permitting … use [of the evidence] upon the trial, we think prejudicial error was committed").

100 *Id.* Although the phrase "exclusionary rule" never appears in the Court's opinion, the remedy may still be accurately described as such since it requires the trial court to not admit the illegally obtained papers into evidence.

101 Again, the Court never dealt with the difference between federal and state actions here. But since the case only held that this action by a federal law enforcement officer should lead to evidentiary exclusion, it was interpreted as such going forward.

102 251 US 385 (1920).

103 *Id.* at 390 and 391 (explaining the facts of the case, including how the US marshal obtained "books, papers and documents" illegally).

104 *Id.* at 391 and 392 (explaining the decision to bar the admission of the evidence at trial).

"fruit of the poisonous tree" doctrine – an extension of the exclusionary rule that held as inadmissible both the illegally obtained evidence and any future evidence obtained as a result of the illegal action.[105] Despite this initial judicial action, it would be decades before the Court expanded the exclusionary rule to state law enforcement. Since almost all American law enforcement officers work at the state level,[106] this functionally meant that even after *Weeks* and *Silverthorne*, virtually all law enforcement could violate the constitution at will without fear that their actions would inhibit a future criminal prosecution. The Court first had the opportunity to extend the exclusionary rule to the states in *Wolf* v. *Colorado*.[107] In that case, Colorado had obtained evidence illegally – evidence that would have been inadmissible under the federal exclusionary rule established in *Weeks*.[108] The Court held that while the Fourth Amendment did apply to state law enforcement, the exclusionary rule did not.[109] It would not be until *Mapp* v. *Ohio* that the Court changed direction.[110] The Court in *Mapp* finally declared that the exclusionary rule applied to all law enforcement agencies – both state and local. Today, violations of the Fourth (unlawful search or seizure) and Fifth Amendments (failure to read a suspect his or her *Miranda* rights) frequently lead to evidentiary exclusion in both state and federal courts.[111]

105 *Id.* at 392 (holding that any holding to the contrary would "reduce the Fourth Amendment to a form of words").

106 *See* Zimring, *supra* note 67 at 102 (describing the decentralization of American law enforcement into around 20,000 smaller state police agencies).

107 338 US 25 (1949).

108 The Court started the opinion by bluntly stating the question: "Does a conviction by a State court for a State offense deny the 'due process of law' required by the Fourteenth Amendment, solely because evidence that was admitted at the trial was obtained under circumstances which would have rendered it inadmissible in a prosecution for violation of a federal law in a court of the United States because there deemed to be an infraction of the Fourth Amendment as applied in *Weeks* v. *United States*?" *Id.* at 26.

109 *Id.* at 33 (holding that "in a prosecution in a State court for a State crime, the Fourteenth Amendment does not forbid the admission of evidence obtained by an unreasonable search and seizure").

110 *Mapp* v. *Ohio*, 367 US 643 (1961) (holding that evidentiary exclusion is proper in cases where state law enforcement illegally obtains evidence).

111 *See, e.g.*, NATIONAL INSTITUTE OF JUSTICE, CRIMINAL JUSTICE REPORT – THE EFFECTS OF THE EXCLUSIONARY RULE: A STUDY IN CALIFORNIA (1982) (finding that the use of the exclusionary rule led to prosecutors dropping complaints in 86,033 felony arrest cases).

Some studies show that the exclusionary rule brought about reform in American police departments.[112] These studies find that police departments faced with the increased cost of evidentiary exclusion are more likely to punish officers engaged in wrongdoing, reward officers who obtain evidence legally, and choose not to promote officers who put cases in jeopardy by obtaining evidence illegally.[113] Nevertheless, another strong current of research suggests that court efforts to alter police department behavior through the judicial decree have been of limited use.[114] For one thing, the Court has also since carved out numerous exceptions to evidentiary exclusion[115] – the silver platter

[112] William C. Heffernan & Richard W. Lovely, *Evaluating the Fourth Amendment Exclusionary Rule: The Problem of Police Compliance with the Law*, 24 U. MICH. J. L. REFORM 311 (1990); Myron W. Orfield, *The Exclusionary Rule and Deterrence: An Empirical Study of Chicago Narcotics Officers*, 54 U. CHI. L. REV. 1016 (1987).

[113] *See, e.g.*, Orfield, *supra* note 112 (finding that the exclusionary rule had at least some positive effect on Chicago police by motivating reform and discouraging violations through policy changes and social norms).

[114] Richard A. Leo, *Inside the Interrogation Room*, 86 J. CRIM. L. & CRIMINOLOGY 266 (1995) (demonstrating how police have learned to negotiate the impact of *Miranda*, lessening the usefulness of warnings and increasing the likelihood of obtaining a confession); Richard A. Leo, *The Impact of "Miranda" Revisited*, 86 J. CRIM. L. & CRIMINOLOGY 621 (1996); GERALD N. ROSENBERG, THE HOLLOW HOPE: CAN COURTS BRING ABOUT SOCIAL CHANGE? SECOND EDITION (2nd ed. 2008) (rejecting the role of courts in instigating social change in various contexts). Gerald Rosenberg famously compiled evidence from numerous empirical studies demonstrating that attempts by the Court to instigate social change often fail. *Id.* at 324–331 (particularly showing his skepticism about the effectiveness of *Miranda* and the exclusionary rule). By holding in *Miranda* that officers must read suspects a set of procedural rights, Chief Justice Earl Warren had two major concerns: police brutality during confessions and psychological coercion that led to innocent people confessing to crimes they did not commit. *Id.* at 324 and 325. But numerous studies after *Miranda* found that individuals were confessing and pleading guilty just as often as they had before the landmark decision. *Id.* at 325 and 326. Police might have simply gotten better at inducing confessions through less-coercive and humane methods, although Rosenberg. Further, Rosenberg argued that many departments still suffered from pervasive brutality. *Id.* at 326. Police have also mediated the impact of judicial regulations. For example, Richard Leo and Charles Weisselberg have both shown how police have found clever ways to limit the effects of *Miranda* warnings, while still avoiding evidentiary exclusion. *Id;* Charles D. Weisselberg, *Mourning Miranda*, 96 CAL. L. REV. 1521 (2008) (illustrating in impressive detail how police training material has taught law enforcement to mediate the impact of *Miranda*).

[115] *See generally* Carol S. Steiker, *Counter-Revolution in Constitutional Criminal Procedure? Two Audiences, Two Answers*, 94 MICH. L. REV. 2466, 2504–2527 (1996) (chronicling the Supreme Court's gradual recognition of numerous exceptions to the exclusionary rule).

doctrine,[116] the inevitable discovery doctrine,[117] and the good faith exception,[118] to name a few.

The exclusionary rule also comes at a high social cost. Many critics have decried the exclusionary rule as "an absurd rule through which manifestly dangerous criminals are let out because the courts prefer technicalities to truth."[119] The Court has also suggested that the need for the exclusionary rule may be waning. In *Michigan* v. *Hudson*, the Court noted that significant improvements in the professionalism and training in American police departments may decrease the need for the exclusionary rule in the future – particularly given the high cost associated with excluding potentially incriminating evidence at trial.[120] This has led many scholars to predict that the Court could someday move to overturn the core of the evidentiary exclusion principle.[121]

Perhaps the biggest limitation of the exclusionary rule, though, is that it only deters police misconduct that actually results in the collection of evidence. This represents only a small fraction of all misconducts. It does little to deter the excessive use of force or unlawful searches and seizures that do not lead to a criminal prosecution.[122] Take, for example, the use of stop-and-frisk by the New York Police Department (NYPD). In 2002, the NYPD reported executing 97,296 stop-and-frisks.[123] In 82 percent of those cases, the officer found no incriminating contraband and did not

[116] *Elkins* v. *United States*, 364 US 206 (1960) (allowing federal law enforcement to use evidence unlawfully obtained by state police).

[117] *Nix* v. *Williams*, 467 US 431 (1984) (permitting law enforcement to use evidence obtained unlawfully so long as the material would have been inevitably discovered through another legal route in the process of the normal investigation).

[118] *United States* v. *Leon*, 468 US 897, 916 (1984) (allowing prosecutors to admit evidence obtained illegally so long as the illegality was done in good faith).

[119] Guido Calabresi, *The Exclusionary Rule*, 26 HARV. J. L. & PUB. POL'Y 111 (2003).

[120] *Hudson* v. *Michigan*, 547 US 586, 599 (2006) (explaining that "we now have increasing evidence that police forces across the United States take the constitutional rights of citizens seriously").

[121] *See, e.g.*, Chris Blair, *Hudson* v. *Michigan: The Supreme Court Knocks and Announces the Demise of the Exclusionary Rule*, 42 TULSA L. REV. 751 (2006); David Alan Sklansky, *Not Your Father's Police Department: Making Sense of the New Demographics of Law Enforcement*, 96 J. CRIM. L. & CRIMINOLOGY 1209 (2006); James J. Tomkovicz, *Hudson* v. *Michigan and the Future of Fourth Amendment Exclusion*, 93 IOWA L. REV. 1819 (2007).

[122] There is a small exception to this general rule. The exclusionary rule would only bar the admission of evidence if the use of force or brutality was a violation of the Constitution and directly contributed to the collection of the evidence.

[123] New York Civil Liberties Union, *Stop-and-Frisk Data*, http://www.nyclu.org/content/stop-and-frisk-data (last accessed on December 3, 2015).

arrest the suspect – meaning that the overwhelming majority of these stops involved completely innocent pedestrians.[124] By 2011, the number of stop-and-frisks increased by *over 600 percent* to 685,724. Roughly 88 percent of those stopped by the NYPD were completely innocent.[125] Around 87 percent of those stopped were black or Latino – despite the fact that blacks and Latinos represent only 52 percent of the city's population.[126] That means that in over 600,000 instances, the NYPD stopped and frisked a completely innocent person. In those thousands of potentially unjustified searches, the exclusionary rule does little good. Since the NYPD discovered no evidence of criminal wrongdoing in those cases, the exclusionary rule provides no avenue for relief. Ultimately, the exclusionary rule is "much narrower than the scope of illegal police misconduct."[127]

2 Private Civil Litigation

The second important regulation that emerged during the Buildup Era is private civil litigation. The recent events surrounding the death of Freddie Gray in the custody of the Baltimore Police Department illustrates the potential value of this regulatory mechanism. Baltimore police arrested the 25-year-old Gray on April 12, 2015, for possession of an allegedly illegal switchblade.[128] When Gray arrived at a police station a half hour later, he could not breathe or talk.[129] Mr. Gray lapsed into a coma after his spine was partially severed from his neck.[130] A week later, Mr. Gray died in a Baltimore hospital.[131] His death sparked rioting and looting.[132] These riots alone may have been enough to spur investigations into potential

124 *Id.* 125 *Id.* 126 *Id.*

127 Rachel A. Harmon, *Promoting Civil Rights Through Proactive Policing Reform*, 62 STAN. L. REV. 1, 11 (2009).

128 Sheryl Gay Stolberg, *Freddie Gray Settlement Approved by Baltimore Officials*, NY TIMES, September 10, 2015, at A24.

129 David A. Graham, *The Mysterious Death of Freddie Gray*, THE ATLANTIC, April 22, 2015, *available at*: www.theatlantic.com/politics/archive/2015/04/the-mysterious-death-of-freddie-gray/391119/.

130 Oliver Laughland & Jon Swaine, *Six Baltimore Officers Suspended Over Police-Van Death of Freddie Gray*, THE GUARDIAN, April 20, 2015, *available at*: www.theguardian.com/us-news/2015/apr/20/baltimore-officers-suspended-death-freddie-gray.

131 *Id.*

132 Scott Calvert, *Freddie Fray's Funeral Draws Thousands in Baltimore*, WALL STREET JOURNAL, April 27, 2015, *available at*: www.wsj.com/articles/freddie-grays-funeral-draws-thousands-in-baltimore-1430147862; Sheryl Gay Stolberg, *Baltimore Enlists National Guard and a Curfew to Fight Riots and Looting*, NY TIMES, April 28, 2015, at A1.

patterns of misconduct in the Baltimore Police Department. But the city of Baltimore had another strong incentive to consider reform – money.

Because of a development during the Buildup Era, Freddie Gray's family had the legal power to file a civil suit via 42 USC § 1983 to seek compensation from the Baltimore Police Department. Under § 1983, individuals can bring federal suit against state law enforcement agents who violate their constitutional rights.[133] For most of the twentieth century, individuals hoping to bring suit for police misconduct faced an uphill battle.[134] Section 1983 states that any "person" who engages in a "deprivation of any rights, privileges, or immunities secured by the Constitution and laws, shall be liable to the party injured in an action at law."[135] On its face, this seems to open up law enforcement officers and administrators to significant liability. However, because of a "misapplication of tort doctrine to constitutional law," the courts held for most of the last century that superiors were immune from liability for the actions of their employees.[136] This meant that, while a private person could file a suit against an individual police officer, holding the police department or municipality responsible was nearly impossible. The Court reaffirmed this holding in *Monroe* v. *Pape*.[137]

Federal courts have made suits against individual police officers challenging. Many officers are protected from civil suits by a legal doctrine known as qualified immunity.[138] This doctrine shields police officers from liability any time they are acting within the scope of their employment and when their behavior does not constitute a violation of clearly established law.[139] In practice, this means that police officers can

[133] 42 USC § 1983 (2000).

[134] This was largely because individuals could not hold a department or municipality liable for much of the twentieth century because of the Court's holding in *Monroe* v. *Pape*, 365 US 167 (1961), which held superiors virtually immune from liability.

[135] The important portions of § 1983 reads:

> "Every person who, under color of [law] ... subjects, or causes to be subjected, any citizen of the United States or other person within the jurisdiction thereof to the deprivation of any rights, privileges, or immunities secured by the Constitution and laws, shall be liable to the party injured in an action at law, suit in equity, or other proper proceeding for redress ... "

[136] Candace McCoy, *Enforcement Workshop: Lawsuits Against Police-What Impact Do They Really Have?* 20 Crime Bull. 49, 49–50 (1984).

[137] *Monroe*, 365 US at 167.

[138] *See generally* Joanna Schwartz, *Police Indemnification*, 89 NYU L. Rev. 885, 892 (2014) (explaining the historical basis and strength of modern qualified immunity doctrine).

[139] The purpose of the qualified immunity doctrine was to prevent the law from over deterring police officers by threatening them with excessive personal liability. *See id*

only be subject to suit under § 1983 when their conduct demonstrates a clear or obvious disregard for civil rights.

Had the Gray family tried to bring such a § 1983 suit in the mid-twentieth century, it would have likely failed. They would have faced an uphill battle to prove that any officers clearly disregarded Mr. Gray's civil rights. And they would have virtually no avenue to hold the Baltimore Police Department responsible for the actions of its officers. But in 1978, that changed. That year the US Supreme Court held in *Monell* v. *New York City Department of Social Services* that a local municipality or police department could be considered a "person" under § 1983 and thus held liable.[140] Courts since *Monell* have articulated a two-prong standard for determining whether a municipality or department would be liable for the actions of an employee like a police officer. Litigants have to prove that the employer was deliberately indifferent in its failure to train or supervise an employee.[141] In these circumstances plaintiffs can reach the employer in civil litigation. The *Monell* decision, no doubt, had important implications for American police departments. Since the case, aggrieved citizens can now levy claims against *both* individual police officers and the police departments that employee them.

In Mr. Gray's case, this meant that his family could file a suit directly against the Baltimore Police Department. Facing significant community pressure, the city of Baltimore agreed to settle with the Gray family for $6.4 million.[142] In theory, such a hefty monetary penalty should motivate a police department like Baltimore to make reforms aimed at reducing police misconduct. But various rigorous examinations of this type of individual-initiated civil litigation against departments have yielded

(quoting *Forrester* v. *White*, 484 US 219, 223 (1988) in stating that "[w]hen officials are threatened with personal liability . . . they may likewise be induced to act with an excess of caution or otherwise to skew their decisions in ways that result in less than full fidelity to the objective and independent criteria that ought to guide their conduct"); *see also Harlow* v. *Fitzgerald*, 457 US 800, 806 (1982) (explaining how the qualified immunity doctrine shields officers from undue interferences with their duties); *Hope* v. *Pelzer*, 536 US 603, 617 (2002) (establishing the "clearly established" law standard for qualified immunity cases).

140 *Monell* v. *New York City Dept. of Social Servs.*, 436 US 658, 695–701 (1978)

141 *City of Canton* v. *Harris*, 489 US 378, 388 (1989) (explaining that a state agent employer may be liable for the actions of an employee under § 1983 if the city's policy or practice was objectively deliberately indifferent to the likelihood that a constitutional violation would occur).

142 Yvonne Wenger & Mark Puente, *Baltimore to Pay Freddie Gray's Family $6.4 Million to Settle Civil Claims*, Baltimore Sun, September 8, 2015, *available at* www.baltimoresun.com/news/maryland/freddie-gray/bs-md-ci-boe-20150908-story.html.

skepticism. This method for regulating law enforcement misconduct "appears to be a weak strategy for achieving police reform, in part because of the structure of local governments and a pervasive pattern of political and administrative irresponsibility."[143] After all, civil litigation is a classic cost-raising regulation tactic. It only works if aggrieved parties regularly litigate, and departments feel the financial consequences of this litigation, thus motivating them to change behaviors and policies.

At least one study has shown that civil litigation has successfully raised the potential cost of misconduct high enough to force a response by local police agencies.[144] Other evidence, though, suggests that decentralization in local municipality government makes legalized accountability difficult: "[O]ne agency of the government, the police department, commits abuses of rights, another agency, the city attorney's office defends the conduct in court, and a third agency, the city treasurer, pays whatever financial settlement results from the litigation."[145] This means that while a police department may suffer from a lawsuit in response to officer misconduct, the department itself may not feel the financial ramifications of the lawsuit. Such a finding means that private civil litigation does not necessarily increase the cost of misconduct, limiting the ability of this litigation to instigate widespread reform.

Further, a recent study by Professor Joanna Schwartz concluded that across virtually every major city in the United States, police departments indemnify officers facing § 1983 suits.[146] So when an individual police officer is held responsible for police misconduct under § 1983, he or she almost never faces any financial consequences. As Professor Schwartz concluded, 99.98 percent of all dollars paid via § 1983 litigation are paid by cities, departments, or municipalities – not by

[143] Samuel Walker & Morgan Macdonald, *An Alternative Remedy for Police Misconduct: A Model State Pattern for Practice Statute*, 19 Geo. Mason U. CR LJ 479, 495 (2008).

[144] Charles R. Epp, Making Rights Real: Activists, Bureaucrats, and the Creation of the Legalistic State 93–114 (2010) (describing the process by which police departments have come to implement reform, due in part to the threat of possible litigation). Epp shows that in November of 1977, when the largest private insurance company that provided police liability insurance withdrew from the market because of unacceptable risk, the prospect of self-insurance motivated many police professionals to develop rules and regulations about police conduct. *Id.* at 95. According to Epp, this contributed to a growing culture of "legalized accountability" in American police departments. *Id.* at 4, 95 and 96 (stating that the "resulting system of legalized accountability has spread widely").

[145] Walker & Macdonald, *supra* note 143 at 495.

[146] Schwartz, *supra* note 138.

individual officers.[147] This means that, not only do cities keep departments from feeling the negative effects of litigation, but officers themselves rarely feel the financial consequences of misconduct.

Even when cities are on the hook for police misconduct, like in the Baltimore case, Professor Schwartz has found that they rarely pay these settlements out of their general funds.[148] Instead, municipalities use a wide range of budgetary mechanisms to lessen the impact of § 1983 settlements.[149] The result is that even cities paying hefty prices for police misconduct via § 1983 litigation may not have a strong financial incentive to invest in police reform.

In addition, in order for financial incentives like § 1983 to be effective, municipalities must grant police supervisors the power to punish or fire officers engaged in misconduct. Emerging empirical evidence, though, suggests that police union contracts, often negotiated outside of public view with minimal community input, frequently handcuff the ability of police supervisors to investigate or punish officers engaged in misconduct.[150] This means that even if an officer engages in misconduct that ultimately results in a costly § 1983 suit, the department may not be able to respond forcefully with internal disciplinary measures.

Finally, individuals hoping to exercise their rights under § 1983 face high entrance barriers and legal fees. The mobilization of legal protections under § 1983 is costly, making them only feasible in cases of serious misconduct. So while it might make financial sense for a person to initiate a § 1983 suit in the case of police misconduct that leads to a wrongful death, a rational individual may choose not to use the statute in the event he or she is unlawfully stopped and frisked. All of this suggests that civil litigation is a useful, but highly imperfect, tool for instigating police reform.

3 Criminal Culpability

A final reform that grew in importance during the Buildup Era is criminal prosecution of police officers. The attempted prosecution of a police officer in Madison, Alabama, provides a useful example of this regulatory mechanism. On the morning of February 6, 2015, Sureshbhai Patel went

147 *Id.* at 1.

148 Joanna C. Schwartz, *How Governments Pay: Lawsuits, Budgets, and Police Reform*, 63 UCLA L. Rev. 1144, 1165–73 (2016) (showing the percentages of police departments in her sample that paid settlements out of their general fund).

149 *Id.*

150 Stephen Rushin, *Police Union Contracts*, 66 Duke L. J. (forthcoming 2017).

for a walk in a residential Madison neighborhood.[151] Mr. Patel, a slender 57-year-old grandfather, was in town from his native India to visit his son's family in the Huntsville suburb.[152] A nearby resident who saw Mr. Patel walking around the neighborhood that morning called 9–11 to report a "skinny black guy" who was "just walking around."[153] The caller explained, "I'd like somebody to talk to him."[154] The police did just that. Moments later a squad car appeared, and two officers began to question Mr. Patel. A dash cam recorded the rest of the encounter.

"Hey bud, let me talk to you real quick. Come here," one officer remarked.[155] While the officers tried to communicate with Mr. Patel, it quickly became apparent that Mr. Patel could not speak English.[156] What happened next is difficult to discern from the dash cam recording. One officer warned Mr. Patel not to "jerk away."[157] The officer told Mr. Patel that if he pulled away again, "I'm going to put you on this ground."[158]

Soon thereafter, Officer Eric Parker swept Mr. Patel's legs and violently slammed him to the ground.[159] Mr. Patel suffered spinal damage, causing paralysis in his arms and legs.[160] After several weeks of therapy, Mr. Patel was able to regain some use of his limbs. Soon after the dash cam footage went public, the local prosecutor in Limestone County, Alabama, filed misdemeanor criminal assault charges against Officer Parker.[161] After all, if a police officer commits an act of misconduct that rises to the level of a criminal offense, prosecutors can always charge him or her with a crime like any other person. But if convicted at the local level, Officer Parker would only face up to a year behind bars and a fine of no more than $2,000. Given the seriousness of Mr. Patel's injury, this relatively minor misdemeanor charge seemed inadequate.

So on March 26, federal prosecutor brought criminal charges against Officer Parker for violating Mr. Patel's civil rights under 18 USC § 242.[162] This statute comes with a far heftier punishment – up to ten years behind bars.[163] In order to secure a conviction under § 242, the federal prosecutor must show that Officer Parker "willfully" deprived Mr. Patel of the

[151] Richard Fausset, *Alabama Police Officer Indicted in Confrontation with Unarmed Indian Man*, NY Times, March 28, 2015, at A11.

[152] *Id.* [153] *Id.* [154] *Id.* [155] *Id.* [156] *Id.* [157] *Id.* [158] *Id.* [159] *Id.*

[160] Challen Stephens, *Defense Says Slamming Down Indian Grandfather Was 'an Officer Safety Issue,'* Birmingham News, September 3, 2015, *available at* www.al.com/news/index.ssf/2015/09/criminal_trial_for_alabama_cop.html.

[161] Fausset, *supra* note 151. [162] *Id.*

[163] 18 USC § 242 (2000) (making it a federal crime for a police officer to "willfully" violate a person's constitutional rights and placing heavy criminal penalties on such behavior that leads to bodily injury).

"rights, privileges, or immunities" guaranteed by the Constitution.[164] For federal prosecutors, the phrase "willfully" represents a significant challenge.

In order to secure a conviction, a prosecutor must ordinarily prove that a suspect acted with a particular mental state. So, for example, in order to secure a conviction for a first-degree murder in most jurisdictions, a prosecutor must traditionally show that a suspect intentionally or purposefully caused another person's death with premeditation or deliberation. Most criminal law statutes require a showing that a criminal suspect committed an act "purposefully," "knowingly," "recklessly," or "negligently." Only a small number of criminal law statutes – including § 242 – require a prosecutor to show that a suspect "willfully" committed a crime. So what must a prosecutor show in order to prove a willful deprivation of civil rights?

In *Screws* v. *United States*, the Supreme Court held that the term "willfully" under § 242 requires prosecutors to demonstrate that an officer knew his or her actions would cause a deprivation of civil rights and that he or she nonetheless took the action with this specific intent.[165] As a result of this interpretation, federal prosecutors have found it extremely challenging to win § 242 cases.[166] In the years leading up to the passage of § 14141, evidence emerged that federal prosecutions under § 242 were rare. Table 1.1 shows the number of civil rights complaints received by the DOJ between 1981 and 1990 and the proportion of these complaints that resulted in investigations or criminal charges.

As the numbers clearly demonstrate, the DOJ investigated only a fraction of civil rights claims under § 242. And the DOJ only sought criminal charges in an extremely small portion of cases – typically under 1 percent. Among those cases where the DOJ actually went to trial on § 242 violations, acquittals were not uncommon.[167] So from the start, federal prosecutors faced an uphill battle in charging Officer Parker with a violation of § 242. Federal prosecutors argued that Mr. Patel had said "No English" and "India" multiple times before trying to guide the officer's back to his son's house. While Officer Parker audibly states that Mr. Patel cannot speak English on the recording, he then continues to issue commands in English. The prosecution also argued that by

[164] *Id.* [165] 325 US 91 (1945).

[166] John V. Jacobi, *Prosecuting Police Misconduct*, 2000 Wis. L. Rev. 789, 809–811 (describing a study by Human Rights Watch which concluded that "*Screws* specific intent element deters federal prosecution of police misconduct.").

[167] *Id.* (showing that in some years, like 1988 and 1989, there were an equal or greater number of § 242 acquittals than convictions).

Table 1.1 *Federal Enforcement of 18 USC § 242 in Years Leading up to Intervention Era**

Year	Complaints	Investigations (%)	Attempted Charges (%)
1981	11,064	30.6	0.6
1982	10,327	31.2	0.8
1983	10,457	31.2	0.6
1984	8,617	39.6	0.7
1985	9,044	32.8	0.8
1986	7,546	37.0	0.8
1987	7,348	38.5	1.0
1988	7,603	38.0	0.7
1989	8,053	39.5	0.9
1990	7,960	38.3	1.0

* Police Brutality: Hearing Before the H. Subcomm. on Civil and Const. Rights of the Comm. on the Judiciary, 102d Cong. 10 (1991) (showing the number of civil rights prosecutions by year as compiled by the DOJ as part of a hearing on police brutality). I calculated these numbers as follows. To determine the percentage of complaints that resulted in investigations, I divided investigations by complaints received. To determine the percentage of times the DOJ attempted to file criminal charges, I added together all times the DOJ presented a case to a grand jury or filed an information.

slamming Mr. Patel to the ground, Officer Parker knew his actions were likely to cause injury and were unconstitutional. The prosecution also provided expert testimony that Mr. Patel will likely never fully recover from the injuries he suffered at the hands of Officer Parker.[168]

In response, the defense portrayed Officer Parker's decision to slam Mr. Patel to the ground as an "officer safety issue."[169] Officer Parker's attorneys argued that Mr. Patel's attempts to walk away from the officers and reach into his pocket put the officer's safety at risk.[170] The defense also argued that Mr. Patel was violating federal law by not carrying his

[168] Challen Stephens, *Deadlocked Jury Favored Acquittal for Officer Who Slammed Down Indian Grandfather*, Birmingham News, September 15, 2015, *available at* www.al.com/news/index.ssf/2015/09/hung_jury_favored_officer_on_t.html.

[169] *Id.* [170] *Id.*

green card.[171] Ultimately, the jury in this trial could not reach a verdict. Ten white male jurors voted to acquit Officer Parker while two black female jurors voted for conviction.[172] Federal prosecutors were not deterred by this mistrial. Shortly thereafter, federal prosecutors again brought charges against Officer Parker.[173] This time, the defense even more passionately blamed Mr. Patel for his injuries because of his failure to "follow our laws and speak our language."[174] As they put it, "Mr. Patel bears as much responsibility for this as anyone." According to the defense, "[t]here are people out there in the world that will kill a police officer just because they are a cop," and "[i]f you act like a criminal you are going to be treated like one."[175] Yet again, the jury failed to reach a verdict.

Why have federal prosecutors struggled to convict Officer Parker? The entire encounter was caught on camera. His own department rejected his conduct and attempted to terminate his employment.[176] His conduct even inspired Alabama governor Robert Bentley to issue a formal apology to Mr. Patel.[177] If all of these outsiders felt compelled to condemn Officer Parker's behavior, why couldn't federal prosecutors secure a conviction? No doubt, the willful mental state requirement under § 242 makes it extremely tough to obtain any conviction in federal court. But this and other recent incidents highlight the fundamental challenges in using criminal prosecution, at both the federal and state levels, to vindicate police misconduct.

Prosecutors are often hesitant to pursue vigorously criminal charges against police officers, and for good reason. Take the example of District Attorney Kari Brandenburg of Bernalillo County, New Mexico. When she filed criminal charges against two Albuquerque police officers for the shooting death of a homeless man named James Boyd, she immediately faced retaliation from other police officers.[178] Within days of filing the

[171] *Id.* [172] Stephens, *supra* note 168.

[173] Challen Stephens, *Defense Blames Indian Grandfather at Start of New Trial, 'Follow Our Laws and Speak Our Language,'* Birmingham News, October 27, 2015, *available at* www.al.com/news/index.ssf/2015/10/defense_blames_indian_grandfat.html.

[174] *Id.* [175] *Id.*

[176] *Officer Calls Alabama's Cop's Takedown of Elderly Indian Man 'Improper' at Trial,* Chicago Tribune, September 3, 2015, *available at* www.chicagotribune.com/news/nationworld/ct-alabama-officer-trial-20150903-story.html.

[177] Fausset, *supra* note 151.

[178] Radley Balko, *Prosecutor's Union Inadvertently Demonstrates Why Local Prosecutors Shouldn't Investigate Police Shootings,* Wash. Post, June 23, 2015, *available at* www.washingtonpost.com/news/the-watch/wp/2015/06/23/prosecutors-union-inadvertently-demonstrates-why-local-prosecutors-shouldnt-investigate-police-shootings/.

charges, city officials shut out one of Brandenburg's deputy prosecutors from a city meeting to discuss another police shooting.[179] The police department claimed that Ms. Brandenburg faced a conflict of interest because of an unrelated case involving a police investigation of her son.[180] Similarly, in Salt Lake County in Utah, District Attorney Sim Gill similarly faced backlash from the local police union when he indicted two officers for the shooting death of Danielle Willard.[181] The police group promised to back Mr. Gill's challenger in the next election and argued that his Indian ethnicity clouded his judgment.[182] Given this sort of backlash, perhaps we shouldn't have been surprised when St. Louis County prosecutor Bob McCulloch seemed "openly and unapologetically sympathetic to [Officer Darren] Wilson and was so hostile to and derisive of protesters" after the shooting death of Michael Brown in Ferguson, Missouri.[183]

The bottom line is that local prosecutors must work with local police officers on a daily basis. When we make these same prosecutors responsible for the prosecution of local police officers, conflicts of interest are inevitable.[184] This may explain why, over the last seven years, local prosecutors have only charged an estimated forty-one police officers with murder or manslaughter for on-duty shootings.[185] Additionally, both juries and grand juries are often more likely to trust and sympathize with police officers than victims of police misconduct.[186] It should come as no surprise, then, that grand juries rarely indict

179 Nancy Laflin, *Bad Blood Brews Between APD, District Attorney*, KOAT Albuquerque, January 15, 2015, *available at* www.koat.com/news/bad-blood-brews-between-apd-district-attorney/30711178.

180 Ryan Boetel, *District Attorney Kari Brandenberg's Office Disqualified From Boyd Case*, Albuquerque Journal, April 9, 2015, *available at* www.abqjournal.com/567045/abqnewsseeker/brandenburg-disqualified-from-boyd-case.html.

181 Radley Balko, *An Unexpected Reformer Fights to Hold Police Accountable*, Huffington Post, October 29, 2013, *available at* www.huffingtonpost.com/2013/10/29/sim-gill-utah-police_n_4164873.html.

182 Balko, *supra* note 178. 183 *Id.*

184 *Id.* at 9 (explaining the hesitance on the part of the prosecutors to bring charges against police officers).

185 Zusha Elinson & Joe Palazzolo, *Police Rarely Criminally Charged for On-Duty Shootings*, Wall Street Journal, November 24, 2014, *available at* www.wsj.com/articles/police-rarely-criminally-charged-for-on-duty-shootings-1416874955.

186 Harmon, *supra* note 127, at 9 (prosecutors generally fail to prosecute police and juries fail to convict); Armacost, *supra* note 7 at 464 and 465 (describing methods to hold law enforcement officers criminally liable for constitutional violations); Livingston, *supra* note 27 at 844 (stating that "criminal prosecution plays some role in holding officers accountable for acts of clear illegality").

cops.[187] By contrast, grand juries almost always return indictments against non-cops. At least one state – Wisconsin – has recently passed a law that requires independent investigations of deaths in police custody.[188] Wisconsin, though, remains the exception, not the norm. In almost all jurisdictions, police prosecutions remain fraught with conflicts of interest.

Perhaps the biggest limitation of police prosecution as a regulatory tool is that the scope of the criminal law is invariably narrower than the scope of police wrongdoing. Even if a jury believes that Sureshbhai Patel, James Boyd, Danielle Willard, and Michael Brown were victims of misconduct, it does not necessarily follow that they were victims of a crime. In order to secure a criminal conviction against a police officer, a prosecutor must prove that an officer violated an existing criminal statute beyond a reasonable doubt. Put simply, the world of police misconduct is far wider than the narrow category of behavior punishable by criminal prosecution. Although necessary and useful in some circumstances, criminal prosecutions are a limited tool for fighting police wrongdoing.

4 The Problems with the Buildup Era

Despite their limitations, the exclusionary rule, private civil litigation, and criminal culpability all represented important steps in gradually building oversight of local police departments. Nevertheless, these Buildup Era regulations simply do not go far enough. None of these mechanisms force a police department to take substantive steps to prevent future misconduct. As a result, these mechanisms generally fail to address the organizational nature of misconduct.

First, the Buildup Era regulations can only make misconduct expensive. They cannot actually force a police department to do anything. That is to say, these regulations attempt to incentivize police reform by raising the costs of non-compliance. If a police department engages in misconduct, the agency risks higher costs – be those the costs of evidentiary exclusion, civil litigation, or criminal prosecution. These cost-raising sorts of regulations have almost certainly had some statistically significant effect on police wrongdoing, even if it is hard to accurately measure. Nevertheless, cost-raising misconduct regulations will always be of

187 Balko, *supra* note 178.

188 Marisol Bello, Greg Toppo, & Peter Eisler, *Grand Jury Charges are Easy, Except Against Police*, USA TODAY, November 25, 2014, *available at* www.usatoday.com/story/news/nation/2014/11/25/ferguson-grand-jury/70098616/.

limited use. A police department can always make a determination that a violation of a cost-raising misconduct regulation is justified. To again use the language of law and economics, a police department is generally free to engage in an efficient breach.[189] That is to say, a police department may determine that the costs associated with a breach – generally monetary penalties or potential evidentiary exclusion – are worth the benefits of violating the law. Much like a contract, cost-raising misconduct regulations give police the duty to follow the law or pay damages, whichever is preferable. As discussed earlier, a city like New York may conclude that by encouraging officers to execute unjustified stop-and-frisks,[190] they can substantially reduce crime in certain high-crime neighborhoods.[191] Such behavior would open the city up to civil litigation. However, the city may conclude that a cost is worth the potential benefit of reduced crime through deterrence.[192] Cost-raising misconduct regulations, therefore, may deter some but not all police wrongdoing. This cost-raising approach to federal regulation of police misconduct has facilitated the rise of police departments that systemically fail to fight misconduct – agencies that make the choice to continue to violate rights, despite the apparent costs.

[189] Robert L. Birmingham, *Breach of Contract, Damage Measures, and Economic Efficiency*, 24 Rutgers L. Rev. 273, 284 (1969) (defining and explaining the concept of efficient breach in the context of contract law).

[190] *Terry* v. *Ohio*, 392 US 1 (1968) (holding that a police officer may engage in a limited stop-and-frisk of an individual if the office has reasonable suspicion that a person is engaged in criminal behavior).

[191] New York is a possible example of a city that has institutionalized the practice of regular *Terry* stops as a possible way to reduce crime. A federal district judge has found that New York City does engage in such an unconstitutional practice and has appointed a federal monitor to ensure changes in departmental policy. *See* Adam Serwer & Jaeah Lee, *Charts: Are the NYPD's Stop-and-Frisks Violating the Constitution?* Mother Jones, www.motherjones.com/politics/2013/04/new-york-nypd-stop-frisk-lawsuit-trial-charts (last visited September 9, 2013) (illustrating the inequality of *Terry* stops in New York City); Joseph Goldstein, *Judge Rejects New York's Stop-and-Frisk Policy*, NY Times, August 12, 2013, *available at* www.nytimes.com/2013/08/13/nyregion/stop-and-frisk-practice-violated-rights-judge-rules.html (last visited September 9, 2013) (detailing district judge's opinion finding that New York City acted unconstitutionally); J. David Goodman, *Bloomberg Calls Court Monitor for Police a "Terrible Idea,"* NY Times, June 13, 2013, *available at* www.nytimes.com/2013/06/14/nyregion/bloomberg-calls-court-monitor-for-police-a-terrible-idea.html (last visited September 9, 2013) (quoting Mayor Michael Bloomberg's objection to judicial intervention in city's use of *Terry* stops as something that may increase crime).

[192] *See, e.g.*, Goodman *supra* note 191 (quoting Mayor Bloomberg, who argues, in response to claims that these stops are unconstitutional, that *Terry* stops are an important part of crime fighting in New York City).

Second, the Buildup Era implicitly treated police misconduct as a "bad apple" problem, rather than a "rotten barrel" problem.[193] The legal system has historically viewed police misconduct as the result of "factual and moral judgments made by officers functioning merely as individuals rather than as part of a distinctive and influential organizational culture."[194] This view focuses on "'notorious incidents and misbehaving individuals'" and "not . . . on the dysfunctional aspects of policing organizations that sustain serious misconduct."[195] When trial courts hear cases of individual officer misconduct in most § 1983 or § 242 cases, they get "no organizational context."[196] During the Buildup Era, judges often have no way to know whether the incident leading to the current claim is the result of one bad officer, or the result of a "diseased organization."[197] Over the last century, policing scholars have started, in earnest, to argue that individual officer misconduct is commonly a symptom of a bigger illness – a diseased organizational culture and lax internal oversight measures that make individual officer misconduct common and routine. The narrative of misconduct as the result of a single cop-gone-rogue is tempting but has been shown consistently to be an oversimplification. Countless real-world examples demonstrate that misconduct thrives when members of an organization are "socialized into membership in a group where the norms favor violation of internal rules, laws, or administrative regulations."[198]

Misconduct becomes routine through the development of an internal organizational culture that passively permits wrongdoing. This sort of culture often develops through a lack of oversight mechanisms and is reinforced through training, punishment, and rewards. Organizational research shows that socialization and on-the-job training can make rule violation routine.[199] Organizational leadership also appears to be critically important to the presence of misconduct. Leaders can apply performance pressure that affects individual action and can support internal cultures that either indirectly or directly condone misconduct.[200] The "willingness [of an organizational member] to use illegitimate means on the organization's behalf is sealed by a reinforcing system of rewards and

[193] Armacost, *supra* note 7, at 457. [194] *Id.* at 455.

[195] Samuel Walker, The New World of Police Accountability 4 (2005).

[196] Armacost, *supra* note 7, at 455. [197] *Id.* [198] Vaughan, *supra* note 60, at 290.

[199] *See, e.g.*, Joseph Bensman and Israel Gerver, *Crime and Punishment in the Factory: The Function of Deviancy in Maintaining the Social System*, 28 Amer. Soc. Rev. 588 (1963); Maurice Punch, Conduct Unbecoming (1985).

[200] Vaughan, *supra* note 60, at 290.

punishments."[201] The incidents in Los Angeles illustrate how this sort of normalization or routinization can facilitate egregious misconduct.

The circumstances surrounding the Rodney King beating in Los Angeles is perhaps the most thoroughly documented case of a police organization normalizing and routinizing misconduct. In the aftermath of the Rodney King events, the city of Los Angeles formed an independent commission to investigate the conditions that precipitated the incident, headed by Warren Christopher.[202] The report filed by this commission came to be informally known as the Christopher Commission Report. The Christopher Commission Report found a wide range of systemic problems affecting the LAPD, including problems with use of force, complaint procedures, training policies, and structural organization. The commission found a startling pattern of excessive use of force among a small portion of officers.[203] The Christopher Commission Report also determined the LAPD used insufficient complaint procedures and improper investigations in cases where citizens levied complaints.[204] Once more, the commission determined that internal policies and procedures used by the Internal Affairs Division make it hard for citizens to file complaints. For example, "[s]ome intake officers actively discourage filing

[201] *Id.* [202] *See generally* Christopher Comm'n Report, *supra* note 26.

[203] While the vast majority of LAPD officers had only 1 or 2 allegations of excessive force, around "183 officers had four or more allegations, 44 had six or more, 16 had eight or more, and one had 16 such allegations." *Id.* at ix and x. Similarly, of the 6,000 police officers involved in use of force incidents between January 1987 and March 1991. *Id.* at x. Again the overwhelming majority of all officers had fewer than five reported uses of force. *Id.* (explaining that " . . . 63 officers had 20 or more reports each . . ." and "[t]he top 5% of the officers [ranked by number of reports] accounted for more than 20% of all reports"). But a small cohort of officers accounted for a large amount of all use of force reports. *Id.* Among the officers that were subject to the most allegations of excessive use of force, "the performance evaluation reports for [these problematic officers] were very positive" as they "document[ed] every complimentary comment received and express[ed] optimism about the officer's progress in the Department." *Id.* at xi.

[204] The commission reviewed "83 civil lawsuits alleging excessive or improper force by LAPD officers for the period 1986 through 1990 that resulted in a settlement or judgment of more than $15,000." *Id.* at xi. This review showed that the majority of "cases involved clear and often egregious misconduct resulting in serious injury or death to the victim." *Id.* Of particular note, the commission found that the LAPD's internal investigation into the events surrounding these eighty-three lawsuits were regularly "light or non-existent." *Id.* The commission also found that the LAPD's internal procedures for handling citizen complaints frequently led to public frustration. Out of 2,152 citizen allegations of excessive force, the LAPD only sustained 42. *Id.* at xix. This means that the LAPD sustained roughly 1–2 percent of all citizen complaints for excessive use of force. This was in part because the part of the police department responsible for investigating these claims – the Internal Affairs Division (IAD) – had limited resources *Id.*

by being uncooperative or requiring long waits before completing a complaint form."[205] The Christopher Commission Report also concluded that the LAPD's training programs were unsatisfactory.[206] The commission believed that the systemic misconduct could be traced back to training programs that emphasized the use of physical force as opposed to verbal skills.[207] And the commission noted several other systemic problems, including startling cases of documented racism.[208] The commission cited several specific examples of racist behaviors by LAPD officers where officers referred to interactions with minority residents as "monkey slapping time," and among other highly offensive comments.[209] Shortly before the King beating, in fact, two of the officers involved were comparing a domestic dispute between two African American individuals to "gorillas in the mist" over the radio.[210] More disturbingly, evidence suggests that leadership within the police department heard or knew of these kinds of statements, but did nothing to stop them or punish those involved.[211]

The LAPD during this time bore all of the hallmarks of a problematic police organization: a lack of internal accountability measures, supervisors who did not punish obvious misconduct, and leadership that either implicitly or explicitly approved of wrongdoing. This made misconduct normal within the organization. External punishment of individual officers – the most common response to police wrongdoing during the twentieth century – merely addressed isolated symptoms. Such a historical approach could not treat the underlying organizational illnesses that contributed to repeated wrongdoing in American police departments.

205 *Id.*

206 As the report explained, LAPD officers go through three different training phases. *Id.* at xvi. Officers get their initial training at the police academy. *Id.* After this, officers then go through a probationary period for one year when they work in the field with more experienced officers. *Id.* After this, officers received continuing in-service training. *Id.*

207 De-escalation, they argued, should be an important component of training at every stage. *Id.* The commission also found that training did not emphasize culture respect and awareness enough. *Id.* Additionally, the commission found that the requirements for training officers were insufficient. *Id.* at xvii. These field training officers (FTOs) "guide new officers' first contacts with citizens and have primary responsibility for introducing the probationers to the culture and traditions of the Department." *Id.* Thus, it should be no surprise that the commission felt that these officers' conduct was critical in ensuring an adequate training program. The requirements for these FTOs were considered insufficient since "there are no formal eligibility or disqualification criteria for the FTO position based on an applicant's disciplinary records." *Id.*

208 *Id.* at xii. 209 *Id.* 210 *Id.* at 14. 211 *Id.* at xii and xiii.

Conclusion

Without the Rodney King incident, Congress may have never initiated the Intervention Era. As described more in Chapter 2, this single event provided a unique political opportunity for members of Congress to push for an expansion of federally initiated structural reform litigation into a new institutional realm. Even so, any description of the Intervention Era must not start with the Rodney King incident. Instead, as this chapter shows, the Intervention Era must be understood as a continuation of a century-long effort to combat structural, political, and organizational conditions that promote systemic wrongdoing within local police departments. In a handful of troubled agencies, a lack of external oversight and permissive organizational cultures make wrongdoing routine. These agencies have shown a systemic unwillingness to control misconduct. Given the unique American approach to law enforcement, the existence of these sorts of problematic policing agencies is inevitable. The Buildup Era brought several new regulations of local police conduct. The exclusionary rule, civil litigation, and expanded criminal culpability almost certainly contributed to a professionalization in American policing. Nevertheless, these Buildup Era reforms have inadequately addressed the problem of police misconduct in the United States. By the late twentieth century, these gaps in the regulatory scheme became highly visible. This created an opening for the beginning of the Intervention Era.

2

The Intervention Era

Introduction

This chapter describes the beginning of the Intervention Era. It starts by describing the legislative maneuvering that led to the eventual passage of § 14141. The beating of Rodney King in 1991 spurred congressional interest in the federal regulation of police misconduct and added urgency to a growing push for a public right of action. Even after Congress expressed serious interest in federal intervention into police departments, it took years for the Intervention Era to become a reality; in fact, it would take another three years before Congress authorized § 14141 as part of a larger omnibus crime bill known as the Violent Crime Control and Law Enforcement Act (VCCLEA). This was a historic moment – a dramatic shift in how the federal government responds to the systemic failure of some police agencies to control misconduct. Yet, amazingly, at the time almost *no one noticed.* Major media outlets all but ignored the passage of § 14141, focusing their coverage instead on more controversial components of the VCCLEA like the federal assault weapons ban. Even the legislative record from the VCCLEA includes no significant mentions of § 14141.

Fast-forward two decades and many of the nation's largest police agencies have been subject to federal intervention, including Los Angeles, Seattle, Washington, DC, Pittsburgh, New Orleans, Cincinnati, Cleveland, Newark, Albuquerque, and Detroit.[1] Other major American cities, like New York, Chicago, Portland, Austin, Columbus, Providence, and Tulsa, have been subject to formal DOJ investigation pursuant to § 14141.[2] Combined, the police departments that have been subject to some sort of DOJ action via § 14141 serve a combined population

[1] *See infra* Appendices A and B. I obtained the information on investigations and structural reform actions directly from the DOJ. The full list of all investigatory actions is available in the appendices of this book.

[2] *Id.*

of over 56 million Americans.[3] That means that nearly *one in five Americans* is served by a law enforcement agency that has been a target for possible federal intervention.[4] All of this suggests that federal intervention is a critical new component of American policing law. In theory, the equitable right of action afforded by § 14141 is uniquely tailored to address the apparent causes of patterns of practices of misconduct in local police agencies. Soon after the measure's passage, a small handful of policing scholars were optimistic that § 14141 could transform the field of American policing law.[5] Some called the passage of § 14141 "more significant, in the long run, than *Mapp* v. *Ohio*, which mandated the exclusion of evidence obtained in violation of the Fourth Amendment."[6]

This sort of optimism was understandable. Upon passage, § 14141 had transformative potential. It gives the federal executive branch authority to define what constitutes legitimate policing within the field of American law enforcement. In a tremendously decentralized field such as American policing,[7] § 14141 is a rare opportunity for one central body to define the boundaries of acceptable policing. Intervention also provides the federal government with the opportunity to demand external monitoring of problematic police agencies.[8] These third-party compliance professionals theoretically allow § 14141 to facilitate real change in problematic police agencies.[9]

[3] This number was calculated by adding up the population served by each law enforcement agency listed as previously or currently under investigation by the DOJ pursuant to § 14141.

[4] I calculated this number by dividing the total number of citizens living in jurisdictions served by a department subject to § 14141 action.

[5] *See, e.g.*, Barbara E. Armacost, *Organizational Culture and Police Misconduct*, 72 GEO. WASH. L. REV. 453, 457 (2003) (stating that § 14141 is "perhaps the most promising mechanism" for reducing police misconduct).

[6] William J. Stuntz, *The Pathological Politics of Criminal Law*, 100 MICH. L. REV. 505, 538–539 n.134 (2001).

[7] BRIAN A. REAVES, U.S. DEP'T OF JUSTICE, CENSUS OF STATE AND LOCAL LAW ENFORCEMENT AGENCIES, 2008, at 2 (2011), *available at* www.bjs.gov/content/pub/pdf/csllea08.pdf (putting the number of state and local law enforcement agencies at 17,985).

[8] *See* Chapter 4 (discussing the appointment of a monitor as a critical component of structural police reform).

[9] In regulating organizations, the law commonly relies upon compliance professionals who act as social filters in interpreting and implementing the tenants of the regulation. These compliance professionals, as is the case in structural reform litigation, normally are individuals with extensive experience in the organizational field being regulated (i.e., former police chiefs or litigators). Compliance professionals are therefore not impartial facilitators of the law but rather encourage regulated organizations to adopt practices

Has the Intervention Era actually lived up to its potential? Has it contributed to widespread reform in American police departments? Despite the law's potential, there has historically been little empirical research on the subject.[10] Until recently, the public knew little about how the DOJ has identified police departments in violation of § 14141. Very little previous research has explored the DOJ's internal enforcement policies. And no work has comprehensively documented how the § 14141 reform process works from beginning to end. This chapter concludes by arguing that these voids in the literature are increasingly indefensible in light of the growing importance of federal intervention into local police departments.

This chapter proceeds in three parts. The first part of the chapter chronicles the legislative maneuvering that led to the beginning of the Intervention Era. The path to the Intervention Era started soon after the Rodney King beating in 1991 when the House Subcommittee on Civil and Constitutional Rights convened a hearing on police brutality. It was in these hearings that expert witnesses, including those from the American Civil Liberties Union (ACLU), emphasized the need for an equitable response to local police agencies that systematically fail to control misconduct within their ranks. The ACLU was not the first group to recommend the use of structural reform litigation to address police misconduct. In 1981, the US Commission on Civil Rights (USCCR) similarly recommended some sort of equitable remedy. Soon thereafter, several members of the subcommittee drafted and submitted legislation that closely mirrored the ACLU and USCCR recommendations. This proposed legislation, known as the Police Accountability Act of 1991, received approval from the House Committee on the Judiciary and was incorporated into the Omnibus Crime Bill of 1991. The measure, though, was derailed via a Republican filibuster. Like dozens of criminal justice measures proposed in the early 1990s, lawmakers revived the proposal in 1993 and incorporated it into the VCCLEA.

common among other organizations in the field. In this way, many regulations of organizations develop endogenously – that is, the meaning of external regulation is "formed in part through the actions of organizations and the models of organizational action that become institutionalized in organizational fields." Lauren B. Edelman, *The Legal Lives of Private Organizations*, Blackwell Companion L. & Soc'y. 231, 244–245 (2004).

[10] *See infra* Part III.B (giving an overview of the available literature on structural police reform).

The second part of this chapter contends that the regulatory model embraced by the Intervention Era – that is, equitable relief permitting court-monitored restructuring – was both historically tested and well-suited to the unique problem facing American law enforcement. In the decades leading up to the passage of § 14141, Congress gave the attorney general authority to initiate structural reform litigation in numerous other institutional contexts, including employment, housing, prisons, education, and voter rights.[11] The Rodney King crisis provided liberal factions in Congress with a highly visible example of misconduct in a local government. In the years leading up to the King incident, civil rights groups had been quietly pushing for an expansion of structural reform litigation. The King beating legitimized congressional interest in expanding structural reform litigation to yet another institutional context. It made sense for Congress to choose equitable relief as the mechanism to address the systematic failures by local police agencies to control misconduct. Two court cases in the late twentieth century, *Los Angeles* v. *Lyons* and *United States* v. *Philadelphia*, made private equitable suits against local police departments practically impossible without congressional approval. This put the impetus on Congress to authorize affirmatively structural reform litigation in the context of police departments. This part also argues that the Intervention Era offers a unique remedy by which the federal government could define the boundaries of legitimate policing behavior and overcome concerns of symbolic compliance.

The third part of this chapter hypothesizes on the importance of the Intervention Era. It uses a range of methodological approaches to demonstrate that the public has not fully appreciated the importance of the Intervention Era, despite its potential to transform the regulation of police misconduct. The DOJ has used its authority under § 14141 to investigate departments across the country serving tens of millions of Americans. This chapter contends that despite receiving virtually no attention during the VCCLEA debates, federal intervention has emerged as one of the most important reforms from the VCCLEA decades later. Nevertheless, few scholars have extensively researched the process by which the federal government intervenes into local police departments.

[11] Rachel A. Harmon, *Promoting Civil Rights Through Proactive Policing Reform*, 62 Stan. L. Rev. 1, 11 (2009).

Thus, this chapter situates this book as an attempt to fill these critical gaps in the literature.

I Legislative Maneuvering

So how did § 14141 end up in the VCCLEA? Although civil rights advocates had recognized the importance of federal intervention for decades, it wasn't until the early 1990s when the issue rose to national importance. This is in large part because of one single incident of appalling police brutality – the Los Angeles Police Department's (LAPD) beating of Rodney King.[12] This event almost immediately spurred congressional investigation into the scope of police misconduct problems in the United States. Within weeks of the event, the House Subcommittee on Civil and Constitutional Rights convened to consider how the federal government could do more to address brutality among the ranks of local police.[13]

The subcommittee members called various experts within the field of policing law, including Paul Hoffman, the legal director of the American Civil Liberties Union (ALCU) of Southern California. Hoffman and his colleagues at the ACLU used the Rodney King incident to illustrate the need for Congress to authorize some mechanism for the federal government to intervene into local police departments.[14] Republican subcommittee members generally opposed such a grant of power to the federal government.[15] Democratic representatives, though, immediately supported the idea.[16] Soon thereafter,

[12] For a detailed account of the Rodney King events, *see* Seth Mydans, *Seven Minutes in Los Angeles – A Special Report: Videotaped Beating by Officers Puts Full Glare on Brutality Issue*, NY Times, March 18, 1991, *available at* www.nytimes.com/1991/03/18/us/seven-minutes-los-angeles-special-report-videotaped-beating-officers-puts-full.html (last visited November 13, 2016).

[13] The Rodney King beating happened on March 3, 1991. On March 20, 1991, the House Subcommittee on Civil and Constitutional Rights of the Committee on the Judiciary called a hearing to discuss the issue of police brutality. At this hearing, discussion of the Rodney King incident clearly dominated. *See Police Brutality: Hearing Before the H. Subcomm. on Civil and Const. Rights of the Comm. on the Judiciary*, 102d Cong. (1991).

[14] *Id.* at 54–118 (showing the transcripts of Hoffman's testimony before the subcommittee, specifically on page 61 when Mr. Hoffman states that "if there is a pattern or practice of abuse, the Justice Department ought to be able to deal with it").

[15] *See id.* at 2 (with Republican Representative Howard Coble stating that he would "like for this sort of misconduct, for want of a better word, to be resolved internally").

[16] *See, e.g., id.* at 131 (Democratic Representative Don Edwards stating that the suggestion that Congress authorize the DOJ to initiate pattern or practice litigation is a "very, very useful concrete thing" that it could do).

a contingent of Democratic leaders – many of which served on the subcommittee – put forward a bill authorizing both public and private parties to initiate structural reform litigation.[17] Labeled the Police Accountability Act of 1991, this measure was ultimately incorporated into the Omnibus Crime Bill of 1991.[18] A Republican filibuster ultimately derailed this first legislative attempt to pass the precursor to § 14141.[19] Three years later, a similar measure found its way into the VCCLEA of 1994 and became law soon thereafter.[20] In addition to authorizing § 14141, the VCCLEA mandated strict truth-in-sentencing requirements, implemented life sentences for repeat violent offenders, banned numerous types of assault weapons, barred juvenile ownership of handguns, added additional penalties for hate crimes, extended the death penalty, and codified the Violence Against Women Act.[21] The overall tone and content of the VCCLEA was remarkably conservative and punitive. Throughout the VCCLEA debates, liberal representatives pushed their peers to include some liberal reforms of criminal justice system. Virtually all of these attempts failed. Section 14141 was one of the few politically progressive measures that found its way into the final version of the VCCLEA.

It is important to recognize that § 14141, as authorized in 1994, was not an innovative idea. "On three separate occasions" before the passage of § 14141, Congress considered giving the attorney general authority to

[17] Police Accountability Act of 1991, HR 2972 102d Cong. (1991). The measure was sponsored by Representatives William Edwards, Howard Berman, John Conyers, Julian Dixon, Mervyn Dymally, Michael Kopetski, Meldon Levine, Craig Washington, and Maxine Waters. Four of those individuals – Edwards, Conyers, Washington, and Kopetski – served on the subcommittee that heard the initial recommendation that Congress expand structural police reform authority to the DOJ.

[18] Omnibus Crime Control Act of 1991, HR 3371, 102nd Cong. (1991); *see also Federal Response to Police Misconduct: Hearing Before the H. Subcomm. on Civil and Const. Rights of the Comm. on the Judiciary*, 103d Cong. at 2 (1992) (Representative Edwards stating that structural police reform measure was incorporated into the Omnibus Crime Bill of 1991).

[19] *Federal Response to Police Misconduct, supra* note 18, at 2 (Representative Edwards stating that after the subcommittee unanimously approved the structural police reform measure and incorporated the measure into the Omnibus Crime Bill of 1991, "there's been a filibuster ever since on the whole bill").

[20] Violent Crime Control and Law Enforcement Act of 1994, Pub. L. No. 103–322, §210401 (1994).

[21] *See* SHAHID M. SHAHIDULLAH, CRIME POLICY IN AMERICA: LAWS, INSTITUTIONS, AND PROGRAMS (2008); DOROTHY V. STICKLE, WOMEN'S ISSUES: ECONOMIC, SOCIETAL, and PERSONAL 2 (2008); RITA HAMMER, FORENSIC NURSING: A HANDBOOK FOR PRACTICE xi (2011).

seek equitable relief against local police departments.[22] Each time Congress rejected such an expansion of federal authority into the realm of local policing.[23] During the same time, Congress expanded the attorney general's authority to initiate structural reform litigation in numerous other institutional contexts, including employment, education, housing, and voter rights.[24] In many respects, local policing was one of the last institutional contexts to come to be regulated by structural reform litigation. The Rodney King crisis legitimized congressional interest in expanding the use of structural reform litigation to yet another institutional context – local policing.

The subparts that follow describe the road to the Intervention Era. The first subpart briefly recounts the role of the Rodney King incident in elevating the issue of police accountability to the national stage. The next subpart then describes the passage of § 14141. This part concludes by elaborating on how the Intervention Era has reimagined the traditional approach to police regulation.

A The Rodney King Incident

Many writers claim that the Rodney King incident ignited concerns about widespread misconduct in the LAPD and built political support for the passage of § 14141.[25] Thus, it seems appropriate to start the Los Angeles story by recounting the events of the Rodney King beating. The Rodney King beating would likely never have become a national

[22] *Id.* at 27 (assistant attorney general of the Civil Rights Division, John R. Dunne, stating in his subcommittee testimony that Congress considered such a proposal in 1957, 1959, and 1964 – rejecting it each time).

[23] *Id.*

[24] Harmon, *supra* note 11, at 11 ("[i]n other civil rights arenas, such as education, voting, housing, and prisons, structural reform litigation has supplemented damages actions and criminal punishment as a tool for generating change in public institutions").

[25] *Id.* at 12–13 (discussing the role of the Rodney King beating in moving Congress to act); *see also* Darrell L. Ross, Civil Liability in Criminal Justice 183–185 (2012) (identifying the King beating as a major turning point in police regulation, precipitating § 14141); Myriam E. Gilles, Reinventing Structural Reform Litigation: Deputizing Private Citizens in the Enforcement of Civil Rights, 100 Colum. L. Rev. 1384, 1401 (2000) (stating that "[i]n 1991, however, the brutal beating of Los Angeles resident Rodney King by six LAPD officers, caught on tape and broadcast repeatedly in the days following the incident, focused national attention on the problem of police abuse and spurred Congress to action" and explaining how Congress opted to grant the attorney general an equitable right of action).

story without the amateur camera work of George Holliday.[26] The Holliday tape showed LAPD officers kicking and striking King "with 56 baton strokes."[27] Within days, video of the beating appeared on national news across the country, sparking public outcry and calls for the resignation of LAPD chief Daryl Gates.[28] Famously, Chief Gates referred to the incident as "an aberration," suggesting that it was not demonstrative of a broader problem with the LAPD.[29]

The pursuit started around 12:30 AM[30] when California Highway Patrol (CHP) officers first observed King's Hyundai speeding in the northeastern San Fernando Valley in Los Angeles.[31] When the CHP officers put on their emergency lights and sirens, King slowed but did not stop.[32] An LAPD squad car – assigned to Officers Laurence Powell and Timothy Wind – then joined the pursuit.[33] At around 12:50 AM, Powell and Ward radioed in a "Code 6," which signifies that a chase had come to a close.[34] The LAPD radio transmission operator then broadcasted a "Code 4," a notification to all officers that no additional assistance is needed at the scene of the pursuit.[35] Despite

[26] *Tape of Police Beating Causes Major Furor*, SEATTLE TIMES, March 6, 1991, at A2 ("The video, shot by amateur photographer George Holliday, shows no indication that King tried to hit or charge the officers.").

[27] INDEP. COMM'N ON THE L.A. POLICE DEP'T, REPORT OF THE INDEPENDENT COMMISSION ON THE LOS ANGELES POLICE DEPARTMENT 3 (1991).

[28] *Id.* at 3 ("Within days, television stations across the country broadcast and rebroadcast the tape, provoking a public outcry against police abuse."); *An "Aberration" or Police Business As Usual?*, NY TIMES, March 10, 1994, at E7 ("More than 1,000 callers from around the country phoned Mr. Gates's office expressing their outrage and demanding that he resign.").

[29] David Parrish, *Activists: L.A. Police 'Street Justice' Brutal*, SPOKESMAN-REV., March 10, 1991, at A3 (quoting Chief Gates as saying that the event was an aberration, and that "[i]t's not the kind of conduct that we have normally from our officers").

[30] Mydans, *supra* note 12 ("Shortly before 12:30 A.M. on Sunday, March 3, Mr. King was driving fast down the Foothill Freeway near San Fernando, at the northern edge of Los Angeles.").

[31] INDEP. COMM'N ON THE L.A. POLICE DEP'T, *supra* note 27, at 4. Notably, King was not alone in the car at the time of the incident. Two other passengers were in the car, both African American. Details also emerged that King was traveling at approximately 110–115 miles per hour, according to the CHP. *Id.*

[32] In addition to not stopping, King allegedly "left the freeway and continued through a stop sign at the bottom of the ramp at approximately 50 m.p.h." *Id.* The CHP also reports that King continued to then drive at a high speed and eventually run a red light at approximately 80 miles per hour. *Id.*

[33] *Id.* In addition to the squad car driven by Powell and Wind, "[a] Los Angeles Unified School District Police squad car which was in the area also joined the pursuit." *Id.*

[34] *Id.*

[35] *Id.* at 5 ("[A] Code 4 notifies all units that 'additional assistance is not needed at the scene' and indicates that all units not at the scene 'shall return to their assigned patrol area.'").

these transmissions, eleven additional LAPD units with twenty-one officers and a helicopter appeared at the scene. At least twelve of the officers arrived after the radio transmission operator had sent out the Code 4 broadcast.[36] The Christopher Commission, an independent panel assigned to investigate the events, found that "[a] number of these officers had no convincing explanation for why they went to the scene after the Code 4 broadcast."[37]

Initially after the stop, the CHP officers attempted to take the lead and arrest King.[38] But LAPD officers soon took over, with LAPD sergeant Stacey Koon telling the CHP officer "that they [the LAPD] would handle it."[39] Sergeant Koon initially perceived King as threatening, disoriented, and potentially under the influence of PCP.[40] Sergeant Koon ordered King to lay flat on the ground, a command that LAPD officers claimed King refused to obey.[41] Officer Powell claimed that as he tried to force King to the ground, King "rose up and almost knocked him off his feet."[42] Sergeant Koon then used an electric stun gun twice on King.[43] The George Holliday video begins around this time.[44] At the start of the tape, King is on the ground and appears to move in the direction of one of the officers.[45] The officer viewed this as a "lunge" in his direction, although the report notes that this move would also be consistent with King simply trying to "get away."[46] At this point, Officer Powell hit King in the head with a baton, causing King to fall to the ground. King then rose to his knees where officers struck King over and over. Sergeant Koon ordered the officers to use "power strokes," telling officers to "hit his joints, hit his wrists, hit his elbows, hit his knees, [and] hit his ankles."[47]

[36] *Id.*

[37] *Id.* For example, "one of these officers told District Attorney investigators that he proceeded to the scene after the Code 4 'to see what was happening.'" *Id.*

[38] *Id.* ("At the termination of the pursuit, CHP Officer Timothy Singer, following 'felony stop' procedures, used a loudspeaker to order all occupants out of King's car.").

[39] *Id.* at 6. This happened after CHP officer Melanie Singer attempted to perform a "felony kneeling" procedure to take King into custody. *Id.*

[40] *Id.* (adding that although he "felt threatened," he still "felt enough confidence in his officers to take care of the situation").

[41] *Id.* ("According to Koon and Powell, King responded by getting down on all fours and slapping the ground and refusing to lie down.").

[42] *Id.*

[43] *Id.* It is unclear from the reports whether or not the stun gun had a serious effect on King. The Christopher Commission reports that Sergeant Koon felt that King did not respond to the stun gun, while another officer's report finds that the stun gun did have an effect as King shook and yelled for approximately five seconds. *Id.*

[44] *Id.* [45] *Id.* [46] *Id.* [47] *Id.* at 7.

In total, officers struck King with batons fifty-six times and kicked him six times.[48] Officers then "dragged [King] on his stomach to the side of the road to await arrival of a rescue ambulance."[49] Although there were some allegations by local news teams that officers yelled racial epithets during the beating, these allegations were deemed inconclusive by the investigators.[50] In the video tape, it appears that only once "did any officer try to intervene."[51] About twenty witnesses from nearby apartments gathered to watch the events.[52] Witnesses told reporters that they were yelling at the police "don't kill him" as the officers beat King.[53]

King received twenty stitches and suffered a broken cheekbone and right ankle.[54] Amazingly, officials initially charged King with both speeding and resisting arrest.[55] But as the video of the incident circulated around the nation, prosecutors decided to drop the charges.[56] After the events, details began to emerge about the background of the officers involved in the beating. A total of twenty-three officers had appeared at the scene of the beating at some point.[57] Four officers were directly involved in the use of illegal force against King – Sergeant Stacey Koon and Officers Laurence Powell, Theodore Briseno, and Timothy Wind.[58] One of the officers involved in the beating had previously been suspended for sixty-six days in 1987 for beating a

[48] *Id.* ("Finally, after 56 baton blows and six kicks, five or six officers swarmed in and placed King in both handcuffs and cordcuffs restraining his arms and legs.").

[49] *Id.* [50] *Id.* at 8. [51] Mydans, *supra* note 12. [52] *Id.*

[53] *Id.* (quoting Elois Camp, a sixty-five-year-old retired school teacher who watched the events from her nearby apartment).

[54] Indep. Comm'n on the L.A. Police Dep't, *supra* note 27, at 8 (noting that in addition to these undeniable injuries, King alleged in his civil complaint that he "suffered '11 skull fractures, permanent brain damage, broken [bones and teeth], kidney damage, [and] emotional and physical trauma'"). It is also worth noting that about five hours after his arrest, King had a blood alcohol level of 0.075 percent, which suggests that he was legally drunk at the time of the events. A blood alcohol level of 0.08 percent is sufficient to prove legal intoxication. Since blood alcohol decreases every hour without alcohol at a relatively constant rate, it can be safely assumed that King's blood alcohol level was above 0.08 percent at the time of the chase and subsequent police misconduct. *Id.*

[55] *An "Aberration" or Police Business As Usual?, supra* note 28.

[56] *Id.* ("But those charges were dropped after the police chief, Darryl F. Gates, conceded that he tape showed unnecessary force being used and said that some of the police involved would face charges instead.").

[57] Indep. Comm'n on the L.A. Police Dep't, *supra* note 27, at 11. The report further clarified that these officers varied in age between 23 and 48. Of the officers at the scene, two were African American, four were Latino, and seventeen were white. *Id.*

[58] *Id.*

handcuffed man.[59] The other three officers had been subject to various complaints for excessive use of force, most of which the LAPD found to be unsubstantiated.[60] Another ten officers were physically present, primarily as bystanders, during the incident.[61] Of these ten bystander officers, four were actually field training officers who were "responsible for supervising 'probationary' officers in their first year after graduation from the Police Academy."[62]

Observers across the country immediately condemned the behavior of the officers involved in the King beating. President George H. W. Bush described the events as "shocking" and called for the Justice Department to investigate the incident.[63] Professor Jerome Skolnick commented that the violent confrontation was "going to be the historical event for police in our time."[64] Skolnick further predicted that the behavior was indicative of a larger problem in the LAPD, explaining that "[t]wo people can go crazy, but if you have 10 or 12 people watching them and not doing anything, this tells you that this is a normal thing for them."[65] Although Chief Gates agreed that the events were "shocking,"[66] he insisted that they were the result of a few bad officers, rather than any systemic problems within the department.[67] The Los Angeles District Attorney's Office secured criminal indictments against Sergeant Koon and Officers Powell, Briseno, and Wind.[68] The District Attorney's Office did not seek indictments against the officers at the scene who "did not attempt to prevent the beating or report it to their

59 Mydans, *supra* note 12, at 3. One officer even told a reporter from the *New York Times* of the "magic pencil" that police officers used to make such misconduct allegations disappear. *Id.*

60 Indep. Comm'n on the L.A. Police Dep't, *supra* note 27, at 12. The full explanation of the officers past misconduct is reproduced below:

> According to press reports, another officer had been suspended for five days in 1986 for failing to report his use of force against a suspect following a vehicle pursuit and a foot chase. (The suspect's excessive force complaint against the officer was held "not sustained" by the LAPD.) A third indicted officer was the subject of a 1986 "not sustained" complaint for excessive force against a handcuffed suspect. Since the King incident, that officer has been sued by a citizen who alleges that the officer broke his arm by hitting him with a baton in 1989. *Id.*

61 *Id.* at 11 ("Ten other LAPD officers were actually present on the ground during some portion of the beating.").

62 *Id.* at 11–12. 63 Mydans, *supra* note 12. 64 *Id.* 65 *Id.*

66 Indep. Comm'n on the L.A. Police Dep't, *supra* note 27, at 12.

67 Parrish, *supra* note 29 (explaining that the events were a mere aberration and not indicative of a broader problem).

68 Indep. Comm'n on the L.A. Police Dep't, *supra* note 27, at 13.

superiors."[69] The prosecution resulted in an acquittal followed by days of chaos and rioting in Los Angeles and surrounding areas.[70] Although federal prosecutors successfully secured convictions against two of the officers involved under § 242, such an effort provided no deterrent for "the dozen officers present for the beating."[71]

B Legislative Response to Rodney King Incident

A little over two weeks after the shocking events in Los Angeles, the House Subcommittee on Civil and Constitutional Rights convened a hearing on police brutality in the United States.[72] While representatives claimed that they did not intend the subcommittee hearing to only discuss the Rodney King incident, discussions of the incident dominated conversation.[73] Throughout the hearing, representatives asked witnesses about the causes of the Rodney King beating and ways that Congress could use federal resources to prevent such events in the future. Democratic representatives quickly suggested the use of structural reform litigation to address systematic patterns of misconduct in local police agencies.[74] In his testimony before the subcommittee, the legal director of the ACLU further reiterated the importance of such a measure.[75] During these initial subcommittee meetings, legislators discussed both laws that would allow the attorney general and private litigants to initiate structural reform litigation.[76] Granting this power to individual litigants was particularly controversial at the time; but the drafters of the law felt that it was "necessary to experiment with new legal theories to reform the way police departments conducted

[69] *Id.* It is worth noting, though, that "[t]he District Attorney . . . referred the matter of the bystanders to the United States Attorney for an assessment of whether federal civil rights laws were violated." *Id.*

[70] Harmon, *supra* note 11, at 12. [71] *Id.* at 13.

[72] *See generally Police Brutality, supra* note 13.

[73] *Id.* at 1 ("Our purpose in this subcommittee is not to focus on that incident [the Rodney King beating] in isolation, but to examine the issues more broadly").

[74] Democratic Representative Washington appears to make the first reference to pattern or practice litigation as a possibility. *Id.* at 27.

[75] *Id.* at 61 (Paul Hoffman suggesting the use of pattern or practice litigation).

[76] The testimony of famous litigator Johnnie L. Cochran is indicative of the subcommittee's contemplated granting of authority to private litigants to initiate structural police reform. In his statement to the subcommittee, Cochran explained that post *Lyons*, Congress had to do more than merely grant private litigants the authority to initiate structural police reform – it needed to make clear the statement about the basis for the private litigants' standing. *Id.* at 75.

themselves."[77] Conservative lawmakers and police advocates claimed that the inclusion of such a measure would lead to frivolous and expensive litigation since "[a]ny individual who feels aggrieved by conduct that [he/she] perceives to be part of a pattern or practice can file a suit."[78] The George H. Bush DOJ and police advocacy groups strongly opposed the inclusion of any such individual right of action.[79]

Despite this conservative criticism, liberal members of Congress soon introduced the Police Accountability Act of 1991 – which would have authorized both private and publicly initiated structural reform litigation. The act was eventually incorporated into the Omnibus Crime Control Act of 1991 (HR 3371) as Title XII.[80] To make the measure more appealing to Republicans, lawmakers in the Conference Committee for the Omnibus Crime Control Act removed the portion of Title XII that authorized individual-intimated claims for equitable relief against police departments.[81] The portion of the law that granted the DOJ the authority to seek injunctive relief was less controversial, likely in part because it was roughly analogous to similar powers granted to the DOJ in other similar contexts: school desegregation, employment discrimination, public housing, and prison condition cases.[82] Even this compromise was not enough to win over conservatives, and Title XII died via filibuster.[83] Democratic legislators soon revived Title XII by inserting a similar measure into the VCCLEA two years later.[84] The VCCLEA, which became law in 1994, was an enormous bill touching on nearly every aspect of the criminal justice system.[85] The inclusion of a provision in the VCCLEA permitting federal intervention into police departments to correct civil rights abuses might initially seem puzzling. After all, the VCCLEA was a largely conservative measure designed to combat the nation's crime epidemic with a host of punitive measures. How did a Congress that authorized such a largely punitive criminal justice measure also come to authorize a significant expansion of federal oversight into local police

77 Gilles, *supra* note 25, at 1403.

78 Terence Moran & Daniel Klaidman, *Police Brutality Poses Quandary for DOJ*, LEGAL TIMES, May 4, 1992, at 1.

79 *Id.* 80 Gilles, *supra* note 25, at 1402. 81 *Id.* at 1403. 82 *Id.*

83 Joan Biskupic, *Crime Measure is a Casualty of Partisan Skirmishing*, 49 CONG. Q. MAG. 3528, 3530 (1991).

84 Violent Crime Control and Law Enforcement Act of 1994, Pub. L. No. 103–322, §210401 (1994).

85 For an excellent summary of these components and a detailed historical account of the VCCLEA's passage, *see* DAVID JAMES GEORGE HENNESSY WINDLESHAM, POLITICS, PUNISHMENT, AND POPULISM (1998).

affairs? The next part provides some background on the VCCLEA and explains why § 14141 was able to garner support in an otherwise conservative piece of legislation.

C The Violent Crime Control and Law Enforcement Act

In the early 1990s, Congress felt considerable authority to act in response to the multidecade-long rise in crime rates. The national concern over the rate of violent crimes is understandable, as it had risen by 106 percent between 1970 and 1993.[86] During this same time period, the number of murders rose by 20 percent, rapes by 120 percent, robberies by 49 percent, and aggravated assaults by 167 percent.[87] Around this same time, the US spending on criminal adjudication and prisons "skyrocketed," while spending on policing increased very little.[88] The total crime control expenditure budget increased from $4.6 billion in 1965 to an astonishing $100 billion in 1993.[89] This represents a 162 percent increase in total spending as a percentage of gross domestic product.[90] "For much of the past three decades [leading up to the VCCLEA], politicians have struggled to identify themelves as tougher than their competitors on crime, delinquency, and drug use."[91]

Even as crime started to recede in the early 1990s, the media paid increased attention to the so-called crime epidemic. Indeed, in "a count by a reputable research organization showed that a record number of crime stories were broadcast [the year before the passage of the VCCLEA] by the three major television networks to a national audience."[92] Even though crime had declined nationwide between 1992 and 1993, the media's coverage of murder stories tripled.[93] Stories on crime topped coverage of both the economy and the healthcare system.

[86] Federal Bureau of Investigations, Uniform Crime Reporting Statistics (1970–2012) (calculating crime rates using data from each year).
[87] *Id.*
[88] William J Stuntz, The Collapse of American Criminal Justice 783–784 (2011).
[89] Katherine Beckett, Making Crime Pay: Law and Order in Contemporary American Politics 3 (1999).
[90] *Id.*
[91] *Id.* Noting as well that "[m]inorities have been especially affected by these developments" as "blacks now comprise over half of all prison inmates in the United States, up from one-third just twenty years ago." *Id.*
[92] Windlesham, *supra* note 85.
[93] *Id.* at 5 (describing a study that demonstrated that news coverage of crime increased precipitously in the time leading up to the passage of the law, thereby potentially affecting the tone of the debate).

Significant improvements in the economy in the early 1990s "open[ed] up space for crime or some other social issue to take its place as the leading topic in media coverage and also in the opinion polls."[94] Whatever the actual reality, by the time when lawmakers introduced the VCCLEA in late 1993, "the fixed perceptions shared by lawmakers and the general public alike were of an ever-rising tide of violence that had started to engulf the United States in the late 1960s and early 1970s."[95] Some scholars believe that this exaggerated portrayal of crime by the media resulted in a disproportionately punitive response in the VCCLEA.[96]

In the midst of a perceived crime epidemic, then-candidate Bill Clinton promised that, if elected, he would push for the adoption of a crime bill during the beginning of his first term.[97] After his election, President Clinton kept to his promise. He turned to chairmen of the Senate and House Judiciary Committees, Senator Joe Biden of Delaware, and Representative Jack Brooks of Texas, to draft a crime bill that focused on "policing and prevention."[98] "On various occasions in the first six months of 1993, Clinton reminded Biden of his desire to see a draft without delay."[99] As then-Congressman Bill McCollum, who served as the chairman of the Subcommittee on Crime in the US House of Representatives' Committee on the Judiciary, explained, Chairmen Biden and Brooks authored bills that reflected the American concern about crime.[100] As he explained in a law review article published contemporaneously with the congressional debate about the VCCLEA, "[o]ver the past decade, when Americans have been asked to identify the biggest problem facing the nation, crime has usually been the answer."[101] According to McCollum's recollection of the events, Congress felt pressure to pass the VCCLEA to address an array of

[94] *Id.* For other useful examples of the country's apparent preoccupation with crime in policymaking, *see* JONATHAN SIMON, GOVERNING THROUGH CRIME (2003) (describing how the policymakers in the United States increasingly use crime and crime metaphors to guide policy).

[95] *Id.* at 8.

[96] *See generally* Sarah Eschholz, *The Media and Fear of Crime: A Survey of the Research*, 9 U. FLA. J. L. PUB. POLY 37 (1997) (detailing how media portrayals of crime have affected public fear and perceptions).

[97] WINDLESHAM, *supra* note 85, at 31. [98] *Id.* [99] *Id.*

[100] Bill McCollum, *The Struggle for Effective Anti-Crime Legislation – An Analysis of the Violent Crime Control and Law Enforcement Act of 1994*, 20 U. DAYTON. L. REV. 561 (1994).

[101] *Id.* at 561.

national crime concerns – high crime rates, a perceived juvenile delinquency epidemic, and a prison system that too frequently released dangerous inmates before they substantially completed their sentence.[102] This mirrored comments made by the Clinton administration at a press conference in 1993, when he, Attorney General Janet Reno, Biden, Brooks, and members of Congress from both political parties announced their intent to pass a crime bill since "[t]he first duty of any government . . . was to try and keep its citizens safe . . . [and] clearly too many Americans were not safe."[103] The Clinton administration initially prioritized the hiring of new police officers and gun control.

Around the same time, Republican lawmakers announced their own proposal, which included the building of more prisons, mandatory minimum penalties for certain crimes, restrictions on habeas petitions for prisons on death row, and a new "three strikes and you're out" proposal mandating life imprisonment for recidivist offenders.[104] In September 1993, Biden and Brooks each introduced nearly identical bills in the House and Senate incorporating components of both the Republican and Democratic proposals.[105] Both of these initial versions included identical sections permitting structural reform litigation in police departments by the Justice Department. And both contained significant elements from previous crime bills that had passed one or both Houses of Congress.[106] These initial versions failed to garner sufficient support, and both died in committee.[107] Republicans found the bill insufficiently punitive, while liberal Democrats demanded additional measures to counter racial discrimination.[108]

After these initial attempts failed, Representative Brooks took a different route. He decided to push the legislation through multiple smaller, single-issue bills. Over the next two months, the House successfully passed eleven shorter bills covering federal drug treatment, state drug treatment, youth gangs, community policing, the Brady bill, prison alternatives, bans on youth handgun ownership, violence against women, violence against minors, kidnapping by parents, and control

[102] *Id.* (explaining in a short casual article his personal views on the motivations behind the bill and why certain components were left in or left out).

[103] Windlesham, *supra* note 85, at 33. [104] *Id.* at 33.

[105] Violent Crime Control and Law Enforcement Act of 1993 (1993S. 1488), GovTrack.us, www.govtrack.us/congress/bills/103/s1488 (last visited July 18, 2013); Violent Crime Control and Law Enforcement Act of 1993 (1993 HR 3131), GovTrack.us, www .govtrack.us/congress/bills/103/hr3131 (last visited July 18, 2013).

[106] Windlesham, *supra* note 85 at 35. [107] *Id.* [108] *Id.* at 34–37.

over child care providers.[109] Meanwhile, in the Senate Biden continued to push an omnibus bill. During the debates that followed, "legislators vied to out-do each other to impress their intended audiences with demonstrations of the toughness of their attitudes."[110] Through these debates, the tone of the VCCLEA began to take a noticeable punitive turn – one distinctly different from the proposals initially offered by Brooks and Biden in September. While the majority of Congress was slowly building the largest and most punitive crime bill in American history, the Congressional Black Caucus (CBC) created its own alternative bill (HR 3315) that emphasized prevention of and alternatives to incarceration, as well as various mechanisms to protect against racial inequality. Although the measure garnered thirty cosponsors (including four of the cosponsors from the Police Accountability Act), it ultimately received little widespread support in Congress. The CBC version of the bill would have authorized structural reform litigation against police departments initiated by both the Justice Department and aggrieved individuals – virtually identical to the initial version of the Police Accountability Act. Even though the CBC version failed, the organization did play a pivotal role in influencing the direction of the final VCCLEA.[111]

Around the end of 1993, one of the single-issue bills passed by the House (HR 3355, authorizing federal funds for increased community policing) became the eventual "vehicle" for the final VCCLEA. Increased spending on police officers was the single issue that united both Republicans and Democrats at the time.[112] The measure easily passed the House on November 3, which sent the bill to the Senate. There, Senators decided to not simply pass the narrow policing bill but instead replace the contents of the bill with their own omnibus legislation.[113] This began a multimonth process of debate as the two houses of Congress attempted to find a middle ground.

By February 1994, Congress had not yet negotiated a compromise. President Clinton responded in the State of the Union Address by scolding Congress for not acting. Clinton also took the opportunity to publicly support the implementation of three-strikes legislation – a policy that Biden had recently dismissed as "wacky." Around this same time Clinton and other Congressmen had come to label "crime" as one of the most urgent problems in American society. This put pressure on Congress to take immediate action.[114] Clinton's sense of urgency was

[109] *Id.* at 36. [110] *Id.* at 37. [111] *Id.* at 39 and 40. [112] *Id.* at 49.
[113] *Id.* at 49 and 50. [114] *Id.* at 76.

understandable, as midterm elections loomed later in the year. For several more months, Congress vehemently debated the terms of the crime bill. Most of the debate and disagreement centered on the inclusion of an assault weapon ban in the bill – an issue from which President Clinton and congressional democrats refused to back down.[115] By August 1994, the House neared a compromise, finally voting to pass a now-extensive, omnibus crime bill by a vote of 235–195, with five representatives abstaining. Four days later, under heavy pressure from the president, the Senate passed the bill by a vote of 61–38.

By the end of the long and complex negotiation process, Congress agreed to an expansive and far-reaching set of reforms in the VCCLEA.[116] In total, the act cost taxpayers an estimated $30 billion.[117] The act provided funding for 100,000 more police officers.[118] It provided billions for new prison construction.[119] The VCCLEA also mandated strict truth-in-sentencing requirements, implemented life sentences for repeat violent offenders, banned nineteen types of assault weapons, banned juvenile ownership of handguns, added additional penalties for hate crimes, and extended the death penalty.[120] Additionally, the act allocated another "$2.6 billion for the Federal Bureau of Investigations, the Drug Enforcement Agency, Immigration and Naturalization Services, United States Attorney Offices, and other Justice Department components."[121] Despite some progressive changes, the overall tone of the bill was remarkably punitive.

So it initially might seem odd that legislators chose to include § 14141 – a measure designed to limit local police authority in the name of civil rights – in one of the largest and most punitive crime bills ever authored. This measure seemed out of line with the overall tone of the VCCLEA. And this measure received no significant attention in public debates from conservative lawmakers, who had opposed the Police Accountability Act in 1991. Once more, § 14141 represented an unprecedented expansion of the federal government's authority into a realm traditionally regulated by local and state governments – policing. This makes the inclusion of

115 *Id.* at 95–99.

116 By August 1994, the House neared a compromise, finally voting to pass a now-extensive, omnibus crime bill by a vote of 235–195, with five representatives abstaining. Four days later, under heavy pressure from the president, the Senate passed the bill by a vote of 61–38. *Id.* at 95–99.

117 *Id.* at 122. 118 *Id.* 119 SHAHIDULLAH, *supra* note 21, at 17. 120 *Id.*

121 ERICA R. MEINERS, RIGHT TO BE HOSTILE: SCHOOLS, PRISONS, AND THE MAKING OF PUBLIC ENEMIES 103 (2007).

§ 14141 even more perplexing. After all, Republican legislators attempted to introduce "far-reaching" amendments to the VCCLA that would "restrict the power of federal courts to set population caps in prison overcrowding lawsuits" and engage in other activist regulation of unconstitutional conduct in prisons.[122] If Republican lawmakers initially insisted on the limitation of the power of the courts to regulate prisons, why would many of these same lawmakers eventually authorize the courts to engage in a very similar regulation of American police department? While the regulation of prisons has been instrumental in "ameliorating the total degradation in many state run prisons and local jails," it has also increased the cost of prison operation.[123] How did § 14141 end up in the VCCLEA, and why did it receive so little attention in the legislative record? There are a couple of possible answers to these questions.

For one thing, many of the other initiatives in the VCCLEA were tied to pricey investments. For example, the VCCLEA required additional investment in prisons at a price tag of around $10 billion.[124] Section 14141 creates no clear financial beneficiaries, nor did it come with the same sort of astronomical price tag as many of the other components of the VCCLEA. This had a couple of possible consequences. It meant that there were a few groups with a strong financial stake to lobby and testify before the Congress about the measure. It also made the measure more palatable as a comparatively low-cost add-in to the VCCLEA to gain some additional support from liberal legislators. In addition, the perceived risk of passing § 14141 was relatively low. The measure did not put any affirmative duty on all police agencies broadly, but instead gave the DOJ a limited right of action against only agencies engaged in a pattern or practice of misconduct. Major police agencies likely viewed the perceived risk of § 14141 post-VCCLEA as relatively low. Combined, these two conditions allowed Congress to pass the VCCLEA with relatively little fanfare and no public debate.

[122] WINDLESHAM, *supra* note 85, at 54. There was one uniting feature that both Republicans and Democrats could agree upon, according to Windlesham: the need to increase the size of America's police force. As he explained, around the end of 1993, one of the single-issue bills passed by the House (HR 3355, authorizing federal funds for increased community policing) became the eventual "vehicle" for the final VCCLEA. Increased spending on police officers was the single issue that united both Republicans and Democrats at the time. *Id.* at 49.

[123] *Id.* at 55. [124] SHAHIDULLAH, *supra* note 119, at 17.

II Why Federal Intervention?

Why did Congress decide to give the federal government the power to intervene into problematic police departments? The choice of federal intervention via § 14141 is a uniquely tailored remedy to the misconduct problem facing American police departments. It also filled a regulatory gap. In *Los Angeles* v. *Lyons*, the US Supreme Court had previously held that private litigants could not pursue structural reform litigation against police agencies unless they could prove that they faced a serious and continuing risk of harm. This high burden of proof operated as a de facto ban on private litigants seeking equitable relief against police agencies, even in cases where the litigant had suffered serious harm due to the existence of a blatantly unconstitutional policy or practice. Around the same time, the DOJ attempted to intervene into the Philadelphia Police Department (PPD) to prevent the municipality from engaging in an apparent pattern of civil rights violations. But the Third Circuit held that, absent congressional authorization, the DOJ lacked the authority for such an intervention. Thus, by the time when Congress considered § 14141, no one – neither the DOJ nor private litigants – had any real authority to intervene into the affairs of a police agency. This made police departments unique. In numerous other institutional contexts, like schools and prisons, the federal government was already actively involved in invasive intervention. Thus, the congressional choice of a public equitable right of action made sense. It filled a regulatory hole left by the *Lyons* decision and the subsequent *City of Philadelphia* case. Congress also had a clear blueprint for how this sort of federal intervention had been used in other institutional contexts. This part concludes by discussing the various regulatory advantages of the Intervention Era.

A The Rise of Federal Intervention via Structural Reform Litigation

No doubt, the congressional authorization of § 14141 was a dramatic shift in policing law. But while the use of a public right of action may have been revolutionary in the policing context, it was already well tested in other institutional contexts. In fact, it may be more accurate to say that policing was one of the last institutional contexts to join the federal intervention party. This is in part because, over the last several decades, law scholars have observed that privately initiated structural reform litigation had fallen out of favor with the courts. For a period of time during the twentieth century, private litigants were able to successfully instigate structural reform of many major state institutions.[125] Many structural reform scholars in the public law field trace this movement back to the famous *Brown* v. *Board of Education* ("*Brown II*") decision when the Supreme Court ordered district courts to implement desegregation.[126] Other famous cases that followed, including *Hutto* v. *Finney*, limiting punitive isolated confinement in prisons,[127] and *Swann* v. *Charlotte-Mecklenburg*, approving an extensive desegregation plan, suggested that the courts were prepared to restructure public institutions when necessary in order to protect constitutional rights.[128] For several decades later, the courts acted as "affirmative, political-activist[s]."[129] Scholars who supported this expansive role of the courts in structural reform praised this activist structural reform as promising to be "*the* central . . . mode of constitutional adjudication" of the future.[130] However, as Professor Myriam E. Gilles has observed, in recent decades, "a number of events signaled the demise of the structural reform revolution."[131]

Changes to procedural rules also made it more difficult for litigants to initiate suits for structural reform. During this time the Court not only has "denied standing to plaintiffs who, it claimed, failed to meet the requirements of causation, redressibility, and injury-in-fact," but it also substantially limited the types of litigants who have standing to pursue injunctive relief.[132] These major changes in recent decades have made individual-initiated structural reform litigation challenging and rare.

125 Gilles, *supra* note 25, at 1390 (explaining how the modern structural reform movement through private litigation began in the 1950s as the federal courts agreed to hear cases alleging the need for equitable relief for various public institutions like schools and prisons).

126 *Brown* v. *Board of Education*, 349 US 294 (1955) (holding that the problems identified in Brown I required multiple different, local solutions; thus Chief Justice Warren urged localities to act "with all deliberate speed" to comply with the Court's order).

127 *Hutto* v. *Finney*, 437 US 678 (1978) (where the Court held that punitive isolation for longer than thirty days in an Arkansas prison constituted cruel and unusual punishment in violation of the Constitution).

128 *Swann* v. *Charlotte-Mecklenburg, Bd. of Ed.*, 402 US 1 (1971) (determining that once a locality had violated a court mandate to desegregate schools, the district court had broad and flexible power to remedy the wrong through equitable relief).

129 Abram Chayes, *The Supreme Court, 1981 Term*, 96 HARV. L. REV. 4(1982).

130 Owen M. Fiss, *The Supreme Court, 1978 Term*, 93 HARV. L. REV. 2 (1979).

131 Gilles, *supra* note 29, at 1393.

132 *Id.* at 1396; *see also Allen* v. *Wright*, 468 US 737, 757, 760 (1984) (holding that the courts are "not the proper forum to press general complaints about the way in which government goes about its business") (citation omitted).

In its place, aggrieved parties have instead relied upon a series of federal statutes that give the attorney general authority to seek injunctive relief through public litigation to address a range of issues.[133] Since then, the Justice Department has brought public litigation claims for a host of different issues – schools desegregation,[134] public housing,[135] employment discrimination,[136] prison conditions,[137] and more. Thus, it is important to recognize that the Intervention Era in policing does not represent a regulatory revolution. Instead, it is the continuation of an existing phenomenon – an extension of structural reform litigation into another institutional context.

B Limited Alternatives

On two separate occasions in the late twentieth century, both private and public litigants sought equitable relief similar to § 14141 in civil lawsuits against local police agencies. In both cases, courts found that the litigants lacked standing to pursue such nonmonetary relief absent a clear statutory authorization. One of these cases happened in 1979, when the DOJ filed a lawsuit against the PPD, alleging a pattern of police abuse that systemically violated residents' constitutional rights.[138] According to the DOJ, the PPD maintained policies and procedures that actively thwarted the investigation and disciplining of officers engaged in constitutional violations.[139] The DOJ requested an injunction to stop the PPD from

[133] *Id.* at 1402 (stating that "[t]he provision granting the Attorney General standing to seek injunctive relief substantially enhances the Justice Department's authority with regard to local police affairs by affording the Civil Rights Division a statutory basis for intervening in police 'pattern and practices' in a way analogous to statutes that have authorized federal government intervention into other spheres").

[134] *Id.* at 1402 n.69 (explaining that "Many school desegregation cases were brought under authorization of the Civil Rights Act of 1964, §407, 42 USC §2000c-6 (1994) . . . which . . . authorizes the Attorney General to sue on behalf of public school or college students for the purpose of assuring their Fourteenth Amendment rights and 'the orderly achievement of desegregation in public education'" (citations omitted)).

[135] *Id.* at 1402 n.71 (citing 42 USC §3614(a) (1994)).

[136] *Id.* at 1402 n.70 (citing 42 USC §2000e-6 (1994)).

[137] *Id.* at 1402 (citing prison conditions as one of the sources of public litigation).

[138] *United States* v. *City of Phila.*, 644 F.2d 187, 190 (3rd Cir. 1980) (explaining at the appellate level that "[t]he government's theory is that the appellees, the City of Philadelphia and numerous high-ranking officials of the City and its Police Department, have engaged in a pattern or practice of depriving persons of rights protected by the due process clause of the fourteenth amendment").

[139] *Id.* (stating that the DOJ alleges that "appellees discourage victims of abuse from complaining, suppress evidence that inculpates police officers, accept implausible

engaging in this kind of misconduct going forward.[140] A federal district judge dismissed the claim, however, holding that the US attorney general had no standing to bring such lawsuits absent an explicit statutory grant of power from Congress.[141] The DOJ appealed the decision, only to have the US Court of Appeals for the Third Circuit uphold the lower court's dismissal.[142] This proved to be a problematic precedent because, as the assistant attorney general testified to the US Commission on Civil Rights, he and his colleagues knew that in Philadelphia they "were dealing with something that went beyond individual acts of misconduct ... [They] were dealing with institutional problems."[143]

The DOJ had previously prosecuted six homicide detectives in Philadelphia for coercing confessions out of possibly innocent suspects.[144] Nonetheless, at least one of those convicted of coercing confessions out of criminal suspects actually received a promotion and support from city leadership.[145] As one member of the DOJ elaborated: "[I]f an officer on the beat perceives that he or she is going to be shielded and protected by the institution from an investigation and from prosecutions ... then I think what we have is a situation where even prosecuting individual officers is not going to change the environment."[146] Complaints aside, *City of Philadelphia* established the precedent that, absent congressional authorization, the DOJ did not have standing to intervene into a local police department.

This rule did not sit well with many civil rights advocates. In 1981, the US Commission on Civil Rights identified *City of Philadelphia* as

explanations of abusive conduct, harass complainants and witnesses, prematurely terminate investigations, compile reports that justify police officers' conduct regardless of actual circumstances, refuse to discipline police officers for known violations, and protect officers from outside investigations").

140 *Id.* at 189 (identifying injunctive relief as the desired remedy).

141 *United States* v. *City of Phila.*, 482 F. Supp. 1248, 1252 (ED Pa. 1979).

142 *City of Phila.*, 644 F.2d at 206 ("We will hold the Attorney General to the same pleading requirements we demand of a private litigant who brings an action under the Civil Rights Acts. The appellant failed to satisfy these standards, and it deliberately rejected an opportunity to amend its complaint.").

143 Bonnie Mathews & Gloria Izumi, U.S. Comm'n on Civil Rights, Who Is Guarding the Guardians?: A Report on Police Practices 135 (1981), *available at* http://catalog.hathitrust.org/Record/007105152.

144 *Id.* at 135 and 136.

145 *Id.* at 136 ("The mayor at the time, of Philadelphia, kept the officers on the force, promoted one of the men who had been convicted, and asserted they were innocent until proven guilty at the Supreme Court level.").

146 *Id.* at 135.

establishing a gap in the regulatory approach to police misconduct.[147] The commission recommended the adoption of legislation to remedy the judicial limitations placed on the use of structural reform litigation.[148] The commission observed that "the volume of complaints of police abuse received by the Commission has increased each year ... and ... [p]atterns of complaints appear to indicate institutional rather than individual problems."[149] The commission also recognized that one of the best possible ways to address these institutional problems was through some type of structural reform litigation that would incentivize police departments to change their behavior.[150] The commission reached this conclusion in part because previous attempts to file for injunctive relief against American police departments had failed.[151] With that in mind, the commission recommended the enactment of a statute similar to § 14141.[152] The commission saw this proposed measure as a novel way to address systemic wrongdoing in police agencies. Nonetheless, the commission did not offer model language, nor did it thoroughly expound on the proposal.

The DOJ was not the only plaintiff attempting to pursue structural reform litigation. A few years before the *City of Philadelphia* case, the US Supreme Court delivered a devastating blow to private litigants attempting to initiate such reform via equitable relief. In 1976, LAPD officers stopped Adolph Lyons for a traffic violation.[153] Even though he did not resist, the officers seized Lyons in a dangerous choke hold.[154] Lyons brought suit against the LAPD, asking in part for the court to enjoin the LAPD from using such choke holds in the future.[155] In a 5–4 decision, the US Supreme Court ruled that private plaintiffs do not have standing to levy a claim for injunctive relief unless they can show that

[147] *Id.* at 135 and 136 (identifying *City of Philadelphia* as the case that has limited DOJ authority to initiate structural police reform and outlining how this has potentially hampered DOJ involvement in police reform).

[148] *Id.* at 134 (identifying the need for "federal litigation aimed at institutional misconduct" in cases where there is a demonstrated "pattern or practice of police abuse").

[149] *Id.* at vi.

[150] *Id.* at 134–136 (detailing the potential usefulness of structural reform litigation).

[151] *Id.* (explaining this failure and linking it to a need for reform).

[152] *Id.* at 164 and 165.

[153] *City of L.A.* v. *Lyons*, 461 US 95, 97 (1983) (identifying a traffic violation as the initial cause of the interaction with the plaintiff).

[154] *Id.* at 97 (saying that Lyons did not resist the officers in any way, nor pose any threat before being put in a choke hold).

[155] *Id.* at 99 and 100 (stating that, at the district level, an order was handed down enjoining the use of the tactic).

they risk real, immediate, or continuing harm from *future* police misconduct.[156] Since Lyons was not in serious risk of being stopped and illegally choked by the LAPD in the future, he lacked such standing.[157] Lyons could seek monetary damages against the police and possibly the city, but he could not seek injunctive relief.[158] After the *Lyons* and *City of Philadelphia* cases, there appeared to be no judicial remedy to force local police departments to adopt proactive reforms to prevent patterns of systemic misconduct.

C Theoretical Advantages of Structural Reform Litigation

Federal intervention via structural reform litigation, as a regulatory mechanism, was tested in other institutional contexts. It also filled a regulatory gap left by *Lyons* and *City of Philadelphia*. But the Congress also passed § 14141 because of the unique, theoretical advantages that structural reform litigation offered as a regulatory mechanism. First, a public right of equitable action via § 14141 gives the DOJ and the federal courts the authority to demand the hiring of an external monitor to ensure that local police agencies actually implement major reforms.[159] Thus, federal intervention via structural reform litigation can potentially induce real change as opposed to mere symbolic compliance.[160] Previously scholars have observed that organizational capacity, organizational commitment, and environmental pressure all affect the organizational response to legal reform.[161] Scholars of organizational theory have predicted that when environmental pressure was low, organizations would have the ability to engage in mere symbolic compliance.[162] Similarly, when environmental pressure was low and organizational

[156] *Id.* at 111 ("Absent a sufficient likelihood that he will again be wronged in a similar way, Lyons is no more entitled to an injunction than any other citizen of Los Angeles").

[157] *Id.* at 102 (explaining that injunctive relief is only appropriate when a plaintiff is "immediately in danger of sustaining some direct injury").

[158] *Id.* at 111–113 (denying injunctive relief).

[159] *See infra* Chapters 4 and 5 (describing the various stages of structural reform and monitor appointment process); *see also infra* Appendix B (showing the structural police reform cases that resulted in the appointment of a monitor).

[160] Mayer N. Zald, Calvin Morrill, & Hayagreeva Rao, *Environment and Responses*, in GERALD F. DAVIS, DOUG MCADAM, W. RICHARD SCOTT, AND MAYER N. ZALD, SOCIAL MOVEMENTS AND ORGANIZATION THEORY 266 (2005) (explaining how high pressure is needed to ensure "maximum compliance" and not mere symbolic compliance, evasion, or resistance).

[161] *Id.* [162] *Id.*

capacity was also low, scholars have predicted that organizations would only exhibit limited compliance.[163] Federal intervention can theoretically increase environmental pressure by mandating the appointment of a monitor and expand organizational capacity by allocating the necessary resources to police reform. Thus, an equitable relief approach may provide the DOJ and the courts with the necessary tools to overcome symbolic compliance.

Second, by giving the DOJ the sole power to instigate § 14141 cases, Congress effectively gave the federal executive branch the power to define the field of legitimate police practices in the United States. Theoretically, each time when the DOJ litigates against an agency, the reforms it demands ought to mirror what the federal executive deems to be best practices – those needed to eradicate a pattern or practice of misconduct and ensure constitutional policing. Before § 14141, there has never been a concerted federal effort to define these sorts of best practices. Section 14141 represents the first real opportunity for the federal government to define the boundaries of legitimate behavior within the field of local law enforcement. This is critically important because, as Professor Joshua Page has previously explained, "players in [a professional] field (often unwittingly) orient their behavior to other players in the field."[164] Fields typically have "guiding principles and values" that orient boundaries of acceptable behavior.[165] Agents within the field come to "grasp the mores, expectations, and acceptable actions" of their respective fields.[166] Within the policing field, § 14141 gives the federal executive enormous authority to transform the definition of acceptable behavior by local law enforcement agencies.

Third, by granting the DOJ an equitable right of action against police departments via federal litigation, Congress may have been harnessing the unique institutional competencies of the judicial and executive branches. One criticism of the court-mandated reform in police departments is that the judiciary lacks the resources to engage in significant lawmaking. As one scholar has argued, "[l]egislative rules tend to be the product of a wide range of inputs, ranging from legislative hearings and poll results to interest group advocacy and backroom compromises."[167]

[163] *Id.*

[164] Joshua Page, The Toughest Beat: Politics, Punishment, and the Prison Officers Union in California (2011).

[165] *Id.* [166] *Id.*

[167] Orin Kerr, *The Fourth Amendment and New Technologies: Constitutional Myths and the Case for Caution*, 102 Mich. L. Rev. 801, 875 (2004).

By contrast, "[j]udicial rules tend to follow a more formal and predictable presentation or written briefs and oral arguments by two parties."[168] The result is that courts operate with an "information" or competency deficit.[169] Section 14141, in theory, could overcome this so-called judicial deficit by putting primary authority in the hands of the DOJ to identify and negotiate settlements with problematic departments. This sort of cooperative federalism allows the executive branch and judicial branch to work together to craft and enforce standards to overhaul systemically flawed police agencies.

Fourth, an equitable relief is theoretically well-suited to address the organizational roots of misconduct. Remember, as discussed in Chapter 1, there is a growing recognition in the available literature that persistent problems within a police agency are often the result of deeply ingrained organizational problems. In one sense, police agencies are bureaucratic organizations. As such, police officers "are expected to make decisions by a universal application of the rules."[170] Even so, police are also frontline bureaucrats who are necessarily afforded "enormous discretionary powers to apply the law."[171] Bureaucratization has attempted to address some of the concerns over police corruption by insulating officers from their environment, but territorially localized and specialized units remain particularly vulnerable to corrupt influences.[172] Within the typical police agency today, "[o]rganizational members believe in the essential rightness of what they do."[173] This is potentially problematic since "this belief can be an obstacle ... to critically

[168] *Id.* [169] *Id.* at 875–882.

[170] Albert J. Reiss, *Police Organization in the Twentieth Century*, 15 CRIME & JUST. 51, 73–74 (1992).

[171] *Id.*

[172] *Id.* at 81. Any external regulation of an organization must deal with the unique characteristics of police departments. Police forces today are larger and more specialized than a century ago, but they spend less time patrolling communities by foot. Technological developments have facilitated the centralization of most law enforcement agencies. As Albert Reiss has observed, police departments today have developed into technocratic bureaucracies. *Id.* Bureaucratization has insulated law enforcement from politics and opened the ranks of police departments to women and minorities. Despite the centralization and bureaucratization of local departments, the American law enforcement community is still comprised of thousands of different, generally small departments. The United States remains exceptional, internationally speaking, in the belief that "local control of police is an essential ingredient of local government." *Id.* at 67. But, as Reiss also observed, there are fundamental tensions in policing organizations between bureaucratization and discretionary authority.

[173] John P. Crank, *Institutional Theory of Police: A Review of the State of the Art*, 26 POLICING INT. J. POLICE STRATEGIC MANAGEMENT 186, 187 (2003).

evaluat[ing] ongoing organizational practices" as many leaders within police departments therefore believe that "corruption is the result of a few bad police officers who slipped through background screening[s]" rather than a problem rooted in organizational inadequacies.[174] The traditional approach to regulating police misconduct – that is, the exclusionary rule, civil litigation, and criminal prosecution – is well-suited to addressing instances of individual misconduct. The traditional approach is poorly suited, however, to respond to organizational pathologies or practices that perpetuate misconduct. By contrast, an equitable relief model is designed to directly combat the organizational roots of systemic misconduct in police agencies. Rather than raising the cost of wrongdoing, an equitable right of action gives the DOJ and the federal courts the authority to force police agencies to implement expansive police and procedural reforms. As discussed more in Chapter 3, these mandated reforms via § 14141 have been extensive – touching on nearly every internal policy in some cases.

Despite these potential advantages, § 14141 was not fully appreciated at the time of its passage. Since the law's passage, academic research has not fully explored the subject.

III Emerging Importance of the Intervention Era

At the time of passage, § 14141 appeared to be an afterthought. Fast-forward twenty years and § 14141 has emerged as arguably the most important component of the VCCLEA. While other parts of the VCCLEA have waned in importance, the impact of the Intervention Era continues to grow today. Despite the apparent modern importance of § 14141, few researchers have empirically analyzed its importance. This is increasingly indefensible, as many of the nation's largest police departments have become subject to intervention via § 14141. This part starts by examining the comparative importance of federal intervention over time. It then briefly evaluates the available literature on federal intervention via § 14141.

A Comparative Importance over Time

One way to judge the perceived importance of legal measures is to analyze media coverage. Theoretically, if the public perceived a legal

174 *Id.*

proposal as more important, the media would reflect this perception by affording the measure more attention. Other researchers have adopted this sort of methodology when judging the perceived importance of a criminal justice measure.[175] To be clear, this methodological approach cannot speak to the actual importance of a law. Rather, it merely attempts to show the perceived importance of a law, as measured by the amount of media attention at the time of passage.

A quick glance at the *New York Times* from the years around the VCCLEA shows that not a single story in the *New York Times* discussed the proposed authorization of § 14141. By contrast, 115 articles addressed the proposed inclusion of the Federal Assault Weapons Ban in the VCCLEA, while dozens more addressed other parts of the VCCLEA like the Violence Against Women Act, truth-in-sentencing reforms, and the proposed addition of 100,000 new police officers. Fifteen years later, the *New York Times* has written dozens of different stories discussing the implementation of § 14141. Coverage of most other components of the VCCLEA has decreased significantly. By 2009–2013, only two other major components of the VCCLEA have received media coverage rivaling § 14141 – the Violence Against Women Act and the Federal Assault Weapons Ban. In addition, there is an important difference in the type of media coverage that these measures had received. Virtually all of the articles discussing these two other parts of the VCCLEA were discussing legislative attempts at their reauthorization. Meanwhile, the recent articles on § 14141 all discussed the continued implementation of this statute. This provides evidence for two assertions.

First, it seems clear that § 14141 has increased in perceived importance today relative to the passage of the VCCLEA, as measured by news coverage. Second, this provides some evidence that, despite a lack of initial media coverage, the Intervention Era has actually had a substantial impact on American policing. But how big an impact has the Intervention Era had on American policing? Chapters 3–5 will dive into this topic in far more depth. To begin a preliminary examination, Appendices A and B show a full list of all actions taken by the DOJ via § 14141. For our immediate purposes, though, it is useful to see how widely the DOJ has utilized § 14141 since the statute's passage. Figure 2.1

175 Franklin E. Zimring, *The Accidental Crime Commission: Its Legacies and Lessons*, 96 Marq. L. Rev. 995, 1001 (2013) (using this sort of syntactical count methodology to judge the perceived importance of certain parts of the Wickersham Commission Report).

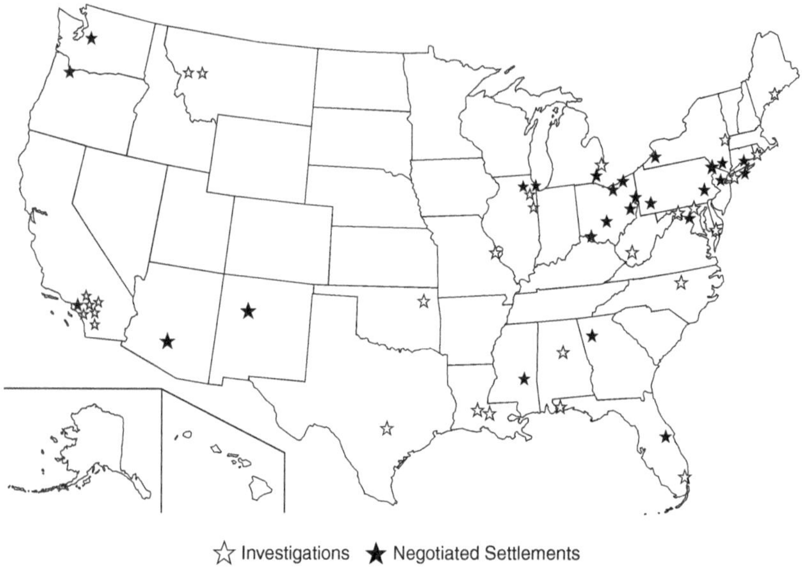

Figure 2.1 Section 14141 Cases Opened by DOJ, 1994–2015

maps out all of the known investigatory actions taken by the DOJ pursuant to § 14141 since 1994.

The white stars identify municipalities where the DOJ has taken some investigatory action – the beginnings of federal intervention. It does not show the action taken by the DOJ in Puerto Rico, where the DOJ has formally investigated the island's central police agency. The black stars note municipalities where the DOJ has settled with the municipality on a set of necessary reforms to avoid further litigation. The figure does not show the Virgin Islands, which has also agreed to a negotiated settlement with the DOJ pursuant to § 14141. Chapter 3 discusses the difference between an investigation and a negotiated settlement in more depth. Overall, Figure 2.1 shows the extent to which federal intervention has touched police agencies in states across the country. At first glance, there do appear to be some unusual patterns in the geographical distribution of investigations – for example, the paucity of action in southern and western United States and the high volume of cases in the mid-Atlantic, Eastern Midwest, and Northeast.

But these more nuanced trends aside, the data shows that the DOJ has targeted sixty-one municipalities for formal investigations and thirty for federal intervention. Agencies across the nation, thus, have been subject

Table 2.1 *Extent of Federal Intervention into Police Departments, 1994–2015*

Type of Action	Number of Municipalities	Total Population Served	Percentage of American Population
Investigation	61	59,897,958	21
Federal Intervention	30	27,459,304	10

to some § 14141 action. Of course, there are around 18,000 police agencies in the United States. This means that only about 0.03 percent of all agencies have been subject to some § 14141 action. This might suggest that the Intervention Era has been a relatively unimportant addition to the field of policing law. But the DOJ has seemingly targeted larger municipalities via § 14141 thus far. As a result, Table 2.1 shows the total population served by the sixty-one agencies targeted for § 14141 action between 1994 and 2015.

Despite the relatively small number of agencies targeted for federal intervention relative to the total number of agencies, the DOJ has identified a cross section of agencies that serve a significant percentage of the American population. The sixty-one municipalities identified thus far serve around 60 million citizens – or about one in five Americans. You could argue that roughly one in five Americans today has had some direct stake in the outcome of a § 14141 action. This realization dramatically recasts the importance of the Intervention Era. This measure that initially received virtually no media attention has today had – at least indirectly – an effect on a large portion of the American population. But despite the apparent growing importance of federal intervention, the empirical literature on the topic is remarkably thin and outcome oriented as explained in the next subpart.

B *Prior Research*

Since the passage of § 14141, very little research in any discipline has empirically analyzed the growing importance of federal intervention into local police departments. And virtually no legal scholarship has done an empirical examination of the topic. Initially, criminal justice observers were optimistic about the potential of § 14141. The late professor William

Stuntz remarked that § 14141 may be one of the most significant historical developments in the regulation of police misconduct.[176] Indeed, there was reason for optimism. Section 14141 seemingly filled a significant hole in the regulatory strategy for police misconduct. As Barbara Armacost explained, "reform efforts have focused too much on notorious incidents and misbehaving individuals, and too little on an overly aggressive police culture that facilitates and rewards violent conduct."[177] If a department wants to engage in "[r]eal reform," it must "accept collective responsibility, not only for heroism, but for police brutality and corruption as well."[178] Indeed, occasional misconduct is an unavoidable consequence of granting police officers the discretion to successfully carry out their jobs. Consistent patterns of misconduct are more commonly rooted in organizational culture, rather than the professional or moral failings of the individual officers. Additionally, cost-raising misconduct regulations can incentivize some reform but have historically proven ineffective at stimulating significant broad policy changes. Thus, most commentators agreed that § 14141 "create[d] an unprecedented opportunity for the federal government to encourage collaborative reform of deficient police institutions."[179] Since then, a small number of empirical studies have assessed the effectiveness of § 14141 in individual cities.

The Vera Institute of Justice completed an empirical evaluation of the long-term effects of the negotiated settlement, sometimes called a consent decree, in Pittsburgh years after monitors left the city.[180] The Vera report found that the reforms implemented as part of the consent decree remained in effect after the monitors departed.[181] Second, Professors

[176] William J. Stuntz, *The Political Constitution of Criminal Justice*, 119 HARV. L. REV. 781, 798 (2006) (calling structural police reform "the most important legal initiative of the past twenty years in the sphere of police regulation").

[177] Armacost, *supra* note 5, at 455. [178] *Id.*

[179] Kami Chavis Simmons, *The Politics of Policing: Ensuring Stakeholder Collaboration in the Federal Reform of Local Law Enforcement Agencies*, 98 J. CRIM. L. & CRIMINOLOGY 489, 528 (2008).

[180] ROBERT C. DAVIS, NICOLE J. HENDERSON, & CHRISTOPHER W. ORTIZ, CAN FEDERAL INTERVENTION BRING LASTING IMPROVEMENT IN LOCAL POLICING? THE PITTSBURGH CONSENT DECREE (2005), *available at* www.vera.org/sites/default/files/resources/downloads/277_530.pdf. There, researchers surveyed over 100 frontline officers, conducted focus groups, interviewed key officials, reviewed monitor reports, surveyed citizenry, and analyzed police statistics. *Id.* at 5 and 6.

[181] *See id.* at 17. The Vera evaluation states that "the officers clearly indicated – as had the command staff – that the accountability mechanisms remained intact after the lifting of the decree." This suggests that the reforms were at least somewhat effective. Even so, the authors

Christopher Stone, Todd Foglesong, and Christine Cole examined the success of the Los Angeles consent decree part of the way through implementation.[182] The preliminary results were extremely positive.[183]

of the study noted some possible problems with the reform strategy used in Pittsburgh. The consent decree negotiation and implementation alienated some officers on the force – many of whom complained that morale sunk after the department agreed to the terms of the consent decree. *Id.* at 42. Other officers believed that the reforms discouraged them from proactively policing the streets for fear of being "disciplined for filling out forms improperly" or being burdened with "duplicative paperwork." *Id.* Supervisors similarly grumbled that the procedures implemented by the consent decree reduced time spent on the street and increased time addressing procedural formalities. *Id.* Vera also noted that one of the primary effects of the consent decree was to centralize decision-making and disciplinary review. The report concluded that the "centralized approach to identifying and responding to officer misconduct makes good sense in the wake of allegations of civil rights violations" but may also run "counter to the decentralizing imperative of the other major police reforms of the past two decades: community policing." *Id.* at 41 and 42. This means that officers in Pittsburgh after the implementation of the consent decree may have exercised less discretion and responsibility over their work.

182 *See* CHRISTOPHER STONE, TODD FOGLESONG, & CHRISTINE M. COLE, POLICING LOS ANGELES UNDER A CONSENT DECREE: THE DYNAMICS OF CHANGE AT THE LAPD (2009), *available at* www.lapdonline.org/assets/pdf/Harvard-LAPD%20Study.pdf. There, researchers undertook participant observation and analyzed administrative data on crimes, arrests, traffic/pedestrian stops, use of force, and personnel. *Id.* at i and ii.

183 Unlike the Vera study, Stone and his colleagues found no evidence for the hypothesis that the implementation of the terms of a consent decree leads to "de-policing" – or "hesitat[ion] to intervene in difficult circumstances for fear that, despite their best intentions, their actions will be criticized and they may even be disciplined." *Id.* at 19. Like in the Vera study, officers "frequently" raised concerns about how the terms of a consent decree can hamper their abilities to exercise discretion, commonly saying that paperwork deterred them from making arrests and arguing that compliance with the terms of the decree hurt their ability to proactively fight crime on the streets. *Id.* at 19 and 20. But the researchers in the Stone study rejected the claim that the terms of the consent decree uniquely burdened the LAPD's ability to fight crime. They showed that since the start of the consent decree, motor vehicle and pedestrian stops actually increased significantly. *Id.* at 22. Once more, comparisons between similar surveys conducted in 1999 and 2003 found that the percentage of officers who reported being afraid that an honest mistake would negatively impact their careers actually decreased. *Id.* at 21. This led Stone and his colleagues to conclude that most of the concern about depolicing was likely misplaced. By all accounts, crime has decreased significantly faster in Los Angeles than other American cities since the implementation of the consent decree. And the traffic and pedestrian stops today lead to arrests more often than in years past. *Id.* at 24. This suggests that Los Angeles police have become even more proactive since the start of the consent decree and have actually become more effective at targeting proactive policing efforts towards actual wrongdoers. More to the point, though, the LAPD has also apparently decreased the use of force since the beginning of the consent decree as well. *Id.* at 32. This is a particularly striking finding since during the same time that use of force declined, the total number of arrests actually increased substantially. *Id.* at 35. The Stone examination of Los Angeles also addressed the concerns expressed in the Vera study about the effect of the consent decree on community relations. Overall, community satisfaction with the LAPD increased during the implementation of the consent decree, and

The third study comes from a doctoral dissertation written by Professor Joshua Chanin.[184] Chanin evaluated the effects of the § 14141 litigation in Washington, DC, Pittsburgh, Prince George's County, and Cincinnati.[185] Unlike the Stone and the Vera case studies, Chanin's dissertation provides analyses of multiple cities, allowing him to make at least some comparative conclusions. Chanin hypothesized that several variables affect the implementation of negotiated settlements, including the complexity of the negotiated settlement, departmental resources, and the support of police administrators as well as local political leaders for the negotiated settlement.[186]

The legal academy has also made several worthwhile contributions to the literature on the Intervention Era.[187] These authors have generally offered normative recommendations on how the DOJ could improve the effectiveness of federal intervention. Professor Kami Chavis Simmons

this pattern continued after the conclusion of the federal intervention. *Id.* at 44. Like in Pittsburgh, the community's satisfaction differed based on the race of the respondent, with the black community somewhat less enthusiastic about the performance of the police department. *Id.* But overall, there was less concern in Los Angeles than in Pittsburgh about the implications of federal intervention on community outreach efforts.

184 Joshua M. Chanin, Negotiated Justice? The Legal, Administrative, and Policy Implications of "Pattern or Practice" Police Misconduct Reform 335 (July 6, 2011) (unpublished Ph.D. dissertation, American University), *available at* www.ncjrs.gov/pdffiles1/nij/grants/237957.pdf.

185 *Id.* at 21 and 22. Chanin hoped to do a retrospective on cities that had completed the terms of the negotiated settlement. *Id.* at 22. Thus, at the time when Chanin started his study, these four cities represented two-thirds of all cities that fell into this category. *Id.*

186 *Id.* at iii–iv (stating that "[s]everal factors help to explain variation between departments, including the complexity of joint action, agency and jurisdictional resources, active and capable police leadership, and support from local political leaders" and hypothesizing that "(1) the policy problem; (2) the policy solution; (3) the environmental context; and (4) the implementing agency" all define the implementation of structural police reform. It is also worth mentioning that, like the Vera study, Chanin worried that the "centralized approach at the heart of the pattern or practice reform template seems to have little in common with the [community-oriented policing] model." *Id.* at 358. Chanin concluded his comparative study with numerous normative recommendations. He argued that the structural reform litigation process ought to include more external oversight and reporting mechanisms after the end of the reform process. *Id.* at 346–349. Chanin also suggested that the development and implementation of consent decrees should be more inclusive, using a bottom-up approach. *Id.* at 350. To this end, he recommended the inclusion of union representatives and key civil rights organizations in the settlement process, the use of community goals in formulating the settlement content, and the regular updating of community and civil rights stakeholders after the start of the implementation process. *Id.* at 351.

187 *See, e.g.*, Armacost, *supra* note 5; Harmon, *supra* note 11; Simmons, *supra* note 179; Samuel Walker & Morgan Macdonald, *An Alternative Remedy for Police Misconduct: A Model State "Pattern or Practice" Statute*, 19 Geo. Mason U. CR LJ 479 (2009).

has targeted a different problem in § 14141 cases – the representation of the various community stakeholders in the negotiation and implementation of settlement agreements.[188] Simmons used Cincinnati, in part, as an example of how the DOJ's implementation process could more effectively incorporate collaboration with various stakeholders.[189] Other legal academics have discussed § 14141, including Professor Debra Livingston, who analyzed the consent decrees in Steubenville, Ohio, and Pittsburgh, Pennsylvania, to identify the types of misconduct that the DOJ targeted in negotiated settlements.[190] Samuel Walker and Morgan Macdonald have recommended the expansion of pattern or practice litigation to the state level.[191]

Overall, these studies fail to answer many important research questions. None of these studies thoroughly examine the process by which the DOJ identifies cities to target under § 14141. Although Professor Rachel Harmon has theorized on how the DOJ could change this selection process,[192] there remains a descriptive gap in the literature on the process by which the DOJ currently identifies cities engaged in a pattern or practice of police misconduct. This is a critical piece of missing information in the scholarship. How does the DOJ go about identifying which of the nation's 18,000 police departments are in violation of § 14141? How does the DOJ define a pattern or practice of misconduct? And can an individual aggrieved by egregious acts of police misconduct go to the DOJ for redress? The available literature is also thin on how the federal intervention process works from beginning to end. Thus, Chapter 3 will empirically examine the DOJ's enforcement of § 14141 and the various stages of federal intervention that follow. Finally, although a small number of studies have examined the apparent outcomes of federal intervention, the scope of these studies has been relatively narrow. The goal of these previous studies was not to identify *why* federal intervention either worked or failed. Thus, while a handful of studies have explored various aspects of the

188 *See generally* Simmons, *supra* note 179.

189 *Id.* at 531. By determining a broad range of potential stakeholders and incorporating them into the structural reform process, Simmons claims that the DOJ can restore the political legitimacy of the process, provide a check on DOJ authority, and create innovative and uniquely tailored remedies. *Id.* at 537–540.

190 See generally Debra Livingston, *Police Reform and the Department of Justice: An Essay on Accountability*, 2 Buff. Crim. L. Rev. 817 (1999).

191 *See generally* Walker & Macdonald, *supra* note 187.

192 *See* Harmon, *supra* note 11.

Intervention Era, the subject remains largely understudied and ripe for more thorough examination.

Conclusion

The passage of § 14141 marked the beginning of an unnoticed transformation in American policing law. Today, the federal executive branch wields considerable authority to define the boundaries of acceptable police practices in local police agencies. The regulatory model adopted by Congress in § 14141 offers considerable theoretical advantages over the traditional approach to local police regulation. But the available literature is remarkably thin on how the Intervention Era works, how the DOJ identifies agencies in violation of § 14141, and how § 14141 works in practice to reform problematic agencies. The next chapter examines these important questions by exploring how the federal intervention operates in action.

3

Federal Intervention in Action

Introduction

"We're an awfully small community," explained Gary Dufour, then city manager of Steubenville, Ohio.[1] Once a thriving steel town, this rust belt city has seen its population fall by over 50 percent since the mid-twentieth century. Today, Steubenville is a town of fewer than 20,000 people, with a police force of around forty sworn officers. In July 1995, Steubenville became the third police department that the DOJ investigated under § 14141. In September 1997, Steubenville would be the second city ever to reach a settlement with the DOJ to correct a pattern of police misconduct. As Mr. Dufour publicly asked, "You see all these problems that have come up at the police departments in Los Angeles and New York and New Orleans, and you've got to wonder, why us?"[2] So why is it that, of all the police departments in the country implicated in apparent patterns of misconduct, the DOJ chose to use its limited investigatory resources in reforming this small Midwest police department? The Steubenville story is symbolic of the difficulties that the DOJ has faced in developing a coherent enforcement strategy for § 14141. At times, the DOJ's enforcement of § 14141 has seemed inconsistent or unfair in the eyes of targeted municipalities. But it is hard to blame the DOJ. When Congress passed § 14141, it gave the DOJ a challenging task.

Soon after the passage of § 14141 and the beginning of the Intervention Era, the DOJ faced many difficult choices. Who in the DOJ would investigate local police agencies? What division of the DOJ would house this new and important responsibility? And how would the DOJ decide which of the nation's roughly 18,000 police departments were engaged in a pattern or practice of unconstitutional misconduct? Soon

[1] Eric Lichtblau, *U.S. Low Profile in Big-City Police Probes Is Under Fire*, LA TIMES, March 17, 2000, at A1.

[2] *Id.*

after the statute's passage, the attorney general vested the DOJ's Special Litigation Section within the Civil Rights Division with the authority to intervene into local police departments. Prior to the passage of § 14141, some litigators in the DOJ's Criminal Division had experience prosecuting individual instances of police misconduct under 18 USC § 242. Others in the DOJ had previously handled structural reform litigation cases in different institutional contexts like prisons and mental health facilities. But no one at the DOJ had any real, substantive experience regulating police. So the head of the Civil Rights Division assigned a small group of litigators to begin a crash course in police regulation. Because of this, it should come as no surprise that enforcement of § 14141 got off to a sluggish start. It took around a year to begin the first investigation of a police department, and it took around three years before the DOJ actually began restructuring a local police agency.

Among the earliest challenges that the DOJ faced in enforcing § 14141 was the identification of police departments in violation of the statute. DOJ personnel quickly realized that they had almost no data on which to make these critical enforcement decisions. The United States keeps very few national statistics on local police behavior. That means that even if these DOJ litigators wanted to develop a fair, transparent, and statistically rigorous method for identifying the nation's worst police departments, the DOJ simply lacked the tools to make it happen.

So why did the DOJ decide to use its limited resources to overhaul Steubenville, Ohio? As one former DOJ litigators explained during an interview, a notable Ohio civil rights attorney "used to litigate against Steubenville all the time."[3] In a previous case, this attorney had "filed a *Monell* count," which included an "affidavit that went through fifty or sixty . . . misconduct incidents" allegedly committed by the Steubenville Police Department.[4] Although this DOJ contact could not remember whether the civil rights attorney "won or lost," the civil rights attorney had "sent the file to the Justice Department. And that's how the case got started."[5] In the absence of national statistics to develop a coherent enforcement strategy, the DOJ has been forced to rely on a range of imperfect indicators. In some cases, like Steubenville, the DOJ relied on existing civil suits filed by private civil rights attorneys. In other cases, the DOJ has relied on media coverage of police misconduct,

[3] Telephone Interview with DOJ Participant #14, at 4 (July 11, 2013) [hereinafter Interview #14] (on file with author).

[4] *Id.* [5] *Id.*

whistle-blowers, and academic studies to guide their enforcement of § 14141. The DOJ has never publicly announced any specific formula for identifying police agencies in violation of § 14141. This lack of transparency is understandable, given the limited tools the DOJ has to make these important administrative decisions, but it also leads some police departments like Steubenville to feel unfairly targeted.

This imperfect enforcement strategy, borne out of necessity, is problematic in and of itself. Politics further complicates the enforcement of § 14141. While § 14141 may have quietly slipped into the VCCLEA, it has been the subject of partisan political wrangling in the years since. In the years immediately after the passage of § 14141, the DOJ had initiated reform efforts in many of the nation's largest police departments, including those in Pittsburgh, Washington, DC, Los Angeles, Cincinnati, Detroit, and Prince George's County. At the time it looked like the Intervention Era was destined to transform American policing forever. Then something changed. Between late 2004 and early 2009, the DOJ initiated few § 14141 investigations and did not pursue full-scale federal intervention into a single police agency.[6] The number of open § 14141 cases also declined precipitously.[7] During this time, public enthusiasm for § 14141 waned, in part because of a prevailing belief that the DOJ had not effectively utilized the statute.[8] This view "attribute[d] the weakness of § 14141 enforcement to insufficient resources devoted to structural reform of police departments and the related absence of political commitment to § 14141 suits, especially on the part of the Bush

[6] *See infra* Figure 3.1. The second term of the Bush administration roughly matches up with this purported time frame.

[7] *See infra* Figure 3.2 (illustrating graphically this decline in open cases over this time period).

[8] Brandon Garrett, *Remedying Racial Profiling*, 33 COLUM. HUM. RTS. L. REV. 41, 100–101 (2001) (stating that "the DOJ lacks the resources" to address problems like racial profiling as demonstrated by the "[f]ew consent decrees" that have resulted from § 14141); Myriam E. Gilles, *Reinventing Structural Reform Litigation: Deputizing Private Citizens in the Enforcement of Civil Rights*, 100 COLUM. L. REV. 1384, 1407–1411 (2000) (arguing that the small number of cases pushed forward by the DOJ via § 14141 is potentially the result of resource and political constraints); John C. Jeffries, Jr. & George A. Rutherglen, *Structural Reform Revisited*, 95 CAL. L. REV. 1387, 1419 (2007) (arguing "that the Department of Justice faces financial and political constraints on its effectiveness" in implementing § 14141); Kami Chavis Simmons, *The Politics of Policing: Ensuring Stakeholder Collaboration in the Federal Reform of Local Law Enforcement Agencies*, 98 J. CRIM. L. & CRIMINOLOGY 489, 493 (2008) ("Citing the expediency and cost-effectiveness of their settlement strategy, U.S. government officials have expressly articulated a preference for avoiding litigation and negotiating with municipalities to ensure compliance with the suggested reforms.").

Administration."[9] And who could blame these pundits? During this time period, it seemed as if the DOJ had simply given up on fighting police wrongdoing.

Previously, scholars observed that "the Special Litigation Section, the arm of the DOJ charged with [initiating federal intervention], changed considerably after the elections of George W. Bush and Barack Obama."[10] With this "came subtle yet important changes in the way pattern or practice initiatives were developed and implemented."[11] There is more to this story. There was a notable dip in the use of federal intervention into police departments during the Bush administration. This apparent dip in enforcement was no accident. The shift in § 14141 enforcement was the result of a deliberate set of decisions made by the DOJ during the Bush administration to deemphasize and discourage the use of federal intervention. Leadership within the DOJ instituted various changes to internal policies and enforcement preferences that directly contributed to the lag in § 14141 enforcement between 2004 and 2009.[12] When President Obama took office in 2009, the DOJ adopted a very different enforcement strategy. At that point, Assistant Attorney General Thomas Perez "told a conference of police chiefs ... that the Justice Department would be pursuing 'pattern or practice' takeovers of police departments much more aggressively."[13] Since then, the DOJ has lived up to its word, intervening into various new police agencies and expansively reading § 14141 to authorize reforms in a wide range of policy arenas – many of which may arguably go beyond the text of the statutory mandate.

Politics aside, across all political administrations, a lack of resources has prevented optimal enforcement of § 14141.[14] Although the DOJ has strategically targeted many of the nation's largest policing forces for federal intervention, it has not been able to initiate structural reform against many departments that appear to be engaged in systemic misconduct. The quantitative data suggests that the DOJ has initiated an average of three investigations of police departments

[9] Rachel A. Harmon, *Promoting Civil Rights Through Proactive Policing Reform*, 62 STAN. L. REV. 1, 21 (2009).

[10] Joshua M. Chanin, Negotiated Justice? The Legal, Administrative, and Policy Implications of "Pattern or Practice" Police Misconduct Reform 335 (July 6, 2011) (unpublished PhD dissertation, American University), *available at* www.ncjrs.gov/pdffiles1/nij/grants/237957.pdf.

[11] *Id.* [12] *See infra* notes 146–150 and accompanying text.

[13] Heather Mac Donald, *Targeting the Police*, WKLY. STANDARD, January 31, 2011, at 26.

[14] *See infra* notes 142–143 and accompanying text.

pursuant to § 14141 per year between 1994 and 2013.[15] During this time, the DOJ only pursued full-scale federal intervention into an average of less than one department per year.[16] Even if we assume that systemic misconduct is present in only a very small percentage of the nation's roughly 18,000 police agencies,[17] the DOJ has only initiated § 14141 investigations against a small fraction of problematic departments. Thus, the limitations to the enforcement of § 14141 stem from both limited resources and internal political pressure to avoid litigation against certain agencies.[18]

In some ways, federal intervention into local police departments is akin to a lottery. This enforcement lottery is messy and imprecise. For a police department to become subject to federal intervention under § 14141, numerous variables must opportunely align. The DOJ must have leadership that is supportive of federal intervention into local police departments, like that of the Clinton or Obama administration. The misconduct of the targeted police department must stand out to the DOJ, above and beyond the nation's other 18,000 police departments. And the DOJ must have enough available resources to investigate the department. The reality is that, for virtually all police departments, these variables will never align. Thus, most agencies will never become subject to federal intervention under § 14141, even if they are engaged in an

[15] *See infra* Table 3.2 (outlining the breakdown of investigations). [16] *Id.*

[17] Brian A. Reaves, US Dep't of Justice, Census of State and Local Law Enforcement Agencies, 2008, at 2 (2011), *available at* www.bjs.gov/content/pub/pdf/csllea08.pdf (putting the number of state and local law enforcement agencies at 17,985).

[18] This chapter adds to the existing literature on agency decision-making in three ways. First, it contributes to a body of literature on how top-down political pressure can lead to "agency slack" or the "tendency of government regulators to underenforce certain statutory requirements because of political pressure." Matthew C. Stephenson, *Public Regulation of Private Enforcement: The Case for Expanding the Role of Administrative Agencies*, 91 Va. L. Rev. 93, 110 and n.48 (describing studies that show the link between politics and "agency slack"). Second, it provides another illustration of how resource scarcity limits virtually all agencies as they attempt to implement statutory mandates. Third, this chapter describes how bottom-up political pressure can also influence agency decision-making. The DOJ's interest in New York City is a paradigmatic example of this sort of political spillover. Despite the DOJ's desire to intervene into the New York Police Department (NYPD), bottom-up pressure by the Southern District of New York prevented this action from going forward. In sum, this chapter illustrates the potential drawbacks of a regulatory model premised on federal intervention. Public rights of action are almost invariably subject to resource limitations and various types of political concerns that limit their potential effectiveness.

egregious pattern of misconduct. This realization underscores the need for some basic reforms in the way that the DOJ enforces § 14141.

The second half of this chapter evaluates the process of negotiated reform that happens after the enforcement lottery. During this process, the DOJ must figure out a way to bring about sustainable change to a targeted police department. At its core, the Intervention Era is about using federal action to bring about both procedural and cultural changes within a targeted police department. The procedural part is comparatively easy. While they can be expensive to implement and maintain, procedural changes are relatively straightforward. Culture, on the other hand, is tricky. As one monitor acknowledged, "it's hard to overcome the culture" of a police department.[19] A problematic culture within a police department can facilitate – either explicitly or implicitly – misconduct by frontline officers. It can be particularly difficult to change the culture of a large, complex organization through forceful external mandates. To bring about sustainable change in a police department, you need both procedural changes enacted through external mandates *and* cultural change that results in organizational buy-in.[20] Realizing these difficulties, the DOJ has taken a unique approach in handling § 14141 cases during the Intervention Era. Rather than going to court to adjudicate a § 14141 case through a trial proceeding, as the DOJ is statutorily authorized to do, the DOJ generally opts to negotiate amicable settlements mostly out of court. This negotiated reform process ensures that federal intervention gets off to a good start. It substitutes contentious, adversarial litigation for quiet, closed-door negotiations.

Negotiated reform is, in many ways, a tactical trade-off by the DOJ. This process may suffer from a lack of transparency and public input. Some may even find the process undemocratic. In these closed-door negotiations, the DOJ and the targeted municipality carve out a package of reforms aimed at curbing wrongdoing and transforming the organizational culture of the troubled agency. On one hand, some may understandably worry that this process does not adequately consider the diverse array of perspectives from within the community. On the other hand, the negotiated reform process has its advantages. Principal

19 Interview with External Monitor #8, at 4 [hereinafter Interview #8].

20 Interview with Police Administrator #11, at 5 ("I had to get rid of the people that didn't buy in to what I was trying to do.") [hereinafter Interview #11]; Interview with Police Administrator #16, at 7 (July 29, 2013) [hereinafter Interview #16] (discussing importance of "buy in from the bottom").

among these, the DOJ and the targeted municipality can avoid costly litigation. The DOJ can also work to build a strong working relationship with city leaders.

This relationship has proven critical to the success of federal intervention in several ways. It can be expensive to implement the terms of a negotiated settlement. The municipality must cover the cost of procedural changes, which sometimes require capital, technological, and personnel investments. In addition, the municipality must frequently pay a team of external monitors to regularly oversee the implementation of the negotiated settlement. By building a cooperative relationship with city leaders, the DOJ can increase the chances that city leaders buy into federal reform efforts by providing the police department with adequate funding to implement the terms of the negotiated settlement.

Additionally, the DOJ has previously leveraged this working relationship with city leaders to bring about changes in leadership within police departments. By working with city leaders to install a police chief who is supportive of federal intervention, the DOJ has attempted to promote buy-in among frontline police officers. Culture may be hard to overcome in a large police department. But through these negotiated reform efforts, the DOJ had attempted to bring about sustainable reform efforts across dozens of American police departments.

I Early Enforcement

After Congress quietly passed § 14141 in 1994, the responsibility to enforce the statute fell to the DOJ. Since the measure dealt with the federal government's response to civil rights abuses, the measure naturally fell under the purview of the Civil Rights Division.[21] The Civil Rights Section is the portion of the DOJ responsible for enforcing statutes that prohibit discrimination.[22] The division was created after the passage of the Civil Rights Act of 1957.[23] The assistant attorney general of the

[21] Brian K. Landsberg, Enforcing Civil Rights: Race Discrimination and the Department of Justice 1 (1998) (talking about the creation and purpose of the Civil Rights Division, which Landsberg describes as the "agent of social justice and change" within the DOJ by enforcing laws against various forms of discrimination and constitutional violations).

[22] *Id.*

[23] *Id.* at 186 n.38 (stating that "the formal order establishing the Civil Rights Division was issued by Attorney General William P. Rogers on December 9, 1957. Attorney General, Order no. 155-57, December 9, 1957").

Civil Rights Division leads this portion of the DOJ, subject to presidential appointment and Senate confirmation.

In 1994, Deval Patrick had assumed the role of assistant attorney general of the Civil Rights Division.[24] Better known as the former governor of Massachusetts, Patrick's background is illustrative of the type of litigators who often work in the Civil Rights Division. Patrick grew up in poverty in South Chicago.[25] Despite a tough childhood, Patrick graduated from Harvard Law School.[26] After graduation, Patrick spent his early years in legal practice working for the NAACP Legal Defense and Educational Fund.[27] Patrick had previously argued several high-profile civil rights cases. Perhaps most famously, Patrick worked on the *McCleskly* v. *Kemp* case, which eventually reached the Supreme Court.[28] In that case, Patrick and the NAACP argued that the death penalty ought to be found unconstitutional because of its disparate racial impact.[29] Immediately before Patrick's nomination as assistant attorney general, President Clinton had unsuccessfully nominated Lani Guinier to head the Civil Rights Division.[30] A law professor from the University of Pennsylvania, Guinier had previously worked at the Civil Rights Division and had litigated cases alongside Patrick at the NAACP.[31] After Republicans rejected Guinier's nomination, Clinton picked Patrick for the post.[32]

During his confirmation hearings, Patrick promised to use his position atop the Civil Rights Division as a "bully pulpit" to "move firmly, fearlessly,

24 *Justice Department Nominees Confirmed*, CHICAGO TRIBUNE March 23, 1994, at 8.

25 Kathy Lewis, *Clinton Defends Rights Nominee; Says Critics of Deval Patrick "Don't Give a Rip About Civil Rights*," SAN FRANCISCO EXAMINER, February 2, 1994, at A14.

26 Lynne Duke, *Civil Rights Is Familiar Terrain for Clinton's Justice Choice*, WASHINGTON POST, February 14, 1994.

27 *Id.* (explaining that Patrick was an associate director-counsel of the NAACP Legal Defense and Educational Fund, where he remained a board member at the time of his appointment atop the Civil Rights Division).

28 *Id.* (Patrick "helped prepare the defense fund's challenge to Georgia's death penalty in 1987 before the U.S. Supreme Court in *McCleskey* v. *Kemp*").

29 *Id.* ("The defense fund analyzed statistics that revealed patterns showing that the death penalty was applied in a racially discriminatory way in Georgia").

30 Timothy M. Phelps, *A "Sensible" Choice: Clinton Taps Boston Lawyer for Top Civil Rights Post*, NEWSDAY, February 2, 1994, at 19 (explaining how Clinton previously appointed Guinier, only to have her withdraw her nomination after controversy over her legal writings).

31 *Id.* (describing Guinier as Patrick's "former colleague").

32 David Johnston, *Clinton Settles on 2 for Long-Vacant Posts at Justice Department*, NY TIMES, February 2, 1994, at N8.

and unambiguously" to enforce civil rights laws.[33] He promised to bring a sea change to the Civil Rights Division and ensure aggressive enforcement of existing laws.[34] The Senate confirmed Patrick on March 17, 1994 – only months before the passage of § 14141.[35] Under his leadership, the Civil Rights Division appeared to ratchet up enforcement of all types of civil rights laws. This aggressive and unabashed approach caught the ire of many conservative commentators. Some publicly expressed concern that the Civil Rights Division was exceeding its statutory authority under Patrick's leadership.[36] Nevertheless, Patrick maintained his belief that the federal government ought to be vigilant in enforcing civil rights protections.

Remember, Congress passed § 14141 with little fanfare and with little apparent expectation that the measure would substantially burden local law enforcement. After passage, the mandate provided Patrick's Civil Rights Division – which was already notorious for aggressively pushing the limits of civil rights litigation – with a seemingly expansive mandate to intervene into the affairs of local police departments. This only further empowered an already progressive and active wing of the DOJ.

Upon passage of § 14141, the Civil Rights Division did not immediately begin intervening into local police agencies. This is because, unlike other civil rights arenas, the Civil Rights Division had no real experience with regulating police agencies. The regulation of police departments was an entirely new challenge for the Civil Rights Division. As one of the early § 14141 litigators at the DOJ explained, prior to working on police reform, DOJ litigators worked on a wide variety of other legal matters.[37] Some worked on voting rights cases.[38] Others worked in the Criminal Division.[39] And still others had handled structural reform litigation under the Civil

[33] *Nominee Pledges to Make Bully Pulpit of Civil Rights Post*, ORLANDO SENTINEL, March 11, 1994, at A10 (using the term "bully pulpit"); Marcy Gordon, *Civil Rights Post Nominee Speaks at Senate Hearing; Attorney Vows to Fight Bigotry, Hate Crimes*, BUFFALO NEWS, March 11, 1994, at A8 (quoting Patrick as saying the department will move "firmly, fearlessly and unambiguously to enforce the anti-discrimination laws").

[34] Gordon, *supra* note 33. [35] *Justice Department Nominees Confirmed, supra* note 24.

[36] *See, e.g.*, Clint Bolick, *Deval Patrick's Legal at Justice*, WALL STREET JOURNAL, May 14, 1994, at A23 (arguing that Patrick's tenure at the Civil Rights Division has been marked with tactics intended to force state and local governments to adopt potentially unpopular reforms).

[37] Interview with DOJ Participant #15, at 1 (July 31, 2013) [hereinafter Interview #15] (on file with author).

[38] *Id.* [39] *Id.*

Rights of Institutionalized Persons Act (CRIPA), which gives the US attorney general the right to seek injunctive relief against mental health facilities, jails, prisons, nursing homes, and other similar governmental institutions that are engaged in a pattern or practice of wrongdoing.[40] However, regardless of where these litigators came from, they all shared one common trait. They all knew little to "nothing ... [about] police matters at all."[41]

There were also no easily accessible outside models that DOJ litigators could turn to in developing an enforcement strategy for § 14141. This made the use of federal intervention particularly challenging in comparison to other comparable statutes. For example, by the time when Congress passed CRIPA, there had already been "dozens of big decrees negotiated mostly by the ACLU" as well as "hundreds" of decrees negotiated by private parties.[42] Once more, the DOJ had already started "negotiating its own prison decrees."[43] So when Congress finally gave the DOJ formalized authority to oversee state prisons, jails, and mental health facilities via CRIPA in 1980, the agency was ready to hit the ground running. Litigators were able to use these previous cases as models of how to go about intervening into and restructuring these organizations.

Again, the policing context was different. As one litigator explained, "there really hadn't been much structural reform litigation [of any kind] involving police departments" before the passage of § 14141 in 1994.[44] Remember back to Chapters 1 and 2. This lack of previous structural reform litigation against police departments was due in part to court decisions in the *Lyons* and *City of Philadelphia* cases, where a federal circuit court and the US Supreme Court blocked attempts by private litigants and the DOJ to intervene into problematic police agencies.[45] Thus, the DOJ had to develop a plan to enforce § 14141 from scratch. This took time.

The first thing that the Civil Rights Division needed to do was to figure out how the agency would go about enforcing this statute. To get this process under way, Patrick handpicked a few experienced litigators to head a taskforce on police misconduct.[46] The obvious choice to begin

[40] Civil Rights of Institutionalized Persons Act, 42 USC § 1997 (1980).
[41] Interview #15, *supra* note 37, at 1.
[42] Interview with DOJ Participant #14, at 7 (July 11, 2013) [hereinafter Interview #14] (on file with author).
[43] *Id.* [44] *Id.* [45] *See supra* Chapters 1 and 2.
[46] Interview #14, *supra* note 3, at 5.

the implementation of § 14141 was the Special Litigation Section.[47] The Special Litigation Section is a smaller component of the Civil Rights Division assigned with enforcing a wide range of civil rights and structural reform litigation statutes.[48] The section has become a sort of "potpourri section" of the DOJ, handling a wide range of specialized civil rights issues.[49] Even as leadership of the Civil Rights Division and the Special Litigation has shifted over time, the Special Litigation Section has remained the home of § 14141 enforcement. At any given time, the Special Litigation Section has since allocated a relatively small number of attorneys to the enforcement of § 14141 nationwide.[50]

Early on in the enforcement process, though, one thing became clear to the litigators tasked with enforcing this new statute. Since there are over 18,000 police departments in the United States, there was no possible way the section could address all of the apparent instances of misconduct.[51] The Special Litigation Section can allocate enough staff and resources to initiate only a small number of § 14141 cases every year.[52] Thus, the section would have to come up with a way to make tough choices – that is, to decide which of the nation's police agencies were engaged in misconduct, how to investigate these agencies, and how to allocate the Special Litigation's scarce resources. No easy task, to say the least. The next part describes in detail the enforcement model that the Special Litigation Section has adopted.

II The Enforcement Lottery

Since § 14141 gives the attorney general sole authority to initiate federal intervention, the DOJ has become a critical gatekeeper. This raises many

47 Interview #15, *supra* note 37, at 1.

48 *Id.* at 2 (explaining that the Special Litigation Section handles a wide range of issues, ranging from structural reform against mental health and detention facilities under the CRIPA, "freedom of access to ... abortion clinics," and other responsibilities).

49 *Id.*

50 Interview #14, *supra* note 3, at 5 (describing how "5 lawyers plus Steve Rosenbaum began to think about how to implement that statute").

51 Telephone Interview with DOJ Participant #5, at 2 (September 4, 2013) [hereinafter Interview #5] (on file with author) (stating that since there are around 20,000 police departments, the DOJ "can't do them all").

52 *Id.* at 3 (stating that "we're gonna be able to only open 2 or 3 cases in the next 1 or 2 years [so] we're gonna be super careful about what those cases are").

important questions. How has the DOJ exercised this authority as the gatekeeper for federal intervention? Has the DOJ more eagerly intervened into problematic police departments during the Clinton and Obama administrations than it did during the Bush administration? Have Republican attorneys general used less invasive alternatives to federal intervention than Democratic attorneys general? And what does this mean for the future of police misconduct regulation? Despite a significant amount of speculation on these subjects,[53] little empirical work has sought to answer these questions. If the DOJ has shifted enforcement policies dramatically from one presidential administration to another, this would suggest that federal intervention is an inconsistent tool for spreading constitutional policing practices in American police departments. If the DOJ rarely exercises its statutory authority to bring pattern or practice litigation – because of either political pressure or budgetary constraints – then federal intervention may not serve as a general deterrent to police misconduct. If political pressures have made the DOJ less likely to negotiate settlements and demand external monitoring of problematic departments, federal intervention may not even serve as an effective tool to reform particularly problematic agencies.

This part presents the findings from an empirical examination of the § 14141 reform process. It focuses on the DOJ's role as the gatekeeper of federal intervention. In doing so, it builds a descriptive account of how the DOJ has used its authority to initiate federal intervention under § 14141. This section also evaluates how political forces have affected the DOJ's use of federal intervention.

Federal intervention is a long and complex process. It is easiest to understand the process of federal intervention into police departments by first taking a macroview of each step. Table 3.1 summarizes the progressive stages.

The subparts that follow describe the first three stages of the federal intervention process – each of which describes a component of the DOJ's enforcement model. These subparts use data from interviews, court documents, media accounts, and monitor reports to provide examples from various localities that have been subject to federal intervention over the last twenty years.

[53] *See* Barbara E. Armacost, *Organizational Culture and Police Misconduct*, 72 Geo. Wash. L. Rev. 453, 513 (2003); Gilles, *supra* note 8, at 1419; Harmon, *supra* note 9, at 21; Simmons, *supra* note 8, at 519.

Table 3.1 *Stages of Federal Intervention into Local Police Departments*

Stage 1: Case Selection
Stage 2: Preliminary Inquiry
Stage 3: Formal Investigation
Stage 4: Settlement Negotiations
Stage 5: Appointment of Monitor
Stage 6: Monitored Reform

A Case Selection

The first step in federal intervention is the identification of problematic police agencies, also known as the case selection process. The process by which the DOJ identifies cities for scrutiny remains somewhat of a mystery – described publicly in mere generalities by the DOJ.[54] This has led many agencies subject to § 14141 litigation to feel unfairly targeted.[55] Professor Michael Selmi has echoed this sentiment, observing that "it doesn't seem like [Justice Department officials] have a very strategic approach – they simply react to cases brought to them."[56] The DOJ has used several major mechanisms to identify problematic departments under this statute.

First, in some cases, the DOJ has used existing civil litigation or private interest group investigations as springboards for § 14141 cases. This appears to have been the motivating factor in the DOJ's initial selections of Steubenville, Pittsburgh, and Columbus, Ohio – "persistent efforts by lawyers and civil rights advocates ... flood[ed] the Justice Department with complaints" that provided the basis for a formal investigation.[57] In the case of existing litigation, DOJ intervention in the case through § 14141 can increase the likelihood of an injunctive remedy. Participants from the DOJ also emphasized how civil rights attorneys and civil liberties groups like the NAACP and ACLU have built sufficiently persuasive

54 *Conduct of Law Enforcement Agencies*, US Dep't Just., www.justice.gov/crt/about/spl/police.php (last visited April 26, 2014) (stating that the DOJ uses "information from a variety of sources" to select cases for § 14141 litigation).

55 Lichtblau, *supra* note 1; *Conduct of Law Enforcement Agencies, supra* note 61 (providing very few details on the case selection process except to say that the DOJ considers community input while also utilizing a variety of other information sources).

56 Lichtblau, *supra* note 1 (alteration in original) (quoting Professor Michael Selmi).

57 Nicole Marshall, *Why Investigate Us? Police Ask*, Tulsa World, April 1, 2001, at A1.

cases of allegedly systemic misconduct to necessitate a DOJ inquiry.[58] For example, as a DOJ insider explained, both the NAACP and the ACLU took part in the initial Pittsburgh allegations; these groups "were in it from the beginning."[59] These organizations have sometimes collected dozens of complaints demonstrating a common or systemic problem in one jurisdiction necessitating DOJ action. As discussed in the introduction, Steubenville exemplified this method, according to one former DOJ litigator. Remember, a notable civil rights attorney "used to litigate against Steubenville all the time," which ultimately motivated the DOJ to take action.[60] This method of case selection saves resources, as it often provides the DOJ with a thoroughly investigated group of allegations ready for further inquiry.[61] Internal policies have varied over the years on whether the DOJ ought to coordinate with traditionally liberal interest groups in formulating targets for inquiries and investigations.

Second, the DOJ regularly monitors media reports of systemic misconduct.[62] While any single, discrete media report of misconduct is insufficient to justify a formal investigation in most cases, a pattern of similar reports or a single report of a particularly serious case of misconduct can spur preliminary inquiries. As one participant explained, "Occasionally [inquiries] get started when there is a big exposé of a big problem in a department."[63]

DOJ litigators identified three examples of cases where outside media attention in particular moved the Special Litigation Section to start a preliminary inquiry – Los Angeles, Cincinnati, and Washington, DC. In Los Angeles, the Rampart scandal made national headlines and, in part, motivated the DOJ to take a hard look at the LAPD.[64] The Rampart

[58] Interview #14, *supra* note 3, at 7 (explaining in detail the role that the NAACP and the ACLU served in early investigations in cities like Pittsburgh).

[59] *Id.* at 7. [60] *Id.* at 4.

[61] *Id.* ("That makes very good sense because it's a huge amount of work to find these incidents and to know that you're talking about something that is systemic enough that there is a point to it.").

[62] Telephone Interview with DOJ Participant #18, at 4 (August 8, 2013) [hereinafter Interview #18] (on file with author) (stating that the DOJ identified cases "through a mix of . . . media reviews [and] newspaper reviews").

[63] Interview #14, *supra* note 3, at 4 (explaining further that when such a major media story breaks, the DOJ will sometimes independently open an inquiry into the matter, or leadership from the affected city may come directly to the DOJ requesting assistance).

[64] *See* Interview #15, *supra* note 37, at 4 ("The LAPD of course, there had been a history of problems. And then the whole controversy broke out in 2000 or 1999, with the Rampart investigation."); Interview #14, *supra* note 50, at 4 (identifying Rampart as an example of

scandal refers to allegations that surfaced in the late 1990s that officers working in the Rampart station in Los Angeles were involved in numerous illegal activities including planting of drugs, making false arrests, and covering up brutality.[65] This massive scandal led the courts to overturn 106 criminal cases and pressured seven officers to retire or resign.[66] Similarly, the *Washington Post* featured a prominent news story on a string of shootings in Washington, DC, which played a role in the DOJ decision to take a closer look at the Washington Metropolitan Police Department (MPD).[67] Eventually, though, the MPD came proactively to the DOJ seeking help.[68] Additionally, in Cincinnati, one DOJ litigator recalled that the local media did an "excellent" job making "credible and repeated" showings of systemic misconduct by the police department.[69] There was already an active class action suit against Cincinnati's police

a prominent news story that motivated the DOJ to focus on Los Angeles); *see also id.* (describing how "a big exposé of a big problem" can spur interest in a police agency for § 14141 litigation).

65 Shawn Hubler, *In Rampart, Reaping What We Sowed*, LA Times, February 17, 2000, at B1 (explaining "the sickening revelations" surrounding the Rampart scandal including "the frame-ups, the dope dealing, the tales of brutality verging on murder"). Other allegations include claims that officers arranged the deportation of witnesses to police abuse. Anne-Marie O'Connor, Activist Says Officer Sought His Deportation, LA Times, February 17, 2000, at A1. The evidence of the Rampart scandal first started to emerge when Rafael Perez, former Rampart division officer, was arrested for cocaine theft charges. *See* Editorial, *A Scandal Hits Home*, LA Times, April 11, 2000, at B8.

66 David Rosenzweig, *3 Sue LAPD over Rampart Scandal*, LA Times, August 7, 2005, at B3 ("More than 100 criminal cases were overturned after former Rampart officer Rafael Perez contended that he and other officers had routinely framed gang members for crimes they did not commit.").

67 Interview #15, *supra* note 37, at 4 (identifying the story in the *Washington Post* as a memorable event that motivated the DOJ to take a deeper look into the District of Columbia); Telephone Interview with DOJ Participant #12, at 2 (July 30, 2013) [hereinafter Interview #12] (on file with author) (noting that the interviewee "think[s] the *Washington Post* actually did an exposé on the shootings," which in part motivated the focus on the Metropolitan Police Department).

68 Interview #12, *supra* note 67, at 1 and 2.

69 *Id.* at 3 and 4. The respondent explained in detail that

> if the media brought attention, shed light on allegations, various allegations in a community and did those in a credible and repeated fashion, I felt that was more powerful than an individual organization or individual complainants calling up ... [T]hat was certainly the case in Cincinnati. There was a lot of excellent reporting by the newspaper there. There was a series of shootings of unarmed African American men. A lot of civil unrest ... happened ... And so, DOJ went in.
>
> *Id.* at 4.

department.[70] And when the shooting of Timothy Thomas, an unarmed teenager, by Cincinnati police made national news and "resulted in about 3 days of civil unrest," it was important enough to spark DOJ interest in the police department's procedures.[71] Indeed, the DOJ appears to rely on media reports to initially identify problematic departments.

Third, research studies have sometimes keyed the DOJ into possible instances of ongoing unconstitutional policing practices. According to one participant in the qualitative interviews, the investigation of the New Jersey State Police demonstrates this phenomenon.[72] The DOJ formally opened an investigation of the New Jersey State Police on April 15, 1996.[73] As this DOJ litigator explained, the Special Litigation Section identified the New Jersey State Police in part because of research presented in an earlier court case on racially disproportionate stop patterns associated with the jurisdiction.[74] Statistician John Lamberth had started studying racial profiling in traffic stops in New Jersey in 1993 after a group of attorneys asked Lamberth to investigate a suspicious and racially disparate pattern of arrests.[75]

Over the following years, Lamberth systematically evaluated whether the New Jersey State Police appeared to be targeting drivers of color on

70 Interview #18, *supra* note 62, at 2 ("[A]t that point, there had already been an ongoing class action lawsuit on racial profiling.").

71 *Id.* ("[W]hen the Timothy Thomas shooting and the subsequent disturbances, some people called them riots, happened; then at that point, also the Justice Department began its § 14141 investigation."); *see also* Police Exec. Research Forum, Civil Rights Investigations of Local Police: Lessons Learned 3 (2013), *available at* http://samuelwalker.net/wp-content/uploads/2013/07/PERFConsent-Decree.pdf (stating that "[i]n Cincinnati, riots were sparked in 2001 by the police killing of Timothy Thomas, a 19-year-old African American with 14 open warrants for minor, mostly traffic-related violations," and identifying this as a major cause of the eventual DOJ investigation of the Cincinnati Police Department).

72 Interview #12, *supra* note 67, at 1 and 2 (giving an overview of how the DOJ became interested in the New Jersey State Police and explaining that "[t]here were maybe tens of years of problems reported by minority drivers on the Turnpike in New Jersey and lots of civil litigation and lots of allegations of abuse and DOJ used the pattern or practice authority to bring the first racial profiling case under that statute").

73 *See infra* Appendix A (listing the starting and ending dates for each investigation initiated by the DOJ).

74 Interview #12, *supra* note 67, at 1 and 2 (explaining the importance of the academic studies in making the DOJ litigators feel more confident in initiating action in New Jersey).

75 John Lamberth, *Driving While Black: A Statistician Proves That Prejudice Still Rules the Road*, Wash. Post, August 16, 1998, at C1.

state highways.[76] He began by sampling the racial distribution of drivers on the road.[77] After twenty-one days of intensive observation, Lamberth concluded that roughly 13.5 percent of automobiles on the studied portions of New Jersey highway contained at least one black occupant.[78] He also concluded that these cars with black occupants made up around 15 percent of all traffic law violators.[79] Yet, about 35 percent of the cars pulled over by police during this same time period contained a black occupant.[80] These "findings were central to a March 1996 ruling by Judge Robert E. Francis of the Superior Court of New Jersey that the state police were de facto targeting blacks, in violation of their rights under the US and New Jersey constitutions."[81] The only remedy that the state judge in that particular case could provide, however, was the exclusion of evidence obtained pursuant to these unlawful stops.[82] The judge was not equipped to provide a more expansive, injunctive remedy. According to participants, these research findings motivated the DOJ to take action. Lamberth's evidence was particularly jarring to some at the DOJ.[83] It also provided an ideal source of evidence to justify further inquiry. Within a month of the state court judge's ruling, the DOJ had opened an official investigation into the use of race in traffic stops by the New Jersey State Police.[84]

Fourth, whistle-blowers within police departments sometimes provided the DOJ with sufficient evidence to open an inquiry.[85] This often happened when officers "themselves ... would contact the division and talk about problems they had witnessed or problems they, themselves, had experienced when they were not in uniform."[86] Interview participants could not always give specific examples of this phenomenon because, as one explained, "We protect the identity of whistleblowers, so we aren't able to talk more about it. But needless to say, in a handful of cases, we relied heavily on files and information given to us by officers inside a department."[87] In other cases, though, a high-level administrator within a police department openly reached out to the DOJ to request a formal § 14141 investigation. This happened, most notably, in Washington, DC. There,

[76] *Id.* [77] *Id.* [78] *Id.* [79] *Id.* [80] *Id.* [81] *Id.* [82] *Id.*

[83] Interview #12, *supra* note 67, at 1 and 2.

[84] The judge in private litigation found there to be a pattern of unconstitutional stops in March 1996. Lamberth, *supra* note 75. The next month, in April 1996, the DOJ began a formal investigation. *See infra* Appendix A (listing all dates of investigations).

[85] Interview #12, *supra* note 67, at 2 ("[S]ometimes there were internal whistleblowers.").

[86] *Id.* [87] *Id.* at 4.

> Charles Ramsey, newly sworn in as chief in Washington's Metropolitan Police Department after a 30-year career in the Chicago Police Department, asked the DOJ to intervene after a series of articles in the *Washington Post* alleged that MPD officers shot and killed more people per capita in the 1990s than any other large U.S. city police force.[88]

Various participants confirmed this story during interviews.[89] Although it is rare to see a police chief so openly request that the DOJ intervene in local affairs, at least one participant remarked that this type of request happens with some frequency.[90] In many of these cases, the DOJ cannot find a sufficiently serious problem as to warrant intervention and instead recommends that the police agency seek alternative assistance through other federal programs or through private accreditation agencies.[91]

Fifth, in a small number of cases, the DOJ relied on particularly egregious individual incidents of misconduct to find possible targets. Of course, § 14141 only provides the attorney general a right of action where there is a pattern or practice of misconduct. This means that a single complaint is typically insufficient to further inquiry.[92] Even so, a single complaint or heinous example of misconduct can convince the DOJ to give a police department a harder look via a preliminary inquiry.[93] In some cases, the Criminal Division of the DOJ sent complaints of officer-involved shootings directly to the Special Litigation

[88] Police Exec. Research Forum, *supra* note 71, at 2 (discussing also how this proactive response in Washington, DC, eventually led to the signing of a memorandum of agreement).

[89] *See, e.g.*, Interview #12, *supra* note 67, at 1 and 2 (stating that Chief Ramsey "very shrewdly asked DOJ to come in and do an investigation"); Interview #14, *supra* note 50, at 4 ("Or they might get started when there's a big exposé and the department itself or, more likely, the mayor responds to that exposé by inviting the Justice Department to come in. That's what happened in D.C."); Interview #15, *supra* note 37, at 4 ("I think this was publicized in the *Washington Post*, there was a settlement with the D.C. police force and that resulted because D.C. actually came to the division and said, we have lots of problems. We want your help. Please investigate us.").

[90] Interview #5, *supra* note 51, at 2 and 3 (explaining that police departments come to the DOJ requesting assistance more often than many outsider observers may believe).

[91] *Id.* (citing Community Oriented Policing Services (COPS) and the CALEA as possible examples of alternative programs that the DOJ may refer a local police agency to in lieu of beginning a formal investigation).

[92] Interview #14, *supra* note 3, at 4 (explaining that the evidence must show that misconduct within a department is systemic enough to justify intervention).

[93] Interview #18, *supra* note 62, at 2 (citing the Timothy Thomas shooting as an example of a particularly egregious incident of misconduct that motivated DOJ action).

Section for additional investigation to determine whether they were part of a pattern or practice of misconduct.[94] In total, the methods by which the DOJ identifies target police departments vary widely.

B Preliminary Inquiry

The second step in the federal intervention process is the preliminary inquiry. If a police agency comes to the attention of the DOJ through one of the manners listed above, the agency will open a preliminary inquiry into that department's conduct.[95] This usually happens when a litigator decides to spend some significant period of time researching claims of misconduct in a particular community.[96] During this initial inquiry, the DOJ only relies on private complaints, news reports of misconduct, and publicly available data.[97] The DOJ also occasionally conducts interviews with citizens from the community.[98] During this initial phase, litigators at the DOJ, both past and present, are careful to describe their actions as inquiries, as opposed to investigations. This distinction matters because of the serious implications of a formal investigation. By identifying a department as "under investigation," the DOJ might expose that department to criticism in the media, which may prove unwarranted after the DOJ concludes its investigation.[99] Moreover,

[94] *Id.* at 4 and 5. This DOJ insider explained the process:

> The criminal section certainly has lots of situations where they've had complaints about officer-involved shootings where they may have done a set of investigations in a particular jurisdiction and said, gee, the policies look pretty bad here. You might want to look at that. They got – they met with and got – feedback from civil rights and community groups.
>
> *Id.* at 4.

[95] *Oversight of the Department of Justice – Civil Rights Division: Hearing Before the Comm. on the Judiciary*, 107th Cong. 18–20 (2002) [hereinafter *Oversight of the DOJ*] (testimony of Ralph Boyd, Jr., Assistant Att'y Gen., Civil Rights Div., US Dep't of Justice).

[96] Interview #5, *supra* note 51, at 2 (explaining the preliminary inquiry process and the assignment of a DOJ number for any activity that takes up at least two hours of time).

[97] *Oversight of the DOJ, supra* note 95, at 18 and 19 (explaining how during this phase, the DOJ typically relies on public information like witness interviews, pleadings, and testimony in court).

[98] *Id.* (stating that the DOJ will conduct interviews in some cases).

[99] Interview #14, *supra* note 3, at 4 ("Opening an investigation is a huge deal. It's a very big moment. You wouldn't want to do that if there turns out not to be enough there to investigate. It would be very detrimental to the police department. Before you open any investigation all through the Department, it doesn't matter what the issue is, you have to figure out if there is a reason to open an investigation.").

Table 3.2 *Total Number of Inquiries, Investigations, and Monitor Appointments from January 1, 2000, to September 1, 2013**

Stage	Cases
Preliminary Inquiry	325
Formal Investigation	38
Negotiated Settlement	21

* I acquired this data from an interview participant with access to DOJ records. The number of preliminary inquiries is approximate, since the Special Litigation Section does not always keep complete records of these inquiries. The participant explained that the number could be anywhere between 300 and 350. Hence, I use 325 as the best approximate estimate. Telephone Interview with DOJ Participant #5 (September 4, 2013) (on file with author).

the investigation process is long and expensive.[100] Thus, the DOJ prefers to advance a case to the investigatory realm only if the litigator finds reason to believe the agency is involved in systemic misconduct, and the leadership at the DOJ believes that such an investigation would be a worthwhile use of limited resources.[101] To illustrate the commonality of initial inquiries, the DOJ provided information on the number of preliminary inquiries registered into the DOJ database since 2000. I recreate that information in Table 3.2, demonstrating the progression of cases from preliminary inquiry through investigation, and settlement.

As Table 3.2 shows, with 325 total cases between 2000 and 2013, the DOJ has initiated an average of around twenty-five or twenty-six preliminary inquiries per year between 2000 and 2013.[102] The vast majority of these preliminary looks fail to become a formal investigation. In fact, only

[100] Jodi Nirode, Doug Caruso, & Bob Ruth, *City, DOJ Draft Pact; The Police Union Will Be Asked To OK Contract Changes to Avoid Suit Over*, COLUMBUS DISPATCH, August 17, 1999, at A1 (stating that in a request for the 2000 budget, the DOJ requested $100 million per year to fund sixteen new investigators annually, putting the estimated cost at around $6 million to $7 million per investigator hired).

[101] Interview #14, *supra* note 3, at 5 (calling this preliminary investigation a "sussing out exercise" used when the DOJ has a suspicion but otherwise has "nothing").

[102] I calculated this by dividing the total number of preliminary inquiries (325) by the number of years in the sample (12.67) to arrive at an average of 25.66 preliminary inquiries per year since 2000.

11.6 percent of preliminary inquiries resulted in a formal investigation. And only 6.5 percent ended up leading to a negotiated settlement.

C Formal Investigation

If this initial inquiry uncovers the possibility of persistent misconduct in a police department, the DOJ may conduct a formal investigation. These are particularly costly endeavors.[103] The average investigation "can take years as investigators wade through piles of internal records and personnel files."[104] Other previous reports suggested that investigations took "as long as a year."[105] Such a slow pace can frustrate police agencies that complain that federal investigation contributes to a cloud of suspicion over the entire department.[106] Full investigations are "comprehensive and far-reaching."[107] In carrying out an investigation, the DOJ takes "inventory of departmental policies and procedures related to training, discipline, routine police activities, and uses of force and conduct[s] in-depth interviews to determine whether the department's practices adhere to formal policies."[108] Litigators from the DOJ do not do these investigations by themselves; instead, they outsource much of the work to police experts and professionals.[109] These police experts "go out and do ride alongs with the police department, review the police policy manuals, [and] observe police training."[110] These experts also evaluate current agency procedure

[103] Nirode, Caruso, & Ruth, *supra* note 100.

[104] Jamie Stockwell, *Rights Investigation of Police Continues*, WASH. POST, December 22, 2002, at C6.

[105] David Hench, *City Police to Get Federal Review*, PORTLAND PRESS HERALD, May 8, 2002, at 1A.

[106] Stockwell, *supra* note 104.

[107] Harmon, *supra* note 9, at 15 (quoting INT'L ASS'N OF CHIEFS OF POLICE, PROTECTING CIVIL RIGHTS: A LEADERSHIP GUIDE FOR STATE, LOCAL, AND TRIBAL LAW ENFORCEMENT 38 (2006), *available at* www.cops.usdoj.gov/files/ric/Publications/e06064100.pdf).

[108] *Id.; see also* INT'L ASS'N OF CHIEFS OF POLICE, *supra* note 107, at 8.

[109] Interview #18, *supra* note 62, at 7 ("[T]he Civil Rights Division and the Special Litigation Section brings on police experts to assist them in the actual investigation."). This participant further elaborated on how the DOJ selects individuals for this role:

> Some individuals are – many of them are – prior chiefs or prior deputy chiefs or involved in maybe heads of internal affairs divisions, some may be academics but I don't think so. I think they're mostly practitioners. There's also been some kind of going back and forth between monitors and the folks who do the investigation.
>
> *Id.* at 8.

[110] *Id.* at 7.

for investigation and commonly "look into and review investigations, both citizen complaints and use of force investigations."[111] Investigations are primarily comparative – that is, the DOJ seeks to compare the policies in the investigated department with "constitutional minimums."[112] In theory, if an investigation reveals a pattern or practice of misconduct and the agency refuses to cooperate, the case could go to trial.[113] In the majority of cases, departments have been reasonably open to cooperating with the investigation to avoid the expense and embarrassment of public litigation.[114]

A Washington, DC, case provides a useful example of a typical investigation. When the DOJ formally investigated the MPD for allegations of excessive use of force, DOJ investigators obtained a "stratified random sample of the use of force incidents."[115] They determined that in approximately 15 percent of these cases, the officer used excessive force.[116] According to DOJ estimates, a "well-managed and supervised" police department should expect only about 1 or 2 percent of all incidents to involve excessive use of force.[117] The survey also found that in 22 percent of the force claims involving firearms, police used deadly force based on the suspicion that the suspect possessed a firearm.[118] And "[i]n each case ... post-incident searches failed to reveal any weapon."[119] Based on these findings, the DOJ provided the MPD with a set of technical assistance

[111] *Id.*

[112] *Id.* This participant's explanation is worth reproduction here to give a fuller explanation of the investigatory process:

> And then to look into and review investigations, both citizen complaints and use of force investigations. That's one of the ways that they compare the police departments or it could be a sheriff or a law enforcement jurisdiction entity. They compare the practices of the investigating – the entity being investigated – with general police practices, model practices and what the expectation[s] are in the field. And review the practices for comparison to constitutional minimums. And as part of the investigation, they examine the systems, the policies, the practices, and the policy systems, compare it to what should be the norm.
>
> *Id.*

[113] Harmon, *supra* note 9, at 15.

[114] *See infra* Appendix B (listing the disposition of each negotiated settlement).

[115] William R. Yeomans, Department of Justice Investigation of Use of Force by the Washington Metropolitan Police Department 2 (2001), *available at* www.clearinghouse.net/chDocs/public/PN-DC-0001-0002.pdf.

[116] *Id.* [117] *Id.*

[118] *Id.* ("22 percent of the sampled incidents involved officers firing their weapons at moving vehicles.").

[119] *Id.*

Table 3.3 *Allegations Made by DOJ Against Local Police Departments, 1994–2015*

Constitutional Violation	Frequency
Excessive Force	48
Discriminatory Policing	38
Unlawful Stops, Searches, or Seizures	29
Unlawful Arrests	5
Poor Jail Conditions	4
Gender Bias in Handling Sexual Assault Reports	2
Improper Detentions	2
Sexual Misconduct	1
Retaliation	1
Improper Treatment of Mentally Ill	1

* Data originally compiled by PBS Frontline

recommendations.[120] In some cases – particularly those involving a small number of problems – this investigation and technical assistance letter ends the DOJ inquiry.[121] If the formal investigation uncovers a more expansive pattern of misconduct, though, the DOJ could theoretically file a lawsuit under § 14141. The types of allegations made by the DOJ after an investigation vary from case to case. But as Table 3.3 shows, the DOJ most commonly finds police departments to be involved in excessive uses of force, discriminatory policing, and unlawful arrests.

This three-step process of internal, investigatory actions by the DOJ sets the stage for federal intervention. It determines which departments are subject to long, costly litigation and which departments get a pass on federal oversight. The DOJ is the gatekeeper to federal intervention. While it remains possible that private litigants can initiate structural reform litigation in a few narrow circumstances after *Lyons*, the DOJ holds the key to virtually all cases of mandatory, top-down oversight.

120 *Id.* at 7 (citing the need for a formal settlement outlining the terms of reform and saying that "[t]he Memorandum of Agreement provides for the development and implementation of updated use of force policies and procedures addressing the issues raised by our investigation as summarized above").

121 Harmon, *supra* note 9, at 16 (writing that, in some cases, the DOJ has "issued a technical assistance letter recommending reform, or taken no action").

In many respects, the current enforcement model makes sense. It attempts to use limited resources to identify and investigate a small number of police departments out of a pool of thousands of possible targets. But in doing so, it uses an imprecise and messy process. As I show in the next part, the agency's enforcement model has also changed over time.

III Changes in Enforcement Policy over Time

In the past, several writers have claimed that both internal and external pressures may affect how aggressively the DOJ pursues cases under § 14141. Professor Joshua Chanin has previously written that the DOJ's enforcement strategy seemed to "change[] considerably after the elections of George W. Bush and Barack Obama."[122] This seems to roughly align with statements made by then candidate George W. Bush as he was campaigning for his first presidential term, when he stated that he did "not believe that the federal government should instruct state and local authorities on how police department operations should be conducted, becoming a separate internal affairs division."[123] This stands in stark contrast to the Obama administration, which has pledged to take on a more aggressive enforcement posture.[124] In many respects, there seems to be something to the notion that the politics affects the § 14141 enforcement strategy. During the Clinton administration, the DOJ sought millions of dollars in additional funds to support § 14141 investigations.[125] And during the Obama administration, the DOJ added nine additional attorneys to facilitate § 14141 enforcement.[126]

Despite many researchers levying theories about changes in enforcement, no study has empirically assessed the validity of these claims. Has § 14141 enforcement changed under different political

[122] Chanin, *supra* note 10, at 334 and 335. Heather Mac Donald, arguing from the conservative standpoint, echoes the view that President Bush's DOJ restricted the number of investigations: "During the Bush Administration, political appointees to the civil rights division reined in the staff's eagerness to investigate police departments for racial profiling, since the profiling studies routinely served up by the ACLU and other activist organizations were based on laughably bogus methodology." Mac Donald, *supra* note 13, at 26.

[123] *See* Eric Lichtblau, *Bush Sees U.S. As Meddling in Local Police Affairs*, LA TIMES, June 1, 2000, at A5.

[124] Mac Donald, *supra* note 13.

[125] Nirode, Caruso, & Ruth, *supra* note 100.

[126] Mac Donald, *supra* note 13.

leadership?[127] Interviewees confirm that the DOJ lacks the necessary resources to respond to every case of apparent systemic misconduct within a police department. The quantitative data in this chapter confirms that, even when the DOJ actively supported § 14141 enforcement, the use of federal intervention has been both limited and inconsistent. These interviewees also attribute the inconsistency in the enforcement of § 14141 to change in internal policies.

First, the data shows that the DOJ has not aggressively pursued federal intervention against a large number of police agencies. In total, the DOJ has initiated around 55 investigations between 1994 and 2013. This means that during this time the DOJ has only formally investigated around three departments per year.[128] The relatively small number of investigations may be the result of a lack of resources, the lack of manpower, a lack of national statistics on local police misconduct, or a combination of these factors. Remember, investigations are costly[129] and can last for several years.[130] As a result, it makes sense that the DOJ can target only a handful of police departments each year. Given that there are around 17,985 state and local police agencies in the United States,[131] this data suggests that the DOJ has historically investigated less than 0.02 percent of all departments in the country each year. Even if patterns or practices of misconduct exist in only one out of every 100 law enforcement departments,[132] then the DOJ has only been able to investigate less than 2 percent of these departments each year. It is fair to assume that, even during the times when the DOJ has aggressively pursued pattern or practice claims, enforcement has been less than

[127] The studies that have alluded to this question have cursorily addressed it by piecing together an answer by relying on interviews, media reports, and news releases. *See, e.g.*, Gilles, *supra* note 8, at 1404–1410 (turning to publicly available information to piece together data on the DOJ's enforcement policies); Simmons, *supra* note 8, at 516 and 517 (describing the lack of aggressive DOJ enforcement through reliance on media reports and publicly available information); Chanin, *supra* note 10, at 24 (describing the use of monitor reports, publicly available data, news reports, and interviews to acquire data).

[128] I calculated this by taking the number of investigations reported by the DOJ in Appendix A and dividing it by the time period covered – approximately eighteen years. This results in an average of approximately three investigations per year.

[129] Nirode, Caruso, & Ruth, *supra* note 100. [130] Stockwell, *supra* note 104.

[131] Reaves, *supra* note 17, at 2.

[132] Unfortunately, there is no good way to estimate the number of police departments that may be engaged in a pattern or practice of misconduct. There is no uniform statistic to measure misconduct – which is part of the reason why the DOJ has developed such a unique and multifaceted case selection method for § 14141 cases.

optimal. As one litigator with the DOJ explained during an interview, "[T]here's no way that the [DOJ] can litigate all of the patterns and practices of police misconduct in this country. There are too many policing jurisdictions ... to do that."[133] In fact, a single, complex § 14141 case alone can nearly exhaust all of the manpower and resources of the Special Litigation Section for an entire year.[134] It is likely that the resources given to the DOJ to investigate § 14141 abuse may never be sufficient to target every city apparently engaged in misconduct.

This is a particularly troubling realization, since only by increasing the frequency of investigations can § 14141 efficiently incentivize widespread reform and generally deter unconstitutional misconduct. As discussed in Chapters 1 and 2, federal intervention has the potential to be the most forceful regulatory tool for overhauling American police departments when used aggressively by the DOJ. Unlike traditional cost-raising mechanisms for misconduct regulation, § 14141 can force noncompliant departments to implement radical reforms to ensure constitutional policing practices. Nevertheless, § 14141 cannot achieve this objective if the DOJ chooses not to invoke the statute's protections. In theory, the statute can only deter misconduct in one of two ways – either it can specifically reform a single problematic department through costly and invasive equitable relief or it can serve as a general deterrent to police departments all across the country, thereby motivating departments to take proactive steps to avoid the cost and embarrassment of DOJ scrutiny.

For this general deterrent rationale to work, police agencies must perceive the possibility of DOJ investigation and oversight as reasonably likely. If agencies view DOJ action under § 14141 to be an extremely remote possibility, then rational choice theory suggests that these departments will have no motivation for reform. As it currently stands, a rational department engaged in systemic misconduct would likely not view a § 14141 suit as a realistic possibility. If this law is to be an incentive for widespread reform, this must change.

Second, the data shows that the DOJ's enforcement of § 14141 has also changed over time. Since commentators previously observed that § 14141

[133] Interview #14, *supra* note 3, at 11. The participant referenced the hard work required in litigating the ongoing case in Maricopa County and further elaborated that even though the Special Litigation Section now has more lawyers than in the past "it's not plausible to think that the [DOJ] can do this by itself" *Id.* at 12.

[134] *Id.* at 11 and 12 (using Maricopa County as an example of a particularly complex and contentious claim that has exhausted significant resources, leaving little left to address other cities).

Table 3.4 *DOJ Action Under § 14141 by Presidential Administration**

Administration	Investigation	Negotiated Settlements
William Clinton Term 1[1]	10	0
William Clinton Term 2	12	3
George W. Bush Term 1	13	11
George W. Bush Term 2	8	0
Barack Obama Term 1	12	8

* *See* Appendices A and B.

1 Section 14141 became law in 1991. The lack of negotiated settlements and monitor appointments before 1997 probably does not represent any administrative unwillingness to use these remedies. After § 14141's passage, the DOJ needed time to develop internal implementation strategies. Enforcement was not fully under way until about a year after Congress passed the VCCLEA. *See, e.g.*, Interview with DOJ Participant #14, at 5 (July 11, 2013) (on file with author) (stating that "it's hard getting a new statute implemented" and detailing the challenging process facing the DOJ in implementing the statute initially in 1994 and 1995). This likely explains the lack of negotiated settlements and monitor appointments during the first Clinton administration.

enforcement seemed to vary by presidential administration, Table 3.4 organizes the total number of investigations and negotiated settlements reached during each presidential administration between 1994 and 2013.

The data shows a decrease in the aggressiveness of § 14141 enforcement between late 2004 and early 2009, which correlates with the second term of the Bush administration.[135] This decrease in aggressiveness manifests itself in several ways. During this time period, there was a noticeable decrease in the number of investigations officially opened by the DOJ. The DOJ did not enter into a single negotiated settlement during this time period. Since

135 It is possible that any effects of political administration on the enforcement policy of the DOJ would only be felt a year or more after a change in executive leadership. *See, e.g.*, Interview #14, *supra* note 3, at 5 and 6 (explaining the time it took to get policies implemented and the possibility of lagged effects of implementation); Interview #15, *supra* note 37, at 2 (explaining that while the statute was not initially enforced, it took a period of time for internal changes to lead to efforts to change enforcement policy). But even when controlling for this possibility, there still appeared to be a noticeable difference in the likelihood of the DOJ to aggressively utilize § 14141 around the second term of the Bush administration.

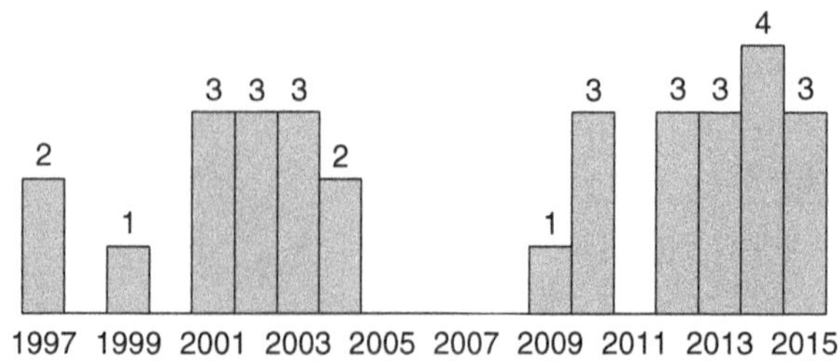

Figure 3.1 Number of Negotiated Settlements by Year

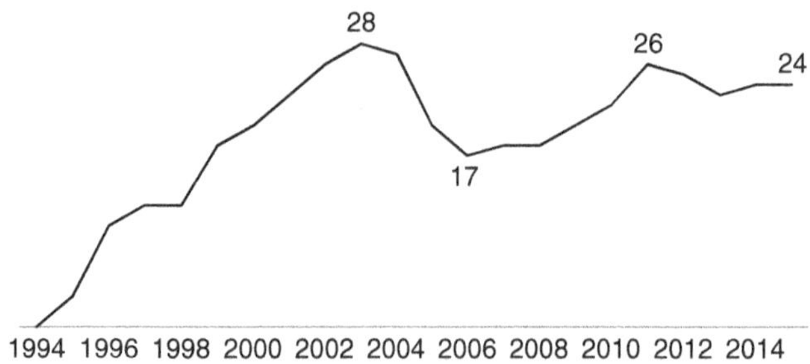

Figure 3.2 Open § 14141 Cases over Time
This data is taken from the list of investigations. *See* Appendix A.

the DOJ did not agree to any settlements during this time period, it also did not push for the monitoring of any police agency. Remember that part of the reason that Congress passed § 14141 in 1994 was to provide the DOJ with the ability to seek injunctive action against police departments – that is, force those police departments to make necessary policy changes aimed at curbing misconduct.[136] During the second term of the Bush administration, though, the DOJ did not force a single police agency to make any policy changes via a § 14141 settlement. The noticeable shift in enforcement is also visible in Figure 3.1, which illustrates the number of negotiated settlements by year, and Figure 3.2, which shows the number of open § 14141 cases over time.

So what caused this apparent shift in the enforcement of § 14141? One experienced DOJ litigator, who left the DOJ around this time, attributed this sharp decline in negotiated settlements to changes in an internal policy that discouraged extensive federal involvement in local police

[136] *See* Chapter 2 (explaining the need for equitable relief to address systemic misconduct issues).

departments.[137] Respondents identified two possible explanations for this change in enforcement policy. First, as one DOJ official detailed, DOJ litigators have often relied on coordination with civil rights groups like the ACLU and the NAACP to determine whether there was sufficient evidence to justify a formal investigation.[138] Remember that, in many cases, coordination with civil rights groups formed the basis for initial inquiries and served as a vital tool for evidence during the formal investigation stage. Litigators continued this method of preliminary inquiry in the early years of the Bush administration. At some point during the Bush administration, an internal policy change allegedly discouraged litigators from coordinating with civil rights groups. This hampered efforts by § 14141 litigators to acquire sufficient evidence to justify invasive federal involvement in local police affairs.

Second, multiple current and former DOJ litigators noted that internal politics around this same time favored the use of § 14141 for technical assistance as opposed to full-scale negotiated settlements and external monitoring.[139] The prevailing belief was that technical assistance letters could provide departments with the necessary guidance to reform internally, without expending additional federal resources monitoring eventual reform efforts.[140] Of course, these technical assistance letters are not

[137] Interview #15, *supra* note 37, at 6 (explaining the changes that happened during the Bush administration). One important change that this participant noted was the removal of the previous leadership within the Special Litigation Section in part because of "his police-related work and the opposition of police unions to the work. Which was very strong." *Id.*

[138] Interview #5, *supra* note 51, at 2 and 3 (explaining the policy that discouraged or even barred the coordination with civil rights groups).

[139] Harmon also provides a useful perspective:

> The technical assistance letters or investigative findings letters represent less formal attempts by the Justice Department to achieve reform. During most of the Justice Department's investigations, it has sent a letter to the investigated police department summarizing its findings at that point in the investigation. In some cases, this letter functioned as a precursor to a later settlement through a consent decree or memorandum of agreement. In other cases – although the letter suggested that the investigation was ongoing at the time – the technical assistance letter was the last public action in the case. In these cases, the letters do not make findings about whether § 14141 has been violated. Instead, they describe departmental deficiencies that may cause misconduct and recommend specific remedial measures to correct those problems.
>
> Harmon, *supra* note 9, at 17 and 18.

[140] Interview #5, *supra* note 51, at 3 (detailing the preference for technical assistance letters); *see also* Harmon, *supra* note 9, at 18 ("[T]he letters do not contain any mechanism for ensuring compliance or for ongoing monitoring.").

binding.[141] Instead, they provide only a voluntary blueprint that agencies can accept if they so choose. These apparent policy changes could explain a substantial amount of the variation in enforcement patterns evident from the data.

In recent years, the DOJ has again started to use § 14141 more aggressively to force police departments to adopt specific policy reforms.[142] In March 2009, less than two months after Eric Holder took over as attorney general, the DOJ approved a consent decree with the Virgin Islands Police Department.[143] This was the first negotiated settlement that the DOJ had approved under § 14141 in over five years.[144] Since then, the DOJ has reached settlement agreements with fourteen different police agencies, including Seattle, Albuquerque, Cleveland, New Orleans, Portland, and Puerto Rico.[145]

In sum, the qualitative and quantitative data suggest that the enforcement of § 14141 varied significantly during a portion of the Bush administration, likely due in part to the adoption of internal policies that discouraged coordination with interest groups and encouraged noninvasive solutions. The Obama administration has, meanwhile, appeared to reverse this trend, ushering in a new era of aggressive enforcement. The evidence also suggests, however, that even when internal policies favor aggressive enforcement of § 14141, the DOJ has only initiated around three new investigations per year. Interviewees argued that this number represented only a fraction of departments seemingly engaged in systemic misconduct.

IV Influence of Politics on Enforcement

The qualitative evidence also suggests that the DOJ faces another potential barrier in initiating action against a municipality that may be engaged

[141] Interview #5, *supra* note 51, at 3.

[142] One way to measure this is to examine the number of investigations per year since President Obama's pick for attorney general – Eric Holder – has assumed office. Holder has served as attorney general for 1,687 days as of September 9, 2013. During this time, the DOJ initiated fifteen investigations. *See* Appendix A. This suggests that the Holder DOJ has averaged approximately 3.25 investigations per 365 days.

[143] *See* Appendix B (detailing the dates of each negotiated settlement reached between the DOJ and local police agencies).

[144] *Id.*

[145] Kimbriell Kelly, Sarah Childress, & Steven Rich, *Forced Reforms, Mixed Results*, WASH. POST., November 13, 2015, *available at* www.washingtonpost.com/sf/investigative/2015/11/13/forced-reforms-mixed-results/.

in patterns or practices of misconduct. An example best illustrates this phenomenon. Multiple interviewees described the Special Litigation Section's interest in intervening into the New York City Police Department (NYPD).[146] The DOJ initiated two separate investigations in New York City – one through the US Attorney's Office (USAO) in the Eastern District of New York and one through the USAO in the Southern District of New York.[147] Neither investigation resulted in a settlement agreement.[148] When asked about this investigation into the NYPD, DOJ litigators suggested that political considerations may have factored into the decision to not formally pursue a settlement agreement. Before the DOJ initiates settlement negotiations under § 14141, the Special Litigation Section relies on the local USAO to facilitate the investigation and to participate in the settlement negotiation. In New York, this meant that the Special Litigation Section needed to work collaboratively with the USAO in the Southern and Eastern Districts of New York. According to interviewees, these two USAO districts are unique in their independence from the central DOJ.[149] Interviewees jokingly referred to the Southern District as the "Sovereign District of New York," a tribute to the district's informal jurisdictional independence from the central authority of the DOJ.[150] Although litigators in the Special Litigation Section felt that a negotiated settlement was needed to address the possible misconduct in the NYPD, multiple interviewees identified the Southern District as a barrier to § 14141 action.[151] Since New York City spans two different USAO districts, the DOJ needed to get the support of both the Southern and Eastern District offices.[152] While the Eastern District seemed

[146] Interview #14, *supra* note 3, at 11–14 (identifying, again, the NYPD as an agency of interest to the Special Litigation Section for § 14141 purposes); Interview #18, *supra* note 62, at 5–7 (explaining the initiation of the New York investigation).

[147] *See* Appendix A (listing all of the investigations pursued by the DOJ).

[148] *See* Appendix B (showing that the NYPD is not among the list of settlement agreements).

[149] Interview #18, *supra* note 62, at 6 (identifying the unique independence of the Southern District in particular); *see also* Interview #14, *supra* note 50, at 12 ("The Eastern District is sort of quasi-sovereign.").

[150] Interview #14, *supra* note 3, at 12; Interview #18, *supra* note 62, at 6 (identifying the independence of the Southern District and stating that "they do all their cases including their civil rights cases").

[151] *Id.* at 12 and 13 (identifying the political concerns that likely motivated the Southern District to oppose formal action); Interview #18, *supra* note 62, at 6 (explaining that the Southern District was the agency most opposed to further action against the NYPD).

[152] Interview #18, *supra* note 62, at 6 ("[I]n order to bring a case against the city, the police department covers all of the boroughs so you'd have to get both US Attorneys on board.").

somewhat willing to pursue the matter further, the Southern District resisted efforts to push further any § 14141 claims against the NYPD.[153] Interviewees disagreed about the extent to which politics factored into the decision by the Southern District to block further action against the NYPD. At least two participants concluded that politics played some role in the decision to not pursue a § 14141 case against the NYPD.[154] One former litigator believed that the DOJ made a tactical choice to not initiate action against the NYPD because of concerns about alienating the agency, thereby hampering future efforts to coordinate as part of law enforcement task forces.[155] As this litigator went on to speculate, federal-state coordination is an increasingly important method for addressing law enforcement issues that traverse jurisdictional borders.[156] Perhaps no local department engages in more federal-state coordination than the NYPD.[157] This suggests that internal politics can also serve as a barrier to DOJ action, in some cases.[158] After all, the DOJ is the ultimate "repeat player."[159] As a repeat player in the legal system, the DOJ must be cognizant of how its actions in one arena may affect its ability to further other, future organizational goals. The result is a sort of political spillover that can hamper otherwise viable efforts to enforce § 14141.

V Negotiated Reform

The rest of this part chronicles the process of negotiated reform in the shadow of the law in American police departments. Historically, this process has been hidden from public scrutiny. Through stakeholder

[153] *Id.* at 6 (identifying the differing opinions between the Eastern and Southern Districts).

[154] Interview #14, *supra* note 3, at 12 and 13 (speculating that the political ambitions of the US attorney of the Southern District of New York may have contributed to the unwillingness to pursue further civil rights actions); *see also* Interview #12, *supra* note 67, at 3 (agreeing during the interview that local politics likely plays an important role in the decision to pursue further action under § 14141).

[155] Telephone Interview with DOJ Participant #23 (September 19, 2013).

[156] *Id.*

[157] *Id.*

[158] Several studies have found that this sort of political spillover can affect agency aggressiveness. Stephenson, *supra* note 18, at 110 n.48.

[159] *See generally* Marc Galanter, *Why the Haves Come Out Ahead: Speculations on the Limits of Legal Change*, 9 Law & Soc'y Rev. 95 (1974). Galanter distinguishes between "repeat players" (those who are engaged in multiple similar litigations over time) and "one shotters" (those who litigate only on rare occasions). *Id.* at 98–104. Since repeat players are engaged in the same type of litigation time and time again, their goals are different than a one shotter. *Id.* at 100. The repeat player wants to establish valuable precedent that will be of use in future cases. *Id.*

interviews, this chapter attempts to build a descriptive account of this negotiation, bargaining, and implementation process. As these stakeholder interviews demonstrate, the reform process typically proceeds in three stages. First, the DOJ negotiates a settlement with the targeted municipality. There does appear to be a good faith negotiation that typically happens between the DOJ and the targeted law enforcement agency. Nevertheless, the DOJ holds an advantageous bargaining endowment during these negotiations. Additionally, since the DOJ is a repeat litigator in the § 14141 context, it negotiates differently than a local police agency. Police unions also commonly attempt to intervene in settlement negotiations with the intent of blocking reforms that may increase oversight or otherwise burden frontline police officers.

Second, with the settlement completed, the parties must next come to an agreement on the appointment of an outside monitor. Without exception, monitors are expensive. The cost of this monitoring falls entirely on the targeted police agency. As a result, the DOJ and local municipality have very different incentives. The DOJ often requests the appointment of a costly external monitor, while the targeted municipality often pushes for lower cost alternatives. There is widespread disagreement between the DOJ and targeted municipalities about the relative importance of a monitor's law enforcement background. During interviews, police executives expressed their strong preference for former police leaders as monitors, while the DOJ has tended to support the appointment of attorneys as external monitors.

Third, with an agreement in place and an outside monitor assigned, the monitored reform begins. The dominant approach used to measure compliance with a negotiated settlement is logical, but also creates openings for confrontation. The relationship between the monitor and the police agency also seems to play a critical role in the speed of reforms, as does the level of institutional and political support within the targeted municipality. Once this reform process has concluded, the goal is for federal intervention to transform both the police department's internal procedures and its organizational culture. While this reform process is far from perfect, it represents an admirable attempt by the DOJ to transform the culture of American police departments through careful, negotiated reforms.

A Settlement Negotiations

"We worked really hard on those early ones," explained a former DOJ litigator when describing the first negotiated settlements in Pittsburgh and Steubenville.[160] When negotiating settlements with police departments first began, the DOJ faced a steep learning curve. The litigator continued, "We worked really hard to figure out what a good [settlement] would look like. As you know, because of *Lyons*, it's not like in the prison setting, where there is a really robust private set of models."[161] On this point, the former DOJ litigator was undeniably correct. Remember that in 1980, Congress passed the CRIPA, which gave the US attorney general the authority to intervene into mental health facilities, prisons, nursing homes, and other similar institutions – provided they were engaged in a pattern of unconstitutional misconduct. But the DOJ had a head start in implementing the CRIPA. In the years leading up to the passage of the CRIPA, a number of private litigants had won suits against prisons and other similar institutions. Prisoners were often able to overcome the *Lyons* standing barrier described in Chapter 2 by proving that they faced an ongoing threat to their constitutional rights from abusive guards and prison wardens absent injunctive relief from federal district courts. Because of this, by 1980 there had been "dozens of big decrees negotiated mostly by the ACLU" as well as "hundreds" of decrees negotiated by private parties.[162] This made the DOJ's job easy. These settlements provided an immediate blueprint. The DOJ needed to merely use its new found authority to demand more prisons adopt these same basic reforms.

The § 14141 context proved to be completely different. There were no existing models for what a good settlement should look like. Almost no private citizens had the legal standing under *Lyons* to seek injunctive relief against local police departments. So the DOJ had to start from scratch. It had to figure out what kinds of reforms were necessary to bring about change in local police departments. And it had to bargain for these reforms with local police departments without the benefit of decades of prior agreements to fall back on during negotiations. This might, in part, explain why settlement negotiations can take anywhere from a few months, to a year or more to complete.[163] The goal of every negotiation

160 Interview #14, *supra* note 3, at 7. 161 *Id.* 162 *Id.*

163 For example, in New Orleans there was approximately a ten-month gap between the conclusion of the investigation and the signing of a consent decree. There, the DOJ issued a report detailing its investigative findings on March 16, 2011, and eventually agreed to a consent decree on January 11, 2013. *United States* v. *City of New Orleans*, No. 2:12-cv-01924-SM-JCW (ED La. July 24, 2013) (consent decree regarding the New Orleans Police Department) [hereinafter New Orleans Consent Decree], *text available at* www.clearinghouse.net/chDocs/public/PN-LA-0001-0001.pdf; INVESTIGATION OF THE NEW ORLEANS POLICE DEPARTMENT, UNITED STATES DEPARTMENT OF JUSTICE,

is to reach a negotiated settlement that outlines all of the necessary policy and procedural changes in a single document. As one DOJ litigator explained, "A negotiated agreement is a compromise."[164] Neither the municipality nor the DOJ gets everything it wants in a negotiated settlement. Remember, very few § 14141 cases actually result in a trial.[165] Both parties typically start a negotiation by making demands that they fully expect the other side to reject.[166] This anchors the negotiation and allows for an eventual compromise somewhere in the middle.[167] The DOJ understands that it will be unable to transform every aspect of a police department's organization or culture in a way that comports with best practices. Instead, the DOJ merely attempts to negotiate a reasonably feasible set of reforms that ought to improve the likelihood that police officers will behave constitutionally.[168] The qualitative interview data provides useful insight into how the negotiation process works. From these accounts, four important trends emerge.

Civil Rights Division v (March 16, 2011) [hereinafter New Orleans Investigation], *text available at* www.justice.gov/crt/about/spl/nopd_report.pdf. In Detroit, that gap was approximately a year. There the DOJ handed down technical assistance letters between March and June 2002 before agreeing to two different consent decrees on June 12, 2003. *See* Detroit Department Use of Force Findings Letter (March 6, 2002), *text available at* www.justice.gov/crt/about/spl/documents/dpd/detroit_3_6.php; Detroit Police Department Holding Cell Findings Letter (April 4, 2002), *text available at* www .justice.gov/crt/about/spl/documents/dpd/detroit_4_4.php; Detroit Police Department Witness Detention Findings Letter (June 5, 2002); *United States* v. *Detroit* 03-72258 (ED Mich. June 12, 2003) [hereinafter Detroit Consent Decree], available at www.justice.gov/crt/about/spl/documents/dpd/detroitpd_uofwdcd_613.pdf. And in Seattle, it took a little over seven months to complete this process. In that case, the DOJ issued a findings letter on December 16, 2011, and entered into a settlement agreement on July 27, 2012. *See United States* v. *Seattle*, no. 2:12-cv-01282-JLR (WD Wa. July 27, 2012) (settlement agreement and stipulated order of resolution) [hereinafter Seattle Settlement Agreement]; Investigation of Seattle Police Department, United States Department of Justice, Civil Rights Division (December 16, 2011), *text available at* www.justice.gov/crt/about/spl/documents/spd_findletter_12-16-11.pdf.

164 Interview #5, *supra* note 51, at 4.

165 Interview #18, *supra* note 62 at 12 ("One of the challenges that the DOJ has is that there hasn't been any litigated pattern or practice cases").

166 Interview #5, *supra* note 51, at 4 (explaining that in past negotiations, the DOJ has started by asking for significantly more reforms than they expect to actually get through a negotiated settlement; "You don't want to begin in your compromise position," but instead start by making lofty demands, thereby allowing each side to meet in the middle).

167 *Id.* (explaining the process of making demands and eventually reaching compromise).

168 In his study of structural police reform from a criminal justice and public policy perspective, Professor Joshua Chanin has called this process "negotiated justice." Chanin, *supra* note 10.

First, there does appear to be a genuine, good faith negotiation that happens between the DOJ and the targeted police agency.[169] As a police administrator involved in the negotiation process explained, on "[t]he negotiation side, there was a lot of give and take in terms of what we thought we could do . . . and in what we thought would still make sense for [our department] as a whole."[170] DOJ litigators also recognize that negotiated settlements require compromise.[171] As one DOJ litigator acknowledged, "[E]very city is different."[172]

Ultimately though, correcting unconstitutional practices through compromise seems counterintuitive. Why, after all, should there be any negotiating about the correction of unconstitutional practices? The answer is at the heart of the complex federal intervention process. There is no perfect formula that a police department can implement to prevent unconstitutional misconduct among its ranks. Instead, there are best practices that leading experts in the field believe encourage lawful behavior. The negotiation process, thus, invites compromise between the targeted police agency and the DOJ – with the DOJ demanding extensive, costly reforms and the police agency attempting to limit the scope of the federal oversight.[173]

Second, even though these settlement agreements do appear to emerge via true negotiation between various stakeholders, the DOJ typically holds an advantageous bargaining position. The DOJ has statutory authority to bring formal litigation in the event that a local municipality refuses to negotiate a settlement agreement. The DOJ has also demanded similar other reforms across different municipalities. According to participants, the federal government has attempted to leverage the contents of previous agreements to gain a bargaining endowment at various times in recent negotiations. As one participant explained, "[T]he DOJ can use the threat of . . . litigation to get [police] departments to settle."[174] Until

169 Interview with Independent Monitor #7, at 3 (July 18, 2013) (transcript on file with author) [hereinafter Interview #7] (stating that police departments are "able to have some form of negotiation about certain things that are placed into the agreement that may just not be operationally sound because of the Department [unique features]").

170 Interview with Police Administrator #16, at 3 (July 29, 2013) [hereinafter Interview #16] (explaining that, "the other side had their own police experts that had that in mind as well").

171 Interview #5, *supra* note 51, at 4 ("A negotiated agreement is a compromise").

172 *Id.* at 4.

173 *See, e.g.*, *Id.* (stating that neither side wants to "begin in [their] compromise position" and also explaining how each side expects to give a little during negotiations).

174 Interview #18, *supra* note 62, at 12.

recently, "no pattern or practice case has come to trial . . . and resulted in a decision one way or the other," in part because "no city has wanted to risk litigation."[175]

Third, since the DOJ is a repeat litigator in the § 14141 context, the DOJ negotiates differently than a local police agency. Marc Galanter has written extensively on the structural advantages that repeat players in the court system have over individuals who litigate only a single case.[176] In the context of § 14141 settlements, it appears that the DOJ is openly concerned with the precedent established by each agreement. While the DOJ does not demand absolute consistency across agreements, it does recognize that inconsistency in settlement terms may be harmful in future negotiations.[177] This suggests that DOJ recognizes it is a repeat player in pattern or practice litigation. As a result, it is concerned not just about securing a satisfactory settlement but also about how that settlement might reflect on the DOJ's bargaining position in future negotiations.[178]

Fourth, police unions commonly attempt to intervene in settlement negotiations with the intent of blocking reforms that may increase oversight or otherwise burden frontline police officers.[179] This makes sense. After all, many policies implemented as part of federal intervention sometimes make the jobs of frontline officers more difficult. An organized labor unit designed to enhance working conditions for

175 *Id.*

176 *See generally* Galanter, *supra* note 159. Galanter distinguishes between repeat players (those who are engaged in multiple similar litigations over time) and one shotters (those who litigate only on rare occasions). *Id.* at 98–104. Repeat players have advanced knowledge and expertise in the area of litigation, economics of scale, and the ability to play the odds over a long series of cases. *Id.* at 98–100. This means that repeat players have a structural advantage in our legal system. As Galanter explains, repeat players have better "information, [the] ability to surmount cost barriers, and [the] skill to navigate restrictive procedural requirements." *Id.* at 109. Since repeat players are engaged in the same type of litigation time and time again, their goals are different than a one shotter. *Id.* at 100. A one shotter simply wants to maximize his or her individual return in any given case. *Id.* The repeat player wants to establish valuable precedent that will be of use in future cases. *Id.*

177 Interview #5, *supra* note 51, at 4 (using the example of how the DOJ wants a clear and cogent answer for why they may change the ratio of supervisors to patrol officers slightly from one jurisdiction to the next, thereby ensuring consistency).

178 *Id.* (stating that "[w]e try to be consistent, or at least know why we are not being consistent").

179 *See, e.g., United States* v. *City of Los Angeles*, 2:00-cv-11769-GAF-RC (CD Cal. November 8., 2000) (notice of interested parties filed by Los Angeles Police Protective League); *see also* Telephone Interview with Police Administrator #30 (November 19, 2013) [hereinafter Interview #30] (describing the union opposition to these sorts of reforms).

its members should rationally want to block such changes – or at minimum be a party to any negotiations. Courts have thus far rejected these union requests and allowed negotiation to proceed exclusively between departmental administration and the DOJ.[180] In interviews, police administrators suggested that this makes structural reform a particularly successful accountability tool.[181] Police chiefs often complain that collective bargaining restrains their ability to implement accountability measures.[182] Thus, federal intervention appears to provide reform-minded police chiefs with legal cover to implement wide-ranging reforms, without having to get union approval.[183] Once these accountability measures are incorporated into a negotiated settlement and enforceable in federal court, police unions have little option but to accept them. In this way, federal intervention reframes the implementation of accountability measures. No longer are these reforms merely annoying encumbrances on the day-to-day lives of frontline workers. Instead, federal intervention imbues these reforms with legal significance, increasing the probability of organizational acceptance. From this negotiation process, the DOJ first reached a settlement on April 4, 1997, when it came to terms with the Pittsburgh Police Department.[184]

180 *See, e.g., United States* v. *City of Los Angeles*, 2:00-cv-11769-GAF-RC (CD Cal. January 4, 2001) (order denying the Los Angeles Protective League's motion to intervene).

181 Telephone Interview with Police Administrator #22 (October 28, 2013) [hereinafter Interview #22] (describing how structural police reform has enabled this police chief to push potentially unpopular, but necessary reforms without having to get union approval).

182 Colleen Kadleck and Lawrence F. Travis, Police Department and Police Officer Association Leaders' Perceptions of Community Policing and Nature and Extent of Agreement, National Institute of Justice 1–3 (September 2004), *available at* www.ncjrs.gov/pdffiles1/nij/grants/226315.pdf (describing the various examples of accountability measures that police unions have resisted across the country).

183 For a further explanation of these concepts in organizational theory, *see* Peer C. Fiss & Edward J. Zajac, *The Symbolic Management of Strategic Change: Sensegiving via Framing and Decoupling*, 49 Acad. Mgmt. J. 1173 (2006). Fiss and Zajac explain that "the success of strategic change will depend not only on an organization's ability to implement new structures and processes, but also on the organization's ability to convey the new mission and priorities to its many stakeholders ... [and] ensuring both understanding and acceptance of new strategies among key constituents." *Id.* at 1173.

184 Stephen Rushin, *Federal Enforcement of Police Reform*, 82 Fordham L. Rev. 3189, 3247 (2014) (listing all of the negotiated settlements reached between the DOJ and individual policing agencies since the passage of § 14141 in 1994).

B Content of Negotiated Settlements

While in theory each agreement should be specifically tailored to the unique needs of the individual municipality, the settlements have proven to be remarkably similar over time. This led one police chief to remark during interviews that today, negotiated settlements "are so cookie-cutter nowadays."[185] This similarity is likely because the DOJ need not reinvent the wheel each time it overhauls a police department. Since most of the police departments targeted for federal intervention have the same core problems, it makes sense that the DOJ would require the same, tested procedural reforms. There are several common issues addressed in negotiated settlements. Most agreements have included sections regulating the use of force by police officers. Virtually all agreements require some change in officer training and the implementation of an early warning system to identify officers engaged in a systematic misconduct. Agreements also frequently regulate the handling of citizen complaints and the internal investigation of officer wrongdoing. About half of the agreements require external auditing or monitoring to ensure compliance. In recent years, though, the DOJ under President Barack Obama expanded the scope of policies demanded as part of federal intervention to cover a wide range of topics, including gender bias, interrogations, lineup procedures, recruitment, crisis intervention, and promotion standards.

1 Use-of-Force Policies

Almost every single negotiated settlement signed by the DOJ pursuant to § 14141 addresses the policing agency's use of force. Some of these use-of-force stipulations regulated many different possible issues related to force.[186] Others more narrowly targeted a particular type of force at issue in the case.[187] In total, virtually all of the negotiated settlements that

185 Interview #16, *supra* note 20, at 7.

186 *See, e.g.*, New Orleans Consent Decree, *supra* note 163, at 19–39 (detailing expansive requirements about the use of force, regulating nearly every possible force usage, including oleoresin capsicum spray, canines, firearms, and electronic control weapons); *United States* v. *Seattle*, No. 2:12-cv-01282-JLR, at 16–40 (WD Wa. July 27, 2013) (settlement agreement and stipulated [proposed] order of resolution) [hereinafter Seattle Agreement], *text available at* www.justice.gov/crt/about/spl/documents/spd_consentdecree_7-27-12.pdf (detailing regulations on the use of firearms, conductive energy devices, oleoresin capsicum spray, and impact weapons).

187 Memorandum of Agreement Between the United States Department of Justice and Prince George's County Police Department, at 6–10 (January 22, 2004) [hereinafter Prince George's County MOA], *text available at* www.clearinghouse.net/chDocs/public/

involved monitors included a section regulating the use of force.[188] The use-of-force stipulations in negotiated settlements fall into three categories.

First, most regulate substantive policy on when officers may and may not use force. These use-of-force sections commonly require a clear delineation of different levels of force.[189] These agreements also normally establish requirements for various types of weapons.[190] Second, virtually every agreement establishes strict reporting requirements for use-of-force incidents.[191] Officers are required to notify their supervisors after

PN-MD-0001-0002.pdf (specifically regulating only the use of force involving oleoresin capsicum spray).

188 This seems to be consistent with the legislative roots of §14141, as the law originated, in part, out of a reaction to the brutal violence against Rodney King. *See* Chapter 2. Remember that the *Lyons* and *City of Philadelphia* cases also involved allegedly repetitive police brutality that private litigants and the DOJ were unable to stop through traditional remedies. As a report by the Police Executive Research Forum (PERF) concluded, "Police use of force is one of the primary issues that the Civil Rights Division investigates ... [and] [u]se of force has been a component in almost all of the DOJ's civil rights investigations to date, including consent decrees/settlements." POLICE EXECUTIVE RESEARCH FORUM, CIVIL RIGHTS INVESTIGATIONS OF LOCAL POLICE: LESSONS LEARNED 12 (2013), *available at* http://policeforum.org/library/critical-issues-in-policing-series/CivilRightsInvestigationsofLocalPolice.pdf. It should be no surprise, then, that even the very earliest agreements, like those in Pittsburgh and Steubenville, included a substantial portion dedicated to the regulation of use of force. *United States* v. *Pittsburgh*, No. 2:97-cv-00354-RJC, at para. 15, 18 (WD Pa. February 26, 1997) (Consent Decree) [hereinafter Pittsburgh Consent Decree], *text available at* www.clearinghouse.net/chDocs/public/PN-PA-0003-0002.pdf (requiring documentation and regular oversight of use of force); *United States* v. *City of Steubenville*, No. 97–0966, at para. 14.b., 21–23 (SD Ohio August 28, 1997) (Consent Decree) [hereinafter Steubenville Consent Decree], *text available at* www.clearinghouse.net/chDocs/public/PN-OH-0002-0005.pdf (requiring written reports on all use of force, the implementation of new policies, training in deescalation, and more).

189 PERF, *supra* note 188, at 13 (stating that agreements often require departments to "clearly identif[y] categorical types and levels of force").

190 *Id.* at 13 ("Policies, procedures, and training that are specific to certain weapons or types of force such as firearms, Electrical Control Weapons, OC spray, canine use, and vehicle pursuit"); New Orleans Consent Decree, *supra* note 172, at 14–22 (including stipulations on the use of firearms, canines, electrical control weapons, and oleoresin capsicum spray); Seattle Agreement, *supra* note 163, at 14–17, 22–33 (regulating various types of weapons and laying out detailed rules on use-of-force reporting, training, use-of-force investigations, and supervisory oversight).

191 PERF, *supra* note 188, at 13 (stating that "reporting, documentation and investigation" requirements are common in negotiated settlements that provide for a supervisor response and period auditing/review). For an example, *see United States* v. *The Virgin Islands Police Department*, no 2008–158, at 6, para. 32 (D. VI November 4, 2009) (consent decree) [hereinafter Virgin Islands Consent Decree], *text available at* www.clearinghouse.net/chDocs/public/PN-VI-0001-0003.pdf (requiring the police department to document all uses of force in writing).

any use of force or upon hearing any allegation of excessive use of force.[192] The same pattern is evident in the Steubenville,[193] Cincinnati,[194] Prince George's County,[195] New Orleans,[196] Washington, DC,[197] and Pittsburgh[198] agreements. Third, most agreements establish detailed procedures for how departments ought to investigate use-of-force incidents.[199] In sum, the negotiated settlements consistently demonstrate a concern for the reporting, regulation, and investigation of use-of-force incidents.

2 Early Intervention and Risk Management Systems

A large number of settlements, including the vast majority of settlements resulting in monitoring, require the development of an early intervention

192 *Id.* at 6, para. 33.

193 Steubenville Consent Decree, *supra* note 188, at 9, para. 22 ("The City shall develop, and require all officers to complete, a written report each time . . . any type of force is used against an individual").

194 Memorandum of Agreement Between the United States Department of Justice and the City of Cincinnati, Ohio and the Cincinnati Police Department, at 11, para. 24 (April 12, 2012) [hereinafter Cincinnati MOA], *text available at* www.clearinghouse.net/chDocs/public/PN-OH-0006-0002.pdf (stating "The use of force report form will indicate each and every type of force that was used, and require the evaluation of each use of force").

195 Prince George's County MOA, *supra* note 187, at 15, para. 47 (explaining the reporting requires for canine use of force in particular).

196 New Orleans Consent Decree, *supra* note 163, at 14 and 15, 28–34 (establishing the use-of-force policy and laying out requirements for use-of-force investigations).

197 Memorandum of Agreement Between the United States Department of Justice and the District of Columbia and the District of Columbia Metropolitan Police Department, at 8 and 9, para. 53–55 (June 13, 2001) [hereinafter Washington, DC MOA] (explaining the reporting requirements for use of force), *text available at* www.clearinghouse.net/chDocs/public/PN-DC-0001-0001.pdf.

198 Pittsburgh Consent Decree, *supra* note 188, at 10, para. 15 (requiring officers to complete written reports on use of force).

199 PERF, *supra* note 188, at 13. For examples of these sorts of stipulations, see *United States* v. *City of Los Angeles*, 2:00-cv-11769-GAF-RC, at 23–27 (consent decree) (CD Cal. June 15, 2001) [hereinafter Los Angeles Consent Decree], *text available at* www.clearinghouse.net/chDocs/public/PN-CA-0002-0006.pdf (laying out the terms of the use-of-force stipulations). The Los Angeles agreement typifies this trend as it mandates the creation of a unit dedicated to the investigation of use-of-force incidents housed in the Operations Headquarters Bureau. *Id.* at 23, para. 55. The Los Angeles agreement also establishes a chain of command when an officer uses categorical force, the investigation process, and the need to notify the district attorney and details the need to interview witnesses, notify the chain of command, and more in the event of a use-of-force incident. *Id.* at 23 and 24, para. 56–68. For other examples of this trend, *see* Prince George's County MOA, *supra* note 187, at 16, para. 51 (applying specifically to canine force use).

system (EIS) to manage risk.[200] The DOJ has required the development of these systems in the Los Angeles,[201] Steubenville,[202] Cincinnati,[203] Pittsburgh,[204] Washington, DC,[205] New Jersey,[206] New Orleans,[207] and Virgin Islands[208] cases. Research suggests that in any given police department, a small number of officers typically use force more often than the rest of the department.[209] One way to limit unlawful uses of force is to identify and monitor these officers with a high proclivity to use force. EIS does just this – "flagg[ing] officers for closer review" by "collect[ing] data and analyz[ing] patterns of activity."[210] These systems go by different names. But their central goal is to "identify opportunities to reduce risky behavior, department liability, and citizen complaints."[211]

The system articulated in the Washington, DC, negotiated settlement is reasonably representative of those required by most settlements. There, the DOJ required the police department to collect numerous data points on officer behavior and catalog this information into a computerized database.[212] Supervisors were then ordered to use this database to

200 PERF, *supra* note 188, at 16 (concluding that a large number of negotiated settlements have inevitably required the development of some type of EIS).

201 Los Angeles Consent Decree, *supra* note 199, at 9–21 (describing the development of the TEAMS II system, the management and coordination of risk assessment responsibilities, and the performance evaluation system).

202 Steubenville Consent Decree, *supra* note 188, at 6–19, para. 12–30 (stating that the city should implement an early warning system within twelve months).

203 Cincinnati MOA, *supra* note 194.

204 Pittsburgh Consent Decree, *supra* note 188, at 16 and 17, para. 23 (describing the annual review process).

205 Washington, DC, MOA, *supra* note 197, at 17–21, para. 106–118 (describing the personnel performance management system).

206 *United States* v. *New Jersey State Police*, 99-5970, at 15–18, para. 40–56 (D. NJ December 30, 1999) (joint application for entry of consent decree) [hereinafter New Jersey Consent Decree] (describing the development of the management awareness program), *text available at* www.clearinghouse.net/chDocs/public/PN-NJ-0002-0001.pdf.

207 New Orleans Consent Decree, *supra* note 163, at 80–83, para. 316–326 (outlining the terms of the new early warning system to be implemented as part of the consent decree).

208 Virgin Islands Consent Decree, *supra* note 191, at 11–16, para. 59–72 (describing the planned implementation of a management and risk supervision system).

209 PERF, *supra* note 188, at 16 ("Research has long suggested that a small percentage of police officers account of a high percentage of use-of-force incidents").

210 *Id.* 211 *Id.*

212 Washington, DC MOA, *supra* note 197, at 17, para. 106 (explaining the definition and requirements of the PPMS). The settlement required the PPMS to include information on use-of-force incidents, canine deployment, officer-involved firearm discharges, vehicle pursuits, complaints, commendations, arrests, investigations, training history, educational background, and more. *Id.* at 17–18, para. 107.

identify "any pattern or series of incidents" that indicate that an officer may be engaged in systematic misconduct.[213] If such a pattern existed, the settlement required the supervisor to take a more intensive review of the behavior.[214]

Law enforcement departments have used these types of early intervention and risk management systems for decades,[215] which have increased in popularity because of the belief that "10 percent of ... officers cause 90 percent of the problems."[216] Initial research demonstrates that these measures also have a positive impact on police agencies as they give supervisors additional information about their officers, foster a climate of accountability, decrease complaints, and help facilitate organizational management.[217]

3 Complaint Procedures and Investigations

Nearly every single monitored settlement provides some stipulations on how the agency ought to collect and process citizen complaints about officer conduct.[218] Settlements that include stipulations on

213 *Id.* at 19, para. 112(a)–(b). 214 *Id.*

215 POLICE EXECUTIVE RESEARCH FORUM, SUPERVISION AND INTERVENTION WITHIN EARLY INTERVENTION SYSTEMS: A GUIDE FOR LAW ENFORCEMENT CHIEF EXECUTIVES 2 (December 2005) [hereinafter PERF EARLY INTERVENTION SYSTEMS], *text available at* www.policeforum.org/library/early-intervention-systems/Chief%27s%20Guide%20EIS.pdf (stating "EIS have been used in the law enforcement community for more than 25 years").

216 SAMUEL WALKER, GEOFFREY P. ALPERT, & DENNIS J. KENNEY, EARLY WARNING SYSTEMS: RESPONDING TO THE PROBLEM POLICE OFFICER (July 2001), *text available* at http://zimmer.csufresno.edu/~haralds/Linkpages/reports/earlywarn.pdf (explaining that in 1999 around 27 percent of departments servicing a metropolitan area of at least 50,000 people had an EIS in place and 12 percent of agencies in 1999 claimed that they would soon implement such a system). Today, around 40 percent of agencies have EIS systems. US DEP'T OF JUSTICE, BUREAU OF JUSTICE STATISTICS, LAW ENFORCEMENT MANAGEMENT AND ADMINISTRATIVE STATISTICS (LEMAS): 2007 SAMPLE SURVEYS OF LAW ENFORCEMENT AGENCIES (2007) [hereinafter LEMAS 2007], *available at* www.icpsr.umich.edu/icpsrweb/ICPSR/studies/31161. This study calculates this number by dividing the total number of departments serving jurisdictions of over 50,000 residents who reported using an EIS (313) by the total number of those agencies that answered the question in the LEMAS survey (774). That resulted in a calculation that approximately 40.4 percent of departments serving jurisdictions with over 50,000 residents have EISs.

217 Walker, Alpert, and Kenney, *supra* note 216, at 4–7 (stating that "[T]he qualitative component of the research found that these systems have potentially significant effects ...," identifying multiple potential benefits).

218 Ten of the eleven monitored negotiated settlements establish some detailed parameters on complaint procedures – with Seattle being the only settlement not requiring such a measure. *See, e.g.*, Washington, DC MOA, *supra* note 197, at 15, para. 92–104

complaints address the same three basic issues – the intake of complaints, the investigation of complaints, and the complaint evaluation process.[219] The process of handling citizen complaints required under these negotiated settlements roughly mirrors those recommended by the International Association of Chiefs of Police (IACP), in coordination with the Office of Community Oriented Police Services (COPS).[220] They also match those identified as best practices by the Commission on Accreditation for Law Enforcement Agencies (CALEA).[221] These organizations argue that improved complaint procedures provide three separate benefits. First, these procedures give administrators a more accurate understanding of the scope and depth of misconduct problems within police agencies.[222] Second, the presence of these procedures may incentivize officers to be accountable for misconduct.[223] And third, these procedures may increase public trust in police agencies.[224]

4 Training Overhaul

Negotiated settlements also commonly require departments to adopt major overhauls of their training procedures. This includes both training for new officers and in-service training for existing officers.[225] The settlements generally require the departments to document the training

(including sections on the receipt of citizen complaints, the investigation of complaints, and the evaluation of these allegations); Los Angeles Consent Decree, *supra* note 199, at 32–38 (detailing rules on the initiation, investigation, and adjudication of complaints).

219 *See, e.g.*, Pittsburgh Consent Decree, *supra* note 188, at 23–32, para. 44–69 (laying out standards for each of these three different phases of the complaint process); Steubenville Consent Decree, *supra* note 188, at 17–22, para. 40–58 (setting requirements for starting an investigation pursuant to a complaint, conducting an investigation, and evaluating a complaint's validity); Prince George's County MOA, *supra* note 187, at 14–18, para. 60–74 (again, including components about the receipt, tracking, investigation, and adjudication of complaints against officers).

220 *See generally* International Association of Chiefs of Police, Building Trust Between the Police and the Citizens They Serve (2008), *text available at* www.theiacp.org/LinkClick.aspx?fileticket=pjRkKQNvkPs%3d&tabid=514.

221 *Id.* at 52 (discussing the CALEA standards for law enforcement agencies).

222 *Id.* at 17–20 (arguing that these improved complaint procedures provide a more "fair, thorough, accurate, and impartial" view of misconduct present in a department).

223 *Id.* (emphasizing the possible improvement in officer morale and behavior).

224 *Id.* (explaining how these measures will "increase trust within the community").

225 *See, e.g.*, Steubenville Consent Decree, *supra* note 188, at 6, para. 14 (identifying the need for both entry and annual in-service training); Cincinnati MOA, *supra* note 194, at 21, para. 82 (noting the need for training for "all new recruits and as part of annual in-service training").

history of each officer.[226] The DOJ normally makes some stipulation as to the subjects of these trainings.[227] The DOJ has not gone to the extent of stipulating the content of the trainings in much specificity.[228] That is to say, the DOJ gives the agency broad discretion to create its own training materials addressing each relevant subject, so long as that training is "consistent with ... [the] law and proper police practices."[229] In some cases, though, the DOJ has gone as far as specifying the length of time that each officer must be trained.[230] The topics covered by the training section of each settlement appear to be uniquely tailored to the apparent problem in the jurisdiction.

Empirical evidence suggests that departments that rigorously train their officers suffer from lower rates of misconduct.[231] And perhaps equally important to the department administrators, enhanced training lowers the likelihood of a department suffering stiff penalties in private litigation.[232] Although there is some academic disagreement about the exact type of training necessary to reduce police wrongdoing, police

[226] *See, e.g.*, New Jersey Consent Decree, *supra* note 206, at 25, para. 108 and 109 ("[T]he State Police will track all training information, including name of the course, date started, date completed, and training location for each member receiving training"); Virgin Islands Consent Decree, *supra* note 191, at 18, para. 77 ("The VIPD shall continue to maintain training records regarding every VIPD officer that reliably indicate the training each officer has received ... [including] the course description and duration, curriculum, and instructor for each officer").

[227] *See, e.g.*, Prince George's County MOA, *supra* note 187, at 12 and 13, para. 54 and 55 (ordering the department to appoint a Training Committee to develop curriculum and stipulating the subjects that ought to be covered); New Jersey Consent Decree, *supra* note 215, at 24, para. 100 (identifying some of the areas that New Jersey must broadly address in trainings).

[228] *See, e.g.*, Prince George's County MOA, *supra* note 187, at 13, para. 55 (listing the areas to be addressed in training, but leaving it up to the department to develop policies that address these topics in accordance with the law); New Jersey Consent Decree, *supra* note 206, at 24, para. 100 (stating that New Jersey needs to develop policies to train recruits and troopers on various issues related to diversity, complaint procedures, professionalism, and many more topics, but not specifically articulating the exact content of these trainings).

[229] Virgin Islands Consent Decree, *supra* note 191, at 18, para. 75.

[230] *See, e.g.*, Steubenville Consent Decree, *supra* note 188, at 6, para. 13(a)–(b) (Identifying field training that must last at least twelve weeks and stating that existing officers must partake in in-service training "for at least 40 hours each year").

[231] James J. Fyfe, *Training to Reduce Police-Civilian Violence*, in AND JUSTICE FOR ALL 163 (William A. Geller & Hans Toch, eds., 1995).

[232] The Court has allowed litigants to hold police departments liable for the actions of their officers in the event that the police department was deliberately indifferent in its failure to train or supervise. *See Monell* v. *City of New York Dept. Social Servs*, 436 US 658 (1978). This case opened law enforcement departments to civil litigation under 42 USC §1983 in

professionals have increasingly recognized the absolute necessity of continual law enforcement training.[233]

5 Bias-Free Policing

A handful of the agreements demonstrate some concern for the prevention of biased policing practices by requiring departments to regularly review and audit officer records to uncover patterns of racial bias.[234] This concern for bias appears particularly evident in the Pittsburgh,[235] Steubenville,[236] New Jersey,[237] and New Orleans[238] consent decrees.[239] For example, in New Jersey, the DOJ required the state police to collect and monitor the racial breakdown of occupants in motor vehicle stops, in hopes of thwarting the use of racial profiling.[240] The agreement then required the monitor to compare the racial breakdown of motor vehicle stops with the racial and ethnic percentage of drivers within the state police's jurisdiction.[241]

6 Community and Problem-Oriented Policing

Another emerging trend in negotiated settlements is the inclusion of community and problem-oriented policing requirements. Even though this component is explicitly mentioned in only one of the negotiated

the event that they failed to provide adequate training that contributed to an officer's violation of an individual's constitutional right.

233 Fyfe, *supra* note 231.

234 *See* Pittsburgh Consent Decree, *supra* note 188, at 13 and 14, para. 20; Steubenville Consent Decree, *supra* note 188, at 31, para. 77.

235 Pittsburgh Consent Decree, *supra* note 188, at 13 and 14, para. 20 ("The City shall conduct regular audits and reviews of potential racial bias, including use of racial epithets, by all officers").

236 Steubenville Consent Decree, *supra* note 188, at 31, para. 77 ("The City shall conduct regular audits and reviews of potential racial bias").

237 New Jersey Consent Decree, *supra* note 206, at 16 and 17, para. 49 and 50 (discussing plans to monitor the racial breakdown of stops in and effort to thwart racial profiling).

238 New Orleans Consent Decree, *supra* note 163, at 48–60, para. 177–222 (laying out terms, in great detail, for how the New Orleans Police Department could avoid racially biased and gender biased policing tactics). The recent settlement in New Orleans, though, has taken a more expansive view of biased policing, expanding bias-free policing to protect undocumented immigrants and LGBT persons. *Id.* at 50, para. 184.

239 The Los Angeles Consent Decree includes some mention of racial bias, too. *See* Los Angeles Consent Decree, *supra* note 199, at 69, para. 138. But this mention of racial bias seems somewhat less significant than other negotiated settlements that discussed the issue. The same can be said for the Washington, DC negotiated settlement. *See, e.g.*, Washington, DC MOA, *supra* note 197, at 12, para. 76.

240 New Jersey Consent Decree, *supra* note 206, at 17, para. 50.

241 *Id.* at para. 54.

settlements – the recent New Orleans agreement[242] – some monitors have openly pushed community and problem-oriented policing during the implementation of structural reform in other cities as a possible solution to aggressive policing strategies that stigmatized minority communities.[243] While there remain some concerns about the disparate benefits of community policing[244] and the general disinterest of law enforcement officers in community policing efforts,[245] criminological research suggests that these measures increase community trust and redefine law enforcement goals along the lines of community interests.[246]

The range of topics covered by negotiated settlements is admittedly broader than the list of topics above. Settlements have also touched on a range of issues related to interrogations,[247] lineup procedures,[248] gang unit management,[249] canine deployment,[250] crisis intervention,[251] and

[242] New Orleans Consent Decree, *supra* note 163, at 60–63, para. 223–233 ("NOPD agrees to reassess its staffing allocation and personnel deployment, including its use of specialized units and deployment by geographic area, to ensure that core operations support community policing and problem-oriented initiatives . . .").

[243] For example, a member of the Cincinnati monitoring team explained that part of the team's goal was to encourage the department to "chang[e] from saturation patrol and aggressive policing to community policing, problem oriented policing and problem solving." Interview #18, *supra* note 165, at 3.

[244] *See generally* Wesley G. Skogan, Disorder and Decline: Crime and the Spiral of Decay in American Neighborhoods 107 (1990) (identifying how minority residents feel less of the positive influences of community policing efforts and explaining that "the lack of positive effects for those at the bottom of the social ladder may be related to their more limited awareness of programs").

[245] *See generally* Anthony M. Pate & Penny Shtull, *Community Policing Grows in Brooklyn: An Inside View of the New York City Police Department's Model Precinct*, 40 Crime & Delinq. 384 (1994) (finding some officers were generally disinterested in the community policing effort).

[246] *See generally* Wesley G. Skogan, *The Promise of Community Policing*, in Police Innovation: Contrasting Perspectives 31 (David Weisburd & Anthony A. Braga, eds.), (2006) ("[A]fter eight years of citywide community policing, Chicagoans' views of their police improved by 10–15 percentage points on measures of their effectiveness, responsiveness, and demeanor").

[247] New Orleans Consent Decree, *supra* note 163 at 46 and 47, para. 163–170 (laying out standards for custodial interrogations).

[248] *Id.* at 47 and 48, para. 171–176 (establishing procedures for photographic lineup administrations).

[249] Los Angeles Consent Decree, *supra* note 199, at 47–50, para. 106 and 107 (requiring the development and administration of gang management policy).

[250] Prince George's MOA, *supra* note 187, at 8–14, para. 29–46 (establishing thorough regulation of canine deployment).

[251] Seattle Agreement, *supra* note 186, at 7–9, para. 23–25 (laying out regulations on crisis intervention via the creation of the crisis intervention committee).

promotion evaluations.[252] One of the most contentious parts of the federal intervention process, though, is the appointment of an external monitor.

C Appointment of Monitor

If the DOJ and the targeted police agency agree to the appointment of an external monitor, the parties next enter the monitor appointment phase. During this stage, the parties must select a mutually agreeable external team of experts to oversee the upcoming structural reforms. This is an important stage since "a city's relationship with the monitor is a critical factor in how swiftly reforms can be made, and a consent decree ended."[253] No research into federal intervention into local police departments has ever evaluated the monitor selection process. This void in the literature is understandable. Generally, this selection process happened through a confidential negotiation process behind closed doors.[254] To better understand how this monitor selection process works, this section supplements interview data with records from the monitor selection process in New Orleans. There, Federal District Judge Susie Morgan of the Eastern District of Louisiana ordered a transparent monitor selection involving public hearings, public disclosure of each monitoring team's proposal, and negotiations between a ten-member panel of officials from New Orleans and the DOJ.[255] From these court records and stakeholder interviews, a couple of trends emerge about the monitor selection process.

First, monitors are expensive. As a result, cost control is a critically important issue in the monitor appointment process.[256] Remember, the

[252] New Orleans Consent Decree, *supra* note 163, at 75 and 76 (establishing both performance evaluations and describing how these evaluations ought to be used in the promotion process).

[253] PERF, *supra* note 188, at 3.

[254] *United States* v. *New Orleans*, No. 2:21-cv-01924, at 3 (ED La. September 6, 2012) (order granting motion for leave to request proposals) [hereinafter New Orleans Monitor Search Order] (stating "[t]he Court further observes that in other cases involving consent decrees negotiated to resolve claims brought pursuant to ... §14141 ... the United States participated in selecting monitors outside of a jurisdiction's standard procurement procedure").

[255] Edmund W. Lewis, *NOPD Consent Decree Moves Forward*, The Louisiana Weekly, August 19, 2013 (explaining the selection process and identifying the ten-person panel entrusted with the selection of a monitor); John Simerman, *Federal Judge Picks Feds' Choice for NOPD Monitor*, The Advocate, July 9, 2013 (explaining the five public hearings held to discuss the appointment of the monitor).

[256] PERF, *supra* note 188, at 42 (stating that "[t]he costs of achieving compliance, and the legal costs paid to monitors, are sometimes contentious" and they are "often high").

Table 3.5 *Approximate Annual Cost of Monitoring Services in Selected Police Agencies*

City	Cost
Seattle	$880,000
Prince George's County	$900,000
Washington, DC	$1,000,000
Oakland	$1,700,000
Detroit	$1,750,000
New Orleans	$2,000,000
Los Angeles	$2,200,000

local police agency has to foot the bill for any monitoring services.[257] Thus, a rational municipality will want to hire the cheapest monitor, so long as that monitor will help that municipality escape the negotiated settlement in an expeditious manner. But the municipality does not have unilateral power to select an external monitor. Instead, the municipality must negotiate with the DOJ to select a monitoring team.[258] Costs are particularly critical for many cities targeted for federal monitoring in part because these communities have finite resources. In some of these municipalities, the high cost of monitoring exacerbates preexisting financial troubles. The annual cost of monitoring typically tops $1,000,000. Table 3.5 shows the average annual yearly cost of monitoring services in several of the cities targeted for federal intervention thus far.[259]

[257] *See, e.g.*, *United States* v. *New Orleans*, 2:12-cv-01924-SM-JCW, at 12–15 (New Orleans Memorandum Regarding Monitor Candidates) (ED La. June 14, 2013) [hereinafter New Orleans Memorandum Recommending Hillard Heintze] (detailing New Orleans's concerns about the relatively high cost of monitoring that they would have to ultimately pay).

[258] *See, e.g.*, Pittsburgh Consent Decree, *supra* note 188, at para. 70 (serving as an example of a typical clause found in negotiated settlements that requires the two sides to negotiate on the selection of a monitor).

[259] PERF, *supra* note 188, at 1, 34 (identifying cost of New Orleans monitoring at 1, and the other costs on 34). These estimates come from city officials, monitors, and media reports discussed at a PERF conference on federal oversight of local police departments. *See also* First Year Budget for Monitoring of Seattle Agreement (November 14, 2012), *available at* www.seattlemonitor.com/uploads/Signed_Nov_2012-Oct_2013_Budget.pdf (stating that the first year budget for the Seattle monitoring will sit around $880,000).

The New Orleans monitor selection process illustrates the tension over allocating costs and burdens. There, the city and the DOJ sharply disagreed on the appropriate choice of monitor, due in large part to substantial difference in cost between the two options; New Orleans advocated for a cheaper monitor, while the DOJ supported the bid from a more expensive team.[260] Ultimately, the Court sided with the DOJ.[261]

Second, there is widespread disagreement about the relative importance of a monitor's law enforcement background. Police agencies frequently push for monitors with law enforcement background. When trying to bring about organizational change, one police chief explained, frontline staff are more willing to accept changes if they know that "the leader bringing about the change has worn those shoes for a while."[262] The chief further clarified that monitors with law enforcement experience are also more credible because former cops "understand [that] if we put accountability measures in place, they [are going to] affect your crime fighting" abilities.[263] As a result, the chief concluded that monitoring teams in the future "should be comprised mostly of people with prior law enforcement experience," and "the top monitor should have very high level police management experience."[264] Conversely, the DOJ has indicated that while monitoring teams should include some individuals with law enforcement experience, lawyers should play an important role in the process. As one DOJ litigator explained, "in all of these cases there are complicated issues of constitutional law [and] criminal procedure involved" including "evidence gathering, data collection, [and] document review that needs to happen."[265] As the participant concluded, "[a]ttorneys are trained to do that" kind of work.[266] The Justice Department official added that "to the extent that there are court

[260] The two finalist options were the Hillard Heintze team and Sheppard Mullin team. The Sheppard Mullin team proposed a four-year monitoring period for approximately $7.8 million with a cap set at $8.9 million. New Orleans Memorandum Recommending Hillard Heintze, *supra* note 257, at 13. Hillard Heintze offered to complete the same basic service for a capped price of around $7 million. *Id.* The United States, though, asserted that the City needs to comply with the Constitution, even if doing so costs money. *United States* v. *New Orleans*, 2:12-cv-01924-SM-JCW, at 17 (United States Memorandum Recommending Sheppard Mullin as Consent Decree Monitor) (ED La. June 14, 2013) [hereinafter US Memorandum Recommending Sheppard Mullin in New Orleans].

[261] US Memorandum Recommending Sheppard Mullin in New Orleans, *supra* note 260, at 1–2.

[262] Interview #16, supra note 20, at 10. [263] *Id.* [264] *Id.*

[265] Interview #12, *supra* note 67, at 8. [266] *Id.*

processes [involved in monitoring], it's helpful to have attorneys that can interface with the court" and explain the "legal ramifications" of the reforms.[267] The court records suggest that this tension was a significant issue in the New Orleans monitor selection process. In that case, New Orleans advocated for the appointment of a monitoring team to lead former law enforcement executives, while the DOJ pushed for a team led by lawyers.[268] New Orleans emphasized the "crucial insight" that former law enforcement administrators could provide to the federal intervention process.[269] The DOJ, though, insisted that lawyers were well suited to "make difficult calls" that are legally "accurate, objective, and credible."[270]

D Monitored Reform

Once a police agency reaches a negotiated settlement with the DOJ, and the parties agree on the appointment of an external monitor, the long and arduous reform process begins. The monitored reform process can take as little as five years.[271] In some cases, though, this stage can take well over a decade.[272] Table 3.6 shows the length of monitoring in all police agencies that have gone through federal intervention.[273]

[267] *Id.* ("It's also very helpful to have attorneys that can sometimes translate, sometimes explain to the legal entity at the jurisdiction, whether that's the city attorney's office or the state attorney's office or county counsel, whatever it will be; what the legal ramifications are of some of these reforms").

[268] New Orleans supported the Hillard Heintze monitoring team led by security and law enforcement experts. New Orleans Memorandum Recommending Hillard Heintze, *supra* note 257, at 1. The DOJ supported the appointment of a monitoring team run by the law firm Sheppard Mullin. US Memorandum Recommending Sheppard Mullin in New Orleans, *supra* note 260, at 8 and 9 (explaining the choice of Sheppard Mullin).

[269] New Orleans Memorandum Recommending Hillard Heintze, *supra* note 257, at 1 and 2 (explaining the importance of "law enforcement experience and expertise" in applying "provisions that are directed toward law enforcement rather than legal analysis").

[270] US Memorandum Recommending Sheppard Mullin in New Orleans, *supra* note 260, at 14 (elaborating further that lawyers are well-suited to be "fair and independent" and "make difficult calls").

[271] *See infra* Table 3.6 (illustrating the length of monitored reform for each city involved in structural police reform thus far, and showing that Cincinnati and Prince George's county took only five years).

[272] *Id.* (showing that Los Angeles, Washington, DC, and Detroit's monitored reforms took over a decade).

[273] This study calculated these monitored reform periods as the number of days between the date that the DOJ entered into a negotiated settlement with the deficient department and the date that the DOJ released the department from the terms of the agreement. *See* Rushin, *supra* note 193, at Appendix (listing the closure date); *see also* Letter from United

Table 3.6 *Length of Reform Process in Selected Police Agencies, 1994–2013*

City	Length of Monitored Reform (years)
Cincinnati	5.0[1]
Prince George's County	5.0[2]
Steubenville	7.5[3]
Pittsburgh	8.2[4]
New Jersey	9.8[5]
Washington, DC	10.7[6]
Los Angeles	11.9[7]
Detroit	12.7[8]

[1] The Cincinnati monitoring lasted from April 12, 2002, to April 12, 2007 – approximately 1,826 days or five years. *Id.*

[2] The Prince George's County monitoring lasted from January 22, 2004, until January 13, 2009 – approximately 1,818 days or 5.0 years. *Id.*

[3] The Steubenville monitoring lasted from September 3, 1997, to March 3, 2005 – approximately 2,738 days or about 7.5 years. *Id.*

[4] The Pittsburgh monitoring lasted from April 16, 1997, to June 16, 2005 – approximately 2,983 days or 8.2 years. *Id.*

[5] The New Jersey monitoring lasted from December 29, 1999, to October 26, 2009 – approximately 3,589 days or 9.8 years. *Id.*

[6] The Washington, DC, monitoring lasted from June 13, 2001, to February 20, 2012 – approximately 3,894 days or 10.7 years. *Id.*

[7] The Los Angeles monitoring lasted from June 15, 2001, to May 16, 2013 – approximately 4,353 days or 11.9 years. *Id.*

[8] The Detroit monitoring lasted from June 12, 2003, to March 2, 2016 – approximately 4,647 days or 12.7 years. *Id.*

The monitored reform process is also costly. The affected police agency must pay the cost of monitoring, which typically runs around \$1–2 million a year.[274] The municipality must then cover the cost of all of

States Department of Justice Responding to Freedom of Information Request (April 24, 2013) [hereinafter Letter from DOJ] (on file with author) (listing agreement). This figure does not include cities that are still under monitoring.

274 PERF, *supra* note 188, at 1, 34 (putting the monitoring costs somewhere between \$900,000 and \$2,200,0000); *see also* US Memorandum Recommending Sheppard Mullin in New Orleans, *supra* note 260, at 8 (describing the competing proposals for

the reforms required by the negotiated settlement. These costs are substantial. For example, in Los Angeles, the cost of implementing reforms likely totaled at least $80–90 million.[275] When factoring in the cost of hiring of the external monitor in Los Angeles, which came in at around $2 million a year,[276] the Los Angeles price tag likely surpassed $100 million, with some estimates placing it substantially higher.[277] This cost might sound startling at first. But considering the size of the city and the length of time it took to implement these changes, the actual cost to each individual Los Angeles taxpayer was fairly low.[278]

During this reform process, the external monitor regularly visits the police agency to audit departmental records and meet with officers.[279] Based on these regular department visits and audits, monitors file public reports every three months evaluating the agency's progress in implementing the terms of the settlement.[280] These quarterly reports are long and detailed, and they describe the department's observed progress in

monitors in New Orleans, with one offering a "four-year capped cost estimate [of] $7,007,542" and the other suggesting a four-year cost of "$7,880,786, with a cap of $8,900,000").

275 Joseph Giordono & Jason Kandel, *Police Union Threatens Suit; LAPD: League President Says Officers to File Federal Case About Consent Decree*, LONG BEACH PRESS-TELEGRAM, November 2, 2000, at A8 (putting the cost of the Los Angeles consent decree at around $40 million to implement in the first year, with an additional $30–50 million in expenses in the years to follow).

276 PERF, *supra* note 188, at 34 (putting the Los Angeles monitoring cost at just north of $2 million a year).

277 This estimate was derived by calculating the cost of monitoring – roughly $2 million a year for over ten years – and adding it to the cost of the reforms. The $100 million figure likely underestimates the actual total cost.

278 Over the 11.9 years that the city of Los Angeles was under a consent decree, the average population was 3,841,881. Given that the estimated cost of the consent decree was around $100 million, then that comes out to $26 a person for the entire time period. Spread out over 11.9 years, this comes out to about $2.19 per resident per year.

279 Interview with External Monitor #3, at 16 (July 2, 2013) [hereinafter Interview #3] (transcript on file with author) (stating that "Fundamentally, the monitoring team goes on site on whatever regular basis is. Some, like ours, we basically go on site one week each quarter to do our on-site review and data analysis, interviews, those kinds of things. We get our reports, data, that we look at").

280 *See, e.g.*, OFFICE OF THE INDEPENDENT MONITOR OF THE LOS ANGELES POLICE DEPARTMENT, FIRST QUARTERLY REPORT 1 (November 15, 2001) [hereinafter FIRST QUARTERLY REPORT FOR LAPD] (stating that the monitors in the Los Angeles case will issue quarterly reports covering approximately three months at a time); OFFICE OF THE INDEPENDENT MONITOR OF THE DETROIT POLICE DEPARTMENT, FIRST QUARTERLY REPORT i [hereinafter FIRST QUARTERLY REPORT FOR DPD] (also describing the plan to issue reports every approximately three months and describing these reports as quarterly reports).

implementing each component of the negotiated settlement.[281] These quarterly reports also include the results of the monitor's regular audits of departmental records.[282]

The DOJ does not expect a police department to achieve 100 percent compliance with all components of a negotiated settlement. Instead, the DOJ monitors generally requires that a police agency achieve "substantial compliance" – defined as the full satisfaction of significant percentage of all components of a settlement agreement – before officially releasing the department from federal oversight.[283] To determine whether a department has reached this critical compliance threshold, monitors break down the negotiated settlement by paragraph and examine whether the department has fully satisfied each term of that paragraph.[284] In doing so, monitors examine both whether a department has instituted the mandatory policy change required by a paragraph and whether the policy change has had the intended effect.[285]

For example, if the monitor finds a department to be in full compliance with 50 out of the 60 paragraphs of a negotiated settlement, then that

281 For reference, the first quarterly report in the New Orleans case was 59 pages. OFFICE OF THE CONSENT DECREE MONITOR FOR THE NEW ORLEANS POLICE DEPARTMENT, FIRST QUARTERLY REPORT (November 29, 2013) [hereinafter FIRST QUARTERLY REPORT FOR NOPD]. The first quarterly report in the Washington, DC, case was sixty-one pages. OFFICE OF THE INDEPENDENT MONITOR OF THE METROPOLITAN POLICE DEPARTMENT, FIRST QUARTERLY REPORT (August 1, 2002) [hereinafter FIRST QUARTERLY REPORT FOR MPD]. And the first quarterly report in the Pittsburgh case was sixty-five pages. OFFICE OF THE AUDITOR OF THE PITTSBURGH BUREAU OF POLICE, FIRST QUARTERLY REPORT (December 15, 1997) [hereinafter FIRST QUARTERLY REPORT for PBP].

282 *See, e.g.*, FIRST QUARTERLY REPORT for PBP, *supra* note 281, at 2 (stating that "Members of the audit team have collected data on-site and have been provided data, pursuant to specific requests, by the Pittsburgh Bureau of Police" and included the findings in the quarterly reports).

283 Telephone Interview with External Monitor #10, at 4 (July 19, 2013) [hereinafter Interview #10] (transcript on file with author) (stating that his team used a 94 percent completion rate to measure compliance because "many of these elements require examination of documents [and] [t]o do that, we really need to do scientific sampling so we know they're representative . . .. so, what we were looking at was this sort of plus or minus 5% error range around that level").

284 Telephone Interview with External Monitor #1, at 9 (July 13, 2013) [hereinafter Interview #1] (transcript on file with author) (explaining controversy surrounding how writers break down settlements into paragraph segments).

285 Telephone Interview with External Monitor #6, at 9 (July 19, 2013) [hereinafter Interview #6] (transcript on file with author) (differentiating between phase one compliance – the measurement of "issuance of policy" – and phase two – "actual implementation" – and stating that both are necessary for the DOJ to agree that a department is in "substantial compliance").

department has achieved 83.3 percent compliance – well short of the targeted 94 or 95 percent range needed for substantial compliance in some cases. Similarly, if a paragraph requires that a department institute an efficient process for residents to file complaints about police misconduct, the monitor would first examine whether the department has adopted a policy consistent with this requirement. Then, the monitor may audit the complaint process via an undercover agent to ensure that the department is actually living up to its new internal complaint policy. Only if the monitor finds a police agency has satisfied both of these requirements – that is, both instituted a policy change internally and subsequently changed organizational behavior consistent with that policy – will the monitor find that the department has fully satisfied the paragraph.

This approach to measuring compliance is logical, but it also creates openings for confrontation. Police administrators complain that some paragraphs in negotiated settlements are long and complex.[286] In these cases, a department may be in full compliance with virtually all components of the paragraph.[287] Nevertheless, because of the department's failure to satisfy one minor element of the paragraph, the monitor will find that the department is not in compliance with the entire paragraph.[288] This can lead to a false appearance that the department is failing to make progress, when in fact the department is only having trouble with a relatively minor part of a large paragraph.[289] Ultimately, measuring compliance is an inexact science that puts considerable authority in the hands of external monitors. This has led to some questions among stakeholders involved in these cases about "who monitors the monitors?"[290]

[286] Interview #1, *supra* note 284, at 9 ("you will have one consent paragraph where you'll have eight or ten subsets to that paragraph").

[287] *Id.* at 9 (using an example from the Detroit monitoring to explain how a department may be in general compliance with virtually all parts of a subsection, but still found to not be substantially compliant because of the settlement organization).

[288] *Id.* at 10 (also recommending that the DOJ should attempt to make every individual requirement a separate paragraph).

[289] *Id.* at 9–10 (again using Detroit as an example of how the division of paragraphs in a consent decree can make measurement difficult and give off the false sense that a department is not making progress).

[290] PERF, *supra* note 188, at 31 (quoting PERF Executive Director Chuck Wexler asking "who monitors the monitor" and showing various responses to this question from ACLU attorney Scott Greenwood, DOJ Deputy Section Chief Christy Lopez, Milwaukee Police Chief Ed Flynn, and Special Litigation Section Chief Jonathan Smith).

The relationship between the monitor and the police agency also seems to play an important role in the speed of reforms.[291] For example, one monitor recalled that the particularly contentious relationship between the monitoring team and the police administration in Oakland slowed down the progress of reforms.[292] Conversely, a police administrator in Los Angeles described how a monitor's good working relationship with the department helped in jointly crafting policy fixes that directly addressed the concerns of the consent decree.[293] And as discussed earlier, stakeholders often disagree on the relative importance of law enforcement experience in the appointment of monitors.[294]

Conclusion

Three lessons emerge from this chapter. First, despite the transformative potential of the statute, it appears that resource limitations and political obstruction have hampered the Intervention Era. Resource limitations have extended from one presidential administration to the next. It is hard to imagine that the DOJ will ever have the requisite resources to fully and rigorously enforce § 14141 against all agencies that appear to be engaged in a pattern or practice of misconduct. But the political obstruction of § 14141 during the Bush administration is yet another reminder of how administrative actors can influence the real-world consequences of law on the books.

Second, in the face of these limitations, the attorneys in the Special Litigation Section have admirably attempted to utilize their limited enforcement power in a way that maximizes the overall effect of § 14141. Yes, the process is messy. The process is also sometimes seemingly inconsistent and

[291] PERF, *supra* note 188, at 7 ("The choice of a monitor is extremely important . . . because] [t]hese officials do more than simply 'monitor' the progress being made; they work to achieve practical and effective outcomes expeditiously").

[292] Interview #16, *supra* note 20, at 9 (describing the link between the "deterioration of the relationship" between the monitor and the police administration and the slow progress of reforms caused by the subsequent "harsh criticism of the chief in one of the reports"); *see also* Interview #1, *supra* note 284, at 7 (describing how Detroit has made progress now that, "four years into it we [monitors] have a respectful working relationship" with the police department).

[293] Interview #22, *supra* note 181. (explaining how in Los Angeles, one of the monitors had a solid working relationship with the LAPD, which facilitated a collaborative effort to jointly write a new policy to satisfy the terms of the consent decree).

[294] *See, e.g.*, Interview #16, *supra* note 20, at 10 ("I do think the majority of monitoring teams should be comprised mostly of people with prior law enforcement experience . . . and the top monitor should have very high level police management experience").

imprecise. These drawbacks are an understandable consequence of an agency taxed with an impossible responsibility. To compensate, the litigators in the Special Litigation Section have strategically investigated many of the largest police agencies in the country, sending a clear message to police departments around the country about the boundaries of acceptable police behavior. But at the end of the day, these attorneys have only been able to push forward an extremely small number of cases relative to the number of police departments in the United States.

Thus, the third lesson that emerges is that, despite the best effort of the attorneys in the Special Litigation Section, outsiders often view the enforcement of § 14141 as nothing more than an enforcement lottery. This is a particularly unfortunate development since a cooperative relationship between the DOJ and a targeted municipality appears critical to the successful and expeditious implementation of mandated reforms. Since enforcement is at times so spotty and inconsistent, municipalities often view their selection for federal intervention as procedurally unjust. This may ultimately be the most troubling and harmful consequence of the § 14141 enforcement lottery.

4

Possibilities and Limitations

Introduction

On November 6, 1997, three men robbed a Bank of America branch in Los Angeles.[1] Such an event is fairly unremarkable. Bank robberies happen all the time. In 2011 alone there were an estimated 5,000 robberies at banks and financial institutions across the country.[2] But this bank robbery was different. This robbery led investigators to discover a shocking pattern of misconduct by LAPD officers. And the evidence uncovered in the years that followed eventually spurred the DOJ to overhaul the LAPD – the nation's third largest police department. A nearly twelve-year reform process followed, costing Los Angeles taxpayers millions of dollars.

In the weeks after the robbery, investigators quickly turned their attention to an assistant bank manager named Errolyn Romero, who appeared to have ordered for an unusually large cash delivery just shortly before the robbery.[3] When Romero eventually confessed to her role in the robbery, she identified her boyfriend, LAPD officer David Mack, as one of the robbers.[4] Officer Mack had previously worked in the Rampart Division as part of the LAPD's elite antigang unit nicknamed CRASH (Community Resources Against Street Hoodlums).[5] While in Rampart

1 Bd. of Inquiry, L.A. Police Dep't, Rampart Area Corruption Incident: Public Report (2000) [hereinafter Rampart Report].

2 *Bank Robbery*, Federal Bureau of Investigations, www.fbi.gov/about-us/investigate/vc_majorthefts/bankrobbery.

3 Rampart Report, *supra* note 1, at 1 and 2 (explaining how Officer Mack's girlfriend Errolyn Romero worked at the bank and helped Mack set up the robbery by ordering $772,000 in unusual denominations the day before the crime); *Rampart Scandal Timeline*, PBS Frontline, *available at* www.pbs.org/wgbh/pages/frontline/shows/lapd/scandal/cron.html.

4 *Rampart Scandal Timeline, supra.*

5 Rampart Report, *supra* note 1, at 1(stating that "David Mack . . . had previously been assigned to Rampart and was a close friend of [another officer implicated in the Rampart Scandal] Rafael Perez").

Division, Officer Mack worked with one of his "best friends," fellow officer Rafael Perez.[6] Officer Mack had even received the LAPD's Medal for Heroism for shooting a drug dealer to protect Perez.[7] In the days immediately after the robbery, investigators learned that Mack and Perez had – perhaps not coincidentally – gambled away thousands of dollars during a weekend trip to Las Vegas.[8] Officer Mack eventually resigned from the LAPD.[9] He was convicted of robbery and sentenced to fourteen years in prison.[10] Mack never revealed the location of the stolen money.[11] Even though circumstantial evidence suggested Perez may have been involved in the robbery, investigators could not definitively prove the identity of the other two robbers. While the robbery implicated one officer with ties with the Rampart Division, it cast a shadow over the entire division – a shadow that grew darker in the coming months when details emerged by the behavior of officers Brian Hewitt and Daniel Lujan.

Evidence emerged that these two Rampart Division officers detained two members of the 18th Street Gang for allegedly violating their parole conditions.[12] The officers brought the men back to Rampart Substation and put each man in a separate interview room.[13] Moments later, Hewitt demanded that one of the suspects provide him with information about gang activity.[14] After the suspect refused to cooperate, Officer Hewitt "choked and beat him until he vomited blood."[15] Although Officer Lujan and another officer were clearly aware of the violence, they released the man without properly reporting the incident to their supervisors and without providing the man with any sort of medical treatment.[16] The LAPD attempted to punish each of the officers involved. But procedural difficulties made it difficult for the chief of police to fire one of the officers involved.[17] Prosecutors also decided to

[6] *Id.* at 2. [7] *Rampart Scandal Timeline, supra* note 3.

[8] RAMPART REPORT, *supra* note 1, at 1 and 2. [9] *Id.* at 2.

[10] *Rampart Scandal Timeline, supra* note 3. [11] *Id.*

[12] RAMPART REPORT, *supra* note 1, at 1 and 2. [13] *Id.* [14] *Id.* [15] *Id.*

[16] *Id.* The report continued by noting that "[t]he man subsequently checked into a hospital and the Department was notified of his allegations" *Id.*

[17] The report explained this procedural complexity as follows:

> Administrative charges were brought against all three officers for the beating and cover-up of the incident. Officers Hewitt and Cohan were eventually terminated at separate Boards of Rights; but, a third Board found the other officer not guilty. (In Los Angeles, a three-member Board of Rights, composed of two staff or command officers and one community member, hears allegations of major misconduct. Each accused

not file criminal charges against the officers because of insufficient evidence.[18]

Only a few weeks after the beating, personnel in the Property Division of the Rampart Division Substation reported that three kilograms of cocaine was missing.[19] The property records stated that an officer in the Rampart Division had checked out the drugs for court on March 2, 1998.[20] When the narcotics were still missing on March 27, the Property Division sent a notice to the officer's supervisor.[21] The officer claimed to have not checked out the drugs; the Property Division officer confirmed that a different person had actually checked out the contraband.[22] An internal investigation identified Rafael Perez – the same officer who spent a weekend gambling away thousands of dollars with a bank robber – as the person who checked out the drugs.[23] The District Attorney's Office then charged Officer Perez with three separate crimes: possession of cocaine for sale, grand theft, and forgery.[24] In the first trial against Officer Perez, the jury deadlocked and could not reach a verdict.[25] As prosecutors prepared for a second trial, further investigation revealed that Officer Perez had been involved in additional cocaine thefts from the Property Division.[26] Even more disturbingly, evidence emerged that Perez had an ongoing relationship with known drug dealers. One of these drug dealers even identified Perez "as having gone to Las Vegas with Perez, Mack, and a third officer immediately after Mack's bank robbery."[27] As the evidence mounted, Perez had no choice but to accept

> officer may select a separate Board and the Chief of Police may impose no greater penalty than the Board recommends.)
>
> *Id.*

18 The report further clarified:

> On two occasions, a criminal filing has been sought against Hewitt, but the case was rejected both times by the District Attorney's Special Investigations Section due to insufficient evidence to convict. The District Attorney's Office is now considering the case for a third time. Criminal filing was also sought from the State Attorney General, but rejected there as well.
>
> *Id.*

19 *Id.* at 3 (stating that it had been reported as checked out for court by an officer who had not actually checked out the large amount of narcotics). This amounts to approximately eight pounds of cocaine. Matt Lait, *A 2nd Rampart Officer Tells of Corruption*, LA Times, January 28, 2000, at 1.

20 Rampart Report, *supra* note 1, at 3. 21 *Id.*

22 *Id.* Further investigation also revealed that the cocaine was not needed for any court hearing.

23 *Id.* at 3. 24 *Id.* 25 The jury was hung 8–4, in favor of conviction. *Id.* 26 *Id.*

27 *Id.*

a plea bargain. In exchange for his cooperation in exposing the extent of corruption in the Rampart Division, prosecutors recommended a reduced sentence.[28]

As part of his plea, Officer Perez then shared "a flood of secrets about his own misconduct and that of others in the Rampart Division, particularly its brutal anti-gang unit."[29] Perez claimed that he and others in the Rampart Division "routinely framed innocent people, falsified documents, and committed perjury in court to send [their] victims to jail."[30] The case of Javier Francisco Ovando perhaps best demonstrates the seriousness of the misconduct present in the Rampart Division.[31] Police shot Ovando in 1996 after an alleged gang raid by Officer Perez and his partner Nino Durden.[32] Perez and Durden then planted a gun on Ovando and accused Ovando of trying to attack them.[33] Ovando was left paralyzed from the waist down as a result of the shooting.[34] Perez later admitted to making up the story and planting a firearm with an obliterated serial number on Ovando.[35] Prosecutors then charged Ovando, and the trial court handed down a twenty-three-year prison sentence as a result of Perez and Durden's testimony.[36] Ovando served two years and six months in prison for a crime he did not commit before he was exonerated by Perez's admissions.[37]

Perez's allegations sent shockwaves through the city of Los Angeles. Less than a decade after the Rodney King incident, the LAPD was embroiled in another, perhaps even more egregious, scandal – what came to be known as the Rampart scandal. Scholars like Erwin Chemerinsky have called the Rampart scandal the "worst … in the history of Los Angeles."[38]

[28] *Id.* At the time of the Rampart report, "Perez's sentencing [was] being held in abeyance and [was] contingent upon his truthful cooperation" *Id.*

[29] John M. Broder, *Los Angeles Paying Victims $70 Million for Police Graft*, NY Times, April 1, 2005.

[30] Greg Gittrich & Beth Barrett, *LAPD Apocalypse? Cop Scandal Cost May be Colossal, Threatening City Services*, Daily News, February 7, 2000, at N1.

[31] Alexa Haussler, *Rampart Victim to Receive $15M*, Daily News, November 22, 2000, at N1 (stating that the Ovando case "has come to symbolize the Rampart police corruption scandal").

[32] *Victim of Police Framing Gets $15 Million: Los Angeles Police Shot a Former Gang Member and Planted a Gun on Him*, Vancouver Sun, November 22, 2000, at A14.

[33] *Id.* [34] *Id.*

[35] Erica Werner, *Perez Gets 2 Years in Prison; LAPD: Federal Sentence Ends Notorious Rampart Figure's Corruption Case*, Long Beach Press-Telegram, May 7, 2002, at A9.

[36] *Victim of Police Framing Gets $15 million*, *supra* note 32, at A14. [37] *Id.*

[38] Erwin Chemerinsky, *An Independent Analysis of the Los Angeles Police Department's Board of Inquiry Report on the Rampart Scandal*, 34 Loy. LA L. Rev. 545, 549 (2000).

As Professor Chemerinsky argued, the misconduct by officers involved in the Rampart scandal is more characteristic of a "repressive dictator[ship]" or a "police state[]" than a democratic society. Because of officer misconduct, a number of innocent people pled guilty to crimes they didn't commit and were successfully convicted by judges and juries based on "fabricated cases against them."[39] The scandal eventually implicated dozens of officers in the LAPD for various types of misconduct, resulting in the overturning of approximately 100 cases and the review of around 3,000 more.[40]

By February 2000, media reports predicted that the Rampart Division scandal would eventually cost the LAPD, conservatively, around $125 million in civil liability.[41] The LAPD and county prosecutors quickly identified around 100 "defendants whose rights were violated by former Officer Rafael Perez."[42] In total, around seventy officers were the subject of formal disciplinary investigation.[43] And by that point, twenty LAPD officers had been suspended without pay or fired for their role in misconduct, connected to Perez's admissions.[44] As the case unraveled, other officers came forward to tell the press of abhorrent incidents of misconduct. One officer, speaking on a condition of anonymity to a *Los Angeles Times* reporter, described an incident where officers shot and wounded two suspects on New Year's Eve of 1995.[45] While the use of force in that case was deemed "in policy" by the Police Commission in 1996, the officer claimed that the incident was more equivalent to "hunting," as the officer suggested that the suspects may not have even been shooting at the officers.[46] Three of the officers involved in this questionable shooting were later relieved of duty after Perez's admissions.[47]

Experts and public officials quickly weighed in on the sheer extent of the Rampart scandal. Los Angeles County district attorney Gil Garcetti openly told the press that the scandal was "the most important case [he had] seen [his] office handle in [his] 31 years ... It goes to the heart of the criminal justice system."[48] Los Angeles supervisor Zev Yaroslavsky argued that the Rampart scandal's importance goes beyond mere

[39] *Id.* at 121.

[40] Beth Shuster & Vincent J. Schodolski, *Poor Morale Rife in LAPD, Survey Finds*, LA TIMES, September 8, 2000, at A22.

[41] Gittrich & Barrett, *supra* note 30, at N1. [42] *Id.* [43] Werner, *supra* note 35, at A9.

[44] Lait, *supra* note 19, at 1. [45] *Id.* [46] *Id.*

[47] *Id.* The newspaper article states, though, that it was unclear whether this incident was among a handful of incidents that the LAPD Corruption Task Force was actively investigating after the Rampart Division corruption became clear.

[48] *Judge Dismisses 10 More Cases in Corruption Scandal*, LODI NEWS-SENTINEL, January 26, 2000, at 2.

concerns about policing, arguing instead that it "is a dagger aimed at the heart of constitutional democracy."[49] Professor Chemerinsky explained that "[n]othing is more inimical to the rule of law than police officers, sworn to uphold the law, flouting it and using their authority to convict innocent people."[50] Chemerinsky bluntly asserted that, "Rampart is the worst scandal in the history of Los Angeles."[51] Professor Jody David Amour commented that the "scale of [this scandal] is unprecedented."[52]

In the wake of the Rampart scandal revelations, the LAPD seemed to be the prime target for federal intervention. This chapter tells the story of the LAPD undergoing federal intervention via § 14141. It seems fitting that the LAPD, which inspired the passage of § 14141 with its traumatizing wrongdoing in the Rodney King case, ultimately became the largest department to date overhauled by the statute. Federal intervention wasn't easy in Los Angeles. But with the help of federal oversight, the LAPD made a significant turnaround. By virtually any measure, the LAPD appears to be a better department today than it was during the Rampart scandal. Given the scope of misconduct in the LAPD and the previous resistance to reform efforts, the LAPD success story is particularly instructive. So how did federal intervention help Los Angeles overhaul its police department?

A confluence of separate circumstances seems to have contributed to the LAPD success story. For one thing, federal intervention forced Los Angeles to invest in costly police misconduct reforms, including additional training, oversight, and a computerized early intervention system. Despite mounting local support for police reform after the Rodney King and Rampart scandals, it was not until federal intervention that the city finally dedicated the necessary resources to combat police misconduct. Federal intervention also contributed to a change in leadership in the LAPD. The importance of this change in leadership can hardly be overstated. Soon after the initiation of federal intervention, Los Angeles named William Bratton as the new chief of the LAPD. Bratton, who was serving as a member of the monitoring team overseeing LAPD at the time, seems to have played a pivotal role in implementing the elements of the consent decree. Various interviewees identified Bratton's appointment as a turning point in the LAPD's transformation.

Additionally, the consent decree in Los Angeles required the appointment of an external monitor to oversee the LAPD for over a decade. This external monitor used innovative methods to measure whether officers

[49] Chemerinsky, *supra* note 38, at 550. [50] *Id.* 549. [51] *Id.*
[52] Gittrich & Barrett, *supra* note 30, at N1.

were complying with stated mandates. This external monitoring also created an extensive database of publicly available information on front-line officer behavior, thereby increasing transparency and accountability. Further, the presence of the federal consent decree allowed leadership in the LAPD to institute potentially unpopular policy reforms. This exemplifies how federal intervention is effective, in part, because of its apparent ability to elevate the importance of oversight and accountability relative to other considerations. And finally, while federal intervention in Los Angeles was expensive, it may eventually pay for itself through reductions in civil liability. Empirical measures suggest that the LAPD was likely engaged in less misconduct at the end of federal intervention. It seems to be no coincidence, then, that the Los Angeles saw an apparent reduction in the number of civil judgments against the city for police misconduct over the period of federal intervention. This is a particularly encouraging development, as it suggests that federal intervention, while costly, may ultimately pay for itself through reductions in civil liability.

Combined, these circumstances – facilitated by federal intervention – helped Los Angeles turn around its troubled police department. Los Angeles is not unique in this respect. The circumstances that helped Los Angeles overhaul its police department appear to be the same factors that have helped numerous police departments across the country achieve similar success with federal intervention. In addition to telling the LAPD story, this chapter weaves in examples from other police departments across the country that have similarly benefited from the unique characteristics of federal intervention.

Nevertheless, it appears that federal intervention is neither necessary nor sufficient for constitutional reform. Federal intervention is not a silver bullet. Real, long-lasting police reform requires local cooperation and dedication to succeed. There is little evidence in Los Angeles or elsewhere to suggest that the DOJ can use federal intervention to overhaul a police agency with defiant and stubborn leadership. This raises serious questions about the viability of federal intervention as a regulatory mechanism. The process also puts a large upfront financial burden on targeted municipalities. Even in smaller departments, the price tag of full-scale federal intervention has commonly exceeded $50 million. The vast majority of this financial burden falls on local police agencies over a relatively short period of time. This raises concerns about the feasibility of federal intervention in poorer communities.

Additional questions remain about whether targeted agencies will sustain reforms after federal intervention ends, and whether intervention correlates with reductions in police aggressiveness. In Los Angeles, there is little evidence that federal intervention correlated with a reduction in police aggressiveness or an increase in crime. In fact, federal intervention correlated with a historic crime decline in the city of Los Angeles. Crime in the city declined far more than the national average and more than virtually any other city in the country during the Intervention Era. But the same cannot be said for all local police departments. In fact, there is some evidence to suggest that federal intervention may be associated with a statistically significant increase in crime rates, particularly in the early years. While these changes are not large, they still represent a potential cost associated with federal intervention – one that shouldn't be dismissed lightly.

Overall, the Los Angeles case study is encouraging. With the help of federal intervention, Los Angeles seemed to experience a reduction in police misconduct at the same time when it underwent a historic crime decline. It appears the LAPD improved the constitutionality of its police actions without compromising public safety or police aggressiveness. More research is needed to determine how exportable the LAPD model is to other municipalities.

I The Bad Old Days in Los Angeles Policing

Two major events precipitated the eventual federal oversight of the LAPD: the beating of Rodney King and the revelations surrounding the Rampart scandal. The national media heavily scrutinized both incidents. The DOJ initiated a formal § 14141 investigation into the LAPD after the Rodney King beating. But the DOJ did not formally determine that the LAPD was engaged in a pattern or practice of misconduct until the Rampart scandal made national news. This section summarizes each of these events and the evidence of systemic misconduct that emerged thereafter.

A Rodney King: The First Evidence of Systematic Misconduct

Chapter 2 has already detailed the specifics of the Rodney King incident. Remember, it was the Rodney King incident that galvanized congressional interest in passing § 14141.[53] Without the George Holliday

[53] Darrell L. Ross, Civil Liability in Criminal Justice 185 (2012) (identifying the King beating as a major turning point in police regulation, precipitating § 14141); Jack

video,[54] § 14141 may have never become law. In Los Angeles, the King incident sparked community demands for action,[55] after LAPD chief Darryl Gates referred to the incident as a mere "aberration."[56] Soon after the King incident, local leaders in Los Angeles convened an independent commission, later referred to as the Christopher Commission, to investigate the event.[57]

While the King beating itself served as a startling example of misconduct, the events that followed also demonstrated the depth of problems facing the LAPD. For instance, immediately after the incident, one of King's passengers alerted Paul King, Rodney King's brother, about the incident.[58] Paul King then went to the Foothill Police Station to file a formal complaint about his brother's treatment.[59] The sergeant who helped King's brother brought him to an interview room where he had King's brother wait for thirty minutes at one point.[60] During the interaction, the sergeant allegedly questioned the brother about whether he had been in any trouble – a question that understandably bothered King's brother, who was there to merely report his brother's mistreatment.[61] The sergeant eventually told King's brother that the LAPD was actively investigating Rodney King.[62] The sergeant then remarked that Rodney King was in "big trouble" for "put[ting] someone's life in danger, possibly a police officer."[63] King's brother left the

R. GREENE, THE ENCYCLOPEDIA OF POLICE SCIENCE: A-I, INDEX 415 (2007) (also pointing to the King incident as a precipitator to § 14141 passage).

54 *Tape of Police Beating Causes Major Furor*, SEATTLE TIMES, March 6, 1991, at A2.

55 *An Aberration or Police Business as Usual?* NY TIMES, March 10, 1994, at 47 ("More than 1,000 callers from around the country phoned Mr. Gates's office expressing their outrage and demanding that he resign"); INDEP. COMM'N ON THE L.A. POLICE DEP'T, REPORT OF THE INDEPENDENT COMMISSION ON THE LOS ANGELES POLICE DEPARTMENT 3 (1991) [hereinafter CHRISTOPHER COMMISSION REPORT] ("Within days, television stations across the country broadcast and rebroadcast the tape, provoking a public outcry against police abuse").

56 David Parrish, *Police "Street Justice" Called Normal Conduct*, DAILY NEWS, March 10, 1991, at N1 (quoting Chief Gates as saying that the event was an aberration and that "It's not the kind of conduct that we have normally from our officers").

57 CHRISTOPHER COMMISSION REPORT, *supra* note 55.

58 *Id.* at 9 (explaining how Bryant Allen awakened Paul King around 4:00 AM to tell him that his brother had been beaten and arrested by the police).

59 *Id.* 9 and 10 ("Paul King said he wanted to make a complaint about his brother").

60 *Id.* at 10 (describing how the sergeant was in and out of the room during the entire forty-minute interaction, with the sergeant once leaving for about thirty minutes).

61 *Id.* In response to this line of questioning, "Paul King responded that he was there to talk about Rodney King, not himself." *Id.*

62 *Id.*

63 *Id.* The officer also told Paul King that his brother "had been caught in a high-speed chase going over 100 m.p.h. or so . . . ." *Id.*

precinct without having the opportunity to formally fill out any complaint form.[64] George Holliday also made an attempt to contact the same Foothill Police Station the following day.[65] Holliday inquired into Rodney King's condition and notified the LAPD that he had witnessed the event.[66] The desk officer he spoke with, though, told him that he could not release information on Rodney King's condition and made no effort to learn any of the details that Holliday had witnessed at the scene.[67] "Confronted with what he viewed as disinterest on the part of the LAPD, Holliday made arrangements with a Los Angeles television station to broadcast the videotape."[68]

After the events, details began to emerge about the background of the officers involved in the beating. Dozens of officers had appeared at the scene of the beating at some point.[69] Four officers were directly involved in the use of illegal force against King – Sergeant Koon and Officers Powell, Briseno, and Wind.[70] One of the officers involved in the beating had previously been suspended for sixty-six days in 1987 for beating a handcuffed man.[71] The other three officers had been subject to various complaints for excessive use of force – most of which had been found to be unsubstantiated by the LAPD.[72] Another ten officers were physically

[64] *Id.* As Paul King later remarked, "I knew I hadn't made a complaint." *Id.*

[65] *Id.* at 9, 11 (stating that Paul King went into the station on March 3 and George Holliday on March 4).

[66] *Id.* at 11. [67] *Id.* [68] *Id.*

[69] *Id.* The Report further clarified that these officers varied in age between twenty-three and forty-eight. Of the officers at the scene, two were African American, four were Latino, and seventeen were white. *Id.*

[70] *Id.*

[71] Seth Mydans, *Videotaped Beating by Officers Puts Full Glare on Brutality Issue*, NY Times, March 18, 1991, at A1. One officer ever told a reporter from the *New York Times* of the "magic pencil" that police officers used to make such misconduct allegations disappear. *Id.*

[72] Christopher Commission Report, *supra* note 55, at 12. The full explanation of the officers past misconduct is reproduced below:

> According to press reports, another officer has been suspended for five days in 1986 for failing to report his use of force against a suspect following a vehicle pursuit and a foot chase. (The suspect's excessive force complaint against the office was held "not sustained" by the LAPD.) A third indicted officer was the subject of a 1986 "not sustained" complaint for excessive force against a handcuffed suspect. Since the King incident, that officer has been sued by a citizen who alleges that the officer broke his arm by hitting him with a baton in 1989.
>
> *Id.*

present, primarily as bystanders, during the incident.[73] Of these ten bystander officers, four were actually field training officers who were "responsible for supervising 'probationary' officers in their first year after graduation from the Police Academy."[74]

The Rodney King events reminded many observers of the Dalton Avenue Case that had happened three years earlier.[75] In that case, dozens of LAPD officers allegedly "invaded the homes of two black families and engaged in what one lawyer called 'an orgy of violence,' ripping out sinks and toilets and smashing windows and television sets, apparently in retaliation for a telephoned threat to a police station."[76] Notably, officers also allegedly wrote the words "LAPD Rules" on the outside wall of the building.[77] The LAPD eventually settled lawsuits by the residents in 1990 for approximately $3 million.[78]

As discussed earlier in Chapter 2, observers widely condemned the behavior of the officers involved in the King beating, [79] while Chief Gates of the LAPD insisted that the events were the result of a few bad officers, not any systemic problems within the department.[80] Later that month Gates announced a "10-Point Plan" intended to understand why the officers involved in the King beating "engaged in such lawlessness."[81] Gates also made various personnel changes,[82] including firing some of the officers involved in the beating.[83] After a failed attempt to prosecute

[73] *Id.* at 11 ("Ten other LAPD officers were actually present on the ground during some portion of the beating").

[74] *Id.* at 11 and 12.

[75] Myrdans, *supra* note 72; *see also* John L. Mitchell, *The Raid that Still Haunts*, L.A. TIMES, March 14, 2001, at 1.

[76] Myrdans, *supra* note 72. [77] *Id.* [78] *Id.*

[79] *Id.* (explaining how President George H. W. Bush called the events "shocking" and called for the DOJ to investigate the incident; also explaining how Professor Jerome Skolnick argued that the violent confrontation "was going to be the historical event for police in our time" and further predicting that the behavior was indicative of a larger problem in the LAPD, explaining that "[t]wo people can go crazy, but if you have 10 or 12 people watching them and not doing anything, this tells you that this is a normal thing for them.").

[80] CHRISTOPHER COMMISSION REPORT, *supra* note 55, at 12 (citing Chief Gates as describing the beating as "shocking"); Parrish, *supra* note 56 (explaining that the events were a mere aberration and not indicative of a broader problem).

[81] CHRISTOPHER COMMISSION REPORT, *supra* note 55, at 13 (referencing the entirety of the 10-Point Plan, which is included as an appendix in the report).

[82] *Id.* ("The Valley Bureau commander was reassigned to the LAPD headquarters and an African American officer was made commander of patrol officers at the Foothill Division").

[83] *Id.* (explaining that one of the officers had been fired and the other three directly involved in the beating were set to face administrative hearings as the department sought their dismissal).

the officers involved in the beating in state court, federal prosecutors ultimately secured convictions against two of the officers.[84]

In the aftermath of these events, the city of Los Angeles formed an independent commission to formally investigate the conditions that precipitated the Rodney King incident, headed by Warren Christopher.[85] The report filed by this commission came to be informally known as the Christopher Commission Report. The Christopher Commission Report found a wide range of systematic problems affecting the LAPD including problems with use-of-force, complaint procedures, training policies, and structural organization. First, the commission found a startling pattern of excessive use of force among a small portion of officers. While the vast majority of LAPD officers had only one or two allegations of excessive force, around "183 officers had four or more allegations, 44 had six or more, 16 had eight or more, and one had 16 such allegations."[86] The overwhelming majority of all officers had fewer than five reported uses of force.[87] Even so, a small cohort of officers accounted for a large amount of all use-of-force reports.[88] Among the officers who were subject to the most allegations of excessive use-of-force, "the performance evaluation reports for [these problematic officers] were very positive" as they "document[ed] every complimentary comment received and express[ed] optimism about the officer's progress in the Department."[89]

Second, the LAPD insufficiently responded to civilian complaints. The commission reviewed "83 civil lawsuits alleging excessive or improper force by LAPD officers for the period 1986 through 1990 that resulted in a settlement or judgment of more than $15,000."[90] This review showed that the majority of "cases involved clear and often egregious misconduct resulting in serious injury or death to the victim."[91] Of particular note, the commission found that the LAPD's internal investigation into the

[84] *Id.* The Los Angeles District Attorney's Office secured criminal indictments against Sergeant Koon and Officers Powell, Briseno, and Wind. The District Attorney's Office did not seek indictments against the seventeen officers who were at the scene and "did not attempt to prevent the beating or report it to their superiors." And the prosecution resulted in an acquittal, followed by days of chaos and rioting in Los Angeles and the surrounding areas. Although federal prosecutors successfully secured convictions against two of the officers involved, such an effort provided no deterrent for "the dozen officers present for the beating."

[85] *See generally* CHRISTOPHER COMMISSION REPORT, *supra* note 55. [86] *Id.* at ix and x.

[87] *Id.*

[88] *Id.* (explaining that "63 officers had 20 or more reports each" and "[t]he top 5% of the officers [ranked by number of reports] accounted for more than 20% of all reports").

[89] *Id.* [90] *Id.* at xi. [91] *Id.*

events surrounding these eighty-three lawsuits were regularly "light or non-existent."[92] The commission also found that the LAPD's internal procedures for handling citizen complaints frequently led to public frustration. Out of 2,152 citizen allegations of excessive force, the LAPD sustained only 42.[93] This means that the LAPD sustained roughly 1–2 percent of all citizen complaints for excessive use of force. This was, in part, because the part of the police department responsible for investigating these claims – the Internal Affairs Division (IAD) – had limited resources.[94] Once more, the commission determined that internal policies and procedures used by the IAD make it difficult for citizens to file complaints. For example, "[s]ome intake officers actively discourage filing by being uncooperative or requiring long waits before completing a complaint form."[95] It seemed Paul King's experience was no aberration.[96] The commission's review of 700 cases found that complaint files regularly included no explanation about whether the investigators had sought to identify or locate witnesses.[97] The files also demonstrated that the LAPD used a "flawed" adjudication process.[98] This, in part, explained the relatively low rate at which the department held officers accountable for accused misconduct.

Third, the LAPD's training programs were unsatisfactory. Normally, LAPD officers undergo through three different training phases.[99] Officers get their initial training at the police academy.[100] After this, officers go through a probationary period for one year when they work in the field with more experienced officers.[101] After this, officers receive continuing in-service training.[102] Such systematic misconduct could be traced back to

[92] *Id.* [93] *Id.* at xix.

[94] *Id.* (explaining that "[g]enerally IAD investigates only a few cases because of limited resources").

[95] *Id.*

[96] *Id.* at 10 (describing how the sergeant was in and out of the room during the entire forty-minute interaction, with the sergeant once leaving for about thirty minutes).

[97] *Id.* at xix. It is worth noting that the commission found that "on the whole ... [the complaint investigations] were of a higher quality than the division investigations," even if they did have many serious problems. *Id.*

[98] *Id.* at xx. The commission reached this conclusion because it found that there was no uniform method for categorizing witnesses as involved or not involved in the incident. It also found that when evaluating the reliability of witness testimony, commanding officers appear to make inconsistent decisions. It also noted that the punishment was typically lenient in cases where a complaint was sustained. Punishment appeared to be more tailored to how embarrassing the punishment was to the department's reputation rather than how the conduct put a citizen's wellbeing in jeopardy. And it found that excessive force was generally treated more leniently than other forms of misconduct. *Id.*

[99] *Id.* at xvi. [100] *Id.* [101] *Id.* [102] *Id.*

training programs that emphasized the use of physical force as opposed to verbal skills. De-escalation should be an important component of training at every stage.[103] Additionally, the commission found that the requirements for training officers were insufficient.[104]

Fourth, the LAPD's structural organization made it difficult for outsiders to hold the police chief responsible for organizational deficiencies. At the time of the King incident, Los Angeles had a unique organizational structure for regulating and monitoring police behavior. The city utilized a "five-member Board of Police Commissioners, which [was] designated the 'head' of the Department and given the express authority to 'supervise, control, regulate, and manage' the Department."[105] The Police Commission also had the authority to appoint, remove, and discipline the police chief.[106] The mayor appointed individuals to the Police Commission and also had the authority to remove individuals.[107] Thus, it became practice for incoming mayors to replace the entire Police Commission upon election.[108] Los Angeles was also unique in that its police chief was insulated from removal or serious disciplinary action absent a showing of "good and sufficient cause."[109] This unique level of job protection came from a 1937 initiative, when voters in the city of Los Angeles "gave the chief the strong civil service job protection previously held only by lower level police officers – a decision that has made Los Angeles one of the few major cities in the country in which the Chief of Police has the prospect of life tenure."[110] This type of civil service protection for the police chief was intended to "provide independence from improper political pressure."[111] But, in practice, it made it nearly impossible to hold a police chief accountable for problems within his or her department.[112] Thus, it should not be a surprise that Chief Gates

103 *Id.* The commission also found that training did not emphasize culture respect and awareness enough. *Id.*

104 *Id.* at xvii. These field training officers (FTOs) "guide new officers' first contacts with citizens and have primary responsibility for introducing the probationers to the culture and traditions of the Department." *Id.* Thus, it should be no surprise that the commission felt that these officers' conduct was critical in ensuring an adequate training program. The requirements for these FTOs were considered insufficient since "there are no formal eligibility or disqualification criteria for the FTO position based on an applicant's disciplinary records." *Id.*

105 *Id.* at 184. 106 *Id.* 107 *Id.*

108 *Id.* ("Police Commissioners are ostensibly appointed for five-year, staggered terms, but in practice, they have served at the pleasure of the Mayor and are usually replaced when a new administration comes in").

109 *Id.* at 185. 110 *Id.* at 186. 111 *Id.*

112 The Christopher Commission Report offers a very thorough explanation of the type of procedural hurdles that would face the city of Los Angeles in the event that the Police

served over fourteen years as the top executive of the LAPD before his eventual resignation. This was, in part, because the Police Commission had generally adopted a "passive role" acting primarily as a "rubber stamp" for the police department.[113] Despite the fact that the Police Commission was supposed to be a check on the LAPD, the head of the Police Commission, known as the commanding officer, often felt that disagreeing with the police chief could put his or her job in jeopardy.[114]

In addition, several other systematic problems existed, including startling individual cases of documented racism.[115] In total, the commission found there was a pattern of misconduct present within the LAPD that was caused by departmental policy, organizational structure, and agency culture. The Christopher Commission Report made several specific recommendations for how the LAPD could correct some of these problems – including the use of more community-oriented forms

Commission wanted to remove the chief of police. City law required that, in order to remove the police chief, the Police Commission needed to go through "protracted and cumbersome procedures." The City Charter provides that the chief's job is a "substantial property right," which cannot be removed without "good and sufficient cause shown upon a finding of 'guilty' of the specific charge or charges assigned as cause or causes therefore after a full, fair and impartial hearing." This hearing was required to occur before a Civil Service Board. The chief is also given the opportunity to appeal his removal via a writ of mandamus in the superior court. The chief may also challenge his removal, since it is a substantial property right, in state or federal courts, as a violation of his procedural due process rights. Combined, these procedural hurdles mean that the cost of removing a police chief is particularly high. *Id.* at 200.

[113] *Id.* at 187.

[114] *Id.* The commission reports that the commanding officer often finds himself in the middle of a battle between the Police Commission and the police chief:

> The Commanding Officer's future transfer and promotion are to a substantial extent at the discretion of the Chief of Police, and he or she is part of the Chief's command structure as well as being answerable to the Police Commission. If there is a conflict between the Police Commission and the Chief, the Commanding Officer can be caught in the middle ... [As a result,] [i]n recent years the Police Commission has gone as far as to require that all commanders apply for the Commission Operations position, out of fear that given a choice, none would apply.
>
> *Id.*

[115] *Id.* at xii. The commission cited several specific examples of racist behaviors by LAPD officers – documented cases where officers referred to interactions with minority residents as "monkey slapping time," and among other choice comments. *Id.* Shortly before the King beating, in fact, two of the officers involved were comparing a domestic dispute between two African American individuals to "gorillas in the Mist" over the radio. *Id.* at 14. More disturbingly, evidence suggests that leadership within the police department heard or knew of these kinds of statements but did nothing to stop them or punish those involved. *Id.* at xii and xiii.

of policing,[116] the recruitment of more minority officers,[117] changes in complaint-processing procedures,[118] improvements in training policies,[119] and some significant structural changes.[120]

Los Angeles adopted some of these recommended reforms. Los Angeles voters passed an amendment giving the city council the authority to review and override the Police Commission.[121] City voters also passed City Charter Amendment F, which "reformed the City's procedures for selection and retention of the Chief of Police."[122] This measure provided that police chiefs were to serve five-year terms and at the pleasure of city officials – effectively ending the civil service protection for chiefs.[123] The measure also barred any individual from serving more than ten years as chief in total.[124] The thoroughness of the Christopher Commission Report itself demonstrated the willingness of the city of Los Angeles to critically explore the problems plaguing the police department. It demonstrated that the city was prepared to take many significant steps to reform departmental policies in a way that would prevent misconduct in the future. Years later, though, the circumstances surrounding the Rampart Division scandal again put the LAPD at the center of a national controversy linked to systemic problems with departmental policies and procedures.

B Five Years after the King Beating: Reform Efforts Begin in Earnest

Five years after the Rodney King incident, the independent commission on the LAPD requested a follow-up report on whether the LAPD implemented the recommended reforms.[125] Overall, this report found that the LAPD had made some substantial changes – including the decreasing of use-of-force incidents, virtually eliminating the use of the baton, improving diversity, and increasing the quality of internal

[116] *Id.* at xiv and xv. [117] *Id.* at xvi and xviii. [118] *Id.* at xix and xx.
[119] *Id.* at xvi and xviii. [120] *Id.* at xxi and xxii. [121] *Id.*
[122] MERRICK J. BOBB, MARK H EPSTEIN, NICOLAS H. MILLER, AND MANUEL A. ABASCAL, FIVE YEARS LATER: A REPORT TO THE LOS ANGELES POLICE COMMISSION ON THE LOS POLICE DEPARTMENT'S IMPLEMENTATION OF INDEPENDENT COMMISSION RECOMMENDATIONS (May 1996) [hereinafter FIVE YEARS LATER REPORT ON LAPD], *text available at* www.parc.info/client_files/Special%20Reports/2%20-%20Five%20Years%20Later%20-%20Christopher%20Commission.pdf.
[123] *Id.* at 68. [124] *Id.*
[125] *Id.* at ii ("This Commission has asked for an investigation and a report on the status of the Christopher Commission reforms").

affairs investigations.[126] This follow-up report, though, mentioned that the LAPD was still spending too much money on civil lawsuits.[127] Perhaps most worrisome, though, is the fact that five years after the Rodney King beating, "there [was] still no comprehensive system in place to collect, analyze, and disseminate data on the risk of excessive force."[128] Consequently, the LAPD could not demonstrate that it had established sufficiently rigorous standards for holding managers and supervisors accountable for their "management of liability risk."[129]

First, after the King incident, the LAPD implemented various reforms that successfully reduced the use of unlawful force – particularly the frequent and unlawful use of the baton.[130] It is challenging to make any definitive conclusions in this regard because of a "lack of an adequate database" on use-of-force claims.[131] But limitations aside, it appears that the amount of use-of-force incidents decreased substantially in the years after Rodney King.[132] Of course, this decline is to be expected, as crime in Los Angeles declined substantially during this time period. The amount of injuries to officers per use-of-force incident remained relatively stable throughout the time period,[133] while the rate of injuries to suspects decreased somewhat.[134] The raw percentage of suspects injured in use-of-force incidents also declined a bit.[135] Overall, this data suggests that the LAPD might have been in the process of improving use-of-force

[126] *Id.* at v. The report also mentions that these reforms have been successfully achieved without a subsequent increase in crime that many residents "feared" would be an inevitable result of such reforms. The report also suggests, though, that demographic decrease in the relative number of young adults may explain the subsequent reduction in crime in Los Angeles – further obscuring the actual effect of these reforms on crime rates. *Id.*

[127] *Id.* (stating that the LAPD spent around $67.5 million on litigation costs between 1991 and 1995, an average of about $13.5 per year).

[128] *Id.* [129] *Id.*

[130] *Id.* at 1 (explaining the central three findings: first, officers appear no less likely to use reasonable force since the King reforms; second, the officers are using batons less frequently – a particular concern raised after the King incident; and third, officers have not replaced baton use with other, more deadly forms of force).

[131] *Id.* at 3.

[132] *Id.* at 4 ("Thus, the number of both use of force incidents and officer-involved shootings declined dramatically between 1990 and 1995").

[133] *Id.* at 13 (showing in figure 6 that the injuries per incident fluctuated over this time period between as low as once per 6.2 incidents to once to 4.3 incidents – with no clear pattern evident).

[134] *Id.* at 12 (showing in figure 5 that the rate of injuries per shooting and deaths per shooting decreased somewhat in the time period after the King incident).

[135] *Id.* at 9 (showing in table 4 that the percentage of suspects injured in use-of-force incidents declined from 54 percent in 1990 to 42 percent in 1995).

procedures after the King incident, although progress was tough to measure because of poor data-recording practices.

Second, the LAPD attempted to address concerns about racism and bias after the King incident by increasing the hiring of minority officers. In June 1990, minorities constituted around 37 percent of the total sworn officer force – with African American officers representing 13 percent of the force and Latinos 21 percent.[136] By March 1996, minority officers made up around 46 percent of the sworn force – with African Americans sitting at around 14 percent and Latinos around 28 percent.[137] Thus, there was measureable improvement in this regard. But there was substantial room for improvement if the LAPD was to roughly match the composition of the community.[138] Unfortunately, subsequent investigations concluded that the department had made "insufficient" progress in training officers in "cultural awareness."[139]

Third, while the LAPD made progress in improving its complaint policies and procedures, many of the basic problems identified by the Christopher Commission remained.[140] Complaint processing in Los Angeles goes through four steps – intake, investigation, classification, and punishment.[141] LAPD officers discouraged residents from filing complaints at the intake stage. And at the investigation and classification stage, LAPD officers almost always adjudicated complaints in favor of the officers.[142] Penalties for excessive use of force were too lenient.[143] While there are ways to measure the appropriateness of internal adjudication of complaints, there is virtually no way to determine how often the LAPD discouraged complaints at the intake stage. If officers were making efforts to discourage complaints at the intake stage, we should expect there to be no formal record of these complaints. Thus, while complaints for excessive use of force appear to have declined significantly after the King incident, it is difficult to conclude whether this is the result of an

[136] *Id.* at 20–22 (mentioning these exact statistics and offering a more detailed breakdown of the numbers in table 1).

[137] *Id.* at 23.

[138] *Id.* ("[I]t appears that with the exception of African-Americans, the LAPD still has a way to go before its composition reflects the diversity either of the City's population or the County's labor pool, although progress continues to be made").

[139] *Id.* at 27 and 28 ("It is insufficient that so few members of the Department have been exposed to cultural awareness training in the five years since the Christopher Report").

[140] *Id.* at 34 (explaining that while many trends suggest improvement in the complaint policies and procedures, "some problems identified by the Christopher Commission persist").

[141] *Id.* at 35. [142] *Id.* at 36. [143] *Id.*

improvement in policy or the continuation of informal policies to discourage residents from filing complaints at the intake stage.[144] A quick reading of the complaint files from the time period suggests a continued pattern of "egregious and disturbing" behavior.[145] Various problems also appeared to continue in the investigation,[146] classification,[147] and punishment.[148] While there may have been some progress in the complaint process, many of the same concerns identified in the wake of the Rodney King incident remained in place years later.

Fourth, years after the King incident, the LAPD had still not adopted a sufficiently thorough early warning and risk management system.[149] The city of Los Angeles paid a substantial amount of money to settle litigation in the years following the Rodney King beating.[150] By attempting to identify and control "at-risk officers and at-risk situations," the LAPD could have saved Los Angeles taxpayers significant amounts of money.[151] At the time of this report, the LAPD utilized a computerized system called TEAMS to monitor at-risk officers.[152] But this system was "weak and inadequate," as it provided only limited data to supervising officers.[153] The system did not provide supervisors with the ability to do "automated trend analysis," and the LAPD sometimes took years to upload data into the system.[154] The LAPD had also not clearly articulated standards by which officers would be held accountable for data loaded

[144] *Id.* at 38 (stating that "we cannot determine from these statistics whether this decline is a result of changed behavior by LAPD officers, a reduction in the public's willingness to purse formal complaints back to pre-Rodney King levels, or a combination of both").

[145] *Id.* at 39 (giving as an example an incident where an officer drove up to an African-American pedestrian and sprayed the individual with pepper spray and called him a racial slur).

[146] *Id.* at 40 and 41 (explaining a host of concerns, including the fact that officers were often not questioned as seriously or rigorously as witnesses or complainants).

[147] *Id.* at 41–43 (identifying any of the persistent concerns about classification identified in the Christopher Commission Report).

[148] *Id.* at 44–47 (showing that punishment for force-related misconduct actually decreased after the King incident, as seen in table 1).

[149] *Id.* at 55 and 56 (explaining that the implementation of such a system is necessary to identify and neutralize officers that pose a high risk of litigation expenses to the city).

[150] *Id.* at 55 (putting this number at $67.5 million between 1991 and 1995, and $13.6 million in 1995 alone).

[151] *Id.* [152] *Id.* at 59.

[153] *Id.* ("At best, TEAMS will provide only limited data – principally raw numbers – on citizen complaints and Internal Affairs investigations, officer-involved shootings, use of force, and some court judgments, . . . among other categories of information").

[154] *Id.* at 59 and 60.

into the TEAMS system.[155] Without a formalized policy on how to use the data in the TEAMS system, the report found that the system did little to formally identify problematic officers.

With all this said, it is worth noting that the LAPD had made some of the reforms recommended in the Christopher Commission. The city of Los Angeles removed the civil service protection that prevented city officials from seriously disciplining or discharging the police chief.[156] As discussed earlier, the new standards established in City Charter Amendment F established that a police chief was to serve at the pleasure of city officials.[157] The chief was to serve one five-year term, renewable only once by the authority of the Police Commission.[158] No chief was permitted to serve more than ten years in total.[159] The city also adopted some of the Christopher Commission recommendations regarding the composition of the Los Angeles Police Commission.[160] One of the notable recommendations not implemented after the Christopher Commission was the hiring of additional staff to assist the Police Commission in investigations and oversight.[161] Another critical recommendation from the Christopher Commission had been implemented five years after the King beating – the appointment of an inspector general responsible for overseeing "receipt of citizen complaints, monitoring the progress of complaints through the Internal Affairs investigation process, and auditing the results of those investigations."[162]

In summary, in the years after the King incident, it appeared that the LAPD made some progress in addressing the systematic problems identified in the Christopher Commission Report. But some of the most egregious issues remained. The LAPD still lacked an early warning and risk management system to ensure accountability and limit civil liability. There remained serious questions about the procedures and policies for dealing with citizen complaints. While the force appeared to be increasingly diverse, training on cultural awareness and sensitivity did not appear to be prioritized. And while the LAPD had made progress, there

155 *Id.* at 60 (explaining that the LAPD "had not issued standards for use of statistical information that adequately address" officers' concerns).

156 *Id.* at 67. 157 *Id.* at 68. 158 *Id.* 159 *Id.*

160 *Id.* (explaining that after the Christopher Commission recommendations, the Police Commission remains a five-person body, but now only includes individuals who can serve a maximum of two five-year terms).

161 *Id.* 68 and 69 (in particular, the Christopher Commission recommended the hiring of auditors, accountants, investigations, and more attorneys – a recommendation that appears to have gone largely unheeded).

162 *Id.* at 69.

remained significant work to be done. In the years after the King incident, there seemed to be significant local support for police reform. This reform, though, had only been partially realized.

C *The Rampart Scandal: Evidence of Systemic Misconduct Reemerges*

Less than a decade later, the LAPD was again embroiled in a major misconduct scandal – the so-called Rampart scandal discussed earlier in this chapter – that implicated over a dozen officers in egregious wrongdoing. Credible evidence emerged that dozens of officers had physically abused suspects, committed violent crimes, and planted evidence to frame innocent people. Remember that Professor Chemerinsky described the LAPD's behavior as more characteristic of a "repressive dictator[ship]" or a "police state[]" than a democratic society.[163] Reforming the LAPD was an extraordinary challenge. The LAPD was (and remains) the nation's third largest police department with over 9,000 sworn officers and over 12,000 employees.

The immediate investigation and public report by the LAPD revealed the seriousness of the scandal. But the report treated the Rampart scandal as a mere incident, rather than symptoms of a broader, systematic problem in the LAPD.[164] An independent evaluation of the Rampart scandal by Professor Chemerinsky found there to be a broader pattern of misconduct. According to his report, the LAPD culture "gave rise to and tolerated what occurred in the Rampart Division."[165] The report written by the Independent Board of Inquiry also "fail[ed] to consider the need for structural reform in the department."[166] And the Board of Inquiry minimized the problems with the department's disciplinary system.[167] Other commentators cited the prevalence of an LAPD "code of silence" described as "a misplaced loyalty system whereby cops who swore to uphold the law stand by as their fellow officers maliciously break the law and shame the city."[168] Indeed, the emerging consensus after the Rampart scandal was that the events were not merely the result of

163 Erwin Chemerinsky, *The Rampart Scandal and the Criminal Justice System in Los Angeles County*, 57 GUILD PRACTITIONER 121 (2000).

164 Chemerinsky, *supra* note 38, at 550 (explaining that the report refers to the events as an "incident," which "fails to convey the unconscionability of what occurred").

165 *Id.* at 559.

166 *Id.* at 589. Namely, the LAPD assessment of the events fails to consider the need for reform in the police commission, the need for independence in the inspector general position, and the need for permanent oversight measures.

167 *Id.* at 597. 168 Gittrich & Barrett, *supra* note 30, at N1.

a handful of bad officers. The events happened because of a pattern and practice of unconstitutional misconduct – tolerated by management, sustained by a dangerous culture of misconduct, and perpetuated by permissive policies that failed to properly oversee officer behavior. Given the significant amount of national attention that the Rampart scandal received, it appeared that the table was set for federal intervention pursuant to § 14141.

D *DOJ Intervention*

The DOJ first opened an investigation into the LAPD soon after the passage of § 14141. In fact, the LAPD was among the first departments officially investigated by the DOJ during the Clinton administration.[169] It took nearly four years for the DOJ to conclude (officially, at least) that the LAPD was engaged in a pattern or practice of misconduct in violation of § 14141.[170] As part of this investigation, the DOJ reviewed LAPD policy statements, examined both reports of officer-involved shootings and nonlethal force incidents, evaluated citizen complaints, and collected data on criminal charges brought against LAPD officers.[171] Investigators also coordinated with the Police Commission and the inspector general in Los Angeles to discuss and analyze possible reforms.[172] And investigators met with representatives from the LAPD.[173] This form of investigation is fairly common in most § 14141 cases, as discussed in Chapter 3. The timing of the investigation strongly suggests that the Rampart Division scandal played a pivotal role in initiating DOJ

[169] *See infra* Appendix A. In total, the LAPD was the ninth investigation initiated by the Justice Department after the passage of § 14141 in 1994. The Justice Department officially opened its investigation of the LAPD on July 31, 1996, according to records I obtained from the Justice Department. Among the investigations of large police departments, only the Pittsburgh and New Orleans investigations predated the Los Angeles investigation. The LAPD investigation was started around the same time as the Montgomery County Maryland Police Department and Beverly Hills Police Department investigations.

[170] The investigation started on July 31, 1996. *Id.* The Justice Department found there to be an officially pattern or practice of misconduct on May 8, 2000. OFFICE OF THE INDEPENDENT MONITOR OF THE LOS ANGELES POLICE DEPARTMENT, FINAL QUARTERLY REPORT, Appendix F, at 3 (June 11, 2009) [hereinafter FINAL QUARTERLY REPORT FOR LAPD].

[171] Letter from United States Department of Justice, Civil Rights Division Acting Assistant Attorney General Bill Hahn Lee to Los Angeles City Attorney James K. Hahn (May 8, 2000), at 1 and 2 [hereinafter Investigations Finding Letter to LAPD], *text available at* www.clearinghouse.net/chDocs/public/PN-CA-0002-0001.pdf.

[172] *Id.* 2. [173] *Id.*

action.[174] Qualitative data from interviews with DOJ officials confirms this suspicion. For example, one former DOJ litigator used the Rampart scandal as an example of a situation where a "big expose of a big problem" motivated the DOJ to take action.[175] Another former DOJ litigator agreed, explaining that while the LAPD had "a history of problems," it took the media attention surrounding the Rampart scandal to finally bring the DOJ to act.[176] While the aftermath of the Rodney King incident appears to have caused the DOJ to initially investigate the LAPD, the national exposure of the Rampart scandal presented an ideal opportunity for federal intervention.

In a letter to the city of Los Angeles, the DOJ alleged that the LAPD engaged in a range of misconduct including excessive force, improper officer-involved shootings, improper arrests, improper stop-and-frisks, improper searches of property without adequate probable cause, and improper seizures of property without probable cause.[177] The DOJ investigation concluded that this pattern of misconduct was the result of the LAPD's failure to properly train and supervise officers, as well as the LAPD's failure to investigate and discipline officers after alleged wrongdoing.[178] This failure to properly supervise officers "created an environment where officers may engage in misconduct without detection and intervention by LAPD supervisors."[179] Even from the earliest investigatory stages, the DOJ noted that the LAPD's failure to develop a "comprehensive risk management system to identify patterns of at-risk conduct by individual officers and groups of officers" was a primary culprit.[180] The computerized risk management system that the LAPD implemented in the years after Rodney King was found

[174] The Rampart scandal made national news in 1998. In early 2000, the Board of Inquiry released its official report detailing the misconduct identified as part of the Rampart scandal. Within a few months of this report, the Justice Department officially concluded that there was a pattern or practice of misconduct present in the LAPD. *See* table 1.

[175] Telephone Interview #14, at 4 (July 11, 2013) (transcript on file with author) [hereinafter Interview #14] (stating that "Occasionally they get started when there is a big expose of a big problem in a department . . . Ramparts, for example").

[176] Telephone Interview with Department of Justice Participant #15, at 4 (July 31, 2013) [hereinafter Interview #15] (on file with author) ("The LAPD of course, there had been a history of problems . . . And then the whole controversy broke out in 2000 or 1999, with the Rampart investigation").

[177] Letter from Bill Lann Lee, Acting Assistant Attorney General, Civil Rights Division of the United States Department of Justice, to James K. Hahn, City Attorney, City of Los Angeles 1–2 (May 8, 2000) (on file with author) [hereinafter Letter from DOJ to LA].

[178] *Id.* at 2. [179] *Id.* [180] *Id.*

to be inadequate by the DOJ investigation at identifying patterns of wrongdoing.[181]

The DOJ investigation also found that the LAPD failed to properly respond to citizen complaints.[182] The internal review mechanisms in the LAPD were also deemed inadequate to provide meaningful oversight of frontline officer behavior.[183] While the LAPD had already established an Office of the Inspector General (OIG) and a citizen-run Police Commission to oversee police behavior, the DOJ found these two oversight branches to have inadequate authority and resources to provide meaningful oversight.[184]

The DOJ's choice to intervene in the LAPD was met with some skepticism. As one DOJ official recalled, "[T]he city and the police department [had] plenty of complaints."[185] But within days of the DOJ announcement, Los Angeles City officials seemed resigned to the fact that the LAPD needed some sort of outside assistance in combatting misconduct. City Councilman Mark Ridley-Thomas candidly opined that the LAPD had "blown it and that's why the DOJ has come in."[186] This sentiment mirrored comments made by many on the Los Angeles City Council.[187] Not all members of the city council were supportive of the DOJ intervention. Councilman Nate Holden accused the DOJ of engaging in a "smear tactic," explaining that "[t]his letter . . . is a boilerplate accusation that could be used against any police department in the country."[188]

181 *Id.* ("As the Police Commission acknowledged several years ago, the LAPD's current 'early warning' system, the Training, Evaluation, and Management System ('TEAMS'), is inadequate").

182 *Id.* at 3. The investigative findings went on to state that "because they are unlikely to be discovered and disciplined, officers are not deterred from engaging in misconduct. Similarly, poorly trained officers are not identified for retraining or counseling. Together with the training and supervision deficiencies identified above, inadequate complaint investigations create an environment that allows police misconduct to occur."

183 *Id.* 184 *Id.*

185 Telephone Interview with Department of Justice Participant #18, at 12 (August 8, 2013) [hereinafter Interview #18] (transcript on file with author).

186 Greg Gittrich, Beth Barrett, & Alexa Haussler, *L.A. Admits P.D. Problem; LAPD: But, Says Riordan: "My Preference is Local Control,"* Long Beach Press-Telegram, May 10, 2000, at A10. The councilman continued by stating that "We have to acknowledge that we have failed. We have failed to push forward an agenda of reform of this city that the citizens said in clear terms was a mandate." *Id.*

187 For example, Councilwoman Laura Chick commented that the Justice Department made it clear it was not happy with the "laissez faire" approach taken by the LAPD. *Id.*

188 *Id.*

Mayor Richard Riordan staked out a moderate position on the reforms from the outset. He argued that while reform was necessary, it should happen through the leadership of local officials – not through a full-scale federal takeover.[189] Mayor Riordan also stood behind then police chief Bernard Parks and the LAPD leadership more broadly. As Riordan argued, "[T]here's no one better to make reforms than the chief, the command staff, the Police Commission, the inspector general, the independent task force, the council and myself."[190] He concluded that the current leadership in the city of Los Angeles "can solve [its] own problems."[191] For the city, one particularly frustrating part of the DOJ's investigative findings letter was that, in its eyes, the letter lacked specific examples.[192] While some city officials complained about the lack of supporting evidence in the findings letter, city leaders eventually realized that federal intervention was inevitable.

E Response by Police Union

While city officials came to accept federal intervention, frontline officers were skeptical. As the DOJ began negotiations with the city of Los Angeles, federal officials made a decision that is relatively common in cases of federal intervention – they generally excluded the police union from negotiations. This move did not sit well with frontline officers. In November 2000, only a few months after the DOJ had officially determined that the LAPD was in violation of § 14141, a union representing rank-and-file police officers, the Police Protective League, attempted to intervene and block a proposed negotiated settlement between the city and the federal government.[193] Union President Ted Hunt claimed that the city of Los Angeles "deliberately excluded" union members from consent decree negotiations.[194] Although objectionable, the exclusion of union leaders from § 14141 settlement negotiations is

[189] *Id.* It is also worth noting that Mayor Riordan walked a careful line after the announcement of the impending federal action in Los Angeles. He both acknowledged the presence of a problem, while also not necessarily agreeing with the Justice Department findings that the LAPD was engaged in a pattern or practice of misconduct.

[190] *Id.* [191] *Id.*

[192] *Id.* (explaining that "There were no specific examples of abuse or evidence of corruption cited by Lee in his correspondence").

[193] Joseph Giordono & Jason Kandel, *Police Union Threatens Suit; LAPD: League President Says Officers to File Federal Case About Consent Decree*, LONG BEACH PRESS-TELEGRAM, November 2, 2000, at A8.

[194] *Id.*

commonplace. The Police Protective League filed the motion to intervene in December 2000, claiming a right to dispute the underlying allegations against the LAPD, a need to protect the terms of the collective bargaining agreement, and a need to prevent violations of police officers' constitutional rights.[195] The district court denied the motion to intervene in January 2001.[196] The crux of the Police Protective League's argument was that the implementation of the proposed settlement between the DOJ and the LAPD could influence the terms of the collective bargaining agreement. This closely mirrors other actions taken by police unions in other cities affected by federal intervention pursuant to § 14141.[197]

As a general rule, federal intervention appears to be uniquely successful because it provides police chiefs with legal cover to implement top-down reforms. The DOJ's involvement imbues these reforms with legal and constitutional significance, which increases the probability of frontline officer buy-in. And perhaps even more importantly, federal intervention allows some municipalities to implement dramatic misconduct reforms without navigating the collective bargaining process.[198] The majority of states require departments to bargain with police unions before imposing new policies that may affect any term or condition of employment.[199] The result is that law enforcement executives are often unable to implement radical reforms, even if they may be necessary to address serious misconduct issues within the department.[200] As Professor Harmon has argued, "[c]ollective bargaining ... functions like an immediate tax" on misconduct reforms.[201] A recent examination of nearly 200 collective bargaining agreements found that a substantial number of these contracts limit officer interrogations after alleged misconduct, mandate the destruction of disciplinary records, ban civilian oversight, prevent anonymous civilian complaints, indemnify officers in the event of civil suits, and limit the length of internal investigations.[202]

[195] *See, e.g., United States* v. *City of Los Angeles*, 2:00-cv-11769-GAF-RC (CD Cal. November 8, 2000) (notice of interested parties filed by Los Angeles Police Protective League).

[196] *Id.*

[197] *See* Telephone Interview with Police Administrator #30 (November 19, 2013) [hereinafter Interview #30] (describing the union opposition to these sorts of reforms).

[198] *Id.* [199] Rachel Harmon, *The Problem of Policing*, 761 MICH. L. REV. 797, 799 (2012).

[200] Other scholars have also discussed how collective bargaining affects police departments. *See, e.g.*, Seth Stoughton, *The Incidental Regulation of Policing*, 98 MINN. L. REV. 2205–2217 (2014).

[201] *Id.* [202] Stephen Rushin, Police Union Contracts, 66 DUKE L. J. (forthcoming 2017).

Because federal intervention often results in the implementation of new procedures that regulate departmental disciplinary procedures, police unions have argued that they should be party to any § 14141 proceedings. In previous cases, courts have generally rejected union attempts to intervene and block negotiated settlements reached via § 14141.[203] By doing so, § 14141 provides a narrow way that police departments can sometimes implement significant misconduct reforms without navigating the cumbersome collective bargaining process.

As the late Professor Clyde Summers argued, "The special political structure and procedure of collective bargaining is particularly appropriate for decisions where [public] employees' interests in increased wages and reduced work load run counter to the combined interests of taxpayers and users of public services."[204] As examples, Professor Summers identified "wages, insurance, pensions, sick leave, length of work week, overtime pay, vacations, and holidays" as topics that were "proper subjects for bargaining."[205] Nevertheless, "[d]emands by policemen for disciplinary procedures which effectively foreclose" reasonable accountability measures like the "use of a public review board further illustrate the need to examine each subject to determine whether it should be decided [by] collective bargaining."[206]

This is not to say that § 14141 reform works best when police unions are excluded entirely from the negotiation process. In other cases like Cincinnati, the terms of the negotiated settlement reflected an unprecedented collaboration between the local police union, police leadership, the DOJ, and community stakeholders.[207] Scholars like Professor Kami Chavis Simmons have persuasively argued that this sort of collaborative approach can improve § 14141 enforcement and increase the probability of political and organizational buy-in.[208] Instead, what seems to make

[203] *See supra* Part I (describing how police unions have attempted to intervene, mostly unsuccessfully, into structural police reform litigation under collective bargaining grounds).

[204] Clyde Summers, *Public Employees Bargaining: A Political Perspective*, 83 YALE LJ. 1156, 1194 (1974).

[205] *Id.* [206] *Id.* at 1196.

[207] Joshua M. Chanin, Negotiated Justice? The Legal, Administrative, and Policy Implications of "Pattern or Practice" Police Misconduct Reform 56 (July 6, 2011) (unpub- lished PhD dissertation, American University), *available at* www.ncjrs.gov/pdffiles1/nij/grants/237957.pdf

[208] Kami Chavis Simmons, *The Politics of Policing: Ensuring Stakeholder Collaboration in the Federal Reform of Local Law Enforcement Agencies*, 98 J. CRIM. L. & CRIMINOLOGY 489, 518–519 (2008) (advocating for measures to increase collaboration during federal reforms).

federal intervention effective is its apparent ability to elevate the importance of oversight and accountability relative to other considerations.

II Terms of the Negotiated Settlement

The terms of the negotiated settlement in Los Angeles roughly mirrored those commonly found in other cities. The LAPD agreement required that the agency adopt new procedures related to use-of-force investigations,[209] search-and-arrest,[210] citizen complaint investigation,[211] and officer disciplinary actions.[212] For example, it mandated the creation of a unit dedicated to the investigation of use-of-force incidents housed in the Operations Headquarters Bureau.[213] It mandated a specific investigative procedure for use-of-force incidents.[214] And it required the LAPD to adopt specific mechanisms for the intake, investigation, and adjudication of citizen complaints – a reform designed to address the kind of problems that Paul King faced when he attempted to file a complaint on his brother's behalf.[215]

Like many consent decrees, the Los Angeles agreement also required the agency to implement an early intervention and risk management system.[216] This new system, described as TEAMS II in the consent decree, was designed as an improvement of the existing TEAMS system that the LAPD already used.[217] One important requirement of the consent decree was that the Police Commission, the inspector general, and the chief of police were all required to have equal and complete access to the new TEAMS II system. This was designed to ensure that all oversight

209 *United States* v. *City of Los Angeles*, 2:00-cv-11769-GAF-RC, at 23–27 (consent decree) (CD Cal. June 15, 2001) [hereinafter Los Angeles Consent Decree], *text available at* www.clearinghouse.net/chDocs/public/PN-CA-0002-0006.pdf (laying out the terms of the use-of-force stipulations).

210 *Id.* at 27 and 28. 211 *Id.* at 29–32. 212 *Id.* at 35–37. 213 *Id.* at 23, para. 55.

214 *Id.* at 23 and 24, para. 56–68.

215 *Id.* at 32–38 (detailing rules on the initiation, investigation, and adjudication of complaints).

216 *Id.* at 9–21 (describing the development of the TEAMS II system, the management and coordination of risk assessment responsibilities, and the performance evaluation system).

217 *Id.* at 9 (stating that "The City has taken steps to develop, and shall establish a database containing relevant information about its officers, supervisors, and managers to promote professionalism and best policing practices and to identify and modify at-risk behavior ... This system shall be a success to, and not simply a modification of, the existing computerized information processing system known as the Training Evaluation and Management System ('TEAMS').").

bodies in the LAPD would have the chance to engage in meaningful regulation.[218] The consent decree clearly labeled all of the types of information that were to be included in the TEAMS II system, including documentation on every time an officer uses force, engages in vehicle pursuits, receives a commendation, conducts an arrest, receives mandated training, is the subject of a civil lawsuit, is the subject of disciplinary action, or is the subject of a complaint.[219] The decree also laid out specifics on how the department ought to review and audit data from the TEAMS II system on a regular basis.[220]

In addition, the consent decree established important changes to the way that the LAPD trained officers.[221] The consent decree added components to the existing training program that notified officers of their ability to report misconduct.[222] Once more, it mandated additional training in cultural diversity, Fourth Amendment law, ethics, and protections available to officers who fear retaliation for reporting misconduct.[223]

One of the most significant components of the LAPD consent decree was the creation of additional oversight mechanisms. Perhaps the most important of these oversight components was the Audit Unit.[224] The purpose of this new unit was to regularly oversee LAPD records to ensure that officers were substantively complying with written mandates. The consent decree specifically required the use of stratified random samples of departmental records to ensure compliance with policy requirements. It also required sting audits, where undercover agents investigate agency compliance covertly.[225] Specifically, the consent decree required the LAPD to audit arrest records, motor vehicle stop records, use-of-force investigations, community complaint investigation records, warrant applications, confidential informant files, and other LAPD work products.[226] To specifically address the problems that

[218] *Id.* at 9.

[219] It is worth noting that this is not an exhaustive list of all information required to be included in the new TEAMS II system. For a complete list, *see id.* at 9–11.

[220] *See, e.g., id.* at 14–16. [221] *Id.* at 54–56. [222] *Id.* at 54. [223] *Id.* at 54 and 55.

[224] *Id.* at 57 ("The Department shall create and continue to have an audit unit within the officer of the Chief of Police (the 'Audit Unit') with centralized responsibility for developing the Annual Audit Plan, coordinating and scheduling audits contemplated by the Annual Audit Plan and ensuring timely completion of audits, and conducting audits as directed by the Chief of Police").

[225] *Id.* at 58 (describing the need for these two types of audits, each under somewhat different conditions).

[226] *Id.* at 58 and 59 (listing these and other audit requirements).

emerged in the Rampart scandal, the consent decree also required audits of financial disclosures made by all LAPD officers who routinely handle valuable contraband or cash.[227] While the Audit Unit was tasked with the responsibility of conducting these audits, the consent decree also required the Audit Unit to turn over their audit records to the OIG for evaluation.[228] The results of these OIG investigations of Audit Division must be forwarded to the Police Commission for further review.[229] This decentralization of responsibility ensures that no one group has complete control over LAPD accountability; responsibility is diffused throughout the organization.

The consent decree also included portions regulating the management of gang units,[230] the development of programs to respond to persons with disabilities,[231] and community outreach.[232] Finally, the consent decree required the DOJ and the LAPD to negotiate in good faith on the selection of an external monitoring team to oversee the implementation of settlement terms.[233] Like all federal intervention, the consent decree made it clear that the city of Los Angeles was responsible for the cost of this monitor and the cost of all necessary reform measures.[234]

III Implementation

By May 2001, the Los Angeles City Council and the DOJ agreed on the appointment of an outside monitoring company – Kroll Associates, Inc. – to serve as the court-mandated independent monitor.[235] While officially US district judge Gary A. Feess had the final say in approving the appointment of the monitoring team,[236] such approval has proven to be somewhat of a formality in many § 14141 cases. The DOJ and the city of Los Angeles selected Kroll out of an initial pool of twenty applicants.[237] The list of applicants included a wide range of talented and experienced

227 *Id.* at 61. 228 *Id.* at 62. 229 *Id.* 230 *Id.* at 47–51. 231 *Id.* at 54–56.

232 *Id.* at 72–74.

233 *Id.* at 71 (further explaining that the monitor was to be selected by March 1, 2001, and ought to meet certain specified requirements). The monitor was supposed to cost no more than $10 million over the first five years in total fees, not counting the cost of "out-of-pocket costs for travel and incidentals." *Id.*

234 *Id.* at 72 ("The City shall bear all reasonable fees and costs of the Monitor").

235 Patrick McGreevy, *N.Y. Firm Chosen to Monitor Reforms*, LA Times, May 19, 2001, at 1.

236 *Id.*

237 Tina Daunt, *Job of Overseeing Reforms at LAPD Attracts Nearly 20*, LA Times, January 17, 2001, at 3.

lawyers and law enforcement professionals.[238] After a lengthy investigation and negotiation process, the monitor selection process proceeded relatively quickly. In fact, some on the Los Angeles City Council complained that the monitor selection process proceeded *too* quickly.[239] By May 17, news reports emerged that the city council had narrowed down its options from twenty to two finalists.[240] And by May 19 news came that the city council had finalized the selection of Kroll as the official monitoring team.[241] Michael Cherkasky, a former prosecutor in New York, led the Kroll team.[242] Cherkasky brought with him a number of highly experienced law enforcement experts, including former New York police commissioner William Bratton.[243] Some in the media portrayed the selection of Cherkasky positively, describing him as "fair but tough."[244]

At least one observer worried that the entire monitor selection process failed to consider community input.[245] The process was largely "secret."[246] A number of applicants suggested that the city of Los Angeles "expressed hostility to aggressive enforcement of the consent decree [during interview questioning]."[247] Objections aside, the Los Angeles City Council eventually approved Kroll's proposed monitoring team by a 9–3 vote.[248] Eventually, even critics like Professor Chemerinsky came to view Cherkasky as a fair monitor, up to the job of overseeing the LAPD.[249] Cherkasky appeared to have something to satisfy all stakeholders. As an outsider from New York who had previously worked as a monitor in other contexts, he brought the kind of impartiality and experience

[238] For example, the list of applicants included Attorney Robert C. Bonner (a former federal prosecutor who served as the head of the Drug Enforcement Administration) and Attorney Stephen Yagman (local attorney who battled with LAPD on previous police cases).

[239] Rick Orlov, *Council Agrees on Monitor in LAPD Probe Consent Decree Nearly Final*, Daily News, May 19, 2001, at N3 (stating that Councilman Mike Hernandez, Nate Holden, and Nick Pacheco all protested the speed at which the council acted to appoint Kroll).

[240] Patrick McGreevy, *City Narrows Choices for Firm to Monitor Police Reforms to 2*, LA Times, May 17, 2001, at 4.

[241] Orlov, *supra* note 239, at N3.

[242] Tina Daunt, *N.Y. Mob Prosecutor to Take on the LAPD*, LA Times, July 24, 2001, at 1.

[243] *Id.*

[244] *Id.; see also* McGreevy, *supra* note 240 (Deputy Mayor Kelly martin calling Cherkasky an "aggressive prosecutor" who was "tough-minded" but "also fair-minded").

[245] Erwin Chemerinsky, *Secretly Naming Police Monitor Ignores Public*, LA Times, May 22, 2001, at 13.

[246] *Id.* [247] *Id.* [248] McGreevy, *supra* note 235, at 1. [249] Daunt, *supra* note 242, at 1.

desired by the DOJ.[250] Los Angeles officials felt that during interviews, Cherkasky "did not prejudge the Police Department" and appeared to be willing to approach the monitoring position "in an objective way."[251]

In addition to Kroll, the city of Los Angeles hired an outside Texas firm to develop criteria for implementing the actual terms of the consent decree.[252] This firm was given the responsibility of translating the terms of the consent decree into useable standards for a law enforcement agency.

Although some city council members held out hope until the very end that "Los Angeles [could] get out of the federal consent decree," it appears that the city generally accepted the need for reform from the beginning.[253] From the outset, the monitor found that the LAPD "took its responsibilities under the consent decree seriously."[254] The LAPD quickly established the Consent Decree Bureau that oversaw the implementation of the consent decree.[255]

In the early years of the consent decree, Cherkasky expressed concern over some failures by the LAPD to meet the standards of the consent decree. For example, only months after Judge Feess officially named Cherkasky as the monitor, his monitoring team found that the LAPD had an unacceptable backlog of misconduct cases and citizen complaints in violation of the consent decree.[256] This sort of problem was typical of the problems facing the LAPD in the earliest days of the consent decree. But early on in the federal intervention process, the LAPD made a change in leadership by appointing William Bratton as police chief.[257] Remember, before becoming chief, Bratton was serving as a policing expert on the Kroll monitoring team overseeing the LAPD.[258] According to the monitor reports, the appointment of Chief Bratton marked the true beginning of institutional reform in the LAPD, in part, because "Chief Bratton raised the level of visibility and dedication to the consent decree."[259]

250 McGreevy, *supra* note 235, at 1. 251 *Id.*

252 Orlov, *supra* note 239, at N3 (explaining how this outside team would be headed by Dr. James Ginger of Public Management Resources, "the only firm in the country that has experience with police department consent decrees").

253 Daunt, *supra* note 237, at 3 (quoting such an objection from Rudy Svorinich, Jr., who tried to rescind the council's approval of the decree until the very end).

254 Final Quarterly Report for LAPD, *supra* note 170, at 5. 255 *Id.*

256 Rick Orlov, *LAPD Reforms Stymied by Backlog Jam*, Daily News, November 20, 2001, at N4.

257 Final Quarterly Report for LAPD, *supra* note 170, at 5. 258 *Id.* 259 *Id.*

The LAPD is not unique in bringing in a new leader around the start of federal intervention. The introduction of federal intervention has also correlated with changes in leadership in a number of targeted municipalities. In fact, Bratton isn't the only *monitor* to be hired to oversee a police department. Soon after the beginning of § 14141 reform, Seattle mayor Ed Murray hired Kathleen O'Toole to oversee the Seattle Police Department.[260] O'Toole had previously worked as a § 14141 monitor in East Haven, Connecticut, where a DOJ investigation had found a pattern of false arrests, discriminatory policing, and excessive force.[261] In Seattle, Los Angeles, New Orleans,[262] and Pittsburgh,[263] federal intervention ushered in the hiring of an outside, seemingly reform-minded police chief who supported the goals of the federal intervention.

To be clear, this is not to say that federal intervention forces any municipality to hire reform-minded leadership. But as one interview participant observed, the beginning of a federal investigation into a police agency "can't help [a police chief's] career."[264] The initiation of federal intervention sends a clear message to local political leaders that their police agency is in need of significant changes. Remember, interview participants emphasized the importance of supportive leadership in the expeditious completion of § 14141 reform. It should come as no surprise, then, that municipalities facing the prospect of long and expensive federal oversight often respond by seeking out a reform-minded leader to oversee their police agency during this challenging time.

One of Chief Bratton's most visible moves in Los Angeles that demonstrated his dedication to the consent decree was his appointment of

260 Gene Johnson, *Kathleen O'Toole Nominated as Seattle Police Chief*, Washington Times, May 19, 2014, *available at* www.washingtontimes.com/news/2014/may/19/mayor-naming-new-seattle-police-chief.

261 *Id.*

262 In May 2014, the same month that the DOJ opened a section 14141 investigation into the conduct of the New Orleans Police Department, Mayor Mitch Landrieu appointed Ronal Serpas to take over the top spot in the department. *Mitch Landrieu Names Nashville Police Chief Ronal Serpas as New Orleans' Top Cop*, The Times-Picayune, May 6, 2010, *available at* www.nola.com/crime/index.ssf/2010/05/new_orleans_native_ronal_serpa.html.

263 Robert McNeilly took over the top-spot in the Pittsburgh Bureau of Police around the same time when the DOJ began a formal investigation of the agency. Chanin, *supra* note 208, at 117.

264 Telephone Interview with External Monitor #13, at 5 (August 5, 2013) [hereinafter Interview #13] (transcript on file with author).

Gerald Chaleff as head of the Consent Decree Bureau. Bratton gave Chaleff, a criminal defense attorney and former member of the Board of Police Commissioners, a position within the LAPD roughly equivalent to a deputy chief.[265] Elevating such a figure like Chaleff – someone from outside the LAPD who had spent much of his professional career critical of police behavior – sent a signal that the LAPD under Bratton was prepared to undergo significant changes if necessary to meet the terms of the decree.[266] When Chief Bratton faced opposition from his own officers over the terms of the consent decree – and there was plenty – he adamantly stood his ground. Bratton continually referred to the decree's provisions as mere best practices.[267]

Despite the existence of supportive leadership atop the LAPD, though, the entire implementation process took nearly twelve years to complete.[268] The federal government spent more time overseeing the LAPD than any other agency in history. This is not surprising, though, given the complexity of the agreement, the size of the department, and the depth of the problems facing the agency before intervention.

Once the reforms had concluded, the LAPD was a remarkably different agency by virtually any metric. The subparts that follow walk through many of these important measures, showing the progress that the LAPD made under federal monitorship. The purpose of the following sections is to examine the progress that the LAPD made during structural reform litigation.

Before doing so, it is important to fully acknowledge the limitations of the available data. Ideally, any test of the Los Angeles consent decree would examine the effects of the decree on rates of police misconduct. Unfortunately, there is no universally accepted way to measure the prevalence of police misconduct. Police misconduct is varied. Additionally, a

[265] *Id.* [266] *Id.*

[267] *Id.* It is worth noting that as is typical in these sort of cases, the federal district court had very little role in the implementation. Perhaps nothing better represents the relatively small role played by the federal district court than the monitoring team's final report. In this report, the monitors described the role played by each party in the process. The sections describing the role of the monitoring team, DOJ, and LAPD included details descriptions of the ways that each party advanced the reform process. The section on the role of the federal district court included a mere single sentence reading, "The Honorable Gary Feess of the United States Court for the Central District of California has presided over this matter for the entire time it has been pending." FINAL QUARTERLY REPORT FOR LAPD, *supra* note 170, at 6.

[268] The Los Angeles monitoring lasted from June 15, 2001, to May 16, 2013 – approximately 4353 days, or 11.9 years. *See* Appendix A and B.

plethora of policies and procedures facilitate misconduct. In a perfect world, the number of complaints filed against a police department would roughly approximate the amount of misconduct present in that agency. Unfortunately, in departments like Los Angeles, one of the key reasons that the DOJ intervened is that internal complaint procedures were inherently flawed. Remember Paul King's experience attempting to file a complaint when his brother Rodney was brutally beaten by several members of the LAPD. Paul King went to the Foothill Police Station to file a formal complaint, only to have the sergeant on duty block his attempts to file a complaint for thirty minutes[269] before questioning him about his possible involvement in criminal activities.[270] The sergeant concluded that there was nothing he could do, absent more conclusive video evidence,[271] since Rodney was in "big trouble" for "put[ting] someone's life in danger, possibly a police officer."[272] These types of barriers to citizen complaints were found to be common in the LAPD and other departments at the start of structural reform litigation. As a result, when departments reform their complaint procedures, it is not uncommon to see complaints actually increase. This is not necessarily because police are engaged in *more* misconduct. Instead this is likely because residents finally have an easy avenue to express their grievances against police officers. Thus, in the case of the LAPD, it is not possible to make any definitive conclusions about the amount of misconduct present by simply comparing the number of complaints before and after the consent decree. Instead, the subparts that follow walk through a range of alternative methods to test the effectiveness of structural reform litigation.

A Citizen Opinions of LAPD

One way to evaluate the impact of the federal consent decree is to see whether public opinion of the LAPD shifted over this time period. Surveys of Los Angeles residents conducted by independent researchers

269 Christopher Commission Report, *supra* note 55, at 10 (describing how the sergeant was in and out of the room during the entire forty minute interaction, with the sergeant once leaving for about thirty minutes).

270 *Id.* In response to this line of questioning, "Paul King responded that he was there to talk about Rodney King, not himself." *Id.*

271 *Id.*

272 *Id.* The officer also told Paul King that his brother "had been caught in a high-speed chase going over 100 m.p.h. or so . . . ." *Id.*

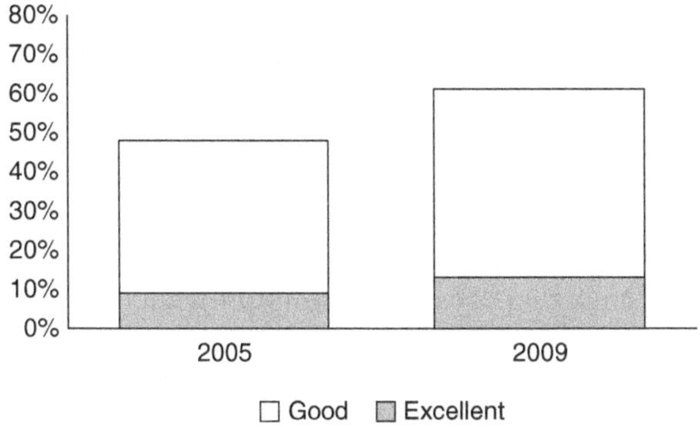

Figure 4.1 Resident Assessment of LAPD Police Services

around the time of federal intervention give some insight into shifts in public opinion. In 2005, a few years into federal intervention, less than 50 percent of residents surveyed said that the "services of the police" were "good" or "excellent" policing services.[273] Several years later in 2009, this number increased to around 60 percent.[274] The proportion of Los Angeles residents who believed the LAPD was doing a "good" or "excellent" job overall also increased during the time of federal intervention. Figure 4.1 illustrates this trend.

By 2009, across all racial groups, Los Angeles residents reported high satisfaction with the overall job done by the LAPD.[275] It is worth noting, though, that black residents still reported somewhat less satisfaction with the LAPD than white, Latino, and Asian residents.[276] Another survey asked respondents whether "compared with the LAPD three years ago, do you believe the police department in Los Angeles today is more likely, less likely, or equally likely to bring offenders to justice while respecting their rights and complying with the law?"[277] A strong majority of black, white, Latino, and Asian respondents answered either "equally likely" or "more likely."[278] And over 80 percent of black, white, Latino, and Asian respondents reported being somewhat or very hopeful about the

[273] Christopher Stone, Todd Foglesong, & Christine M. Cole, Policing Los Angeles Under a Consent Decree: The Dynamics of Change at the LAPD 44 (2009), www.lapdonline.org/assets/pdf/Harvard-LAPD%20Study.pdf (showing these statistics in figure 29).

[274] *Id.*

[275] *Id.* at 45 (showing in figure 30 that Hispanic, white, black, Asian, and other racial groups all showed a strong majority assessing the LAPD as either "good" or "excellent").

[276] *Id.* [277] *Id.* at 46 (displaying these statistics in figure 31). [278] *Id.*

direction of the LAPD in 2009.[279] Perhaps most interestingly, in interviews with detainees – those taken into custody by the LAPD – the majority reported that the LAPD was doing a "good" or "excellent" job.[280] All of this data suggests that the LAPD may have made some meaningful progress over the federal intervention term. This data is also similar to the experience of other cities that underwent federal intervention. In Pittsburgh, for example, a survey of 400 residents found that a significant number reported visible improvements in policing services and fair treatment.[281]

But, in Los Angeles, some troubling patterns remain in the survey data. For instance, some surveys in Los Angeles showed significant racial divides. When residents were asked whether the LAPD "treat[ed] all racial and ethnic groups fairly," a strong majority of white respondents answered "almost always" or "most of the time."[282] By contrast, only around half of Latino and around 40 percent of black respondents expressed similar optimism.[283] Similar disparities existed when interviewers asked Los Angeles residents "Based on your personal experiences, how many of the LAPD officers you encounter treat you, your friends, and your family members with respect?" and "How would you describe relations between the LAPD and the community where you live?"[284] It is worth noting that Los Angeles is not alone in witnessing an apparent disparity in citizen satisfaction based on race. The same basic pattern emerged in the surveys done in Pittsburgh after federal intervention.[285]

Of course, citizen survey responses are hardly dispositive. It is often unclear how familiar any given respondent is with the changes made during a consent decree. And an individual citizen is not necessarily well positioned to judge changes in the frequency of police misconduct. Overall, though, these surveys in Los Angeles should inspire tempered optimism. Some racial disparities aside, these results are consistent with a police department that may have made observable improvements during federal intervention.

[279] *Id.* (providing this data in figure 32). [280] *Id.* at 48 and 49.
[281] *See generally* Robert C. Davis, Christopher W. Ortiz, Nicole J. Henderson, Joel Miller, & Michelle K. Massie, Turning Necessity into Virtue: Pittsburgh's Experience with a Federal Consent Decree (2002), *available at* www.vera.org/sites/default/files/resources/downloads/Pittsburgh_consent_decree.pdf.
[282] Stone, Fogelsong, & Cole, *supra* note 273, at 50. [283] *Id.* [284] *Id.* at 51–53.
[285] Davis, Ortiz, Henderson, Miller, & Massie, *supra* note 281, at 39.

B Complaint Management

The LAPD substantially improved the complaint intake, review, and investigation process. Remember, complaint procedures were a problem identified after the King incident and in the subsequent consent decree. Before the DOJ intervened, the LAPD made preemptive efforts to improve the complaint intake, documentation, and review process.[286] Nevertheless, despite having various procedures in place to ensure supervisor review of complaint intake and review, "the LAPD struggled to comply with the requirements" of the consent decree, particularly "complaint notification requirements."[287] The consent decree required the LAPD to make several changes to the complaint procedures. The consent decree required that, after a complaint investigation finished, a supervisor was to evaluate the quality and completeness of the report.[288] The supervisor was then to identify the underlying deficiency or training problem that may have led to the issue.[289] And the supervisor was responsible for implementing nondisciplinary changes or recommending an officer for formal disciplinary action.[290] The LAPD was also required to notify any complainant of the resolution, including a full explanation of the general allegations and disposition.[291]

Federal intervention gave the LAPD a unique method for testing whether the LAPD had corrected some of the problems associated with its complaint procedures. The monitors in coordination with the OIG for the LAPD regularly audited a sample of citizen complaints to determine whether the LAPD had properly handled these complaints in accordance with the terms of the consent decree.[292] Through this process, the monitor "reviewed thousands of complaint investigations and the related manager review and letters to complainants" to ensure they were following departmental policy.[293] The monitors also worked with the LAPD to send undercover informants to police stations around the city; these informants attempted to file complaints and monitor

[286] Final Quarterly Report for LAPD, *supra* note 170, at 59 ("Prior to the Consent Decree, the LAPD had established a practice of having managers review complaint investigations for quality and completeness and to identify training needs").

[287] *Id.* at 59. [288] *Id.* at 58. [289] *Id.* [290] *Id.* [291] *Id.*

[292] *Id.* at 103–128 (detailing how the LAPD progressed over time in conducting internal audits to ensure that officers were engaged in constitutional policing); Los Angeles Consent Decree, *supra* note 210, at 40 (describing the requirement that the LAPD utilize audits as part of the consent decree).

[293] Final Quarterly Report for LAPD, *supra* note 170, at 59.

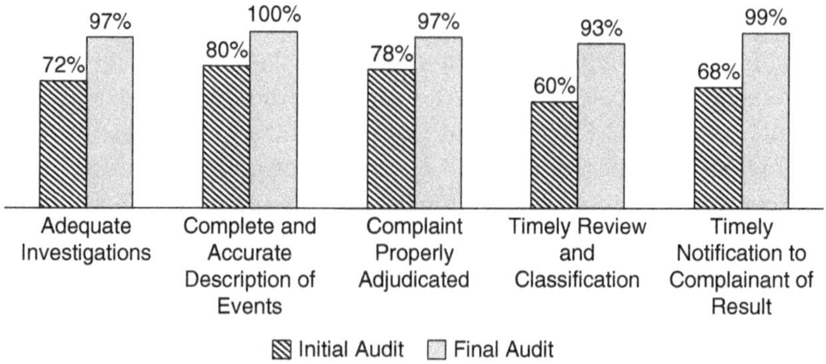

Figure 4.2 Percentage of Audited Complaints Handled Properly
The LAPD's audit division completed these audits on a staggered schedule. Thus, the dates of the initial audits varied by a year or more in some cases. And the dates of the final audits also varied by a year or more.

their progress.[294] Figure 4.2 shows the results of these audits of the complaint process.[295]

[294] Los Angeles Consent Decree, *supra* note 209, at 40 (stating that "the City shall develop . . . a plan for organizing and executing regular, targeted, and random integrity audit checks, or 'sting' operations . . . to identify and investigate . . . at-risk behavior, including: unlawful stops, searches, seizures . . ., uses of excessive force, . . . [and] to identify officers who discourage the filing of a complaint or fail to report misconduct").

[295] This data comes from a variety of quarterly reports filed by the LAPD monitor between 2001 and 2010. The initial audit for the adequacy of investigations is from 2005, and the final audit is from 2010. *See* Andre Birotte, Jr., Office of the Los Angeles Inspector General, Complaint Investigations Audit for Fiscal Year 2005–2006 ii (December 28, 2005) [hereinafter OIG Complaint Audit 2005–2006], *available at* www.oiglapd.org/Reports/complt_Invsts_12-28-05.pdf (describing how in 2005 of the forty-six complaints audited, thirteen gave the Office of the Inspector General "significant concern related to the adequacy of the investigation"); Nicole C. Bershon, Office of the Los Angeles Inspector General, Complaint Investigations Audit for Fiscal Year 2010–2011, 2–3 (April 13, 2011), [hereinafter OIG Complaint Audit 2010–2011] *available at* www.oiglapd.org/Reports/Compl-A_FY10-11_4-13-11.pdf (showing that between 97 percent and 100 percent of all complaints audited showed that officers conducted proper interviews, completed each investigatory step). The initial audit for the completeness and accuracy of the complaint description happened in 2006 and the final audit in 2009. *See* Andre Birotte, Jr., Office of the Los Angeles Inspector General, Complaint Investigation Audit for 2006–2007 (December 28, 2006) [hereinafter OIG Complaint Audit 2006–2007], *available at* www.oiglapd.org/Reports/06-Complaint_Audit_12-28-06.pdf (describing how "eleven investigations had a paraphrased statement that was either incomplete or inaccurately depicted significant information stated in the tape-recorded interview of a complainant and/or witness"); OIG Complaint

The LAPD demonstrated remarkable improvement in the adherence to all citizen complaint procedures – achieving nearly perfect compliance by the end of the auditing periods in most categories. Given the rigor of the monitor's audits into the complaint process over the years of federal intervention, it seems apparent that the LAPD mostly corrected this endemic problem that plagued the department for years.

C TEAMS II

Remember that an additional requirement of the consent decree was that the LAPD ought to develop a new EIS system[296] called TEAMS II to keep track of "risk-oriented data (uses of force, complaints, etc.), [and] operational data (arrests, traffic stops, citations, etc.)" and "automatically notify supervisory personnel when officers in their command deviate significantly from the norms of their sworn peers."[297] The monitoring team found that the LAPD not only developed a satisfactory EIS system in TEAMS II but "incorporated [it] into the LAPD manual and in the daily business practices ... including promotions, pay-grade advancement, selections to specialized units, annual performance evaluations, transfers to new commands, ... and complaint investigations."[298] The monitoring team audited dozens of monthly reports created by this new data system and found the department was generally using

AUDIT 2010–2011, *supra*, at 2 and 3 (showing that 100 percent of all complaints reviewed in 2010 were properly identified and framed, and 100 percent were also accurately summarized in writing on complaint forms). The initial audit, discussing whether issues were properly adjudicated, happened in 2005, with the final audit in 2009. OIG COMPLAINT AUDIT 2005–2006, *supra*, at ii (stating that in 2005, 10 out of 46 complaints reviewed, there was some evidence of a significant allegation not properly framed or adjudicated); OIG COMPLAINT AUDIT 2010–2011, *supra*, at 2 and 3 (demonstrating that in an audit completed by the Office of the Inspector General, 97 percent of complaints were found to have reached a reasonable adjudicatory result). The initial audit for the proper forwarding of complaints occurred in 2001 with the final audit happening in 2006. FINAL QUARTERLY REPORT FOR LAPD, *supra* note 170, at 50 and 51 (showing the change over time in the complaint face sheet review). And finally, the first audit testing whether complainants were notified of the results of the complaint happened in 2002, with the final audit handed down in 2006. *Id.* at 62 (showing in figure entitled "Notification to Complainant" the progressive improvement in this category).

[296] This EIS involved five separate systems that were integrated together: "the Complaint Management System (CMS), the Use of Force System (UOFS), the STOP database, the Risk Management Information System (RMIS) and the Deployment Planning System (DPS)." FINAL QUARTERLY REPORT FOR LAPD, *supra* note 170, at 10.

[297] *Id.* at 9. [298] *Id.*

this new data system properly.[299] An event in 2008 illustrates just how useful these kinds of data-driven warning systems can be in improving the constitutionality of local policing. The LAPD in coordination with the monitoring team conducted an assessment of data collected by the new data system and found that the Central Area Narcotics unit appeared to engage in statistically unusual behavior.[300] The unit was disproportionately taking advantage of a narrow exception in LAPD policy that permitted officers to avoid completing a field data report after stopping a suspect.[301] Thanks to the data-driven system mandated via federal intervention, the LAPD was able to notice this potentially unconstitutional pattern of behavior and take actions to correct it.

D Use of Force

The LAPD's improved use-of-force policies and procedures were "the single most encouraging aspect" of the federal intervention era.[302] Recall, the consent decree identified a pervasive pattern of unlawful use of force present in the LAPD at the time of the federal investigation. Starting in August 2002, the monitoring team began documenting various measures to test whether the LAPD was using force in a constitutional manner. First, the LAPD made dramatic improvements in properly reporting use-of-force incidents to superiors.[303] Second, the consent decree mandated that all so-called categorical use-of-force incidents be reviewed by a use-of-force

[299] *Id.* at 11 and 12 ("the Monitor reviewed 34 different monthly reports produced by RMIS, including four individual summary and comparison reports, 15 different summary and comparison reports for units and/or workgroups and 15 different incident reports … [and] determined that these reports met the Consent Decree requirement").

[300] *Id.* at 13 (explaining how, after a staff review of "total Department-wide action items for the second quarter of 2008," they determined that the Central Area Narcotics division "appeared to be statistically higher than the average of other specialized units for RMIS threshold").

[301] *Id.* The monitors also observed that supervisors appeared to be engaged directly in use-of-force incidents rather than serving in a merely supervisory capacity. *Id.*

[302] Final Quarterly Report for LAPD, *supra* note 170, at 20.

[303] Office of the Independent Monitor of the Los Angeles Police Department, Fourth Quarterly Report 6–7 (August 15, 2002) [hereinafter Fourth Quarterly Report for LAPD] (stating "[n]otification and a prompt response by CIID is critical to preserve evidence and maintain integrity"). The Fourth Quarterly Report stated that, "The CIID's overall response time ranged from approximately 25 to 106 minutes, with an average mean arrival time of 69 minutes. This response time is judged to be within acceptable limits and not an impairment to the investigation." *Id.* at 6. The report also stated that the police chief was properly notified in 22 out of 23 cases, or 95.7 percent of the time. *Id.* at 7. Final Quarterly Report for

review board.[304] Categorical use of force refers to any lethal force used by law enforcement or any force resulting in injury requiring hospitalization, all head strikes, and deaths in custody.[305] The monitors observed the process by which the use-of-force review board hears cases of categorical use of force and found them to be in line with the requirements of the consent decree.[306] The LAPD continued these full board reviews for categorical use of force throughout the period of the consent decree.[307] Similarly, the consent decree required the LAPD to review noncategorical use-of-force incidents within fourteen calendar days.[308] The LAPD initially had a tougher time abiding by this requirement. When the monitoring team first audited use-of-force files in December 2002 to determine whether noncategorical use-of-force incidents were being properly investigated within the requisite fourteen days, the team found that only 75 percent of cases were evaluated in the proper time frame.[309] This was deemed

LAPD, *supra* note 170, at Appendix D, p. 2 (showing that paragraph 58 is in compliance throughout the period of the consent decree).

[304] Office of the Independent Monitor of the Los Angeles Police Department, Fifth Quarterly Report for LAPD, at 20 ("Paragraph 69 requires the LAPD to continue its practice of presenting every Categorical Use of Force investigation before the Use of Force Review Board").

[305] Los Angeles Police Department, Use of Force Annual Report for 2009, 4 (2009) [hereinafter Use of Force Report for LAPD 2009], *available at* www.lapdonline.org/assets/pdf/2009YearEndReportFinal.pdf. The LAPD's full definition of categorical use of force is as follows:

> All incidents involving the use of lethal force such as intentional Officer Involved Shootings; Unintended Discharges of a firearm; all uses of Carotid Restraint Control Holds; all uses of force resulting in an injury requiring hospitalization, commonly referred to as Law Enforcement Related Injuries; all Head strikes with an impact weapon; all other uses of force resulting in death; all deaths while the arrestee or detainee is in the custodial care of the LAPD referred to as an In-Custody Death; or a K-9 Contact which result in hospitalization.
>
> *Id.*

[306] Fifth Quarterly Report for LAPD, *supra* note 304, at 20 and 21.

[307] Final Quarterly Report for LAPD, *supra* note 170, at Appendix D, p. 2 (showing under paragraph 69(a) that the LAPD was in compliance with this portion in the fifth quarterly report and remained in compliance over the duration of the consent decree).

[308] Office of the Independent Monitor of the Los Angeles Police Department, Sixth Quarterly Report 19 (February 15, 2003) [hereinafter Sixth Quarterly Report for LAPD] (explaining that the consent decree requires "LAPD Division . . . to review each use of force within 14 calendar days of the incident, unless a deficiency in the investigation is detected, in which case the review shall be completed within a reasonable time period").

[309] *Id.* ("The Monitor found that 21 of the 85 investigations selected for review were not reviewed within 14 calendar days of their submission" and "[f]or all 21 incident

insufficient.[310] By June 2003, the LAPD had dramatically improved this figure. By then, the LAPD processed approximately 94 percent of noncategorical use-of-force cases within fourteen days.[311] This figure increased to 95.6 percent in December 2003 and remained above 95 percent thereafter.[312]

Third, another part of the consent decree required the LAPD to utilize specific procedures in investigating both categorical and noncategorical use-of-force claims. For example, the consent decree required the audio and video recording of interviews conducted after categorical use-of-force incidents.[313] It barred the use of group interviews after both categorical and noncategorical use-of-force events.[314] It also established requirements for the collection and preservation of evidence and mandated officer interviews with all supervisors after use-of-force incidents, among other requirements.[315] The monitoring team first measured compliance with these requirements in September 2002. In this initial examination, the monitors examined thirty-seven categorical force investigations.[316] While this initial assessment found the LAPD in compliance with most of the categorical force investigation requirements, it did find that the LAPD had failed to adequately tape or video-record interviews[317] and failed to collect and preserve adequate evidence.[318] The monitors similarly found the noncategorical investigations to be insufficient in multiple ways

investigations the Monitor noted no extenuating circumstances and the LAPD did not document any extenuating circumstances that would have precluded the investigation from reasonably being reviewed as required").

310 *Id.*

311 Office of the Independent Monitor of the Los Angeles Police Department, Eighth Quarterly Report 18 (August 15, 2003) [hereinafter Eighth Quarterly Report for LAPD] ("During the current quarter, the Monitor reviewed the merits of 87 NCUOF incident investigations ... [and in] all but five investigations, LAPD Division Management reviewed the incident within 14 days and the investigations were completed within a reasonable time period thereafter").

312 Office of the Independent Monitor of the Los Angeles Police Department, Tenth Quarterly Report 23–24 (August 15, 2003) [hereinafter Tenth Quarterly Report for LAPD] (stating that 87 out of 91 cases of non-categorical use of force were properly handled within fourteen days).

313 Final Quarterly Report for LAPD, *supra* note 170, at Appendix D, at 3 (describing the conduct of investigation requirements in paragraph 80i for categorical and non-categorical use-of-force incidents).

314 *Id.* 315 *Id.* 316 Fifth Quarterly Report for LAPD, *supra* note 304, at 36–39.

317 *Id.* at 38 ("For the 37 incidents reviewed, two contained witness statements that were not captured on tape and one contained a suspect's statement that was not captured on tape").

318 *Id* ("In two separate Categorical Use of Force incidents the Monitor identified a key witness to the incident who was not interviewed by the investigating officers").

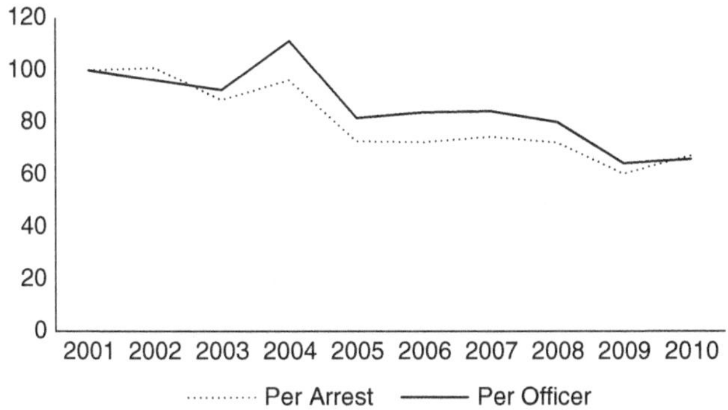

Figure 4.3 Categorical Uses of Force per Officer by LAPD

during the first examination.[319] Soon, though, the LAPD corrected these problems and generally maintained compliant use-of-force investigation procedures from that point forward.[320]

Combined, these various measures suggest that the LAPD's reporting and investigation of use of force improved substantially during the consent decree period. What is surprisingly absent, though, from the monitoring report is some measure of how these changes impacted the LAPD's proclivity towards using force against criminal suspects. The OIG, though, does provide some consistent measure of use of force over time. During the time when the monitors were regularly overseeing the categorical use-of-force report procedures, the total number of categorical use-of-force incidents declined. Figure 4.3 shows the decline in categorical use-of-force incidents during the monitoring period.

The decrease in categorical use-of-force incidents during the monitoring time period may be a mere coincidence. It may be a side effect of decreased crime. Or it may represent a genuine change in officer behavior to use categorical force less often, since officers are aware that the OIG and the external monitor are observing their behavior. It is tough to make any definitive conclusions from the data, although the general trend is encouraging.

[319] Final Quarterly Report for LAPD, *supra* note 170, at Appendix D, at 3 (noting that the LAPD was not in compliance in the first audit of the non-categorical investigation procedures in the sixth quarterly report for paragraph 80i).

[320] *Id.* (showing a move from noncompliance to compliance for various categories listed under 80i for categorical and noncategorical use-of-force investigations).

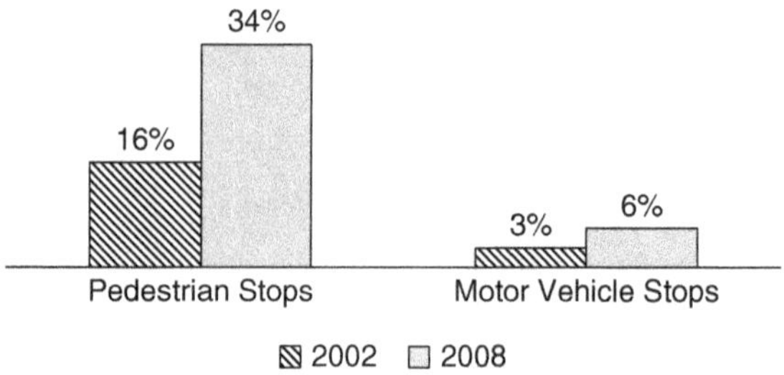

Figure 4.4 Percentage of Stops by LAPD Resulting in Arrests

It is important to note that two years after the external monitoring team stopped monitoring categorical uses of force, the total number of categorical use-of-force incidents increased by about 37 percent.[321] Most of this uptick was tied back to an increase in officer-involved shootings, which increased by 58 percent in just one year.[322] The LAPD has not publicly provided any definitive or persuasive explanation for this sudden jump in officer-involved shootings. This is a potentially discouraging development worthy of further study.

E Stops and Arrests

Another way to evaluate the effectiveness of federal intervention into the LAPD is to look at stop-and-arrest data. "When stops increase greatly without an increase in the number that lead to arrests, the pattern suggests that suspicions are being aroused too easily and the decision to interfere with people's liberty is being made too lightly, even if the stops are constitutionally justifiable in each individual instance."[323] Conversely, when a higher percentage of stops result in arrest, this suggests that "police officers stopped people for good reasons and were willing to have the district attorney scrutinize those reasons."[324] Figure 4.4 shows data on the change over time in the percentage of stops that lead to arrest in Los

[321] Alexander A. Bustamante, Office of the Inspector General, Quarterly Use of Force Report: First Quarter 2012, 3 (June 27, 2012), [hereinafter 2012 Use of Force Report] *available at* www.oiglapd.org/Reports/6-27-12_UOF-Rprt1stQ-2012.pdf. I reached the 37 percent statistic by comparing the 2009 number of categorical use-of-force incidents with the 2011 number (84 and 115, respectively).

[322] *Id.* at 3 (explaining the rise in officer-involved shootings and giving the 58 percent statistic).

[323] Stone, Foglesong, & Cole, *supra* note 273, at 24.

[324] *Id.*

Angeles, as collected by Professors Christopher Stone, Todd Foglesong, and Christine M. Cole.

In 2002, only around 16 percent of pedestrian stops and 3 percent of vehicle stops ended in an arrest. By 2008, these numbers had increased to 34 percent and 6 percent, respectively. In addition to looking at the arrest rate in police stops, we can analyze the frequency by which these arrests led to charges by the prosecutor. In theory, if the rate at which prosecutors bring charges against those arrested by the LAPD increased, then the LAPD is likely making better arrest decisions. Conversely, if the prosecutor is choosing to bring fewer charges per arrest, then we might suspect that the LAPD is making a higher proportion of unjustified arrests. So how prosecutors file charges more or less frequently during the federal intervention era? Among those arrested, the rate at which prosecutors levied charges in Los Angeles actually increased.[325] This suggests that not only did LAPD officers arrest more individuals after stops, but, increasingly, the prosecutor agreed with these arrest decisions. This is consistent with a police department that is more judiciously using its authority to stop pedestrians and motorists.

F *Bias-Free Policing*

One controversial subject during the federal intervention era was the LAPD's adherence to the consent decree's mandated nondiscrimination policy for automobile and pedestrian stops. The Christopher Commission Report found significant evidence of racial bias in the LAPD's ranks, and investigations after the Rampart scandal revealed similar problems.[326] To measure the presence of possible racial profiling, the LAPD began collecting demographic statistics on vehicle and pedestrian stops starting in November 2001.[327] The Audit Unit then began auditing this data in August 2003.[328] By 2005, Los Angeles

[325] Stone, Foglesong, and Cole used filing rate as a measure of the "quality" of police decisions to make an arrest. They showed that, "[f]or Part One arrests, the felony filing rate increased while both the release rate and misdemeanor filing rate fell. For Part Two arrests, the felony filing rate increased, the misdemeanor filing rate fell, and the release rate remained steady, at 14 percent." *Id.* at 31.

[326] Final Quarterly Report for LAPD, *supra* note 170, at 69.

[327] *Id.* at 70 ("The Decree also mandated that the Department require LAPD officers to complete a written or electronic report each time an officer conducted a motor vehicle or pedestrian stop by November 1, 2001").

[328] *Id.* at 71 (the Audit Unit "completed its first *Motor Vehicle and Pedestrian Stop Data Collection Audit* in August 2003").

released a major public report detailing the results of these audits.[329] It found that, even when controlling for several variables, racial disparities remained.[330] A few years later, Professor Ian Ayres worked with the ACLU of Southern California to conduct an additional study of this same data set.[331] Ayres found apparent racial bias in how LAPD officers exercised authority post-stop.[332] In response to these reports, the LAPD leadership instituted additional protocols that require officers to fully articulate detailed reasons for conducting traffic and pedestrian stops.[333] Complaints against officers for racial profiling were not closed unless the officer had provided such a full explanation.[334]

As is the case in many police departments targeted for federal intervention, though, proving the frequency of racial bias in the ranks of the LAPD is an extremely challenging empirical enterprise. That said, the LAPD appeared to make several good-faith attempts to identify and respond to potential racial bias. First, the LAPD put in place an automated reporting system that recorded stop data into the TEAMS II system.[335] This way, even if it was difficult to reach conclusions on the presence of racial bias via aggregate statistics, the LAPD hoped to identify individual officers who may be engaged in a more visible pattern of race-based stops. Second, the LAPD began installing cameras in squad cars.[336] The LAPD has also agreed to conduct regularized audits of audio and video from these cameras.[337] Thus, while some claims of racial bias remain in the LAPD, it appears that the department may have taken steps to correct these problems.

329 *Id.* at 72 ("The City, working with the Analysis Group, Inc. prepared and released the 'Final Pedestrian and Motor Vehicle Stop Data Analyses Methodology Report,' dated December 8, 2005").

330 *Id.*

331 Ina Ayres and Jonathan Borowsky, American Civil Liberties Union of Southern California, A Study of Racially Disparate Outcomes in the Los Angeles Police Department (October 2008), *available at* http://islandia.law.yale.edu/ayers/Ayres%20LAPD%20Report.pdf.

332 *Id.* at i. 333 *Id.* at 73. 334 *Id.* at 73 and 74.

335 *Id.* at 74 ("This system incorporates the collection of stop data as approved by DOJ and provides for its storage in TEAMS II").

336 *Id.* (explaining that "... the City and Department have continued to move towards Department-wide implementation of cameras in cars (DICVS), which the Monitor has strongly endorsed and recommended as a best practice in monitoring potential bias in stops").

337 *Id.* at 75 (stating that the LAPD planned to "conduct regular audits of the audio and video, in addition to periodic inspections by supervisors").

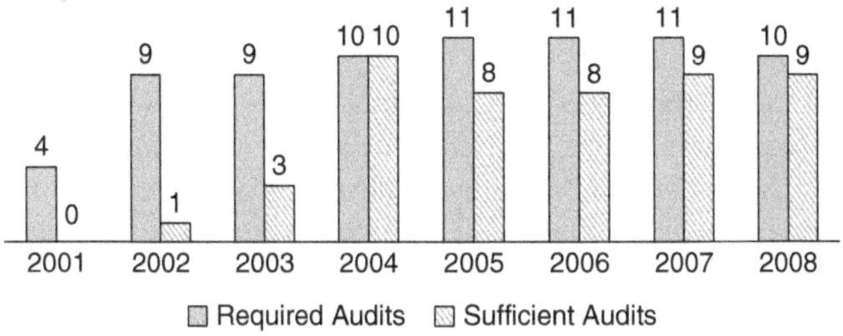

Figure 4.5 Number of Required and Sufficient Audits

G Auditing

Perhaps the single most important change made in the LAPD was the structural change in monitoring police behavior via auditing. Remember that before the initiation of federal intervention, the LAPD had some mechanisms in place to monitor police behavior – namely, the Police Commission and the OIG. The federal investigation of the LAPD found that these two oversight mechanisms lacked the authority and skills to properly oversee LAPD behavior. Thus, as part of the consent decree, the federal government demanded that the LAPD create a new Audit Unit, which served under the chief of police. This new Audit Unit was given the responsibility of conducting stratified, randomized audits of various police practices. Under the consent decree, the chief of police was to submit to the Police Commission and the OIG a list of planned audit targets. The Audit Unit was then responsible for conducting these regular audits and submitting the results to the Police Commission and OIG for review. The consent decree mandated several required subjects for these regular audits – warrants, arrests, use of force, stops, complaints, financial disclosures, and police training. Figure 4.5 shows the trend in the number of completed audits and sufficiency of these audits.

During the federal intervention era, the external monitoring team examined the quality of the audits conducted by the Audit Unit. At first these audits were frequently flawed. For example, the monitoring team found that many of these early audits "used inadequate samples and included questions that yielded improper results."[338] Over time, and with the help of both the external monitors and additional newly hired personnel, the LAPD dramatically improved the quality of these regular audits. After only a few years, the Audit Unit began submitting timely audits that met quantitative and

[338] *Id.* at 109.

qualitative expectations. This is not to say that the Audit Unit has been perfect. In fact, in the later years of monitoring, the Audit Unit still had some issues with timeliness, as seen by the slight dip in compliance between 2005 and 2007. But overall the LAPD – an agency that once suffered from a serious inability to monitor its own officers – made tremendous improvement in this regard over the federal intervention era. In fact, the LAPD made so much progress that the agency "participat[ed] as founding members of the International Law Enforcement Audit's Association (ILEAA) and coordinat[ed] the first ILEAA conference in August 2007."[339] The LAPD Audit Unit even participated in peer reviews of other similar systems that have been installed in cities like Phoenix, Dallas, and Richmond.[340]

H Additional Measures

The monitoring team also found that the LAPD made substantial progress in improving its management of gang units,[341] handling of persons with mental illnesses,[342] policies on confidential informants,[343] and broader training programs.[344] Monitors also audited warrant applications and arrest records to verify legal sufficiency and authenticity of officer behavior.[345] The monitors found that the LAPD made substantial progress in both areas.[346]

IV Costs of Reforms in Los Angeles

By most measures, federal intervention appears to have been successful in reducing apparent misconduct in Los Angeles – but at what cost? What did the city of Los Angeles have to sacrifice to make this apparent improvement in its police force? Surprisingly, it appears that Los Angeles may have

339 *Id.* at 112. 340 *Id.*

341 FINAL QUARTERLY REPORT FOR LAPD, *supra* note 170, at 76–83 (stating that, although early on the LAPD struggled with the gang unit requirements, the "Department has made substantial strides towards a better trained and supervised gang unit").

342 *Id.* at 89–93 (claiming that the LAPD has made "significant advances" in this area and now "continues to be in the national forefront of this important policing issue").

343 *Id.* at 84–88 ("The Department released a Confidential Informant Manual in 2002 that incorporated all of the requirements of the Consent Decree").

344 *Id.* at 93–99 ("The LAPD has been tremendously successful in its effort to improve its training function").

345 *Id.* at 34–38 (stating that initially audits only found 55.5 percent of arrest packages to be in line with policy, but 88 percent were in line with policy after the monitoring; also noting that compliance rates significantly increased for warrants as well).

346 *Id.*

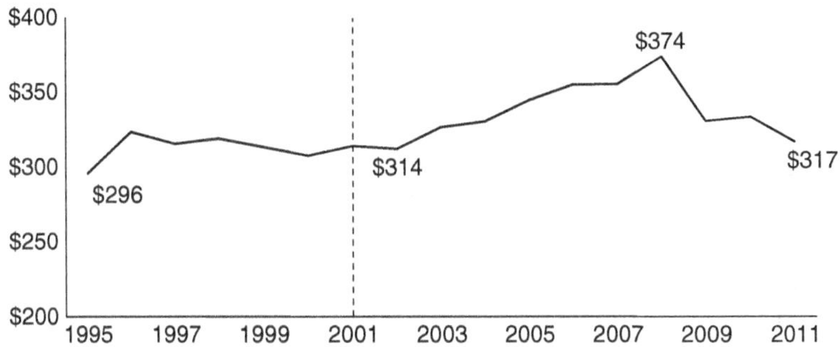

Figure 4.6 LAPD Inflation-Adjusted Expenditures per Resident
The dotted vertical line signifies the beginning of the structural police reform era.

made less of a sacrifice than previously expected to achieve these improvements in constitutional policing. Although the City of Los Angeles spent a considerable amount of money to pay for initial investments into misconduct reforms, there is reason to believe that the city may have been able to recoup at least some of these costs through reductions in police misconduct. Police officers also worried that the consent decree may result in a decrease in police aggressiveness – a phenomenon sometimes called depolicing. In actuality, though, little statistical evidence exists to verify this depolicing hypothesis in Los Angeles. In fact, available statistics suggest that the LAPD may have become more aggressive and more effective at combatting crime relative to other municipalities during the federal intervention era. Combined, these two observations suggest that the real cost of federal intervention was lower than critics assumed. This realization makes Los Angeles a fascinating case study – an instance where the law may have helped facilitate meaningful improvement in police conduct without significant cost.

A *Upfront Financial Costs*

The consent decree appears to have directly affected the overall budget of the LAPD. As seen in Figure 4.6, around the time when the LAPD entered into a consent decree with the DOJ, the city of Los Angeles spent around $314 (adjusted for inflation) per resident on policing services. By 2008, that number ballooned to around $374. Most of this cost appears to be tied to a temporary investment in equipment and administrative tools necessary to satisfy the terms of the consent decree. By the end of the consent decree period, average expenditures per resident had receded somewhat – possibly because of the waning implementation costs of the consent decree and the nationwide recession that strapped city budgets across the nation. Initial estimates suggested that the consent decree would cost around $40 million to implement in the first year, with an additional $30–50 million in expenses in the years to follow.[347] In total, this would suggest that the LAPD ought to have spent somewhere between $80 and $90 million in equipment and administrative costs to fully implement the terms of the consent decree. Further investigation into the details of the LAPD budget suggests that these estimates were approximately correct. Between 2001 and 2011, the LAPD expenses on equipment and administrative investments related to the consent decree totaled between $83 and $84 million.[348] When combined with the cost of monitoring, which amounted to an average of around $2 million per year,[349] the total cost of federal intervention was over $100 million. Other estimates have placed the cost of the LAPD consent decree at over $300 million.[350] Figure 4.6 shows the trend in the LAPD's inflation-adjusted expenditures per resident, with the dotted line signifying the beginning of federal intervention.

As is the case in many communities facing federal intervention, the cost of the monitor was also particularly controversial in Los Angeles. Towards the end of the consent decree monitoring, the then president of the Police Protective League Tim Sands argued publicly that the Kroll was "wast[ing] taxpayer dollars [with] incessant, meaningless auditing that does nothing to enhance public safety or 'reform' the LAPD."[351] Political critics of the consent decree also focused their attacks on the high cost of monitoring services. Council Dennis Zine publicly criticized the cost of things like airfare and food paid to monitors who needed to travel from out of state to perform their duties.[352]

[347] Giordono & Kandel, *supra* note 193, at A8. [348] *Id.*

[349] *Id.* (citing the cost of monitoring and auditing services as around $10 million for a five-year period). The monitoring period actually continued for several years more than initially predicted.

[350] Kimbriell Kelly, Sarah Childress, & Steven Rich, *Forced Reforms, Mixed Results*, WASH. POST, Nov. 13, 2015, *available at* http://www.washingtonpost.com/sf/investigative/2015/11/13/forced-reforms-mixed-results.

[351] Rick Orlov, *Police Want End to Consent Decree, LAPD: Union Protests Cost of Using New York Monitoring Team*, DAILY NEWS, February 1, 2008, at A3.

[352] *Id.* Mr. Zine explained that "I don't know why we had to hire a New York firm to do this work. And I don't know why they couldn't hire someone in Los Angeles to serve as monitor." *Id.*

The fact that federal intervention forces municipalities to allocate scarce resources to the cause of police reforms and monitoring cuts both ways. On one hand, federal intervention forces cities to make investments into constitutional police reform that may not be otherwise possible without outside stimulus. Gaining local political support for a multimillion dollar investment in the LAPD over a relatively short period of time would be extremely challenging without the impetus of federal intervention. But federal intervention transforms heightened investment in the police department from a luxury to a legal necessity. As a result, various interview participants suggested that police chiefs in cash-strapped cities would be wise to turn to the structural reform litigation as a strategic avenue to force a municipality to dedicate more money to fighting misconduct through investments in accountability measures.[353] This highlights the fact that preventing police misconduct costs money. When local political actors are unwilling to make the necessary investments in police reform, federal intervention uses the threat of equitable relief under § 14141 to force the reallocation of scarce resources in a way that no other regulatory mechanism can.

On the other hand, this forced allocation of scarce municipal resources raises some serious concerns. Decentralization in American policing leads to wide resource disparities between municipalities.[354] The result is that some jurisdictions lack the necessary resources to invest in policies and procedures to reduce misconduct.[355] While the forced allocation of scarce resources may be an advantage of federal

[353] Telephone Interview with DOJ Participant #12, at 2 (July 30, 2013) [hereinafter Interview #12] (on file with author) (positively describing the decision by a municipal police chief to invite the DOJ to intervene and provide the department with "resources and the expertise" to "take a look and come up with some solutions").

[354] Several decades ago, estimates wrongly put the number of policing agencies at around 40,000. President's Commission on Law Enforcement and Administration of Justice, The Challenge of Crime in a Free Society 91 (1967) [hereinafter President's Commission on Law Enforcement], *available at* www.ncjrs.gov/pdffiles1/nij/42.pdf Subsequent studies have reduced this number substantially. Modern estimates place the number at around 17,985 state and local law enforcement agencies in the United States. Brian A. Reaves, U.S. Dep't of Justice, Census of State and Local Law Enforcement Agencies 2 (2011), *available at* www.bjs.gov/content/pub/pdf/csllea08.pdf.

[355] President's Commission on Law Enforcement, *supra* note 354, at 91 (highlighting how spending for urban departments was found to be around $27.31 per resident per year, while spending in smaller departments was only $8.74 per resident per year).

intervention, it represents a potential limitation as well. What happens when a particularly poor community chooses not to invest in costly police reforms out of necessity because of a lack of overall resources? Take the example of Camden, New Jersey, discussed in Chapter 1. Remember, the average Camden resident only makes around $29,118 per year, resulting in over a third of all Camden residents living below the poverty line.[356] The entire city of Camden took in only around $24 million in tax revenue in 2011, despite the fact that the Camden police force alone cost around $65 million that year.[357] Camden has historically lacked the resources to hire enough police forces to man the streets, let alone to invest in proactive misconduct regulation mechanisms. When faced with the prospect of federal intervention, other financially strapped communities like New Orleans have been forced to consider tax increases.[358] As a result, the DOJ may understandably face significant backlash in using federal intervention in poor communities.

B Long-Term Savings through Reductions in Civil Liability Exposure

Admittedly, federal intervention comes with some high upfront costs. But what if federal intervention could compensate for this upfront price tag by reducing the amount of police misconduct long term, thereby reducing the number of civil rights suits filed against a city? Unfortunately, testing this hypothesis is tricky. Communities often keep poor records on the

356 United States Census Bureau, American Community Survey (2006–2010).

357 Matt Taibbi, *Apocalypse, New Jersey: A Dispatch From America's Most Desperate Town*, Rolling Stone, December 11, 2013, *available at* www.rollingstone.com/culture/news/apocalypse-new-jersey-a-dispatch-from-americas-most-desperate-town-20131211. Camden has responded to this budgetary crisis by consolidating its police department with the county-level agency to lower costs and avoid duplicative expenditures. *See generally* Heather Haddon, *Crime Dips in Camden as New County Police Force Replaces City Officers*, The Wall Street Journal, August 5, 2013, *available at* http://online.wsj.com/news/articles/SB10001424127887323968704578650171849946106 (detailing the so-called experiment whereby Camden has closed its citywide police department and instead relied on the newly expanded county department).

358 Richard Rainey, *Mitch Landrieu Requests a Doubling of Tax Rates for New Orleans Police and Fire*, The Times-Picayune, May 1, 2014, *available at* www.nola.com/politics/index.ssf/2014/05/mitch_landrieus_tax_hike_plan.html; Tyler Bridges, *Legislature Approves Property Tax Hike for New Orleans Police and Fire; Now Heads to Voters*, The Lens, May 29, 2014, *available at* http://thelensnola.org/2014/05/29/legislature-approves-property-tax-hike-for-new-orleans-police-now-heads-to-voters.

actual costs of litigating and settling civil rights suits related to police misconduct.

The LAPD has provided some preliminary data on the relationship between federal intervention and reductions in civil liability exposure by disclosing a complete dataset of all civil liability related to police conduct between January 1, 2002, and October 5, 2011.[359] This data comes from a comprehensive list of all lawsuits and payouts made by the LAPD and released to the *Los Angeles Times*. When reporting the information, the LAPD categorized each case into a category based on the type of lawsuit. Many of these suits involved employment litigation, including claims of wrongful termination or sexual harassment.

In order to test the effects of federal intervention on civil liability exposure, though, it is important to limit our inquiry to the kinds of civil rights cases that federal intervention sought to eliminate – that is unlawful uses of force, claims of excessive uses of force, unlawful searches, unlawful seizures, and other situations where civilians allege that a police officer violated his or her civil rights. Because of the way that the LAPD reported this data, it is possible to isolate these particular cases. Categorizing cases in this manner leaves a dataset of 353 civil rights suits

[359] This data comes from a comprehensive list of all lawsuits and payouts made by the LAPD and released to the Los Angeles Times. *See Legal Payouts in LAPD Lawsuits*, LA TIMES, January 22, 2012, *available at* http://spreadsheets.latimes.com/lapd-settlements. This data shows all suits settled between January 1, 2002, and October 5, 2011. When reporting the information to the LA Times, the LAPD categorized each case into a category based on the type of lawsuit. Thus, many of these suits involved employment litigation, including claims of wrongful termination, sexual harassment, and the like. This figure only uses lawsuit data from this spreadsheet in cases where the LAPD categorized it as either a civil rights violation case or a use-of-force related case. These are the kind of misconduct that the consent decree should have reduced. This resulted in a set of 353 civil rights lawsuits against the LAPD settled between 2002 and 2011. The average of these civil rights or use-of-force cases took 486 days to settle, or about 1.33 years. And twenty-four of these cases took over three years to settle. Of course, litigation can take years to complete. A claim filed in 2001 may not be resolved until 2002 or 2003. To correct for this, the figure includes data on the number of cases resulting in payoffs organized by both the date of settlement and the date of filing. If the LAPD is engaging in less misconduct, the total number of misconduct cases should decrease by year and the total amount paid by the LAPD for misconduct cases also decrease. Although the dataset runs through 2011, the figure ends at the year 2009. This is to ensure that the data takes into account the length of time it takes to settle civil rights lawsuits. The final dataset may slightly underrepresent the number of civil rights suits filed in 2006 and the expected payoff. Some suits filed in 2006 may still be unsettled as of October 15, 2011 – approximately 1749 days later. But based on the full dataset provided by the LAPD, 346 out of 353 suits (or about 98 percent) were settled in less than 1749 days. Data on file with author.

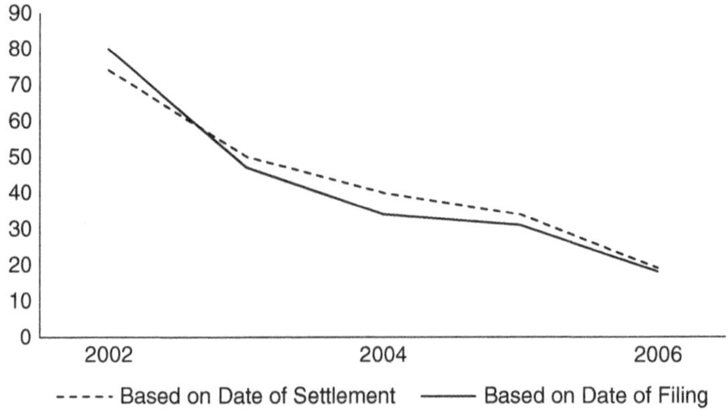

Figure 4.7 Number of Civil Rights and Use-of-Force Lawsuits Against LAPD Resulting in Financial Payouts

against the LAPD settled or fully adjudicated between 2002 and 2011. Of course, litigation can take years to complete. A claim filed in 2001 may not be resolved until 2002, 2003, or later. The average of these civil rights or use-of-force cases took 486 days to settle, or about 1.33 years. Another twenty-four of these cases took over three years to settle. This means that we cannot simply look at the number and pay off for suits by year from 2002 through 2011. Some instances of misconduct that happened in the later years of this sample may not have resulted in a final adjudication or settlement by October 5, 2011. For accuracy, we should narrow our inquiry to look at a shorter time window. Figure 4.7 shows the number of cases filed against the city of Los Angeles for police misconduct between January 1, 2002 and December 31, 2006. In the sample of 353 cases, 346 or 98 percent took less than 1,749 days to settle or reach a final adjudication. Thus, Figure 4.7, which draws on a sample that runs through 2011, should include adjudicatory results for virtually all civil rights cases filed between 2002 and 2006.

Figure 4.7 suggests that the number of civil rights suits against the LAPD declined between 2002 and 2006. The total payouts for civil rights suits based on the date of filing also decreased from $13,187,100 in 2002 to $3,325,054 in 2006, an annual savings for the city of Los Angeles of nearly $10 million. The number of civil rights cases filed each year that resulted in payouts also declined, from a peak of eighty cases filed in 2002 to a low of only eighteen cases in 2006. While this trend is consistent with a conclusion that federal intervention contributes to lower civil liability, it is far from dispositive. For example, a change in the number of civil rights police cases that resulted in a payout might be indicative of a change in litigation strategies, independent of the introduction of federal intervention. If a change in litigation strategy was driving the decline in civil rights lawsuits resulting in financial payouts, this change in strategy should have similar effects on other types of lawsuits against the LAPD. Nevertheless, the number of successful lawsuits against the LAPD for other matters, like traffic accidents, has remained relatively constant during the federal intervention era.[360] This is consistent with the conclusion that federal intervention exerted a unique and significant influence on the volume of civil rights abuses by the LAPD.

Ultimately, the LAPD data on civil liability is encouraging but inconclusive. This time period is simply too short to provide definitive data. Even so, this very short trend is consistent with remarks made by a knowledgeable official in Detroit during an interview, who claimed that "the amount of money that we have saved on lawsuits that we had endured for years ... have paid for the cost of implementation of the monitoring two or three times" over.[361] If it were proven true that federal intervention consistently reduced civil liability exposure, this would have profound implications.

Take the city of Chicago, for example. On December 6, 2015, the DOJ announced that it had begun a § 14141 investigation of the city's police force.[362] A little over a year before this announcement, on the evening of October 20, 2014, Chicago police responded to a report that a man wielding a knife was breaking into vehicles in the city's Archer Heights neighborhood.[363] According to officers on the scene, the seventeen-year-old suspect Laquan McDonald used the knife to slash the tires of a squad car.[364]

[360] In 2003, private litigants filed thirty-six civil suits related to traffic accidents against the LAPD that eventually resulted in a monetary payout. In the years that followed, the number of traffic-related civil suits filed against the LAPD that resulted in financial compensation remained stable – always between 32 and 42 cases. *Legal Payouts in LAPD Lawsuits, supra* note 360.

[361] Telephone Interview with City Official and External Monitor #20, at 6 (September 5, 2013) (transcript on file with author) [hereinafter Interview #20].

[362] Monica Davey & Mitch Smith, *Justice Officials to Investigate Chicago Police Department After Laquan McDonald Case*, NY TIMES, December 7, 2015, at A10.

[363] Jeremy Gorner & Jason Meisner, *FBI Investigating Death of Teen Shot 16 Times by Chicago Cop*, CHICAGO TRIBUNE, April 14, 2015, *available at* www.chicagotribune.com/news/local/breaking/ct-feds-probe-police-shooting-met-20150413-story.html.

[364] Josh Sanburn, *Chicago Releases Video of Laquan McDonald Shooting*, TIME, November 24, 2015, *available at* http://time.com/4126670/chicago-releases-video-of-laquan-mcdonald-shooting.

A seven-minute dash cam video caught by one of the squad cars on the scene shows Mr. McDonald standing in the middle of a four-lane street when one officer exits his squad car and shoots McDonald from a distance of approximately 10–15 feet.[365] At the moment of the shooting, McDonald appears to be walking diagonally from the officer.[366] After the seventeen-year-old falls to the ground, the video shows the officer shooting McDonald several more times.[367] In total, the officer shot McDonald sixteen times.[368] The officer involved in the shooting – Officer Jason Van Dyke – was not initially charged with Mr. McDonald's murder.[369]

On the night of shooting, a police union spokesman argued that McDonald was a "very serious threat to the officers and he le[ft] them no choice at that point but to defend themselves" since McDonald "was coming at the officer."[370] And for over a year, the public knew very little about the case – other than the fact that the city of Chicago agreed to pay Mr. McDonald's family a $5 million settlement even before the family had brought a suit.[371] The settlement also included a highly controversial clause that required the family to keep quiet about the video.[372] It would take another thirteen months for the video to become public – after Mayor Rahm Emmanuel had successfully won a second term as Chicago's mayor.[373] Only then did the video go public and the Cook County State's attorney Anita Alvarez file charges against Officer Van Dyke.[374] In fact, it wasn't until one week after Mayor Emmanuel won reelection that the city of Chicago formally agreed to the settlement with Mr. McDonald's family.[375]

The Laquan McDonald shooting was hardly the first instance of alleged organizational misconduct by the Chicago Police Department. The city has recently considered a $5.5 million reparations package to compensate the victims of police torture from the 1970s and 1980s.[376] Much of this torture allegedly happened under the watchful eye of police

[365] *Id.* [366] *Id.* [367] *Id.* [368] *Id.*

[369] Monida Davey & Mitch Smith, *Chicago Protests Mostly Peaceful After Video of Police Shooting is Released*, NY Times, November 25, 2015, at A1.

[370] *Id.*

[371] Monica Davey, *Chicago Pays $5 Million to Family of Black Teenager Killed by Officer*, NY Times, April 16, 2015, at A15.

[372] Davey & Smith, *supra* note 370, at A1.

[373] Bernard Harcourt, *Cover-up in Chicago*, NY Times, November 30, 2015, *available at* www.nytimes.com/2015/11/30/opinion/cover-up-in-chicago.html.

[374] *Id.* [375] *Id.* [376] Davey, *supra* note 371, at A15.

commander Jon Burge.[377] After Chicago fired Burge in 1993, the city paid an estimate $85 million in settlements and other costs.[378]

If the DOJ finds a pattern or practice of misconduct, Chicago would be the largest police department to ever undergo federal intervention – even larger than Los Angeles. In the wake of the DOJ's announcement, many speculated about the possible costs of DOJ intervention into the Chicago Police Department. If Chicago ends up like Los Angeles, the city may be on the hook for a bill of over $100 million in the coming decade. But it is important to take a step back and ask – what would Chicago get in return for such an investment? Obviously, Chicago should get a police force that engages in less unconstitutional misconduct. What many fail to realize is that, from a purely fiscal perspective, unlawful police behavior is expensive.

Over the last decade, the city of Chicago has paid out a jaw-dropping $500 million on civil rights settlements, judgments, and legal fees.[379] In 2013 alone, the city paid $84.6 million – more than triple the amount that the city had anticipated in its budgetary projections.[380] What if federal intervention could meaningfully reduce the amount of misconduct committed by police officers, thereby reducing the amount of money a city spends each year handling civil rights suits? Presumably, such a realization would have profound effects. It would suggest that federal intervention is actually an investment – not just an investment in reducing the dignitary harms of police wrongdoing, but a financial investment capable of saving a municipality money over the long run.

C *Did Federal Intervention Hurt Police Effectiveness?*

Some critics of federal intervention allege that this regulatory mechanism causes police departments to become less aggressive.[381] This accusation was particularly loud in the LAPD case. According to this view, federal intervention reduced the amount of encounters between LAPD

377 *Id.* 378 *Id.*

379 Andrew Schroedter, *Beyond Burge*, BETTER GOVERNMENT ASSOCIATION, April 3, 2014, *available at* www.bettergov.org/news/beyond-burge.

380 *Id.*

381 *See, e.g.*, DAVIS, HENDERSON, & ORTIZ, *supra* note 282, at 16 (explaining how officers in Pittsburgh felt "hesitant to intervene in situations involving conflicts because they were afraid of having citizens file an unwarranted anonymous complaint against them").

officers citizenry, either because oversight makes officers hesitant or because it forces officers to spend valuable time completing procedural hurdles.[382]

This so-called depolicing hypothesis is not unique to Los Angeles. Recall from Chapter 1 that the NYPD has got into hot water through the use of stop-and-frisk. On August 12, 2013, US district judge Shira Scheindlin ruled that the New York City stop-and-frisk program violated the constitutional rights of minority residents, as it constituted a "policy of indirect racial profiling."[383] As part of her decision, Judge Scheindlin ordered New York City to change its stop-and-frisk policy.[384] She also ordered the appointment of an external monitor to oversee mandated changes to the NYPD stop-and-frisk procedures.[385] Mayor Michael Bloomberg strongly objected to the decision to appoint a monitor, calling it a "terrible idea" and arguing that it would be "disruptive."[386] According to Bloomberg, any court-appointed monitor

[382] Chanin, *supra* note 207 (quoting a leader from the Washington, DC police union as saying that structural reform litigation leads to more time-consuming paperwork).

[383] Joseph Goldstein, *Judge Rejects New York's Stop-and-Frisk Policy*, NY Times, August 12, 2013, *available at* www.nytimes.com/2013/08/13/nyregion/stop-and-frisk-practice-violated-rights-judge-rules.html (last visited September 9, 2013) (providing details about Judge Scheindlin's ruling); *see also* John Cassidy, *Judge Scheindlin Stops and Frisks N.Y.C. Mayoral Candidates*, The New Yorker Blogs, August 12, 2013, *available at* www.newyorker.com/online/blogs/johncassidy/2013/08/judge-scheindlin-stops-and-frisks-ny-mayoral-candidates.html (last visited September 23, 2013) (mentioning Judge Scheindlin's decision that stop-and-frisk constitutes a violation of the Constitution); *New York City's "Stop and Frisk" Policy Does Violate the Constitution and Leads to "Indirect Racial Profiling," Federal Judge Rules*, Mail Online, August 12, 2013, *available at* www.dailymail.co.uk/news/article-2390077/New-York-stop-frisk-federal-judge-Shira-Scheindlin-rules-policy-violates-constitution-orders-changes.html (last visited September 23, 2013) (explaining Judge Scheindlin's opinion).

[384] Daniel Beekman, *Ivy League Law Professors to Help Implement Stop-and-Frisk Reforms*, NY Daily News, September 19, 2013, *available at* www.nydailynews.com/news/crime/ivy-league-law-professors-implement-stop-and-frisk-reforms-article-1.1459589 (last visited September 23, 2013) (explaining the dozen individuals that); J. David Goodman, *Bloomberg Calls Court Monitor for Police a "Terrible Idea,"* NY Times, June 13, 2013, *available at* www.nytimes.com/2013/06/14/nyregion/bloomberg-calls-court-monitor-for-police-a-terrible-idea.html (last visited September 9, 2013).

[385] Goodman, *supra* note 384 (explaining the judge's appointment of external monitor Peter L. Zimroth); *see also* Beekman, *supra* note 384 (describing the various academics appointed to the twelve person monitoring team tasked with reforming New York City's stop-and-frisk program).

[386] Goodman, *supra* note 384; *see also* Yoav Gonen, *De Blasio Calls NYPD's Federal Monitor a Temporary Reality*, New York Post, http://nypost.com/2013/09/20/de-blasio-calls-nypds-federal-monitor-a-temporary-reality/ (last visited September 23, 2013) (referring to Bloomberg's conclusion that the appointment of a monitor would be "terrible");

would not understand "the streets of New York City."[387] Citing Philadelphia's experience with a police department monitor, Bloomberg also claimed that the decision could contribute to higher crime, thereby putting the safety of all New Yorkers at risk.[388] Bloomberg, and many critics of Judge Scheindlin's decision, has argued that judicial efforts to reform police departments negatively affect the department's efficiency and effectiveness.[389] No doubt, in the same period of time when the NYPD rapidly expanded the use of stop-and-frisks, crime rates plummeted, with violent crime rates falling by approximately 66 percent and property crime declining 62 percent.[390] Indeed, there is strong correlation between the increase in stop-and-frisks and the decline of crime in New York City. But these stops appeared to have come at a high and possibly unconstitutional cost. The proliferation of stop-and-frisks started after the US Supreme Court issued the *Terry v. Ohio* case. There, the Court permitted a law enforcement to execute a limited stop-and-frisk when the officer had reasonable suspicion that a group of individuals were engaged in criminal

Colleen Long, *NYC Stop-and-Frisk Policy Wrongfully Targeted Minorities, Judge Rules; Outside Monitor Appointed*, MINNEAPOLIS STAR TRIBUNE, August 12, 2013 (identifying Bloomberg as a strong critic of the decision, and citing Bloomberg's concern that the law will hurt crime fighting efforts).

387 Goodman, *supra* note 384; *see also* Michael Howard Saul, *Bloomberg Calls Stop-and-Frisk Ruling "Dangerous,"* THE WALL STREET JOURNAL, September 21, 2013 (also quoting Mayor Bloomberg criticizing the decision, in part, because of the court's failure to understand the streets of the city).

388 *See, e.g.*, Goodman, *supra* note 384; Damien Gayle, *Shootings up 13% in New York City After Federal Judge Rules Police "Stop and Frisk" Tactics Unconstitutional and Racist*, MAIL ONLINE, September 19, 2013, *available at* www.dailymail.co.uk/news/article-2425055/Shootings-10-New-York-City-federal-judge-rules-stop-search-unconstitutional-racist.html (last visited September 23, 2013) (detailing how New York City officials are pointing to a 13 percent increase in shootings over the last twenty-eight days as evidence that the Judge's orders have contributed to higher crime).

389 *See e.g.*, Tom Howell Jr., *NYC Mayor Bloomberg Staunchly Defends Stop-and-Frisk Program*, THE WASHINGTON TIMES, August 12, 2013, *available at* www.washingtontimes.com/news/2013/aug/12/judge-says-nyc-stop-and-frisk-policy-violated-righ/ (last visited September 23, 2013) (summarizing Mayor Bloomberg's objections to the Judge's ruling); *New York Police Commissioner Ray Kelly Calls Stop-and-Frisk Decision "Disturbing and Offensive,"* NY DAILY NEWS, August 12, 2013, *available at* www.nydailynews.com/news/politics/new-york-police-commissioner-ray-kelly-comments-stop-and-frisk-decision-article-1.1424689 (last visited September 23, 2013) (quoting Police Commissioner Ray Kelly, who calls the allegations made in the court case "recklessly untrue").

390 FEDERAL BUREAU OF INVESTIGATIONS, UNIFORM CRIME REPORTING STATISTICS (1970–2011), *available at* www.fbi.gov/about-us/cjis/ucr/ucr.

activity.[391] Since the issuance of this decision, the use of these so-called *Terry* stops has raised accusations of racial profiling in cities across the country. And perhaps nowhere have those accusations of wrongdoing been greater than in New York City.[392] In 1990, the New York Police Department (NYPD) officers recorded only 41,438 *Terry* stops.[393] By 2011, this number had risen to an astonishing 685,724 – an increase of over 1,300 percent.[394] Of those stopped by the NYPD pursuant to this policy, an estimated 87 percent were either Latino or African American.[395] And these stops rarely led to an arrest or yielded illegal contraband.[396] On average, the NYPD seizes illegal contraband once for every 143 stops of African Americans and 99 stops for Latinos.[397]

Despite these concerning patterns, many New York officials like Mayor Bloomberg worried that any court-ordered reform of the city's stop-and-frisk program would hurt law enforcement's ability to fight crime. Bloomberg is not alone in this belief that court-ordered reform of police departments can hurt the efficiency and effectiveness. Critics have challenged nearly every single attempt to reform police departments by alleging that such efforts would hurt policing quality and result in higher crime. For example, critics levied such claims after

[391] *Terry* v. *Ohio*, 392 US 1 (1968) (holding that a police officer could perform a stop of a limited time and scope if he or she had reasonable suspicion that a person was engaged in a criminal act).

[392] *See generally* Goldstein, *supra* note 383; Stop and Frisk Data, New York Civil Liberties Union, *available at* www.nyclu.org/content/stop-and-frisk-data (last visited September 23, 2013) (giving a detailed breakdown of the seemingly racially disparate pattern of stop-and-frisks in New York City).

[393] Franklin E. Zimring, The City That Became Safe: New York's Lessons for Urban Crime and Its Control 128 (2012).

[394] Dylan Matthews, *Here's What You Need to Know About Stop and Frisk – And Why The Courts Shut It Down*, Washington Post, August 13, 2013, *available at* www.washingtonpost.com/blogs/wonkblog/wp/2013/08/13/heres-what-you-need-to-know-about-stop-and-frisk-and-why-the-courts-shut-it-down/ (last visited September 9, 2013).

[395] Zimring, *supra* note 393 at 129.

[396] Adam Serwer & Jaeah Lee, *Charts: Are the NYPD's Stop-and-Frisks Violating the Constitution?* Mother Jones, April 29, 2013, *available at* www.motherjones.com/politics/2013/04/new-york-nypd-stop-frisk-lawsuit-trial-charts (last visited September 9, 2013) (detailing the highly imprecise nature of stop-and-frisk in New York City).

[397] *Id.* By contrast, when police officers in New York City *Terry* stop against a white suspect, they find contraband about one in every twenty-seven cases. This means that *Terry* stops against Latino suspects are around 3–4 times less accurate than stops of white suspects. And *Terry* stops of black suspects are around five to six times less accurate. This, according to many, is clear evidence that police officers in New York view minorities with more suspicion than their criminality warrants.

the implementation of the exclusionary rule[398] and the *Miranda* decision,[399] just to name a few.

The reforms implemented as part of § 14141 litigation raise the same fundamental concern. Police officials' objections to this method of reform typically involve complaints about burdensome procedural requirements forced on departments during monitoring – procedural headaches that make police less aggressive. For example, a Vera Institute study of the federal oversight in Pittsburgh found that officers felt "hesitant to intervene in situations involving conflicts because they were afraid of having citizens file an unwarranted anonymous complaint against them."[400] The study concluded that three in every four officers felt that federal oversight contributed to reduced aggressiveness.[401] Similarly, the head of Washington, DC's Police Union claimed that federal oversight led to more paperwork, thereby making officers less equipped to fight crime.[402] Previous researchers have called this theory the depolicing hypothesis.[403]

Various critics have claimed that federal intervention into the affairs of local police agencies decreases police efficiency, thereby increasing crime.[404] One of the most common arguments made by depolicing

[398] *See, e.g.*, Raymond A. Atkins & Paul H. Rubin, *The Effects of Criminal Procedure on Crime Rates: Mapping Out the Consequences of the Exclusionary Rule*, 46 J. L. & Econ. 157 (2003) (finding that the exclusionary rule's passage was associated with a uptick in national crime); National Institute of Justice, Criminal Justice Report – The Effects of the Exclusionary Rule: A Study in California National Institute of Justice, Criminal Justice Report - The Effects of the Exclusionary Rule: A Study of California (1982) (finding that the use of the exclusionary rule led to prosecutors dropping complaints in 86,033 felony arrest cases).

[399] *See, e.g.*, Paul G. Cassell & Richard Fowles, *Handcuffing The Cops? A Thirty-Year Perspective on Miranda's Harmful Effects on Law Enforcement*, 50 Stan. L. Rev. 1055, 1062–66 (1998) (linking Miranda to decreased clearance rates in the United States); *see also More Criminals to Go Free? Effect of High Court's Ruling*, U.S. News & World Rep., June 27, 1966, at 32, 33 (quoting Los Angeles mayor as saying the *Miranda* decision would handcuff police and contribute to more criminals going free); S. Rep. No. 90–101097, at 25 (1968), *reprinted in* 1968 USCCAN 2112, 2123 (determining that "crime will not be effectively abated so long as criminals who have voluntarily confessed their crimes are released on mere technicalities"); Liva Baker, Miranda: Crime, Law and Politics 248 (1983) (citing Nixon's campaign speeches criticizing *Miranda* as a decision that will increase crime).

[400] Davis, Ortiz, Henderson, Miller, & Massie, *supra* note 281, at 16.

[401] *Id.* at 21.

[402] Chanin, *supra* note 207 (quoting the head of Washington, DC's police officer union).

[403] *Id.* at 185. Stone, Todd Fogelsong, & Cole, *supra* note 273, at 19–36 (describing the depolicing hypothesis before thoroughly rejecting it in the case of the LAPD).

[404] *See, e.g.*, Colleen Long, *NYC Stop-and-Frisk Policy Wrongfully Targeted Minorities, Judge Rules; Outside Monitor Appointed*, Minneapolis Star Tribune, August 12, 2013 (identifying Mayor Bloomberg as a strong critic of a federal district court decision to

advocates is that federal intervention decreases police aggressiveness. According to this view, federal intervention reduces the amount of encounters between police and citizenry, either because structural reform makes officers hesitant or because it forces officers to spend valuable time completing procedural hurdles.[405] Some officers suggest that depolicing is most likely to affect the number of police contacts and arrests for minor street crimes.[406] This is because arrests for serious crimes normally happen after lengthy investigations, while arrests for minor crimes happen as police officers proactively monitor the streets and respond to visible wrongdoing. The depolicing hypothesis suggests that policies and procedures mandated by federal intervention inhibit an officer's abilities to engage in this type of proactive, order maintenance policing. As a result, some worry that federal intervention will lead to higher crime rates.[407]

If depolicing were happening in Los Angeles during federal intervention, we should see a corresponding drop in police aggressiveness. After all, a number of on-the-ground actors in Los Angeles worried that the introduction of federal intervention would result in depolicing. Did this happen? In order to measure whether federal intervention impacted the aggressiveness of LAPD officers, Table 4.1 shows the change in the frequency of total arrests, minor arrests, pedestrian stops, and car stops during the federal intervention era.[408]

overhaul New York City police department's stop-and-frisk program, and citing Bloomberg's concern that the law will hurt crime fighting efforts); Michael Howard Saul, *Bloomberg Calls Stop-and-Frisk Ruling "Dangerous,"* THE WALL STREET JOURNAL, September 21, 2013 (also quoting Mayor Bloomberg criticizing the court decision overhauling stop-and-frisk, in part, because of the court's failure to understand the streets of the city).

405 *See, e.g.*, Chanin, *supra* note 207 (quoting a leader from the Washington, DC, Police Union as saying that structural police reform leads to more time-consuming paperwork).

406 STONE, FOGELSONG, & COLE, *supra* note 273, at 19–20. (showing in figure 10 that a high proportion of LAPD officers believed that the threat of community complaints would hurt proactive street policing; also stating that "concerns have been raised that the consent decree would lead to de-policing or what one law enforcement official describe to us as the 'drive-and-wave syndrome'").

407 As discussed earlier, one of the most prominent recent examples of this depolicing hypothesis was the response by Mayor Michael Bloomberg to the New York City stop-and-frisk litigation. *See supra* notes 384–85.

408 This chart uses the best available data to represent the start and end of federal intervention. Data is drawn from several sources. Los Angeles Police Department, Statistical Digest (2001–2011), *available at* www.lapdonline.org/crime_mapping_and_

Table 4.1 *Change in LAPD Officer Aggressiveness during Federal Intervention*

Stage of Federal Intervention	Total Arrests	Index Arrests per Crime	Minor Arrests	Minor Arrests per Officer	Pedestrian and Car Stops	Pedestrian and Car Stops per Officer
Start	114,355	0.178	82,227	8.95	587,200	65.7
End	101,167	0.215	78,382	7.85	875,204	88.8

The LAPD saw a slight downtick in total arrests by the end of federal intervention – dropping from 114,355 reported arrests to only 101,167. At first this is discouraging. But it is important to remember that crimes in Los Angeles also decreased significantly over this time period. When factoring in this precipitous crime decline, LAPD officers actually appear to be engaged in more index arrests per crime reported at the end of federal intervention. However, the number of minor arrests executed per sworn officer fell somewhat during this time period. Additionally, the number of reported vehicle and pedestrian stops per officer actually increased from around 65.7 near the start of federal intervention to 88.8 near the end – an increase of 35.2 percent.[409] Then again, this apparent uptick in pedestrian and car stops may be the result of better reporting by LAPD officers, which merely coincides with the implementation of the federal consent decree. Overall, the picture is mixed. Nevertheless, it seems safe to

compstat/content_basic_view/9098 (click on "statistical digest" under the requisite year) (providing the number of serious, or type I arrests, and the number of minor, or type II, arrests for 2001 and 2011 in Los Angeles); U.S. Dep't of Justice, Bureau of Justice Statistics, Uniform Crime Reports (UCR): Crime in the United States (2000–2012) [hereinafter FBI UCR Statistics], *available at* www.fbi.gov/about-us/cjis/ucr/ucr-publications (to access, click on requisite year under "Crime in the United States," then click "Police Employee Data," "Table 78," and navigate to the data for Los Angeles, California). For Arrests, this figure used data from 2000 to represent the start of structural police reform and 2012 to represent the end of federal intervention – the most recent date when data is easily accessible. For pedestrian and vehicle stops, this figure uses 2002 to represent the state of structural police reform, since it was the first date that there was good data available. It uses 2008 as the end date for motor vehicle and pedestrian stops since it was the most recent date when the LAPD released thorough data that was easily accessible to the public.

409 The LAPD had approximately 9,056 sworn police officers in 2002 and 9,743 sworn officers in 2008. *Id.*

say that this data is not indicative of a police department that significantly reduced aggressiveness in response to federal intervention. Even if some officers did reduce the aggressiveness of their patrols somewhat, it seems unlikely that this contributed to any increases in crime rates.

The data from Los Angeles is at least partially corroborated by an empirical study conducted in Pittsburgh. There, the introduction of federal intervention did not correlate with any apparent reductions in traffic citations or DUI arrests.[410] This is not to say that federal intervention is without negative side effects. It is fully possible that § 14141 intervention leads to more complex externalities that are not readily apparent from these statistics.[411] The next obvious question is whether federal intervention has correlated with any changes in crime outcomes. To tackle this question, Figure 4.8 first looks at the experience of the LAPD during its consent decree era. It graphs the change in the rate of index crimes reported in Los Angeles, California, and the United States between 2000 and 2012.

Over the federal intervention period, Los Angeles saw reported index crimes rates decline more precipitously than the state of California or the United States as a whole. But how did Los Angeles fare during this time period compared to other large American cities? Figure 4.9 compares the change in violent crime rates in Los Angeles to the change in violent crime rates in the other largest cities over the time period in the United States.[412]

During the same time when Los Angeles was undergoing federal intervention, the city saw a tremendous decrease in violent crime relative to other major American cities. In total, violent crime rates in Los Angeles dipped by 65 percent between 2000 and 2012.[413]

[410] Davis, Ortiz, Henderson, Miller, & Massie, *supra* note 281, at 56 (showing in figure 12 the progression of these two trends during the structural reform litigation era).

[411] For instance, it remains possible that structural police reform reduces total police contacts via *Terry* stops or traffic stops. Measuring this sort of reduction statistically is challenging. In many cases, municipalities do not, or have not, kept good records on the number of these minor interactions with law enforcement. Thus, making accurate determinations changes in the rate of these minor contacts over time is often impossible.

[412] FBI UCR Statistics, *supra* note 408 (to access, click on requisite year under "Crime in the United States," click on "Violent Crime," select "Table 8," and navigate to the requisite police agency). Chicago is not included in this sample because it has not collected data on rape offenses in a manner that is consistent with the rest of the country.

[413] *Id.* (as Los Angeles's violent crime rate dropped from 1359.8 crimes per 100,000 residents to 481.1 crimes per 100,000 residents).

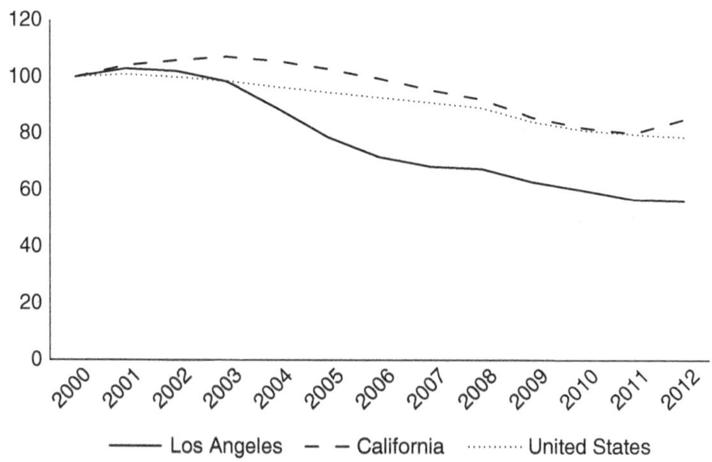

Figure 4.8 Change in Rate of Reported Index Crimes (2000 set equal to 100)

By comparison, violent crime in the United States fell by around 24 percent during this time period,[414] and the median large American city in Figure 4.9 saw violent crime fall by about 28 percent.[415] Figure 4.10 similarly compares changes in property crime in Los Angeles and other large American cities.[416]

Although not as impressive as the violent crime numbers, Los Angeles still outperforms the typical large American city during the federal intervention era in property crime prevention.[417] Los Angeles also outperformed the United States as a whole.[418] Combined, these statistics demonstrate that after the start of federal intervention in Los Angeles *the sky is not falling*. Of course, it is not immediately

[414] The violent crime rates in the United States over the time period started at 506.5 per 100,000 residents and fell to 386.9 by 2012. *Id.* (to access, click on requisite year under "Crime in the United States," click on "Violent Crime," and select "Table 1").

[415] Using the data from Figure 5.6, San Diego and San Antonio are jointly the median cities. San Diego's violent crimes fell by 29 percent and San Antonio's by 27 percent, resulting in an approximate median of 28 percent.

[416] *Id.* (to access, click on requisite year under "Crime in the United States," click on "Property Crime," select "Table 8," and navigate to the requisite police agency).

[417] The median city – San Diego – saw a decline of 26 percent in property crimes. Los Angeles saw a decline of 36 percent in property crime. *Id.*

[418] The United States saw property crime decline from a rate of 3618.3 in 2000 to a rate of 2859.2 in 2012, an overall drop of about 21 percent – significantly lower than Los Angeles at 36 percent. *Id.* (to access, click on requisite year under "Crime in the United States," click on "Property Crime," and select "Table 1").

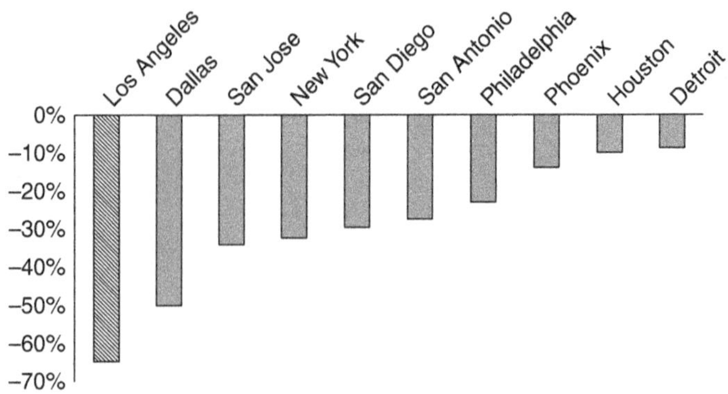

Figure 4.9 Changes in Violent Crime Rates from 2000 to 2012

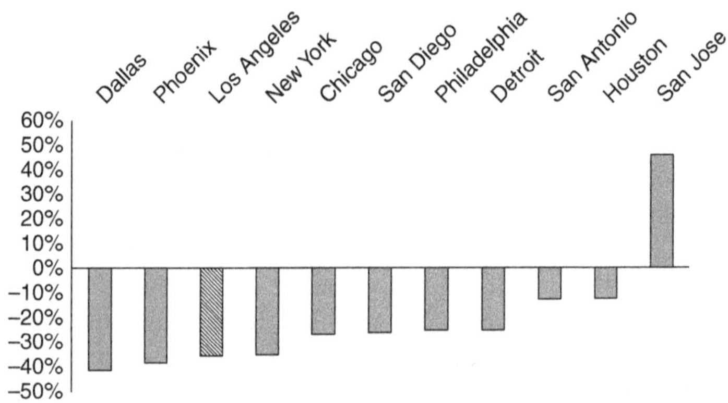

Figure 4.10 Changes in Property Crime Rates from 2000 to 2012

clear whether the LAPD had an effect on these changes in crime outcomes. Criminologists have theorized that a number of demographic, legal, and socioeconomic factors may affect crime rates.[419]

[419] Historically, criminologists explained the causes of crime in four ways. Classical criminologists generally argued that individuals are rational actors; thus, in order to deter crime policymakers ought to raise the costs of crime through increasing the length or certainty of criminal penalties. *See generally* CESARE BECCARIA, ON CRIMES AND PUNISHMENT (1764); James Q. Wilson, *On Deterrence*, in THINKING ABOUT CRIME (1975). Sociological criminologists contend that society defines and creates crime through poverty, income inequality, and culture. Adolphe Quetelet, *Of the Development of the Propensity to Crime*, in A TREATISE OF MAN (1842); John Lea and Jock Young, *Relative Deprivation*, in WHAT IS TO BE DONE ABOUT LAW AND ORDER (1984). And situational criminologists have argued that society can deter criminal deviance by adjusting situational incentives for illegal behavior. Ronald V.G. Clarke, *"Situational" Crime Prevention: Theory and Practice*, 20 BRITISH J. CRIMINOLOGY

Since 2000, the demographic profile of Los Angeles remains fairly stable,[420] as has the median income when adjusted for inflation.[421] Poverty rates have not changed noticeably.[422] Incarceration in Los Angeles County has actually decreased.[423] Overall, it is hard to find any obvious socioeconomic, legal, or demographic change in Los Angeles that should explain the unusually dramatic decline in crime over the federal intervention era.[424]

This chapter does not offer any affirmative explanation for the dramatic crime decline in Los Angeles during federal intervention. It is

136 (1980); Marcus Felson, *The Routine Activity Approach as a General Crime Theory*, in S.S. Simpson, of Crime and Criminality (2000).

420 Criminologists commonly associate trends in crime with trends in the relative size of the adolescent population. *See, e.g.*, Franklin E. Zimring, American Juvenile Justice 92–93 (2005) (showing that the most common age for an offender to commit various crimes is around late adolescence). The adolescent population in Los Angeles represented 21.8 percent of the total city population in 2000, and 21.8 percent in 2010. Thus, any changes in crime cannot be attributed to changes in the size of the adolescent population. By contrast, the relative size of the adolescent population in the United States has declined over the same time period by 5.8 percent. *See* United States Census Bureau, State and County Quick Facts (2010), *available at* http://quickfacts.census.gov/qfd/index.html (select "California" and browse to "Los Angeles" to find 2010 statistics); United States Census Bureau, Los Angeles City, California QuickLinks (2000), *available at* http://quickfacts.census.gov/qfd/states/06/0644000lk.html (select "economic characteristics" under the "Census 2000 population, demographic, and housing information" subsection to find 2000 statistics).

421 Adjusting for inflation, median income in Los Angeles has gone from $47,934 in 2000 to $50,028 in 2010 – a relatively small increase of 4.3 percent. *Id.*

422 In 2000, the poverty rate in Los Angeles was 18.3 percent. In 2010, that number ballooned to 20.2 percent, an increase of just under 2 percent. *Id.*

423 In 2000, approximately 54,180 of the California inmates in state prison came from Los Angeles county. State of California Department of Corrections, California Prisoners and Parolees, table 10 (2001), *available at* www.cdcr.ca.gov/Reports_Research/Offender_Information_Services_Branch/Annual/CalPris/CALPRISd2001.pdf. By contrast, in the most recent survey of California prisoners in 2013, that number had actually dropped to 46,341. Prison Census Data, California Department of Corrections and Rehabilitation, table 7 (August 26, 2013), *available at* www.cdcr.ca.gov/Reports_Research/Offender_Information_Services_Branch/Annual/Census/CENSUSd1306.pdf.

424 Los Angeles saw a substantially larger decrease in crime between 2000 and 2012 than the United States. Thus, if demographic or sociological explanation could explain the uniquely large crime drop in Los Angeles, then Los Angeles should see substantially better outcomes in these categories than the United States. As seen below, there is not a significant difference between the two locales. Given that most traditional method for explaining crime do not seem to explain the Los Angeles decline, we are left with policing and situational criminology as the most likely remaining theoretical explanation. For an example of this sort of methodology in work, *see generally* Zimring, *supra* note 393.

entirely plausible that exceptional crime decline in Los Angeles is entirely unrelated to the changes in the LAPD. Instead this chapter offers a narrower, but nonetheless important claim. The LAPD case study suggests that constitutional policing need not come at the price of crime control. In fact, Los Angeles was able to introduce significant constitutional reforms that curbed apparent police misconduct while the city also underwent one of the largest crime drops in American history. Whether this model is exportable to other communities over different time periods is an open empirical question. A cursory examination of other large agencies that have also undergone federal intervention suggests that this pattern may not necessarily be unique to the LAPD – although the overall evidence is mixed.

Appendices C and D show the change in violent crime and property crime rates in communities that have undergone or are currently undergoing federal intervention via § 14141 between 1994 and 2015. On average, these municipalities have been little changed in property or violent crime rates, relative to the national average. Nevertheless, there is wide variation from one community to the next.

A recent empirical study provides a more thorough analysis of the depolicing hypothesis across the entire population of cities to undergo federal police intervention. That study finds that the depolicing effects of federal intervention may be greater in the years immediately after federal intervention and diminish over time.[425] The study relied on a panel of American law enforcement agencies and difference-in-difference regression analyses to examine whether federal intervention via § 14141 had any effect on police aggressiveness (as measured by arrests) or crime rates. It focused specifically on federal intervention cases that took place between 1994 and 2012. While it failed to find any statistically significant relationship between federal intervention and arrest rates, it did find a statistically significant relationship between federal intervention and crime rates. Specifically, it found that communities faced with § 14141 intervention saw a measurable increase in crime rates in the first few years of the oversight process, even when controlling for other potentially explanatory variables.[426] This effect

[425] Stephen Rushin & Griffin Edwards, *De-Policing*, 102 Cornell L. Rev.(forthcoming 2017).

[426] The study attempted to control for demographics by including variables for urbanization rate, the proportion of the population that is male, the proportion of the population that is nonwhite, and the proportion of the population that is between the ages of 10 and 49. In addition, the study included controls for the economic condition of each community by adding in variables for unemployment rate and median real income. Finally, the study

diminished over time. This suggests that police departments may experience some growing pains when faced with external regulation via § 14141.

Ultimately, though, more empirical analysis will be necessary in the future to understand the complex relationship between federal intervention and depolicing.

V Remaining Questions and Concerns

Overall, the LAPD appears to have made significant and meaningful changes during structural reform litigation. But not every city has been so lucky. Take the DOJ's recent battle with Sheriff Terry Johnson in Alamance County, North Carolina. For years, civil rights advocates in Alamance County argued that Sheriff Johnson targeted unfairly targeted Latino residents.[427] One local newspaper reporter described Sheriff Johnson as "a white Southern sheriff prone to saying things every so often a white Southern sheriff shouldn't say."[428] So it came as no surprise to many when the DOJ initiated an investigation into the conduct of the Alamance County Sheriff's Department via § 14141. This investigation, like dozens before it, relied heavily on interviews, statistical analyses, and witness statements to conclude that Alamance County was engaged in a pattern of "systemic racial profiling of Latinos."[429] Prominent civil rights organizations like the American Civil Liberties Union took an interest in the Alamance County case, urging Sheriff Johnson to comply with DOJ requests.[430] Among the more inflammatory findings, the DOJ investigative report cited evidence that an Alamance County Sheriff's Office captain sent "his subordinates a video game premised on shooting Mexican children, pregnant women, and other 'wetbacks.'"[431]

included variables to capture the specific characteristics of each police department, including the number of sworn officers, the number of male officers, the number of female officers, and the ratio of male to female sworn officers.

427 Billy Ball, *"Bring Me Some Mexicans!"* Independent Weekly, January 2, 2013, at 11.

428 David Zucchino, *A North Carolina Lawman Practices Discriminatory Policing, the Justice Department Says*, LA Times, November 24, 2012, at 13.

429 Michael Biesecker, *US Files Civil Rights Complaint Against NC Sheriff*, Associated Press, December 20, 2012; Emery P. Dalesio, *Attorney: NC Sheriff Won't Settle Racial Profiling Claims*, Associated Press, September 26, 2012 (stating that the DOJ's investigation of the Alamance County Sheriff's Department lasted two years).

430 *ACLU Urges Alamance Sheriff to Comply with DOJ Requests in Light of Lawsuit*, States New Service, December 20, 2012.

431 *Justice Department Documents Discriminatory Practices by Alamance Sheriff's Office in Latest Court Filing*, States New Service, March 4, 2014.

By 2012, the table was set for the Alamance County Sheriff's Department to settle with the DOJ. After all, the DOJ had never brought a single § 14141 case to trial. It never needed to. Remember that all previous § 14141 cases had ended in settlements. Most cities thought § 14141 cases were too risky to go to trial. A full trial could cost taxpayers hundreds of thousands of dollars. And the findings from a DOJ investigation seemed difficult to refute. So most cities rationally determined that they'd lose a court battle with the DOJ. A settlement has proven to be the path of least resistance. But Alamance County proved to be different from the start. The events that followed have raised serious questions about the usefulness of federal intervention as a regulatory mechanism.

A *The Need for Organizational Cooperation*

When the Justice Department "invited the Sheriff's Office to negotiate a court enforceable agreement to remedy the violations" Sheriff Johnson refused.[432] According to the DOJ, Sheriff Johnson even withheld documents and falsified records.[433] Other Alamance County officials quickly came to the defense of Sheriff Johnson. "The Alamance County commissioners, all white," strongly supported Sheriff Johnson's resistance to federal intervention, "praising his hard-line stance against illegal immigration."[434] And in the midst of the dispute, North Carolina's Republican governor Pat McCrory honored Sheriff Johnson with the Order of the Long Leaf Pine award, one of North Carolina's top civilian honors.[435] The table was set for the most significant showdown to date between the federal government and a local police department.

432 *Cost of Alamance Sheriff Terry Johnson's Trial Continues to Grow*, Greensboro News & Record, August 26, 2014.

433 Michael Biesecker, *Terry S. Johnson, North Carolina Sheriff, and Deputies Accused of Discrimination and Targeting of Latinos for Deportation*, Huffington Post, September 19, 2012, *available at* www.huffingtonpost.com/2012/09/19/sheriff-terry-s-johnson-discrimination-charges_n_1896343.html ("The agency also said that Johnson obstructed the federal investigation launched in 2010 by withholding requested documents and falsifying records.").

434 *Id.*

435 Colin Campbell, *McCrory Honors Alamance County Sheriff Facing Federal Allegations of Racial Profiling*, The News & Observer, December 19, 2014 (it is worth noting that Government Pat McCrory claimed that the award was unrelated to the ongoing federal suit against Sheriff Johnson and this was the second time that Sheriff Johnson received this sort of an honor).

At this point, the DOJ had two choices. The DOJ could declare defeat. Why use limited resources to reform a department that will fight tooth-and-nail to block reform efforts? But opting for this path would make the DOJ look weak in the eyes of many departments across the country. It would essentially put the nation's police departments on notice – resist hard enough, and the DOJ will leave you alone.

Conversely, the DOJ could file suit against Alamance County in federal district court. Doing so would be risky. The DOJ would need to convince a federal judge that the Alamance County Sheriff's Department was engaged in a pattern or practice of unconstitutional misconduct. If the DOJ were to lose its case against Alamance County, this failure could embolden other police departments to resist federal intervention in the future. Worse yet, a loss in federal court could establish an unfavorable precedent that harms future cases.

In a sense, the DOJ is what sociolegal scholars would call the classic "repeat player."[436] That is to say the DOJ will inevitably handle many § 14141 cases in the future. Because of this, the DOJ must think about how its behavior in the Alamance County case may influence future cases. A loss against Alamance County could set a harmful legal precedent that impairs DOJ reform efforts in other cases. Alamance County, though, is what sociolegal scholars would call a "one shotter."[437] Sheriff Johnson doesn't care about future cases. Nor does he care about the precedent set by this case. Sheriff Johnson's only goal is to resolve this single dispute in a way that benefits him most and satisfies his constituents.

This imbalance of goals is nothing new. In every § 14141 case before Alamance County, the same imbalance existed. Every local police department that the DOJ targets for § 14141 reform is a one shotter. This has not kept the DOJ from bringing these one shotters to the negotiation table. So what makes Alamance County different? Why was Alamance County one of the first cases where a municipality refused to negotiate with the DOJ?

The answer possibly lays in the difference between municipal police departments and sheriff's departments. In most § 14141 cases, the DOJ has carefully leveraged the structure of local government to obtain favorable settlements – settlements that give one shotter municipalities

436 *See generally* Marc Galanter, *Why the Haves Come Out Ahead: Speculations on the Limits of Legal Change*, 9 L. & Soc'y Rev. 95, 98–104 (1974) (distinguishing between repeat players and one shotters).

437 *Id.*

sufficiently favorable terms to justify settlement, while also protecting the long-term interests of the DOJ in obtaining precedents that benefit them as repeat players. One way that the DOJ accomplishes this is by negotiating with city officials – city attorneys, mayors, or city council members – rather than with the police chief directly. In many cases, this tactic has resulted in both settlement and the firing of potentially problematic police chiefs. But when the DOJ negotiates with a sheriff department, like Alamance County, it may be forced to negotiate directly with the sheriff. In most states, sheriffs are directly accountable to their constituents. And in Alamance County, it seemed that Sheriff Johnson's constituents fully supported his unwillingness to negotiate with the DOJ. This suggests that the DOJ may be less effective in obtaining § 14141 settlements against one shotter sheriff's departments than one shotter police departments.

Despite the risks, the DOJ ultimately opted to bring Alamance County to trial. So in August 2014, the DOJ and Alamance County began the first § 14141 trial since the statute's passage in 1994. The trial itself lasted only for a few days.[438] US district judge Thomas D. Schroeder took nearly a year to issue his opinion in the case.[439] When he eventually released his opinion, Judge Schroeder concluded that the DOJ had failed to demonstrate a pattern or practice of unconstitutional misconduct.[440] In a detailed 253-page opinion, Judge Schroeder concluded that "with no evidence that any individual was unconstitutionally deprived of his or her rights under the Fourth or Fourteenth Amendments, the Government's case rested largely on vague, isolated statements attributed to Sheriff Johnson and on statistical analyses."[441]

Judge Schroeder did recognize that the Alamance County Sheriff's Department had some problems. The department was inconsistent in its use of discipline against officers engaged in misconduct.[442] Judge Schroeder harshly criticized officers for their "abhorrent"

438 Michael D. Abernethy, *Judge Dismisses DOJ Case Against Johnson, Finds No Evidence of Unconstitutional Practices*, Times-News, August 7, 2015.

439 *Id.* ("Five days shy of a year since the case was tried, a federal judge Friday found for Alamance County Sheriff Terry Johnson and ruled that the U.S. Department of Justice failed to show a pattern or practice of racial profiling against Latinos.").

440 Abernethy, *supra* note 438. 441 *Id.*

442 *Id.* ("The evidence at trial highlighted inconsistencies in ACSO's discipline. Some conduct violating ACSO's policies was disciplined, while other conduct was not. A competent, efficient, and professional functioning law enforcement organization requires consistent, regular discipline.").

decisions to circulate racist e-mails that used ethnic slurs.[443] Nevertheless, he concluded that the government still presented insufficient evidence to prove that any of these actions resulted in a pattern or practice of unconstitutional behavior by frontline officers.[444] Even if the DOJ could prove that Sheriff Johnson and his subordinates had used highly offensive language in reference to Latinos, the district court was more hesitant to conclude that this necessarily resulted in a "pattern or practice of misconduct." Judge Schroeder rejected statistical evidence presented by DOJ experts that purported to show a pattern of discriminatory policing.[445]

In its first real showdown with a defiant police department under § 14141, the DOJ lost. Before the Alamance County case, police departments facing § 14141 litigation were hesitant to go to trial, as they weren't certain what legal standard courts would use in interpreting a so-called pattern or practice of misconduct. If the Alamance County case is any indication, some municipalities may have underestimated their chances of success against the DOJ in a § 14141 trial.

Perhaps most unsettling about the Alamance County case, though, are the allegations by one deputy in the Alamance office about how Sheriff Johnson responded to dissent within his ranks during and after the DOJ inquiry. One of Sheriff Johnson's deputies – Jeffrey Randleman – testified on behalf of the DOJ, claiming that Sheriff Johnson had asked him to check the immigration status of people not yet in custody.[446] Deputy Randleman had been worked at the sheriff's department in Alamance County for twenty-two years under numerous different sheriffs.[447] But soon after testifying on behalf of the DOJ, Sheriff Johnson chose "not to re-swear Randleman as a deputy, effectively firing him."[448] This apparent firing stood in stark contrast to how Sheriff Johnson treated other officers after the lawsuit. Even though the DOJ lawsuit uncovered undisputed incidents of some of the sheriff's department's "highest-ranking supervisors" circulating highly offensive jokes based on ethnic stereotypes, there has been no evidence that Sheriff Johnson reprimanded or fired

[443] *Id.* ("He admonished officers who circulated racist emails and jokes, and said epithets and slurs used by some officers were 'abhorrent.'").

[444] *Id.*

[445] *Id.* (explaining that the judge "found as matters of fact that the statistical analyses proffered by the DOJ were unpersuasive and in instances scientifically unsound.").

[446] Kenwyn Caranna, *Former Deputy Sues Sheriff Terry Johnson Over Firing*, Greensboro News & Record, February 18, 2015.

[447] *Id.* [448] *Id.*

any of these employees.[449] Instead, Randleman appears to be "the sole deputy dismissed."[450] When questioned about the firing, Sheriff Johnson argued that "North Carolina deputies serve at the pleasure of the Sheriff."[451]

The Alamance County case is a cautionary tale about the importance of local support in effective federal intervention. Interview participants suggested that local support for the negotiated settlement are critical to the speed at which the police agency can implement the mandated reforms.[452] According to nearly every single interview participant, the supportiveness of the police executives in the targeted departments was the single greatest predictor of the overall success of the reforms.[453] Participants pointed to Oakland as an example of a case where departmental leadership has not always supported the ongoing structural reform efforts.[454] Perhaps not coincidentally, structural reform litigation has dragged on at a painfully slow rate in Oakland.[455]

Police chiefs that have embraced the structural reform efforts normally have had an easier time implementing the changes expeditiously.[456] Interviewees emphasized that supportive leadership was necessary if a department was to change its organizational

449 *Id.* 450 *Id.* 451 *Id.*

452 *See, e.g.*, Interview with Police Administrator #16, at 7 (July 29, 2013) [hereinafter Interview #16] (describing the slow pace of reforms in Oakland and saying that "a lot of that had to do with the dysfunction of our city council and the change in leadership in City Hall . . . [c]hanges in direction . . . [a]ll that kind of stuff").

453 *Id.* at 7 (stating that, "leadership, stable leadership and commitment of that leadership to get it done"); Telephone Interview with DOJ Participant #5, at 6 (September 4, 2013) [hereinafter Interview #5] (on file with author) (claiming that "a huge part of the success of these agreements is the leadership"); Interview with Independent Monitor #7, at 5 (July 18, 2013) (transcript on file with author) [hereinafter Interview #7] (emphasizing the overall importance of leadership).

454 Interview #12, *supra* note 353, at 6 (explaining how Oakland leadership within the department and within the broader city government has ebbed and flowed and how this likely had some effect on the consent decree implementation).

455 Henry K. Lee, *Oakland Police Slammed for Slow Pace of Reform*, San Francisco Gate, January 18, 2012, *available at* www.sfgate.com/crime/article/Oakland-police-slammed-for-slow-pace-of-reform-2594489.php (describing the complaints about the slow speed of reform in the Oakland PD).

456 Telephone Interview with External Monitor #13, at 9 (August 5, 2013) [hereinafter Interview #13] (transcript on file with author) (giving advice to any chief whose department was under structural police reform that he or she ought to "welcome it with open arms and make it a positive experience because if you become perceived as part of the solution instead of part of the problem, you'll survive . . . . And if you're not part of the solution, you'll definitely be a casualty").

culture.[457] This is particularly relevant since scholars have increasingly tied misconduct within a department to underling trends in organizational culture.[458]

While not surprising, this realization has significant implications for the usefulness of federal intervention as a regulatory mechanism. It suggests that federal intervention is not a silver bullet. Police reform ultimately requires local cooperation and dedication to succeed. The DOJ cannot use federal intervention to instantly transform a police agency with defiant, obstinate leadership. Remember that, at the start of the Obama administration, Assistant Attorney General Thomas Perez "told a conference of police chiefs ... that the Justice Department would be pursuing 'pattern or practice' takeovers of police departments much more aggressively than the Bush administration, eschewing negotiation in favor of hardball tactics seeking immediate federal control."[459] During the second half of the George W. Bush administration, the DOJ had taken a more cautious approach to enforcing § 14141, opting for cooperative arrangements.[460] Policing scholars criticized this Bush administration approach, saying that it demonstrated a lack of political commitment to the issue of police misconduct.[461] The evidence gathered in this study raises questions about whether the DOJ can effectively use § 14141 in a manner that the Obama administration has advocated.

Can the DOJ force reform on a municipality that adamantly opposes it? This represents that most important question facing federal intervention in the future. The answer to this question will define the future usefulness of this regulatory mechanism. The early results from Alamance, County North Carolina are particularly worrisome.

[457] Telephone Interview with External Monitor #11, at 9 (July 1, 2013) [hereinafter Interview #11] (transcript on file with author) (stating that organizational leaders and commanders play a pivotal role in transforming organizational culture within a police department).

[458] *See, e.g.*, Barbara E. Armacost, *Organizational Culture and Police Misconduct*, 72 Geo. Wash. L. Rev. 453 (2003) (generally tying organizational culture of a police department to police misconduct).

[459] Heather Mac Donald, *Targeting the Police*, Wkly. Standard, January 31, 2011, at 26.

[460] Stephen Rushin, *Federal Enforcement of Police Reform*, 82 Fordham L. Rev. 3189, 3228–3235 (2014).

[461] Rachel Harmon, *Promoting Civil Rights Through Proactive Policing*, 62 Stan. L. Rev. 1, 21 (2009) (explaining the "absence of political commitment to § 14141 suits, especially on the part of the Bush Administration").

The Los Angeles case study also sharply contrasts with the experience of another large California police department that underwent similar structural reform litigation around the same time period – Oakland. On December 2000, a plaintiff filed a § 1983 suit against the Oakland Police Department (OPD) alleging that a group of officers known as "the Riders" engaged in a pattern of misconduct.[462] Among the allegations, the plaintiff alleged that these officers kidnapped him, beat him, and planted drugs on him.[463] A few months later, the federal district court consolidated this case with a number of other pending OPD misconduct cases.[464] These consolidated cases came to be known as the "Riders" cases and involved a total of 119 plaintiffs.[465] As part of the consolidated suit, these plaintiffs sought equitable relief against the OPD.[466]

Soon after consolidation, Judge Thelton Henderson took over the cases.[467] Judge Henderson ordered the OPD and the plaintiffs to try to negotiate a settlement.[468] The negotiation process was prolonged, lasting "about 2 and half years start to finish" during which time the two sides exchanged dozens of settlement drafts.[469] Eventually, in March 2003, the parties agreed to a $10.9 million settlement.[470] The parties also agreed that the OPD would implement an extensive package of reforms with the oversight of a monitoring team appointed by the court.[471] Like many consent decrees before it, this agreement required the OPD make changes to internal affairs investigations, discipline procedures, field supervision, management oversight, use-of-force investigations, training, and the auditing of officer performance records.[472]

While the DOJ was not officially involved in the OPD case, it is worth noting that the monitoring team appointed by the court included two former DOJ litigators – Kelli Evans and Christy Lopez – who had handled § 14141 cases in the past.[473] The lack of official DOJ involvement in the OPD case seemed to make the process somewhat different than the LAPD. The court took on a much more prominent role in this process. And the process appeared to be far

[462] *See, e.g., Allen et al.* v. *City of Oakland et al.*, 3:00-cv-04599-TEH (ND Cal. December 7, 2000) (complaint filed).

[463] David Postel, The Civil Rights Litigation Clearinghouse, *Allen v. City of Oakland*, February 10, 2014, *available at* www.clearinghouse.net/detail.php?id=5541.

[464] *Id.* [465] *Id.* [466] *Id.* [467] *Id.* [468] *Id.*

[469] Interview #16, *supra* note 453, at 3–4. [470] Postel, *supra* note 463. [471] *Id.*

[472] *Id.*

[473] Other members of this monitoring team included Charles Gruber and Rachel Burgess.

more adversarial than other § 14141 cases. According to some respondents, the process was also slowed down by the city of Oakland's "dysfunctional" leadership.[474] This problematic leadership, according to stakeholders involved in the case, came from both instability in the police department and volatility in the city government. As one knowledgeable insider remarked during an interview, the OPD case has moved slowly, and "[a] big chunk of it has to do with dysfunction and the inability to get things processed through quickly" by city management.[475]

The OPD also had a number of different police chiefs during the structural reform litigation era – some of which had "a decent relationship with the monitors" and others that did not.[476] As the interviewee explained, "[W]e've had so many . . . changes in leadership."[477] These sorts of "changes in direction" have made it hard for the OPD to deliver a consistent message to frontline officers.[478] The OPD went through six different police chiefs in the last twelve years. By contrast, William Bratton and eventually Charlie Beck provided stable leadership for the LAPD throughout their federal intervention era. This unstable leadership, both within the OPD and in city hall, made implementing some parts of the OPD consent decree challenging. For example, according to one respondent, the OPD does not handle its own "technology stuff."[479] These sorts of technological upgrades come directly from the city. At times, the city's failure to provide necessary technological upgrades has brought the reform process "to a grinding halt."[480]

On multiple occasions, the court has extended the negotiated settlement in the OPD case. What was supposed to be a five-year oversight period grew to over a decade. Recently, the court announced that it would consider the possibility of receivership.[481] Judge Henderson even ordered the parties to prepare briefs on the issue.[482] Eventually, Judge Henderson opted for to appoint a compliance director. This compliance director is "appointed by and answerable to the Court" and has "'directive authority' over Oakland PD, relevant to the existing consent decree."[483] This compliance director can direct individual expenditures up to $250,000 and

[474] Interview #16, *supra* note 452, at 8; Interview #18, *supra* note 185, at 5.
[475] Interview #16, *supra* note 453, at 8.
[476] *Id.* at 9 (explaining how the relationship between one chief and the monitoring team deteriorated, "[w]hich ultimately resulted in the monitor levying some very harsh criticism of the chief in one of the reports").
[477] *Id.* at 7. [478] *Id.* [479] *Id.* at 8. [480] *Id.* [481] Postel, *supra* note 463. [482] *Id.*
[483] *Id.*

can directly discipline, demote, or remove the chief of police and assistant/deputy chiefs.[484] Today, the compliance director continues to work with the monitor to reform the OPD. The OPD consent decree has now been in place for over twelve years, and there is still considerable work to be done.

Indeed, Oakland and Los Angeles are two cities that have taken dramatically different paths. According to the monitors and other stakeholders involved in the Los Angeles case, the appointment of William Bratton as police chief represented a turning point. As Monitor Cherkasky explained, "It was . . . under the leadership of a new Chief, William J. Bratton, who had served as a policing expert on the Monitoring team prior to his appointment in October 2002, that reform truly began its institutionalization throughout the Department."[485] After his appointment on October 28, 2002, the monitoring team immediately applauded the city's decision.[486] According to Cherkasky, Bratton's appointment was a signal that the city of Los Angeles, including "the Police Commission, the Mayor and the City Council," was dedicated to the success of the consent decree.[487] And almost immediately after his appointment, Bratton began making significant changes. Only months after his appointment, Bratton proposed a fundamental reorganization of the LAPD's management structure.[488] "Among other things, the plan elevate[d] day-to-day responsibility for the Consent Decree to the Bureau level, headed by the equivalent of a two-star chief reporting directly to Chief Bratton."[489] Chief Bratton was also vigilant in ordering random audits to ensure that his department was abiding by the terms of the consent decree.[490] Bratton pushed the LAPD to install "state of the art video cameras in patrol cars," a move that received enthusiastic support from the monitoring team.[491] Because of these moves, among others, the monitoring team believed that "Chief Bratton raised the visibility and dedication to the [d]ecree."[492]

We may never know whether the consent decree in Los Angeles would have been successful without Bratton's leadership. But

[484] *Id.* [485] Final Quarterly Report for LAPD, *supra* note 170, at 5.

[486] Sixth Quarterly Report for LAPD, *supra* note 308, at 4. [487] *Id.*

[488] Office of the Independent Monitor of the Los Angeles Police Department, Seventh Quarterly Report 4 (May 15, 2003) [hereinafter Seventh Quarterly Report for LAPD] (stating that this plan was proposed on February 25, 2003).

[489] *Id.* [490] *Id.*

[491] Office of the Independent Monitor of the Los Angeles Police Department, Fifteenth Quarterly Report 4 (May 16, 2005) [hereinafter Fifteenth Quarterly Report for LAPD].

[492] Final Quarterly Report for LAPD, *supra* note 170, at 5.

stakeholders involved in the LAPD case all agreed that departmental and city leadership are the most important elements to the successful implementation of a consent decree in a police department. As one interviewee commented, leadership is "a huge part of the success of these agreements."[493] Another explained how the successful implementation of a consent decree requires "leadership, stable leadership, and commitment of that leadership to get it done."[494] Leadership must be supportive not just in the police department but also within the broader city government. As another respondent remarked, "[Y]ou have to have leadership at the highest level of a city in order to get success."[495]

The LAPD made steady progress under stable, supportive leadership during the federal intervention era. City officials generally supported federal intervention. The city allocated the necessary resources to get the job done. And LAPD leadership showed genuine commitment to making substantive reforms. Oakland, by contrast, suffered from death by delay under inconsistent and unsupportive leadership. The OPD seemed so opposed to external change that the first court-appointed monitoring team actually "walked away," because they believed they could not bring about substantive change.[496] That monitoring team just "didn't feel as a team that [they] could get it done with the leadership that was in place there."[497] Even after the new monitoring team took over, they quickly realized that the OPD would "not [be] an easy department to deal with."[498] Consistently, all the monitors involved in the OPD case report that the city has been more "contentious" and "resistant" than any other department in the past, making progress challenging.[499] All of this suggests that the key to successful structural reform litigation in a police department may be

[493] Telephone Interview with Department of Justice Participant #5, 6 (September 4, 2013) (transcript on file with author) [hereinafter Interview #5].

[494] Interview #12, *supra* note 353, at 7. [495] Interview #20, *supra* note 361, at 6.

[496] Telephone Interview with External Monitor #2, at 6 (July 21, 2013) [hereinafter Interview #2] (transcript on file with author).

[497] *Id.*

[498] Telephone Interview with External Monitor #6, at 9 (July 11, 2013) [hereinafter Interview #6] (transcript on file with author).

[499] Telephone Interview with External Monitor #8, at 3 (July 14, 2013) [hereinafter Interview #8] (transcript on file with author); Telephone Interview with External Monitor #11, at 4 (July 1, 2013) [hereinafter Interview #11] (transcript on file with author) (stating "Oakland is a little more resistant to change and resistant to reform"); Telephone Interview with External Monitor #9, at 4 (July 26, 2013) [hereinafter Interview #9] (transcript on file with author) (stating that the "relationship between

the department's receptivity to outside reform. There is no evidence so far that the DOJ can use § 14141 to overhaul a police department with intransigent leadership. It seems that in each successful case of structural reform litigation in American police departments, supportive leadership has played a critical role in the measure's success. And perhaps nothing better illustrates this point than the slow and painful process of structural reform litigation currently underway in the OPD. Federal intervention can bring about change – that is, if a police department *wants* to change.

B *Sustainability*

Once more, because of the importance of organizational buy-in to the success of federal intervention in American police departments, serious questions remain about the ability of a police department to sustain reforms after federal regulators leave. The Pittsburgh case provides a cautionary tale about what can happen after external monitoring ends. The Pittsburgh Bureau of Police was the nation's first local police agency to reach a § 14141 settlement with the DOJ on April 16, 1997.[500] Both external monitoring and independent evaluation by the Vera Institute for Justice demonstrated that the Bureau made substantial progress in reducing apparent unconstitutional misconduct during federal intervention.[501] The DOJ ended oversight of Pittsburgh around June 16, 2005.[502] During this entire period, Police Chief Robert McNeilly oversaw the Bureau.[503] Throughout his time as Chief, McNeilly was an ardent supporter of the DOJ intervention, claiming that the changes mandated by the consent decree all "mirrored his own plans" for the agency.[504] This resulted in fierce backlash by frontline officers. When McNeilly

the city administration and the monitoring team . . . has been much more strife-laden" than other cases).

500 Rushin, *supra* note 460, at 3247.

501 *See generally* Davis, Ortiz, Henderson, & Massie, *supra* note 281.

502 Rushin, *supra* note 460, at 3247.

503 Michael A. Fuoco, *The Mayoral Transition: Police Chief Out*, Pittsburgh Post-Gazette, December 29, 2005, *available at* www.post-gazette.com/local/city/2005/12/29/The-mayoral-transition-Police-chief-out/stories/200512290284 (stating how Chief McNeilly was sworn in on April 2, 1996, and was removed around December 29, 2005).

504 Michael A. Fuoco, *Police Chief McNeilly's Tenure Saw Wrenching Changes*, Pittsburgh Post-Gazette, January 9, 2006, *available at* www.post-gazette.com/local/city/2006/01/09/Police-chief-McNeilly-s-tenure-saw-wrenching-changes/stories/200601090107.

received voter approval to create a Citizens Police Review Board, "which holds hearings on police misconduct and can recommend disciplinary action," the police union issued a vote of no confidence in McNeilly's leadership.[505] Despite this sort of opposition, McNeilly pressed ahead with implementing each requirement of the negotiated § 14141 settlement, including a computerized early warning system.[506] Throughout this time, Mayor Thomas Murphy, Jr. generally supported Chief McNeilly and ongoing federal intervention.

In 2006, when Robert O'Connor, Jr., took over as mayor, things changed.[507] Mayor O'Connor fired Chief McNeilly and sided with local police union leaders, who claimed that McNeilly's use of excessive disciplinary action hurt officer morale.[508] In the years since this change in leadership, civil rights advocates have worried that the Bureau "is now sliding back towards where it was" before federal intervention.[509] During federal oversight, for example, the number of civil rights complaints against the Pittsburgh police brought to the ALCU fell dramatically.[510] In the years after McNeilly's removal, the volume of these complaints has increased.[511]

Perhaps most troubling of all, Pittsburgh mayor Bill Peduto recently acknowledged that the Bureau had regressed so much that it may be "on the verge of another consent decree."[512] This latest problem has emerged after Pittsburgh police chief Nathan Harper was indicted in March 2013 on corruption charges,[513] which spurred another federal investigation of the agency. The entire Pittsburgh

[505] *Id.* (explaining how the Fraternal Order of Police, the local police union that represents the Pittsburgh Police Bureau, issued this order during the consent decree time period).

[506] *Id.* (this "computerized early-warning system that analyzes all aspects of an officer's job performance so that hints of trouble can be detected and dealt with quickly").

[507] Fuoco, *supra* note 503.

[508] Fuoco, *supra* note 504 (describing the change in philosophies under the new mayoral administration).

[509] Laura Maggi, *Pittsburgh Bureau of Police was First in Nation with Official Federal Intervention*, THE TIMES PICAYUNE, October 16, 2011, *available at* www.nola.com/crime/index.ssf/2011/10/pittsburgh_bureau_of_police_wa.html.

[510] *Id.* [511] *Id.*

[512] Jeffrey Benzing, *Pittsburgh Police Could Face Second Federal Consent Decree, Peduto Says*, PUBLIC SOURCE, July 1, 2014, *available at* http://publicsource.org/from-the-source/pittsburgh-police-could-face-second-federal-consent-decree-peduto-says.

[513] Jonathan D. Silver, Liv Narvatil, and Richard Lord, *Attorney: Ex-Pittsburgh Police Chief Nate Harper to Plead Guilty*, PITTSBURGH POST-GAZETTE, March 23, 2013, *available at* www.post-gazette.com/local/region/2013/03/22/Attorney-Ex-Pittsburgh-police-chief-Nate-Harper-to-plead-guilty/stories/201303220153.

story demonstrates how quickly reforms can unravel without institutional support.

Conclusion

Two lessons emerge from the Los Angeles case study. The first lesson is that, under the right conditions, federal intervention appears to be a reasonably effective tool in facilitating organizational reform in police departments. Even after the Rodney King beating and Rampart scandal, the LAPD seemed unwilling to dedicate significant amounts of money to the cause of police misconduct reform.[514] Federal intervention forced Los Angeles to make a concerted investment in police reform measures. The use of external monitoring led to extensive data on frontline officer behavior in the LAPD. It also led to improvements in how the LAPD internally audited and responded to officer behavior. The initiation of federal intervention also correlated with a change in leadership atop the LAPD. Interviewees and monitor reports suggest that Bratton's support for federal intervention contributed to the measure's success in Los Angeles. But perhaps the most important revelation from Los Angeles is that the city was able to make substantial improvements in the quality of its police force without significant overall cost. Admittedly, the upfront financial costs of federal intervention appear to be steep. Over the long haul, though, interviewees suggest that the LAPD may have been able to recoup some of this cost through reductions in civil liability for civil rights violations. There is also little evidence to suggest that federal intervention correlated with reductions in police efficiency or effectiveness in the city. The evidence suggests that Los Angeles improved the constitutionality of its police force with little compromise. More research is needed to determine whether this pattern is isolated to Los Angeles or more broadly applicable to other federal intervention cases. This hypothesis – that federal intervention may contribute to constitutional policing without compromise – is a promising finding that deserves substantially more investigation in the future.

The second lesson from the LAPD case study is less encouraging. The LAPD case study, especially when viewed in light of the Oakland, Alamance County, and Pittsburgh experiences, suggests that federal

[514] *The Lame Duck Truth Mayor Riordan's Final Budget Speaks to the Sad State of the LAPD*, DAILY NEWS, April 23, 2001, at N12.

intervention is most effective in agencies that are supportive of external intervention and when local political leaders are dedicated to the improvement of the police department over the long term. Of course, the police agencies most in need of the DOJ's assistance may be the least supportive of federal intervention. This is a particularly dispiriting realization. External intervention is a powerful tool for facilitating organizational change in some cases. It remains unclear as to whether the DOJ can use this mechanism to reform a police department that strongly opposes such intervention.

5

Moving Forward

Improving Oversight of Local Police

Introduction

Police misconduct represents a serious national problem perpetuated by numerous local police departments. Through the Buildup Era, the federal government began a gradual pushback against local police misconduct. During the Intervention Era, the federal government has become more aggressive. But during both eras, fighting police misconduct has proven to be difficult. It is important to remember, though, that this is not the first time that Congress has faced such a regulatory challenge.[1] As I recently argued in a coauthored article with Professor Jason Mazzone, the United States faced a similarly serious problem that threatened to undermine the very foundation of our democracy between the mid-nineteenth and twentieth centuries. During this time period, southern states had enacted a number of barriers, like literacy tests, good character tests, and property requirements, designed to keep blacks from exercising their right to vote. Congress tried to discourage this behavior by passing a number of federal laws designed to criminalize voter suppression efforts.[2] The Supreme Court also attempted to invalidate state laws that deterred black voters.[3] Ultimately, however, these valiant efforts were

[1] For a more detailed discussion of the historical parallels between voter suppression efforts in the mid-twentieth century and police misconduct today, *see* Jason Mazzone & Stephen Rushin, *From Selma to Ferguson: The Voting Rights Act as a Blueprint for Police Reform*, 105 CAL. L. REV. (forthcoming 2017).

[2] Specifically, Congress passed two federal laws – the Enforcement Acts of 1870 and 1871 – that criminalized state-sanctioned discrimination in voter registration and interference by private individuals with the right to vote. 16 Stat. 140 (1870); 16 Stat. 433 (1871).

[3] The Supreme Court stepped in several times to invalidate specific tactics used by states to discourage black voter registration, like grandfather clauses that allowed white voters to circumvent voting barriers like literacy tests and poll taxes. *See Guinn & Beal* v. *United States*, 238 US 347 (1915); *Myers* v. *Anderson*, 238 US 368 (1915). In addition to these 1915 cases, the Supreme Court invalidated grandfather exemptions to a registration deadline in 1939. *See Lane* v. *Wilson*, 307 US 268 (1939). *See also Smith* v. *Allwright*, 321 US 649 (1944)

mostly ineffective at increasing black voter turnout. Around the middle of the twentieth century, Congress took a more aggressive approach, passing multiple laws that empowered the US attorney general to compile statistics on state voting and to bring civil suits against state actors that deprived individuals of the right to vote based on race.[4]

Again, Congress found these measures to be ineffective in significantly reducing voter suppression. These early federal attempts only permitted the federal government to act in piecemeal fashion. The attorney general could stamp out wrongdoing in only one individual municipality at a time. These measures did not give the federal government the power to regulate voting procedures proactively.

In hopes of addressing voter suppression once and for all, Congress ultimately authored one of the most transformative statutes in the history of American civil rights: the Voting Rights Act of 1965. The measure came soon after the horrific events in Selma, Alabama, where state-troopers and private citizens on the Edmund Pettus Bridge ruthlessly beat civil rights demonstrators.[5] A little more than a week after the events of "Blood Sunday" in Selma, President Lyndon B. Johnson presented his version of the Voting Rights Act (VRA) of 1965 before a nationally televised joint session of Congress,[6] which became law in August 1965.[7]

(invalidating so-called white primary laws); *United States* v. *Thomas*, 362 US 58 (1960) (overturning racially discriminatory registration limitations); *Gomillion* v. *Lightfoot*, 364 US 339 (1960) (limiting gerrymandering); *Alabama* v. *United States*, 371 US 37 (1962) (per curiam) (limiting voting tests).

[4] The Civil Rights Act of 1957 gave the US attorney general the authority to bring civil suits against state actors that deprived individuals of the right to vote based on race. Civil Rights Act of 1957, Pub. L. No. 85–315, § 131, 71 Stat. 637 (codified as amended at 52 USC § 10101 (2014)). However, it quickly became apparent that in order to win these sorts of suits, the attorney general needed access to voting records. The attorney general also needed the power to obtain more than a simple order demanding reform. So, in 1960, Congress passed another Civil Rights Act, this time giving the attorney general the authority to compile state voting statistics. *See Civil Rights Act of 1960: Hearings Before the S. Comm. on the Judiciary*, 86th Cong. 9 (1960) (stating that "In many cases, discrimination in registration can be proved only by comparing the records of Negro applicants with those of white applicants. At the present time, the Government lacks any procedure by which to compel the production of these records before a suit is filed."). Civil Rights Act of 1960, Pub. L. No. 86–449, 74 Stat. 86 (codified as amended at 52 USC § 10101 (2014)).

[5] Gary May, Bending Toward Justice: The Voting Rights Act and the Transformation of American Democracy, 85–89 (2013).

[6] President Lyndon B. Johnson, Voting Rights Act Address (March 15, 1965).

[7] Voting Rights Act of 1965, Pub. L. No. 89–110, 79 Stat. 437 (codified as amended in scattered sections of 42 and 52 USC).

The act moved the federal government from a reactive to a proactive role in regulating local voting procedures. It did so, in part, by establishing something called a coverage formula.[8] Congress developed this formula to decide which state and local governments were to be bound by the rigorous oversight mechanisms included in the act. Based on the terms of the coverage formula, the limitations of the act applied to jurisdictions that used any potentially unlawful device to limit voting as of November 1, 1964, and to jurisdictions with unusually low numbers of registered voters relative to their population.[9] Using this formula, in the years that followed, the DOJ identified over a dozen states that, either in part or in whole, required further regulation to prevent voter suppression.[10] If any jurisdiction covered by this formula wanted to change their voting procedures, the act required the jurisdiction to obtain approval from the federal government.[11]

In addition, the act established frequent invasive oversight of local voting precincts covered by the federal formula. The act permitted federal courts to appoint examiners to oversee jurisdictions in violation of the act.[12] And the act authorized the appointment of election observers to any jurisdiction subject to examiner oversight.[13]

The act proved to be enormously successful in increasing black voter registration and turnout, with nearly one million black voters registered within four years of the act's passage.[14]

From a regulatory perspective, the challenges that Congress faced in combating voting discrimination in the 1950s and 1960s mirror the challenges that Congress faces today in battling local police misconduct. To be clear, this is not to say that the current problems with police misconduct are as invidious as the systematic deprivation of voting rights in the mid-twentieth century. From a regulatory perspective, however, these two civil rights challenges are surprisingly similar. Both involve attempts by the federal government to limit the presence of unconstitutional misconduct perpetuated by thousands of local governments. So what can we learn from the Congress's response to voting discrimination in the 1960s? And how can we harness those lessons to improve our

[8] § 4, 79 Stat. 438. [9] § 4(b), (e).

[10] Jurisdictions Previously Covered by Section 5, U.S. Dep't of Justice, *available at* www.justice.gov/crt/jurisdictions-previously-covered-section-5 (last visited January 7, 2016).

[11] § 5, 79 Stat. 439.

[12] Fannie Lou Hamer, Rosa Parks, & Coretta Scott King Voting Rights Act Reauthorization and Amendments Act of 2006 § 3(a).

[13] § 8. [14] US Comm'n on Civil Rights, Political Participation 13 (1968).

response to police misconduct? This chapter argues that it is time for Congress to improve the federal oversight of local police departments.

In the years leading up to the passage of the VRA, Congress initially passed the Civil Rights Act of 1957 – a law that gave the US attorney general the authority to bring civil suits against state actors that violated a person's voting rights. Like § 14141, the Civil Rights Act of 1957 represented an important step in gradually expanding the role of the federal government into a traditionally local function. By giving the US attorney general the power to intervene into police departments engaged in a pattern or practice of misconduct via § 14141, Congress has already laid the groundwork for expanded federal oversight of local police departments.

But like the Civil Rights Act of 1957, this first step has ultimately proven insufficient. In order for the federal government to become a meaningful protector of civil rights from police misconduct, Congress must do more. This chapter lays out three ambitious reforms that Congress could pass in order to fight local police misconduct.

First, it is time for Congress to collect additional data on local police conduct. Again, the voting rights context is instructive. In the Civil Rights Act of 1960, Congress empowered the federal government to collect data on voting registration to assist in federal suits against local jurisdictions. Similarly, it is time for Congress to give the US attorney general the authority to collect data on police misconduct to assist in § 14141 suits. As Chapter 3 demonstrated, the lack of national statistics on police misconduct has thwarted the DOJ's efforts to enforce § 14141. The DOJ currently lacks the necessary data to determine definitively which of the nation's police departments are engaged in the most serious misconduct. The DOJ has been forced to rely on imperfect proxies to make such determinations. If we want the DOJ to engage in meaningful oversight of local police behavior, then the federal government must give the DOJ the necessary data to do the job. This chapter lays out several new types of data that the federal government could obtain from local municipalities.

Once obtained, the DOJ could use this data to incentivize widespread reform in local police departments by harnessing data to improve the enforcement of § 14141. For one thing, the federal government could make this sort of data publicly available. By making this data publicly accessible, the federal government could empower the public, the press, and interest groups to identify problematic patterns of potentially troubling police misconduct. This could, in turn, motivate local police departments to institute proactive reforms aimed at reducing the frequency of police misconduct.

The DOJ could also develop a transparent system for analyzing this newly amassed data on police behavior. During the Intervention Era, the federal government has failed to explain how it identifies police departments in need of § 14141 reform. As a result, some have perceived federal intervention via § 14141 as procedurally unjust. This lack of perceived fairness has real consequences. If a police department believes that they have been arbitrarily selected for federally initiated reform efforts, the targeted agency may be less likely to cooperate with federal regulators. Transparency has another added benefit. If the federal government transparently announces its methodology for identifying problem police departments, it can create incentives for police agencies across the country to make reforms proactively.

To this end, this chapter proposes a novel approach by which the federal government could harness transparency to incentivize widespread reform in American police departments. The DOJ could also use this newly amassed data to maintain some limited oversight of local police departments after § 14141 reform ends. Remember from Chapter 4 that a major drawback of § 14141 reform is that there is no guarantee that municipalities will maintain reforms after the federal intervention ends. Combined, these reforms could harness the power of this newly amassed data to facilitate widespread reform in American police departments.

Second, the federal government should look for ways to increase the frequency of § 14141-style interventions in local police departments. Remember from Chapter 3 that the DOJ simply lacks the resources to rigorously oversee the nation's 18,000 police departments. Congress could conceivably provide the DOJ with substantially more funding to increase oversight. But perhaps there is another, less costly way for the federal government to increase the frequency of these sorts of top-down interventions into local police departments. Other scholars have offered creative proposals for how the Congress could authorize private litigants to fill the regulatory gaps left by DOJ underenforcement of § 14141, or how states could enact their own statutes similar to § 14141. Either measure would help ensure that more police departments undergo this sort of top-down reform aimed at curbing police wrongdoing.

Third, it is time for the federal government to regulate police misconduct proactively. The federal government should provide additional incentives for local police departments to adopt policies and procedures aimed at deterring wrongdoing. One immediately feasible way that

Congress could accomplish this is by tying federal funding to local police departments to the enactment of reforms aimed at curbing police misconduct. Dozens of existing federal statutes permit "federal agencies to give money and power to local police departments."[15] But virtually none of these federal grant programs subsidize the cost of misconduct regulations. Instead, the vast majority of federal money spent on local policing services goes to promotion of public safety, encouragement of agency coordination, and purchase of new equipment. These federal grants "do little to promote lawfulness, accountability, or fairness in policing."[16] While the federal government has subsidized community-oriented policing, these expenditures account for a tiny percent of the overall expenditures on policing services.[17] Thus, the federal government could do more to incentivize the adoption of reform efforts through reorienting the stated goals of federal grants.

A more ambitious and controversial way the federal government could incentivize widespread reform in police department is by taking a page from the VRA, as recommended in my recent coauthored study.[18] When Congress passed this act, it fundamentally transformed how the federal government regulated voting rights. In the past, the federal government had waited for the state or locality to enact a problematic voting regulation before it acted. When the federal government did act, it did so through piecemeal litigation against individual jurisdictions. This created two problems. This piecemeal litigation process was slow. And the federal government had trouble keeping up with the pace at which states and localities enacted harmful voting restrictions. By establishing coverage formulas and preclearance requirements, Congress went from reactive regulation to proactive regulation. In addressing the national police misconduct problem, Congress could similarly turn to coverage formulas or preclearance requirements.

Such a proposal is certain to be controversial. Small government advocates will likely claim that coverage formulas or preclearance requirements similar to the Voting Rights Act of 1965 constitute an unreasonable limitation on local autonomy. After all, policing tactics have almost always

15 Rachel Harmon, *Federal Programs and the Real Cost of Policing*, 90 NYU L. Rev. 870 (2015).

16 *Id.* at 890.

17 U.S. Gov't Accountability Office, GAO-06-104, Community Policing Grants: COPS Grants Were a Modest Contributor to Declines in Crime in the 1990s 11–12 (2005).

18 *See generally* Mazzone & Rushin, *supra* note 1.

been considered an issue for local decision-making. At minimum, the history of the VRA presents a radical alternative to the traditional way the federal government has overseen local police wrongdoing.

None of these measures alone will necessarily transform the regulation of police misconduct. Together, though, this package of reforms could expand the top-down oversight of local police departments. These reforms could correct some of the remaining problems of the Intervention Era. They represent a real commitment to the reduction of local police misconduct.

I The Value of More Data

Several recent, high-profile police killings of civilians have ignited a national debate about the regulation of law enforcement[19] and have specifically increased calls by advocates for better documentation of police behavior through national statistics.[20] Although the federal government keeps records on everything from "how many people were victims of

[19] Most notably, the killings of Michael Brown in Ferguson, Missouri, Eric Garner of New York, New York, and Tamir Rice of Cleveland, Ohio, have sparked national outrage. *See, e.g.*, Julie Bosman & Emma G. Fitzsimmons, *Grief and Protests Follow Shooting of a Teenager*, NY TIMES, August 10, 2014, *available at* www.nytimes.com/2014/08/11/us/police-say-mike-brown-was-killed-after-struggle-for-gun.html (providing an early account of Michael Brown's death at the hands of the Ferguson Police Department); J. David Goodman & Al Baker, *Wave of Protests After Grand Jury Doesn't Indict Officer in Eric Garner Chokehold Case*, NY TIMES, December 3, 2014, *available at* www.nytimes.com/2014/12/04/nyregion/grand-jury-said-to-bring-no-charges-in-staten-island-chokehold-death-of-eric-garner.html (providing a detailed account of Eric Garner's death after being choked by police); Richard A. Oppel Jr., *Police Gave Boy No Aid After Shooting in Cleveland*, NY TIMES, January 8, 2015, *available at* www.nytimes.com/2015/01/09/us/police-in-cleveland-boys-fatal-shooting-did-not-give-medical-aid.html (explaining how Cleveland officers shot and failed to offer any medical assistance to a twelve-year-old named Tamir Rice, who was shot while holding a toy gun, after a 911 call reported "a guy" holding a "probably fake" pistol).

[20] Blake Fleetwood, *Congress Finally Acts to Prevent Police Killings, But Will It Make a Difference?* WASH. MONTHLY, December 17, 2014, *available at* www.washingtonmonthly.com/ten-miles-square/2014/12/congress_finally_acts_to_preve053348.php (describing how Rand Paul was a prominent supporter of the Death in Custody Reporting Act, which calls on local law enforcement agencies to report all people killed during arrests or while in their custody); Jon Swaine, *Eric Holder Calls Failure to Collect Reliable Data on Police Killings Unacceptable*, THE GUARDIAN, January 15, 2015, *available at* www.theguardian.com/us-news/2015/jan/15/eric-holder-no-reliable-fbi-data-police-related-killings (stating "[t]he troubling reality is that we lack the ability right now to comprehensively track the number of incidents of either uses of force directed at police officers or uses of force by police," and saying "[t]his strikes many – including me – as unacceptable").

unprovoked shark attacks ... to the number of hogs and pigs living on farms in the U.S., there is no reliable data on how many people are shot by police officers each year,"[21] let alone any data on other law enforcement action. This part argues that Congress should empower the federal government to collect detailed statistics on local police behavior.

In collecting data on local police behavior, the federal government faces a handful of hurdles. For one thing, there is no easy way to measure police misconduct.[22] There is no single statistic that can capture the full range of police misconduct, from unlawful stop-and-frisks, to unconstitutional searches or seizures, to excessive uses of force. Misconduct varies too much. Any effort to document the presence of police misconduct comprehensively is a significant undertaking. In addition, it is difficult to judge the correctness of police behavior after the fact. In many cases, the only witnesses to an alleged act of misconduct are the police officer and the alleged victim. While technological tools like body cameras are beginning to address this problem, it remains extraordinarily difficult to keep tabs on the unstructured behavior of frontline police officers. Finally, given the extensive decentralization of American law enforcement, as discussed in Chapter 1,[23] the collection of uniform statistics

[21] Wesley Lowery, *How Many Police Shootings a Year? No One Knows*, WASH. POST, September 8, 2014, *available at* www.washingtonpost.com/news/post-nation/wp/2014/09/08/how-many-police-shootings-a-year-no-one-knows; *see also* Rob Barry & Coulter Jones, *Hundreds of Police Killings Are Uncounted in Federal Statistics*, THE WALL STREET JOURNAL, December 3, 2014, *available at* www.wsj.com/articles/hundreds-of-police-killings-are-uncounted-in-federal-statistics-1417577504; Eugene Robinson, *What America's Police Departments Don't Want You to Know*, WASH. POST, December 1, 2014, www.washingtonpost.com/opinions/eugene-robinson-its-a-crime-that-we-dont-know-how-many-people-police-shoot-to-death/2014/12/01/adedcb00-7998-11e4-b821-503cc7efed9e_story.html (stating "no one can say for sure" how many people police officers kill every year). This sentiment was perhaps best summed up by FBI director James B. Comey, who remarked that, "It's ridiculous that I can't tell you how many people were shot by the police last week, last month, last year." Michael S. Schmidt, *F.B.I. Director Speaks Out on Race and Police Bias*, NEW YORK TIMES, February 12, 2015, *available at* www.nytimes.com/2015/02/13/us/politics/fbi-director-comey-speaks-frankly-about-police-view-of-blacks.html.

[22] For an example of the trouble federal regulators have faced in identifying misconduct in local police departments, see the difficulty faced by DOJ officials while attempting to identify police departments in violation of 42 USC § 14141. Stephen Rushin, *Federal Enforcement of Police Reform*, 82 FORDHAM L. REV. 3189, 3219–3224 (2014).

[23] LARRY E. SULLIVAN, MARIE SIMONETTI ROSEN, DORTHY MOSES SCHULZ, & M.R. HABERFELD, ENCYCLOPEDIA OF LAW ENFORCEMENT (2007), *available at* knowledge.sagepub.com/view/lawenforcement/n517.xml (explaining how the United States is fairly unique in its decentralized policing model, contrasting it with other more centralized policing models in France, Italy, Sweden, Finland, China, Vietnam, Cuba, and others).

from the nation's 18,000 police departments presents a significant regulatory challenge.[24]

Thus, as Congress tries to identify statistical measures it can obtain from local police departments, it is important to limit expectations. Any federal database on police behavior will be imperfect and will, out of necessity, make compromises. At times, Congress will only be able to obtain incomplete data. Traditionally, when the federal government has obtained data from local police departments, it has relied on local agencies to self-report information.[25] Take, for example, three of the major datasets on local police departments – the Uniform Crime Reports, the National Incident Based Reporting System, and the Law Enforcement Management and Administrative Statistics. These national databases rely on local police departments to self-report information on everything from crime rates,[26] to the incidents surrounding criminal acts,[27] to administrative policies.[28] This self-reporting procedure has predictably led to some problems.[29] Social scientists and reporters have documented numerous cases of police departments altering or manipulating data via these self-reported metrics.[30]

[24] Brian A. Reaves, U.S. Dep't of Justice, Census of State and Local Law Enforcement Agencies 2 (2011), *available at* http://www.bjs.gov/content/pub/pdf/csllea08.pdf.

[25] The federal government has collected information from police departments in several different databases. Perhaps most prominently, the Federal Bureau of Investigation collects information on crimes reported in most jurisdictions in the United States through the Uniform Crime Reports (UCR). These annual statistics report the number and rate of different crimes in each reporting jurisdiction. UCR is self-reported and voluntary. *See Uniform Crime Reports*, Fed. Bureau of Investigation, *available at* www.fbi.gov/about-us/cjis/ucr/ucr-publications [hereinafter UCR reports]. Crime data is also aggregated in the National Incident Based Reporting System (NIBRS). *See* Lynn A. Addington, *Studying the Crime Problem with NIBRS Data: Current Uses and Future Trends*, in Handbook on Crime and Deviance (Marvin D. Krohn et al., eds., 2009). And the federal government collects information on police department policies, procedures, and behaviors through the Law Enforcement Management and Administrative Statistics (LEMAS). U.S. Dep't of Justice, Bureau of Justice Statistics, Law Enforcement Management and Administrative Statistics (LEMAS): 2007 Sample Surveys of Law Enforcement Agencies (2007) [hereinafter LEMAS 2007], *available at* www.icpsr.umich.edu/icpsrweb/ICPSR/studies/31161 [hereinafter LEMAS].

[26] *See generally* UCR Reports, *supra* note 25.

[27] *See generally* Addington, *supra* note 25.

[28] *See generally* LEMAS, *supra* note 25.

[29] For a detailed explanation of how this methodology can lead to problems, see Barry and Jones, *supra* note 32, describing apparent discrepancies between self-reported numbers on justifiable homicides in various jurisdictions and numbers obtained by the Wall Street Journal during their own independent investigation.

[30] *See, e.g.*, Steve Thompson & Tanya Eiserer, Experts: Dallas Undercount of Assaults Builds "Artificial Image," Dallas Morning News, December 15, 2009 (showing how the Dallas

No doubt, if the federal government simply asked police departments to self-report metrics on police misconduct, departments would be highly incentivized to underreport. This incentive may be irresistible if it were clear that unusually high rates of apparent misconduct could result in federal intervention. What department, after all, would voluntarily admit to engaging in a pattern of misconduct that could result in costly federal intervention? To be clear, this chapter does not articulate every possible statistical database that Congress could develop on local police behavior. Instead, it suggests a range of plausible statistics Congress might consider collecting in the future.

The subparts that follow propose several possible statistics that Congress could acquire from local police departments. None of these statistics, on their own, would necessarily demonstrate that a police department was engaged in a pattern of unconstitutional behavior. Instead, each would provide federal regulators with statistical proxies that may suggest a systemic pattern of misconduct within a police department. In the case of some of these proposed databases – like civilian deaths associated with local law enforcement agencies – Congress has already acted to make this data more readily available in the near future. Other databases – like internal disciplinary records, payouts from civil rights suits, civilian complaints, traffic stop data, and search data – would require additional acts by Congress.

A Civilians Killed by Law Enforcement

How many civilians die at the hands of law enforcement each year? And how often do police use deadly force against black suspects relative to suspects of other races? These are the questions that reporters and civil rights advocates asked after numerous highly visible and controversial cases in recent years.[31] Police union leaders and "law-and-order

Police Department has allegedly underreported assault statistics); Corey Rayburn Yung, *How to Lie with Rape Statistics: America's Hidden Rape Crisis*, 99 Iowa L. Rev. 1197 (2014) (describing how police departments systemically underreport or manipulate rape statistics); Michael Matza, Craig R. McCoy, & Mark Fazlollah, *U.S. Review Set for Philadelphia Crime Reports*, Philadelphia Inquirer, November 14, 1998 (describing investigations into a pattern of underreporting of crime statistics in the Philadelphia Police Department); Fox Butterfield, *As Crime Falls, Pressure Rises to Alter Data*, NY Times, August 3, 1998, at A16 (describing the pressure on local police departments to alter self-reported crime statistics).

31 *See, e.g.*, Wesley Lowery, *How Many Police Shootings a Year? No One Knows*, Wash. Post, September 8, 2014, *available at* www.washingtonpost.com/news/post-nation

conservatives insist that shootings by officers are rare and even more rarely unjustified," while civil rights groups claim that police more frequently utilize unnecessary, lethal force against people of color.[32] It has proven nearly impossible to reach any firm conclusions, though, because the federal government currently keeps no national statistics on the number of individuals killed by law enforcement officers each year. For years before this, the FBI had voluntarily collected data on "justifiable homicides."[33] But these counts appeared to vastly underreport the number of actual police killings in the United States. This lack of data has puzzled and frustrated even FBI director James B. Comey.[34]

Advocates and legislators have called for the federal government to collect this sort of data.[35] In recent years, these calls have crossed traditional political party lines.[36] Critics have claimed that it is inconsistent for the federal government to keep detailed records on the number of law enforcement officers killed or assaulted in the line of duty,[37] but not keep comparable records on citizens killed or assaulted by law enforcement. Without official federal statistics, various media outlets like *The Guardian*[38] and the *Washington Post*[39] have relied on crowdsourcing and online searches to approximate the number of civilians killed annually by police – with somewhat uneven results.

/wp/2014/09/08/how-many-police-shootings-a-year-no-one-knows/ (bringing up the Michael Brown shooting as one of several that have inspired a national conversation on police shootings); Martin Kaste, *System for Reporting Police Killings Unreliable, Study Finds*, NPR, March 26, 2015, *available at* www.npr.org/2015/03/06/391269342/system-for-reporting-police-killings-unreliable-study-finds (using Eric Garner as one example of a police killing that has inspired a national conversation about police statistics); Allen G. Breed, *Police Killing Data Filled With Many Unknowns*, HUFFINGTON POST, December 7, 2014 (describing the shooting of twelve-year-old Tamir Rice as one of many examples of police killings that have sparked calls for more detailed national statistics).

32 Lowery, *supra* note 31. 33 *Id.*

34 Michael S. Schmidt, *F.B.I. Director Speaks Out on Race and Police Bias*, NY TIMES, February 12, 2015, at A1.

35 The Times Editorial Board, *One Thing the U.S. Government Doesn't Count: How Often Police Kill Civilians*, LA TIMES, December 16, 2014, *available at* www.latimes.com/opinion/editorials/la-ed-police-statistics-20141217-story.html (editorial board of the LA Times calling for a comprehensive, national database on police killings).

36 Fleetwood, *supra* note 20.

37 The FBI currently records detailed data on any assault or killing of a police officer in the line of duty as part of the Uniform Crime Reports. *See* UCR Reports, *supra* note 36.

38 *The Counted*, THE GUARDIAN, *available at* www.theguardian.com/us-news/series/counted-us-police-killings.

39 *Fatal Force*, WASH. POST, *available at* www.washingtonpost.com/graphics/national/police-shootings-2016.

To help address this information gap, Congress recently passed the Death in Custody Reporting Act ("DCRA"), which requires police departments to document the death of any person "who is detained, under arrest, or is in the process of being arrested."[40] Under the law, police departments must report the manner and circumstances of these deaths.[41] States that fail to report these statistics to the DOJ "could be stripped of up to 10 percent of the federal money they receive for local law enforcement purposes."[42] The DCRA also requires the U.S. attorney general to study the resulting data and make recommendations to Congress on how the federal government can reduce the number of deaths in custody.[43] In addition, the FBI has announced that it will "sharply expand" its system of tracking fatal police shootings.[44] As part of this push, the FBI will attempt to track not just civilian deaths but "any incident in which an officer causes serious injury or death to civilians, including through the use of stun guns, pepper spray and even fists and

[40] Death in Custody Reporting Act of 2013, Pub. L. No. 113–242, 128 Stat. 2860 (2014) (to be codified at 42 U.S.C. § 13727). Technically, this law is simply a reauthorization of an earlier measure passed in 2000. It took several years for law enforcement agencies to report data via the original version of this law. And the original version expired shortly thereafter, in 2006. As a result, the DOJ did not release any comprehensive statistics from the first attempt at this sort of database. Allie Gross, *Congress Is Finally Going to Make Local Law Enforcement Report How Many People They Kill*, MOTHER JONES, December 17, 2014, *available at* www.motherjones.com/politics/2014/12/death-custody-reporting-act-police-shootings-ferguson-garner.

[41] Eli Hager, *The Ferguson Bill*, MARSHALL PROJECT, December 12, 2014, *available at* www.themarshallproject.org/2014/12/12/the-ferguson-bill ("Each report must include 'the name, gender, race, ethnicity, and age of the deceased; the date, time, and location of the death; the law enforcement agency' involved and a description of how the death occurred.").

[42] *Id.* (elaborating that the funds local law enforcement would lose would be through "so-called Byrne grants, which account for about $500 million a year"). For more information on how Byrne grants are awarded and distributed, see *How Byrne JAG Grants Are Awarded and Distributed*, NAT'L CRIMINAL JUSTICE ASS'N, *available at* www.ncja.org/how-byrne-jag-grants-are-awarded-and-distributed (explaining how these grants are "awarded to states and territories by a formula based on population and Part 1 violent crimes").

[43] 42 U.S.C.A. § 13727(f) (West 2014) (stating "[t]he Attorney General shall carry out a study of the information reported under subsection (b) and section 3(a) to ... determine means by which such information can be used to reduce the number of such deaths").

[44] Kimberly Kindy, *FBI to Sharply Expand System for Tracking Fatal Police Shootings*, WASH. POST, December 8, 2015, *available at* www.washingtonpost.com/national/fbi-to-sharply-expand-system-for-tracking-fatal-police-shootings/2015/12/08/a60fbc16-9dd4-11e5-bce4-708fe33e3288_story.html.

feet."[45] The new FBI data may be available as early as 2017.[46] While the FBI database relies on police departments to self-report information on police behavior, the Bureau of Justice Statistics (BJS) has recently unveiled a pilot program that relies on open-source data to document the frequency of police use of deadly force. The BJS is currently dedicating two computer servers to "combing the internet 24 hours a day for reports of anything that looks like someone dying in an interaction with a police officer."[47] As part of this BJS initiative, analysts have begun contacting "police, medical examiners and other local officials to check the accuracy of the information and gather additional facts."[48] The BJS hopes to convert this pilot project into a "full-fledged" program that will produce annual data by the end of 2016.[49]

Admittedly, each of these planned databases may have problems. The financial penalty states face if they fail to report DCRA data is relatively small.[50] The FBI database will rely on police departments to self-report data voluntarily.[51] And the BJS database may only identify police killings that result in a news story.[52] Despite their individual shortcomings, these three databases may soon combine to provide the best available information on the frequency of civilian deaths at the hands of law enforcement.

45 *Id.*

46 *Id.* (explaining that "[t]he FBI's system for tracking fatal police shootings is a 'travesty,' and the agency will replace it by 2017").

47 Tom McCarthy, *US Government Database Hopes to Tell "Whole Story" of Police Killings after Year of Guardian Count*, The Guardian, December 13, 2015, *available at* www.theguardian.com/us-news/2015/dec/13/justice-department-database-police-killings-counted-statistics.

48 Kindy, *supra* note 44.

49 *Id.* (stating that "The bureau plans to convert the pilot into a full-fledged program in the spring and produce its first full year of data by the end of 2016.").

50 Editorial, *Data on Officer-Involved Shootings Will Finally Get Compiled Under State and Federal Laws*, LA Times, January 3, 2016, *available at* www.latimes.com/opinion/editorials/la-ed-police-shooting-data-20160103-story.html (explaining that "The latest version of the law is superior to its predecessor in that it has teeth, albeit not terribly sharp ones.").

51 Kindy, *supra* note 44 (explaining that "The new database will continue to rely on the voluntary reports of local police departments; FBI officials said they lack the legal authority to mandate reporting."). It is worth noting, though, that the FBI has expressed an intention to offer federal grants to local police departments that need additional resources to comply with this data request. And the FBI has gotten support from "the nation's largest police organizations [who] have agreed for the first time to lobby local departments to produce the data." *Id.*

52 McCarthy, *supra* note 47.

There is good reason to believe that these sorts of databases on civilian deaths could provide useful information in identifying problematic police departments. Police killings data should be difficult to manipulate. The existing social science data offers numerous examples of law enforcement agencies manipulating self-reported data.[53] This is in part because there is no way for a third party to accurately authenticate some of the self-reported law enforcement statistics. By contrast, the media would likely be able to partially authenticate the number of deaths allegedly caused by each law enforcement agency each year. Many times when a police officer is involved in a civilian death, this event makes headlines. Because of this, reporters and social scientists have been able to estimate the frequency of police killings based on media reports alone.[54] In addition, the collection of police killings should not be particularly expensive or burdensome, given that police already provide the federal government with a range of other, more complex statistical datasets each year.[55]

Admittedly, these emerging data sources on civilian deaths at the hands of law enforcement will not be a perfect measure to identify problematic police departments. It should go without saying that a police officer's decision to use deadly force is often justified. Sometimes police simply have no choice but to use deadly force. And police officers in some jurisdictions – particularly more dangerous jurisdictions – might be forced to use deadly force more often than others. The available data on police injuries in the line of duty only bolsters this conclusion. This data shows that police officers in larger cities typically face a higher risk of

[53] *See supra* notes 27–30 (describing multiple examples of police departments manipulating, underreporting, or otherwise altering self-reported crime statistics).

[54] Rueben Fischer-Baum, *Another (Much Higher) Count of Homicides by Police*, FIVE THIRTY EIGHT, August 25, 2014, *available at* http://fivethirtyeight.com/datalab/another-much-higher-count-of-police-homicides/ (citing databases of police killings put together by the Gun Violence Archive, Deadspin, Fatal Encounters, and even a Facebook page – each of which tends to rely heavily on media reports to document the number of police killings of civilians); *see also* Kyle Wagner, *We're Compiling Every Police-Involved Shooting in America. Help Us*, DEADPSIN, August 20, 2014, *available at* http://regressing.deadspin.com/were-compiling-every-police-involved-shooting-in-americ-1624180387.

[55] The Times Editorial Board, *One Thing the U.S. Government Doesn't Count: How Often Police Kill Civilians*, LA TIMES, December 16, 2014, *available at* www.latimes.com/opinion/editorials/la-ed-police-statistics-20141217-story.html (explaining how "The FBI [already] compiles statistics from 18,000 law-enforcement agencies for its annual 'Crime in the United States' report, but it doesn't include 'use of force' data. Separately, the bureau collects voluntarily supplied data on 'justifiable homicide' by police, defined as 'the killing of a felon by a law enforcement officer in the line of duty'").

injury in the line of duty than rural officers.[56] As a result, it would be unfair to judge any police department solely on the basis of this sort of statistic. But it can provide useful information for Congress in overseeing local police behavior.[57]

Nevertheless, the frequency of civilian deaths at the hands of law enforcement can serve as a valuable proxy for the presence of systemic misconduct in a police department. An apparent "pattern or practice of excessive force, including deadly force," is the single most common justification for the DOJ to intervene into a local police department via § 14141.[58] In fact, according to one estimate, of the sixty-eight formal investigations that the DOJ has initiated into local police departments since 1994, forty-eight of them – or a little more than 70 percent – have involved claims of excessive force.[59] Take the investigation in Ferguson as an example. There, the DOJ found that the "FPD engages in a pattern of excessive force in violation of the fourth Amendment."[60] The DOJ went on to find that officers in Ferguson are "quick to escalate encounters with subjects they perceive to be disobeying their orders or resisting arrest."[61] FPD officers deploy "canines to bite individuals when the articulated facts do not justify this significant use of force,"[62] turn to force in cases where a suspect's behavior is "annoying or distasteful but

[56] In 2012, for every hundred police officers in metropolitan counties, about eight were victims of assault in the line of duty. By contrast, only about 4.9 out of every hundred officers in nonmetropolitan counties were victims of assaults over the same time period. *See* UCR reports, *supra* note 36 (navigate to the Law Enforcement Officers Killed or Assaulted [LEOKA] database and navigate to table comparing the frequency of assaults in different-sized metropolitan areas).

[57] For example, one possible way to accomplish this would be to weight the frequency of police killings against the relative dangerousness of each jurisdiction. Dangerousness could be measured by using some combination of available statistics of each jurisdiction's homicide rates or the rate at which officers in each jurisdiction suffer injuries in the line of duty.

[58] U.S. Dep't of Justice, Civil Rights Div., Investigation of the Albuquerque Police Department, at 1 (2014), *available at* www.justice.gov/crt/about/spl/documents/apd_findings_4-10-14.pdf [hereinafter Albuquerque Investigative Findings Letter].

[59] *Fixing the Force*, PBS Frontline, *available at* apps.frontline.org/fixingtheforce/#allegations (showing a breakdown of the number of formal investigations and the basis of these investigations).

[60] U.S. Dep't of Justice, Civil Rights Div., Investigation of the Ferguson Police Department, at 28 (2015) [hereinafter Ferguson Investigative Report], *available at* www.justice.gov/sites/default/files/opa/press-releases/attachments/2015/03/04/ferguson_police_department_report.pdf.

[61] *Id.* [62] *Id.* at 31.

does not pose a threat,"[63] and overrely on force when dealing with "vulnerable populations, such as people with mental health conditions or intellectual disabilities and juvenile students."[64] The Ferguson findings were similar to a number of other cases where the DOJ identified a pattern or practice of misconduct. In a number of these cases, this pattern of excessive use of force ultimately resulted in an unusually large number of civilian deaths at the hands of law enforcement.[65]

B *Additional Data on Officer Behavior*

In addition to collecting data on civilians deaths at the hands of law enforcement, the federal government could also collect a range of other data on officer behavior, including arrests, stops, searches, and officer use of nondeadly force. If available, such data may prove useful in identifying patterns of nondeadly, nonetheless suspicious behavior by local law enforcement.

Some of this data is already available, albeit imperfectly. A decent number of police departments already report arrest data to the federal government.[66] Typically, this data shows the number of arrests made each year.[67] And in some cases, these arrest statistics are broken down into offense category and searchable by suspects' age, gender, and race.[68] In addition, the DOJ has recently taken steps to create a national police

[63] *Id.* at 33. [64] *Id.* at 35.

[65] For example, the DOJ investigation of the Albuquerque Police Department found that the agency had a hand in an unusually large number of civilian deaths – twenty individuals – in the preceding three years. Albuquerque Investigative Findings Letter, *supra* note 58, at 2 and 3.

[66] The FBI collects data on arrests made by local law enforcement through the UCR. The current arrest databases are voluntarily reported by local law enforcement. Some agencies fail to report arrest data for all twelve months of the year. Between 1980 and 2012, the FBI obtained complete arrest data on police departments that serve anywhere from 72 to 86 percent of the national population. Thus, the current arrest database provides a fairly complete but, ultimately, imperfect view of the frequency of arrests by law enforcement in the United States. For more information, *see* Bureau of Justice Statistics, *Arrest Data Analysis Tool, available at* www.bjs.gov/index.cfm?ty=datool&surl=/arrests/index.cfm (navigate to "Methods" tab to learn more about the methodology for the presently available arrest statistics).

[67] *Id.* (navigate to "Agency-Level Counts" to see the number of arrests by individual jurisdiction and year or navigate to "National Estimates" to see the estimated number of arrests by all law-reporting law enforcement agencies on an annual basis).

[68] *Id.* (navigate to "Definitions" tab to see the sortable variables available for analysis using the online arrest analysis tool).

use-of-force database.[69] The acquisition of other self-reported data on officer behavior would require an act of Congress. For instance, the federal government currently keeps no national data on police stops or searches.

This sort of data could be helpful in identifying police departments engaged of systemic misconduct that may benefit from federal assistance. First, if the federal government had access to the racial breakdown of police use of force, arrest, stops, and searches, it could use this information to target federal action against police departments that appear to be engaged in racially disparate behavior. For example, in Ferguson, the DOJ concluded that, "[d]ata collected by the FPD from 2012 to 2014 shows that African Americans account for 85% of vehicle stops, 90% of citations, and 93% of arrests made by FPD officers."[70] Black drivers were twice as likely to be searched during vehicle stops as white drivers.[71] All of this suggests that black drivers experience disparate impact from the FPD's use of arrests, stops, and searches.

Second, even without evidence of potential racial bias in police behavior, a high number of stops, searches, arrests, and uses of force relative to the national average may suggest that a police department is engaged in unconstitutional conduct. Again, the Ferguson example is instructive. The DOJ report in Ferguson found that the FPD engaged in a significant number of minor arrests for things like "Failure to Comply, Disorderly Conduct, Interference with Officer, or Resisting Arrest."[72] While one would expect to see some arrests under these categories, a large number of these arrests are consistent with a police force that "reflexively resort[s] to arrest immediately upon noncompliance with their orders, whether lawful or not" and a police force that is "quick to overreact to challenges and verbal slights."[73] As the DOJ concluded, "[t]hese incidents – sometimes called 'contempt of cop' cases – are propelled by officers' belief that arrest is an appropriate response to disrespect."[74] Thus, one way that Congress could use arrests data in a national coverage formula is to include some measure of the proportion of arrests for seemingly minor, "contempt of cop" offenses. This might serve as a proxy for unlawful or unjustified arrests.

[69] Sari Horwitz & Mark Berman, *Justice Department Takes Steps to Create National Use-of-Force Database*, Washington Post, October 13, 2016, *available at* www.washingtonpost.com/world/national-security/justice-department-takes-steps-to-create-national-use-of-force-database/2016/10/13/6d0ea7ac-9166-11e6-9c52-0b10449e33c4_story.html.

[70] Ferguson Investigative Report, *supra* note 60, at 4. [71] *Id.* [72] *Id.* at 25. [73] *Id.*

[74] *Id.*

There are other ways that Congress could identify potentially suspect patterns in arrest, stop, and search data. As one group of scholars have previously argued, "[w]hen stops increase greatly without an increase in the number of that lead to arrests, the pattern suggests that suspicions are being aroused too easily and the decision to interfere with people's liberty is being made too lightly, even if the stops are constitutionally justifiable in each individual instance."[75] Conversely, if a higher percentage of stops result in arrest, this suggests that "police officers stopped people for good reasons and were willing to have the District Attorney scrutinize those reasons."[76] Thus, Congress could use data on stops and arrest to investigate the rate at which stops materialize into arrests. This may provide a measure of the frequency of unjustified stops by police.

While there is little doubt that additional data on officer behavior would be useful, serious questions remain about whether Congress could obtain reliable data on these fronts – particularly when it comes to stops and searches. Unlike arrests, which create additional records through the need to book and jail a suspect, stops and searches do not always create such paper trails. Thus, it may be easy for a police department to manipulate or underreport these statistics.

C Civil Rights Suits

In addition, Congress could acquire data on the number of civil rights suits filed by private parties alleging unconstitutional officer misconduct via 42 USC § 1983 and the amount paid out from these suits. These statistics may provide a useful proxy for the presence of misconduct within a police department. Theoretically, if a police department is engaged in misconduct, a certain portion of this wrongdoing will result in civil suits.

Remember that victims of police misconduct have two options for filing federal civil rights suits under § 1983. If victims can overcome the qualified immunity doctrine, they can file suits directly against a police officer. Thereafter courts may order police officers to compensate victims of police misconduct. But, in reality, police officers are rarely, if ever, on the hook for these judgments. Instead, police departments and

75 Christopher Stone, Todd Foglesong, & Christine M Cole, Policing Los Angeles Under a Consent Decree: The Dynamics of Change at the LAPD 24 (2009), *available at* www.lapdonline.org/assets/pdf/Harvard-LAPD%20Study.pdf.

76 *Id.*

municipalities, with their deeper pockets, almost always indemnify officers. This means that most police departments provide officers with legal representation and pay for any judgments against them. As a result, suits against police officers almost always result in a payout by the municipality, not by an individual officer. Alternatively, victims of police misconduct have the ability to file suit directly against police departments. In order to do so after *Monell*, a victim must show that the police department failed to adequately train or supervise the officer in question.

In either instance – whether a victim files a civil suit against a police officer or the entire police department – the municipality is ultimately on the hook for any civil judgments. And the municipality should ultimately have records on this sort of suits and settlements. Because of this, municipalities are well positioned to compile and report data on civil rights suits to federal regulators. But absent any sort of a federal regulation, private parties have found it difficult to obtain accurate data on the frequency of civil rights suits against police departments. In a small handful of cases where this sort of data has gone public, it has revealed a startling pattern of apparent civil rights abuses. Take the example of the Chicago Police Department (CPD). Remember, the city of Chicago has paid out a jaw-dropping $500 million on civil rights settlements, judgments, and legal fees related to police misconduct.[77] In 2013 alone, the city paid $84.6 million – more than triple the amount that the city had anticipated in its budgetary projections.[78] It should come as no surprise, then, that the DOJ announced an investigation of the CPD for a civil rights investigation under § 14141 soon after the release of this data and the shooting of Laquan McDonald.[79]

The federal government could conceivably collect data on all the number of civil rights suits filed against municipalities across the country and the amount paid out from these cases. To force compliance with such a mandate, Congress could tie federal funding to local police departments to the release of this data. Of course, such a congressional mandate would sure be controversial. It could have adverse effects on litigants by discouraging municipalities from offering expeditious settlements in cases of police misconduct. And the release of this data to federal regulators could also raise privacy concerns.

[77] Andrew Schroedter, *Beyond Burge*, Better Government Association, April 3, 2014, *available at* www.bettergov.org/news/beyond-burge.

[78] *Id.*

[79] Monica Davey & Mitch Smith, *Justice Officials to Investigate Chicago Police Department After Laquan McDonald Case*, NY Times, December 7, 2015, at A10.

Perhaps most concerning though, civil suits are an admittedly imperfect proxy for the presence of police misconduct. Victims of serious police misconduct like excessive uses of force may be highly incentivized to bring a suit against a police officer or a police department. Such a suit is typically worth the time and resources that litigation requires. Victims of minor misconduct rarely turn to cumbersome litigation as a remedy, given the high entrance barriers. Thus, data on civil rights suits would provide a useful, but, ultimately, imperfect proxy for the presence of police misconduct in local police departments.

D *Officer Disciplinary Records*

Congress could also try to collect police officer internal disciplinary records. To do this, Congress could create incentives for states and localities to release police officer disciplinary records. All fifty states have freedom of information laws that generally grant some sort of public access to state records. Nearly all of these laws carve out exceptions that prevent the government from disclosing information that may violate a person's reasonable expectation to privacy. Take the example of the Chicago. Even before the DOJ formally announced its investigation of the police department in Chicago in December of 2015, activists had been demanding that the city of Chicago release its internal database of citizen complaints. It took seven years of litigation for University of Chicago law professor Craig Futterman to win a protective order requiring Chicago to release some of these records.[80] What they showed was startling. The data encompassed various years from 2001 through 2015.[81] During these time periods, the CPD determined that 95.34 percent of the 56,371 citizen complaints were unsubstantiated.[82] And less than 2 percent of the 28,567 allegations of misconduct complaints filed against the CPD between 2011 and 2015 resulted in some sort of discipline.[83] During these time periods, the most common punishment in the small number of

[80] Rob Wildeboer, *Complaints Against Chicago Police Published After 20-Year Saga*, WBEZ Chicago, November 9, 2015, *available at* www.wbez.org/news/complaints-against-chicago-cops-published-after-20-year-saga-113715 (describing the "seven years of litigation" that Futterman underwent to obtain access to these records).

[81] Citizens Police Data Project, *available at* http://cpdb.co (navigate to the "Methods" tab to find the detailed description of how the Citizens Police Data Project obtained this data and the years it covers).

[82] *Id.* (navigate to findings and scroll to find this data).

[83] *Id.*

substantiated complaints was a short suspension or a letter of reprimand.[84] Black residents made up 61 percent of those making complaints, but only 21 percent of sustained complaints.[85] By contrast, White residents made up only 21 percent of those making complaints, but 58 percent of sustained complaints.[86] And a small number of officers – less than 10 percent – also made up a disproportionate number of the complaints.[87] This small cohort of officers received an average of 3.7 times more complaints than the rest of the force.[88] This specific pattern is particularly indicative of a police department that is not adequately overseeing its officers. The same pattern existed in the LAPD before federal intervention. A study of the LAPD concluded that while the vast majority of LAPD officers had only one or two allegations of excessive force, around "183 officers had four or more allegations, 44 had six or more, 16 had eight or more, and one had 16 such allegations."[89] And a small cohort of officers in the LAPD made up a disproportionate number of the department's use of force cases.[90] The Chicago and LAPD cases are consistent with the belief among many academics that "10 percent of . . . officers cause 90 percent of the problems."[91]

The data from Chicago, though, only goes back a few years. An ongoing legal battle could determine the fate of disciplinary records going as far back as 1967.[92] Two years ago, police unions in Chicago filed a labor grievance arguing that the terms of the collective bargaining agreement require most documentation about complaints against police

[84] *Id.* (335 of the sustained cases resulted in no penalty, 580 resulted in a reprimand, 797 resulted in a suspension of less than one week, 254 resulted in a suspension of more than one week, and thirty-three resulted in termination).

[85] *Id.* [86] *Id.*

[87] *Id.* ("Complaints are disproportionately filed against a small subset of the Chicago Police Department. Repeat officers – those with 10 or more complaints – make up about 10% of the force but receive 30% of all complaints. They average 3.7x as many complaints per officer as the rest of the force.").

[88] *Id.*

[89] Indep. Comm'n on the L.A. Police Dep't, Report of the Independent Commission on the Los Angeles Police Department ix–x (1991).

[90] *Id.*

[91] Samuel Walker et al., *Early Warning Systems: Responding to the Problem Police Officer*, Nat'l Inst. Just. Res. Brief, July 2001, at 1, *available at* www.ncjrs.gov/pdffiles1/nij/188565.pdf.

[92] Rosa Flores & Mallory Simon, *Chicago's Next Fight: Trying to Purge Police Misconduct Records*, CNN, December 20, 2015, *available at* www.cnn.com/2015/12/18/us/chicago-police-misconduct-records.

officers to be destroyed within five years.[93] Excessive use of force and criminal conduct complaints can be held by the city for seven years.[94] The agreement also specifies that internal disciplinary records of any kind cannot be used by the CPD after the five- or seven-year period ends.[95] Union leaders argue that many of these internal disciplinary records are for minor offenses, like failure to file a report, that hold little value after five years.[96] But civil rights advocates argue that these records can help outsiders uncover patterns of misconduct.

The Chicago case is hardly unique. For example, when the DOJ initiated its investigation of the Cleveland Police Department for a possible pattern or practice of unconstitutional misconduct, it quickly found that "its [collective bargaining] contract said that disciplinary actions or penalties should be removed [from departmental databases] after two years."[97] And an ambitious project by the citizen oversight group Check the Police found that police union contracts in Austin, Baltimore, Columbus, Jacksonville, Louisville, Miami, Minneapolis, New York City, Seattle, and Washington, DC, all had some provisions requiring the department to purge disciplinary files that could be used to identify patterns of unconstitutional misconduct by officers.[98] This pattern has been further demonstrated through a more recent and exhaustive empirical study of police union contracts.[99] Across the country, civil rights advocates face significant barriers in gaining access to internal police disciplinary records. In many places, labor contracts prevent the retention and the release of this information.

93 Andy Grimm, *Activists Say Now Is Wrong Time to Destroy CPD Disciplinary Records*, CHICAGO SUN TIMES, December 3, 2015, *available at* http://chicago.suntimes.com/news/7/71/1149585/lawsuit-seeks-stop-police-discipline-files-destroyed ("A decision by an arbitrator earlier this month gave a partial victory to police unions, which want the city to destroy most disciplinary files after five years have passed").

94 *Id.* (A Chicago police union previously wanted "to destroy complaint files alleging excessive force or criminal conduct after seven years").

95 Flores & Simon, *supra* note 92 ("The agreement, which is effective from July 1, 2012, to June 30, 2017, says in part: 'All disciplinary investigation files, disciplinary history card entries, IPRA [Independent Police Review Authority] and IAD [Internal Affairs Division] disciplinary records, and any other disciplinary record or summary of such records other than records related to Police Board cases, will be destroyed five [5] years after the date of the incident.'").

96 *Id.* ("If the complaint involves alleged excessive force, it is to be destroyed after seven years, according to the contract.").

97 Flores & Simon, *supra* note 92.

98 *Police Union Contract Project*, CHECK THE POLICE, *available at* www.checkthepolice.org (scroll down to find a table showing a chart that compares union contracts and navigate to "Police Contracts Database" to find a full database of these union agreements).

99 Stephen Rushin, *Police Union Contracts*, 66 DUKE L. J. (forthcoming 2017).

In other states with a less significant union presence, open records laws carve out exceptions that limit or ban the release of these sorts of disciplinary records. State open record laws typically approach public access to police disciplinary records in three ways. In twenty-three states and the District of Columbia, police personnel records and disciplinary histories are considered confidential under existing open records laws.[100] Some of the nation's largest states are among the states that protect the confidentiality of police personnel, including four of the largest ten states in the United States – California, New York, Pennsylvania, and North Carolina.[101] In another fifteen states – including large states like Texas, Illinois, and Michigan – these records are available to the public in limited circumstances.[102] Only twelve states make these sorts of records publicly available in most circumstances.[103]

In total, state laws ban access to the disciplinary records for approximately 323,556 police officers in the United States. This represents about 51.2 percent of nation's state and local police force.[104] The disciplinary records of another 172,658 officers, or about 27.3 percent of nation's state and local police force, are subject to limited availability.[105] In total, state laws limit or bar access to the disciplinary records of around 496,214 police officers, or about 78.6 percent of the nation's police force.[106]

[100] Robert Lewis, Noah Veltman, & Xander Landen, *Is Police Misconduct a Secret in Your State?* WNYC, October 15, 2015, *available at* www.wnyc.org/story/police-misconduct-records/ (showing a full list of all states where police personnel records are confidential either under a specific state statute – as in Delaware, California, and New York – or under privacy exemptions or public employee personnel records exemptions to state open record laws).

[101] *Id.* (listing these states in the first figure).

[102] *Id.* (stating that in these states, "some of these states, only records of severe discipline, like a suspension or termination, are public while the rest is confidential. In others, responses vary by department because of evolving court precedents or ambiguity in the law.").

[103] *Id.* (explaining that, "In these states, police disciplinary records are generally available to the public. Many of these states still make records of unsubstantiated complaints or active investigations confidential.").

[104] I calculated these numbers by comparing the states categorized as having confidential, limited, and open personnel records with the UCR database on police personnel statistics. *See* UCR Reports, *supra* note 25 (navigating "Crime in the United States," selecting 2014, and navigating to "Police Employee Data" to uncover the number of officers employed in each state); Lewis, Veltman, & Landen, *supra* note 100 (using the figures to determine which states have confidential, limited, or open police personnel records).

[105] *Id.* [106] *Id.*

But what if states across the country granted open access to internal disciplinary records? What if civil rights advocates didn't have to go to court, like Professor Futterman had to do, to gain access to even the most basic information about these disciplinary records? Such openness would empower civil rights advocates to identify potentially problematic police practices. Perhaps if Chicago had allowed open public access to their disciplinary records from the beginning, the DOJ could have opened an investigation of the CPD years ago.

It may be impractical to expect states across the country to alter their open records laws to facilitate the release of this information. And even in states that grant public access to disciplinary records under open records laws, some municipalities would still reach agreements with local police unions to limit access to these records. Thus, it may take an act of Congress to gain access to this sort of information. If obtained, Congress could then use this information as a trigger for federal intervention.

E Citizen Complaints

Finally, Congress could sidestep local police departments and simply obtain data on police misconduct directly from the public. There is an existing historical precedent for such an act. Under Section 6 of the VRA, if the DOJ received at least twenty validated complaints about a jurisdiction infringing upon voting rights, the attorney general could assign federal examiners to prevent continuing misconduct.[107] Such a model is not unlike how the DOJ currently utilizes external monitors under § 14141 to target police departments engaged in a pattern or practice of misconduct.[108] Thus, it is conceivable that the DOJ could create a national database for complaints against local and state police departments. Individuals who have been victims of misconduct at the hands of local or state police departments could then file a report with this database. Federal regulators could then use this database to identify agencies with the highest number of complaints per capita.

This sort of a database has obvious appeal. It would be difficult for police departments to manipulate with such a database in any meaningful

[107] *See supra* Part I.D.2 and accompanying text (describing how the VRA established a system whereby the attorney general could mandate the appointment of an examiner in the event it received twenty meritorious complaints about voting suppression).

[108] *See* Stephen Rushin, *Structural Reform Litigation in American Police Departments*, 99 MINN. L. REV. 1343, 1391–1396 (2015) (describing the use of external monitoring as part of SRL initiated via § 14141).

way. This database would presumably encompass the entire scope of police misconduct. Citizens could file complaints about everything from unjustified traffic stops, to perceived racial profiling, to excessive use of force. But herein lays the primary drawback of such an approach – resources. Validating police complaints from jurisdictions all across the country would be an extraordinarily resource-intensive endeavor. In a sense, the DOJ already has this power. Under § 14141, the DOJ has the authority to intervene into local police departments that are engaged in a pattern or practice of misconduct.[109] In enforcing § 14141, the federal government has struggled with limited resources. The DOJ has only been able to investigate an average of about three police agencies every year between 1994 and 2013.[110] Getting selected for investigation or restructuring under § 14141 is so rare that it can feel akin to "winning a terrible lottery."[111] History tells us that in order for such a complaint database to be successful, Congress must be prepared to make a far more substantial investment in the federal investigation of local police misconduct.

II Harnessing Data to Incentivize Reform

Once the federal government has acquired useful data on local police behavior, there are several ways it could use this data to discourage local police misconduct. To begin with, the federal government could make this sort of data transparently available to the public. Doing so may promote bottom-up reform in some local police departments. But as Chapter 1 illustrated, mere transparency alone may be insufficient to motivate all police departments to implement costly reforms. It often takes some additional, outside incentive to motivate police departments to implement costly reforms aimed at curbing misconduct. This part discusses how the DOJ could publicly prioritize § 14141 litigation against police departments based on the statistical databases described in the previous section – civilian deaths, frequency of civil rights suits, internal disciplinary records, and citizen complaints. By publicly prioritizing litigation in such a way, the DOJ can create a race to the top, as

[109] 42 USC § 14141 (1994) ("Whenever the Attorney General has reasonable cause to believe that [a police department is engaged in a pattern or practice of unconstitutional conduct] the Attorney General . . . may in a civil action obtain appropriate equitable and declaratory relief to eliminate the pattern or practice").

[110] *Id.* [111] Rushin, *Federal Enforcement of Police Reform*, *supra* note 22, at 3194.

departments try to avoid expensive and stigmatizing federal intervention. This could expand the regulatory effect of § 14141. This part also describes how the DOJ could use these new databases to keep an eye on police departments after federal intervention ends, thereby promoting sustainability.

A Using Transparency to Promote Bottom-Up Reform

One way that the federal government could accomplish this is by making all of this data on local police behavior publicly accessible. Mere access to this information may motivate some police departments to take proactive steps to implement policies that reduce police violence. Transparency will also empower the public, the press, and interest groups to oversee local police conduct. In recent years, the United States has seen an explosion of public interest in police conduct. In many major cities, "copwatching" groups – "groups of local residents who wear uniforms, carry visible recording devices, patrol neighborhoods, and film citizen-police interactions" – have taken an active role in overseeing police behavior.[112] These copwatching groups have emerged in cities like Berkeley, Los Angeles, Austin, New York, Richmond, Portland, Atlanta, and Minneapolis.[113] The Black Lives Matters movement has produced protests in cities and on college campuses across the country.[114] These groups add to the list of existing civil rights groups

[112] Jocelyn Simonson, *Copwatching*, 104 CAL. L. REV. 391, 391 (2016).

[113] *Id.* at 445 (showing a full list of copwatching groups that Professor Simonson interviewed as part of her article. Presumably, this list is not inclusive of the entire field of copwatching, but rather an indication that copwatching groups exist in, at minimum, these listed communities).

[114] *See, e.g.*, Sandhya Somashekhar, *How Black Lives Matter, Born on the Streets, Is Rising to Power on Campus*, WASH. POST, November 17, 2015, *available at* www.washingtonpost.com/national/how-black-lives-matter-born-on-the-streets-is-rising-to-power-on-campus/2015/11/17/3c113e96-8959-11e5-be8b-1ae2e4f50f76_story.html (describing the rise of Black Lives Matter groups at Columbia University, Kalamazoo College, Wesleyan University, Georgetown University, and the University of Cincinnati); Charlotte Alter, *Protests Erupt in Minneapolis After Police Shoot Black Man*, TIME, November 16, 2015, available at http://time.com/4114447/minneapolis-black-lives-matters-protests-police-shooting/ (describing protests in Minneapolis by Black Lives Matter Activists after the shooting of unarmed twenty-four-year-old Jamar Clark); Shelby Grad, *How Black Lives Matter Became a Thorn in the Side of L.A. Leaders*, LA TIMES, October 20, 2015, *available at* www.latimes.com/local/lanow/la-me-ln-how-black-lives-matter-became-a-thorn-in-the-side-for-l-a-leaders-story-so-far-20151020-htmlstory.html (describing Black Lives Matter protests in Los Angeles).

with a longtime interest in police violence, like the American Civil Liberties Union.[115]

Historically, we have seen a troubling pattern in how some police departments respond to incidents of misconduct. A video emerges of alleged misconduct by a police officer.[116] Community groups immediately express outrage and demand reform. In response, police leaders deflect these calls for reform by arguing that misconduct was an isolated incident.[117] After all, every large organization will have a few bad apples. In the absence of any national statistics on local behavior, it can be difficult for the public, the press, or interest groups to prove that an individual act of police misconduct is connected to a broader problem within a police department.

By making data on local police behavior – including the frequency of police killings, internal disciplinary records, civilian complaints, and civil rights suits – the federal government can break this cycle. If made available to the public, the press and interest groups could use these statistics to compare the frequency of apparent misconduct from one jurisdiction to the next. Of course, none of these statistics would necessarily be dispositive. But combined, they could provide advocates with compelling evidence to ground demands for change. Transparency could also motivate local police departments to institute proactive reforms aimed at reducing the frequency of police misconduct.

Transparency alone, though, will likely not be enough to stimulate widespread reform in a significant number of police departments. Remember from Chapter 1 that a number of political, structural, and organizational barriers prevent bottom-up police reform, even in cases where misconduct appears to be a problem. Transparency may spur

115 For an example of the work done by the ACLU to investigate and lobby against police misconduct, see Robinson Meyer, *Film the Police: A New App Makes it Easier*, THE ATLANTIC, May 6, 2015, *available at* www.theatlantic.com/technology/archive/2015/05/film-the-police/392483/ (describing an app that encourages people to film police conduct and have the video automatically uploaded to "servers owned by the American Civil Liberties Union" ensuring that "[e]ven if the phone is destroyed, the video will survive"). The ACLU has also been instrumental in lobbying against the use of stop-and-frisk by police officers. For an example of this, see *Chicago Stop-and-Frisk to Be Monitored*, NY TIMES, August 8, 2015, at A19.

116 *See, e.g.*, Rachel A. Harmon, *Promoting Civil Rights Through Proactive Policing Reform*, 62 STAN. L. REV. 1, 12 n.31 (describing the release of the George Holliday video in Los Angeles showing the beating of Rodney King).

117 *See, e.g.*, David Parrish, *Police "Street Justice" Called Normal Conduct*, DAILY NEWS, March 10, 1991, at N1 (quoting Chief Gates as saying that the event was an aberration, and that "It's not the kind of conduct that we have normally from our officers").

some bottom-up reform in some local police departments. But history suggests that transparency enough may not be enough to bring about change in all police departments. Instead, we should be looking for ways to use these new data sources to stimulate reform in local police departments.

B Publicizing Potentially Problematic Police Departments to Promote Proactive Reform

The DOJ could use these new data sources to improve the enforcement of § 14141. Specifically, the DOJ could use these new data sources to create an enforcement approach that incentivized police departments to enact proactive reforms. Remember, the DOJ has only been able to investigate an average of around three law enforcement agencies police department each year – or less than 0.02 percent of the nation's police departments.[118] Section 14141 action is extremely rare, leading some to feel that the process lacks procedure fairness. The goal, then, for the DOJ is to establish, with limited resources, an enforcement strategy that appears procedurally fair, while also ensuring widespread compliance. This task has been a virtually impossible one without some national statistics on police behavior.

To help accomplish these goals, the DOJ could adopt an enforcement approach similar to a proposal originally made by Professor Rachel Harmon. She argued that the DOJ could use data on local police behavior to create a national list of police departments that may be engaged in a pattern or practice of misconduct.[119] The DOJ could make this list publicly available. The DOJ could then issue an ultimatum that gives these police departments two choices – either explain the unusual statistics patterns in your department, or provide evidence that your department has taken steps to address these problems. Thereafter, the DOJ could enforce this ultimatum by prioritizing

118 Rushin, *Federal Enforcement of Police Reform, supra* note 22, at 3230. Of course, this current enforcement approach makes sense, given the lack of hard data available to justify intervention into one police department over another. Historically, there has been little hard evidence to support the DOJ's choice of using § 14141 over one jurisdiction rather than another. Since the DOJ has only had the resources to investigate around three police departments in the United States each year, getting selected has felt akin to "winning a horrible lottery." *Id.* at 3194.

119 *See generally* Harmon, *supra* note 116 (similarly recommending that the DOJ develop a public list of the most problematic police departments as a way to stimulate widespread change).

§ 14141 investigations against police departments that fail to either justify or correct these problems. Similarly, the DOJ could offer safe harbor to police departments that proactively explain or correct their pattern of suspicious behavior. The DOJ might even consider offering police departments a specific list of policies and procedures they must implement to obtain such safe harbor under such an enforcement provision.[120]

This approach would have two likely benefits. First, it would improve the perceived fairness of the § 14141 case selection process. Unlike the current system, this proposed case selection process methodology would be more transparent. Municipalities would also have ample, public opportunity to respond to their ranking on the DOJ's watch list. Second, and perhaps most importantly, this enforcement approach could motivate a larger number of police departments to reform proactively, despite the DOJ's limited resources.[121] As it currently stands, the DOJ is careful not to publicly suggest a police department may be engaged in any misconduct before the formal investigation stage in § 14141 cases.[122] The stated reasoning for this policy is that the DOJ does not want to unfairly implicate a police department that may not be

[120] For example, the DOJ could require that police departments implement at least a few of the policies or procedures typically mandated under § 14141 consent decrees – like early intervention systems, training initiatives, complaint management protocols, or use-of-force investigation procedures. *See* Rushin, *Structural Reform Litigation in American Police Departments, supra* note 108, 1378–1395.

[121] At least one scholar has previously made a similar argument. *See* Harmon, *supra* note 116 at 4 ("The Justice Department can induce reform in police departments that are engaged in substantial misconduct, even if it does not sue them, by making the proactive adoption of reforms a less costly alternative for these departments than risking suit ... This strategy seeks to leverage whatever Justice Department litigation resources exist to motivate problematic departments to adopt recommended reforms without incurring the costs to the Justice Department of additional suits.") Although similar, this proposal is nevertheless distinct from previously made recommendations. Those recommendations did not present a specific methodology for police departments to identify problematic police departments. This article agrees with the core idea. The DOJ should rank police departments through some publicly transparent list. This article goes beyond previously made arguments. It claims that the DOJ should use the DCRA in constructing this list of problematic police departments. This would provide even more transparency and give police departments a clear metric by which they ought to improve.

[122] Rushin, *Federal Enforcement of Police Reform*, supra note 22, at 3225 (stating that "[d] uring [a preliminary look into a police department's behavior], litigators at the DOJ, both past and present, are careful to describe their actions as inquiries, as opposed to investigations [because by publicly] identifying a department as 'under investigation,' the DOJ would expose that department to immediate criticism in the media.").

engaged in wrongdoing.[123] This rationale is understandable. The DOJ does not want to unfairly suggest that a police department is engaged in systemic misconduct without first conducting a thorough investigation. But this caution has also severely limited the national impact of § 14141.

By adopting such an enforcement strategy, the DOJ can substantially increase the perceived risk of § 14141 reform. A hypothetical may better illustrate this point. Assume the city council and police chief in the fictional city of Pleasantville are trying to decide whether they should fund additional police misconduct reforms to prevent DOJ intervention via § 14141. Under the current enforcement approach, Pleasantville would have little motivation to make proactive reforms for fear of § 14141 intervention. As one scholar has previously argued, "The expected cost of § 14141, *E*, to any municipality is at least *p*, the probability perceived by the municipality that its police department will be subject to a full investigation under § 14141 (regardless of the outcome) multiplied by *c*, the cost a municipality expects to incur as a result of that investigation."[124] Given that the DOJ only has historically investigated around three municipalities per year, the probability, *p*, that the DOJ would target Pleasantville appears to be around 0.02 percent.[125] Even if we assume that the ultimate cost, or *c*, of § 14141 reform in Pleasantville could run as high as $50 million – as it has in many other communities – the risk of § 14141 reform may still be too remote for Pleasantville to justify such any significant police reform expenditure. Under such circumstances, the expected cost, or *E*, of § 14141 amounts to no more than $10,000 – or the probability of § 14141 action (0.02 percent) multiplied by the possible cost of this DOJ action ($50 million). And that assumes that an investigation of Pleasantville would amount to a full-scale § 14141 reform.

Now assume that the DOJ were to adopt the enforcement strategy proposed in this chapter. Assume the DOJ identified twenty police

[123] *Id.* at 3225 n.253 (quoting a knowledgeable DOJ insider who said that, "Opening an investigation is a huge deal. It's a very big moment. You wouldn't want to do that if there turns out not to be enough there to investigate. It would be very detrimental to the police department. Before you open any investigation all through the Department, it doesn't matter what the issue is, you have to figure out if there is a reason to open an investigation.").

[124] Harmon, *supra* note 116, at 23 and 24.

[125] Again, this is based on the presumption that the DOJ investigates an average of around three departments each year out of the nation's 18,000 total law enforcement agencies.

departments on its annual list of problematic police departments. And assume that the DOJ announced that it would formally investigate and pursue § 14141 reform in three of these departments each year. If Pleasantville were included on this list of suspicious police departments, city officials would be highly motivated to take proactive steps to avoid DOJ intervention. Rather than a 0.02 percent probability, or *P*, of DOJ intervention, Pleasantville is now facing a 15 percent chance of a DOJ investigation.[126] Given this probability of DOJ action, and the possible price tag associated with this intervention, Pleasantville may rationally conclude that it makes sense to allocate significant resources to proactive police reform. Using the deterrence theory formula, we may expect Pleasantville to invest up to $7.5 million to misconduct reforms after being included on a list of suspicious police departments – that is the probability of § 14141 action (15 percent) multiplied by the possible cost of this DOJ action ($50 million).

Under the current enforcement strategy, rational police departments will wait until the DOJ has publicly selected them for § 14141 investigation. The result is that the DOJ can only force a small number of departments a year to make changes. By adopting this enforcement strategy, the DOJ could induce many more police departments to make at least some proactive reforms aimed at curbing police violence. Doing so would expand the net of police departments affected by § 14141. And by also giving these police departments with an opportunity to alternatively justify or explain their unusually large number of police killings, the DOJ could also avoid unfairly stigmatizing agencies without some procedurally fair process.

C *Monitoring Police Departments after Federal Intervention*

The DOJ could also use these new databases to monitor police departments that have already undergone § 14141 reform. Remember that § 14141 reform typically takes anywhere from five to ten years or longer to complete.[127] Once a police department has demonstrated substantial compliance with the terms of the negotiated settlement, the DOJ will

[126] This figure is calculated by taking the number of police departments targeted each year for an investigation (three) and dividing it by the number of departments identified in the annual list of "Police Departments Engaged in the Most Civilian Deaths" (twenty).

[127] Rushin, *supra* note 108, at 1392 (showing the lengths of time each settlement took to complete in figure 5).

officially stop monitoring the department.[128] This raises a very serious concern. What is to keep a police department from abandoning the reforms mandated by the DOJ immediately after § 14141 oversight ends? This concern is especially salient because, in the absence of national statistics on police behavior, the DOJ has no mechanism to oversee police departments after the end of a consent decree. And given the high cost of police reforms, municipalities may be highly incentivized to drop these procedures as soon as external oversight ends.

This is not to say that these data sources would give the DOJ all the information it needs to engage in long-term oversight after monitoring concludes. But they would give the DOJ significantly more information to keep an eye on police departments after § 14141 reform ends. The DOJ could use these databases to monitor these agencies for several years thereafter. The DOJ could even mandate in future § 14141 settlements that a suspicious pattern in these databases after monitoring ends would trigger another investigation of the agency. Importantly, this sort of continual oversight would not be resource intensive for the DOJ. And it could provide police agencies with additional incentives to keep § 14141 reforms in place after the terms of the settlements conclude. Thus, these datasets could present a unique and cost-effective opportunity for the DOJ to conduct some limited monitoring of police departments after § 14141 intervention ends.

III Increasing the Frequency of § 14141-Style Interventions

Given the apparent inability of the DOJ to consistently or aggressively utilize § 14141, policymakers should take steps to increase the number of structural police reform cases. One way that Congress could achieve this is by granting private litigants a limited equitable right of action against police departments engaged in a pattern or practice of unconstitutional misconduct, as recommended by Professor Myriam Gilles.[129] Some

[128] *Id.* at 1394 (describing how a police department can demonstrate substantial compliance to end external monitoring – generally a standard that requires at least 94 percent compliance with the terms in the consent decree).

[129] Professor Myriam Gilles has argued that, in light of the DOJ's limited enforcement ability, Congress ought to amend § 14141 to allow the DOJ to deputize private citizens to bring public pattern or practice suits seeking injunctive relief. Myriam E. Gilles, *Reinventing Structural Reform Litigation: Deputizing Private Citizens in the Enforcement of Civil Rights*, 100 Colum. L. Rev. 1384 (2000). Gilles tempers her recommendation that the DOJ must formally deputize any private individual seeking § 14141 relief. *Id.* at 1417. She says that this deputation model thrives in other similar

scholars have argued that granting such a private right of action would interfere with active public claims.[130] This is a reasonable concern.

In order to alleviate this concern, though, Congress could provide the attorney general with narrow authority to intervene and block private § 14141 claims against agencies where the DOJ has already initiated a public § 14141 investigation. In theory, this statutory change would permit the DOJ to continue the important job of structurally reforming problematic police departments, while empowering a new group of plaintiffs to fill the gaps left by the DOJ's historically uneven enforcement policies. Congress considered this possibility in the original Police Accountability Act of 1991 and considered another bill that would do just this in 1999 and again in 2000.[131] Such a private right of action would be "especially valuable when the reigning presidential administration's financial and political commitment to § 14141 enforcement is low."[132] Chapter 2 demonstrated that during a period of the Bush administration, there appeared to be a lesser commitment to § 14141. In the absence of DOJ action, this statutory change would permit private individuals to fill the gaps during times of underenforcement. Further, this would likely increase the number of total § 14141 claims brought against American police departments,[133] as DOJ officials openly acknowledge that they cannot possibly litigate in most agencies where there may be a pattern

litigation contexts. *Id.* at 1418. Scholars have also recognized that agencies often "lack the capacity to enforce the law adequately," making private enforcement valuable in some contexts. Matthew C. Stephenson, *Public Regulation of Private Enforcement: The Case for Expanding the Role of Administrative Agencies*, 91 VA. L. REV. 110, 107–109.

130 Harmon, *supra* note 116 at 63 ("[P]rivate suits would not only likely result in weaker reforms than government suits, but would effectively inhibit the [DOJ] from pursuing more effective reforms in the same departments in the future.").

131 *Id.* at 58 ("[S]everal members of Congress introduced in 1999 and then again in 2000 the Law Enforcement Trust and Integrity Act (LETIA) to amend § 14141 to allow any aggrieved person to bring a civil action for declaratory and injunctive relief for violations of the statute."); *see* Law Enforcement Trust and Integrity Act of 2000, HR 3927, 106th Cong. § 502; Law Enforcement Trust and Integrity Act of 1999, HR 2656, 106th Cong. § 501.

132 Harmon, *supra* note 116, at 59.

133 *Cf.* Telephone Interview with DOJ Participant #14, at 11 (July 11, 2013) [hereinafter Interview #14] (on file with author). The participant explained in depth:

> I think that a private cause of action would obviously be transformative. And I think if Congress was nervous about creating a private cause of action and thought that it's too radical, that there would be ways to have some kind of gatekeeping function around the private cause of action. I think that would be – there's no way that the Justice Department can

or practice of misconduct.[134] This change would empower civil rights groups to bring pattern or practice claims independently, rather than having to convince the DOJ that action is warranted. One litigator commented that adding a private right of action to § 14141 would "obviously be transformative."[135] This proposed change would also potentially overcome concerns about political cooptation of public rights of action and political spillover, as the power would be directly in the hands of private litigants to seek equitable action against local law enforcement agencies.[136]

Nevertheless, this approach would suffer from drawbacks. Private parties may "pursue a resolution to the § 14141 suit that maximizes their expected financial gain rather than a resolution that maximizes effective reform."[137] As Professor Harmon has argued, private parties could use § 14141 claims as leverage in § 1983 cases.[138] And such a grant of power to private litigants is constitutionally suspect after *Lyons*.[139] In light of the potential shortcomings of a private right of action, policymakers may understandably look for other ways to increase the number of structural police reform cases. For instance,

> litigate all of the patterns and practices of police misconduct in this country. There are too many policing jurisdictions for them to do that.
>
> *Id.*

134 *Id.* at 12 (stating that "[i]t's just, it's not plausible to think that the Justice Department can do this by itself" in arguing that the Special Litigation Section cannot possibly litigate all pattern or practice claims).

135 *Id.* at 11.

136 Stephenson, *supra* note 129, at 110–112 (stating that "private enforcement is most associated with legislative distrust of the executive branch" and can potentially correct "agency slack").

137 Harmon, *supra* note 116, at 60.

138 *Id.* at 59. Harmon concludes that the availability of § 14141 remedies will make local municipalities

> more receptive partners for private actors seeking to maximize § 1983 awards: some public officials will seek to avoid intrusive reforms, even at the expense of financial payouts by the city, while some private actors will seek to maximize financial awards from the city, even at the expense of less reform. In such cases, both parties would have reason to reach a settlement that avoids many best practice reforms. Even private plaintiffs with good motives may be influenced by local agents intent on avoiding intrusion. These incentives for collusion suggest that private suits are unlikely to produce results consistent with the public interest.
>
> *Id.* at 60.

139 Gilles, *supra* note 129, at 1414 (arguing that any attempt to grant a private right of action under § 14141 would face "insurmountable constitutional problems under the equitable standing rule of *Lyons*").

state legislatures could permit state attorneys general to initiate structural police reform in state court. Professor Samuel Walker and Morgan Macdonald have recommended the addition of such a state-level structural police reform measure.[140] Any state statute could roughly mirror § 14141 and give state attorneys general the ability to bring suit against police departments within their state that are engaged in a pattern or practice of unconstitutional misconduct. This could dramatically increase the number of structural police reform cases. While state attorneys general may be susceptible to the same resource limitations, political cooptation, and political spillover effects evident in the federal government's enforcement of § 14141, structural police reform initiated by state attorneys general may be more rigorous than reforms requested by private litigants.

IV From Reactive to Proactive Federal Oversight

Improving the enforcement of § 14141 would be an important first step in bolstering federal oversight of local police departments. Section 14141 cases, though, represent one of many weapons the federal government has to influence local police conduct. This part outlines some ways that the federal government could move more broadly from reactive to proactive oversight of local police departments – that is, how the federal government could gradually break away from the limited oversight of the Hands Off and Buildup Eras and take on a more direct regulatory role in fighting police wrongdoing.

A Moving from Sticks to Carrots: Proactive Federal Investment in Police Reform

The federal government could move from reactive to proactive regulation of local law enforcement by reallocating federal grants to support the reduction of local police misconduct. The federal government currently gives states and local police departments hundreds of millions of dollars in funding each year through the Edward Byrne Justice Assistance Grants (Byrne JAG) and the Community Oriented Policing Services (COPS) Hiring Program grants.[141] Additionally, the federal government also

[140] *See generally* Samuel Walker & Morgan Macdonald, *An Alternative Remedy for Police Misconduct: A Model State "Pattern or Practice" Statute*, 19 Geo. Mason U. CR LJ 479, 549 (2009).

[141] Harmon, *supra* note 15, at 872.

allocates significant resources to support local policing through grants administered by the Department of Homeland Security and the Department of Agriculture.[142] Federal efforts to directly subsidize local policing efforts began with the Law Enforcement Assistance Act (LEAA) of 1965. Then Attorney General Nicholas Katzenbach explained during congressional hearings that the LEAA represented "a new concept of Federal assistance to State and local law enforcement."[143] Given the "alarming rise in crime," the purpose of the LEAA was to provide financial assistance to localities so they could "meet the problem more effectively."[144] The LEAA was never intended to "build police academies, raise police salaries, or enable a city to double the size of its police force."[145] Instead, as Attorney General Katzenbach explained, the LEAA was designed to "provide selective support for model programs" that can effectively combat crime.[146] This focus on using federal funds to improve crime reduction was also evidenced three years later in the passage of the Omnibus Crime Control and Safe Streets Act of 1968. The stated purpose of this law was "to assist State and local governments in strengthening and improving law enforcement at every level by national assistance" and to encourage "the development of new methods for the prevention and reduction of crime and the detection and apprehension of criminals."[147] During the 1970s, these block grant programs "faded" in part because of "criticisms of their effectiveness and a declining national focus on crime."[148] But by the late 1980s, Congress again turned its attention to efforts to subsidize local crime fighting efforts, this time in the form of the Byrne JAG program.[149] Even the Violent Crime Control and Law Enforcement Act (VCCLEA) of 1994 which gave us § 14141 also included a substantial component dedicated to the subsidization of local crime fighting efforts. While the federal government has dedicated substantial resources to funding local crime fighting and antiterrorism efforts, there has not been a similar approach in supporting the detection and prevention of officer misconduct.

[142] *Id.*
[143] *Law Enforcement Assistance Act of 1965: Hearing Before the Subcomm. of the Committee of the Judiciary*, 89th Cong. 6 (1965) [hereinafter *LEAA Hearing*].
[144] *Id.* [145] *Id.* at 7.
[146] *Id.* It is also worth noting that Attorney General Katzenbach emphasized a range of other goals in his testimony, including a need to provide better training on cutting edge crime control methods, install more fairness into the criminal trial process, and a number of other criminal justice related goals.
[147] Pub. L. No. 90–351, Title I, 82 Stat. 197. [148] Harmon, *supra* note 15, at 882.
[149] *Id.*

Policymakers often argue that there are two major ways to induce a desired behavior. You can rely on punishment – colloquially referred to as "sticks." That is you can increase the cost of bad behavior in hopes of bringing about more good behavior. Conversely, you can turn to rewards – sometimes called "carrots." So why has the federal government turned to sticks in deterring officer misconduct, but has provided carrot after carrot in its effort to combat crime? The federal government has rarely subsidized and rewarded police departments for adopting cutting-edge policies or technologies aimed at combatting misconduct. Instead, it has provided penalties for police officers and police departments that are engaged in wrongdoing. Things could be different.

It is not difficult to imagine the federal government more broadly subsidizing local police efforts to address misconduct. We have already seen small efforts on this front. In 2015, the DOJ initiated a pilot project to subsidize the purchase and implementation of body cameras by local police departments.[150] After announcing this program, the DOJ's Office of Justice Programs received applications from 285 agencies in forty-two states, the District of Columbia, and tribal governments.[151] These agencies requested 55,000 body cameras at a cost of $56 million.[152] The DOJ was only able to award $23 million in federal funds – enough to support the implementation of 21,000 body cameras in seventy-three agencies across thirty-two states.[153] Even if the DOJ was unable to meet the local demand, this is an important step. It suggests that policy-makers are beginning to recognize the value in subsidizing efforts to combat local police misconduct. The Byrne JAG program also listed grants for body cameras as a priority in its annual grant solicitation notice.[154]

In sum, the federal government could use its current grant-giving apparatuses to fund more police reform efforts. However, this sort of a policy suffers from an obvious drawback. Police departments must generally take the initiative in applying for federal assistance. This reform

[150] *Justice Department Awards Over $23 Million in Funding for Body Worn Camera Pilot Program to Support Law Enforcement Agencies in 32 States*, Department of Justice, September 21, 2015, *available at* www.justice.gov/opa/pr/justice-department-awards-over-23-million-funding-body-worn-camera-pilot-program-support-law.

[151] *Body-Worn Camera Program Fact Sheet*, Bureau of Justice Assistance, *available at* www.bja.gov/bwc/pdfs/BWCPIP-Award-Fact-Sheet.pdf (last visited January 12, 2015).

[152] *Id.* at 1. [153] *Id.*

[154] *Edward Byrne Memorial Justice Assistance Grant (JAG) Program FY 2015 Local Solicitation*, Department of Justice, May 12, 2015, *available at* www.bja.gov/Funding/15JAGLocalSol.pdf.

effort would not bring about change in local police departments that remain opposed to the implementation of oversight mechanisms. Addressing these problematic agencies may require some out-of-the-box solutions, like the one discussed next.

B The Voting Rights Act as a Blueprint for Police Reform

A final and controversial way that Congress could fight local police misconduct is by taking a page from the Voting Rights Act (VRA) of 1965, as I have argued in a recent coauthored article with Jason Mazzone.[155] Remember that Congress faced a challenging regulatory dilemma in combatting voter suppression. Localities were actively thwarting federal efforts to ensure equal access to the polls. In response, Congress created a statute that proactively regulated a large number of localities. The VRA created a coverage formula that triggered oversight of any municipality with a low voter registration and any municipality that used tests or devices that suppressed voter participation. In these covered jurisdictions, local officials had to receive federal preclearance before making any changes to voting procedures. The measure also provided for the appointment of federal monitors to oversee voting practices.

What if Congress crafted a similar statute to regulate local police departments? Congress could craft a coverage formula to identify potentially problematic police departments. To do so, Congress would need to collect substantially more data on local police behavior. Requiring local police departments to report the kind of data discussed earlier – data on use of force, civilian deaths, civil rights payouts, arrests, stops, searches, disciplinary records, and citizen complaints – would be a good start. From this data, Congress could conceivably put together a formula that identifies police departments that may be engaged in systemic misconduct. Congress could then mandate that all of these covered police agencies adopt specified prophylactic measures. Congress could turn to previous § 14141 settlements to develop these prophylactic measures. Thus, Congress could force covered police departments to implement early warning systems, citizen complaint management reforms, use of force policy reforms, or even body cameras.

[155] For an expanded and more nuanced articulation of this argument, *see* Mazzone & Rushin, *supra* note 1.

Some may argue that such a coverage formula for local police departments violates the principles of federalism. According to this view, coverage formulas for police departments would arbitrarily and unfairly penalize some municipalities but not others.[156] A coverage formula would also be a radical extension of the power granted to the attorney general under § 14141. In order to intervene into a local police department under § 14141, the attorney general has the burden of proving in federal court that a police department was engaged in a pattern or practice of unconstitutional misconduct. A coverage formula would turn the tables. It would establish an arguably less rigorous test to trigger federal oversight. In the eyes of some, this would violate due process and equal protection.[157] Critics may also contend that no coverage formula could possibly determine the likely presence of systemic misconduct within a police department.

But the Supreme Court has heard and rejected a similar challenge to the VRA in the past in *South Carolina* v. *Katzenbach*.[158] In their opinion, the Court noted that previous, piecemeal efforts to fight these civil rights abuses had failed.[159] The Court concluded that, "[a]s against the reserved powers of the States, Congress may use any rational means to effectuate

[156] During the congressional debate about the VRA, this same concern emerged. *See, e.g.*, S. Rep. No. 89–162, *reprinted in* 1965 USCCAN 2508, 2517 (1965) ("The dates are purely arbitrary. The percentage used is equally arbitrary. The events are purely arbitrary. The supposed result from the facts determined is purely arbitrary.") (statement of Sen. Charles J. Bloch).

[157] Again this same issue came up during the VRA debates. *See, e.g.*, 111 Cong. Rec. 8107 (1965) ("The present bill, in my opinion, denies due process and equal protection of the law, as guaranteed by the 14th amendment, to a large segment of our people in the States to which it applied.") (statement of Rep. Joel T. Broyhill).

[158] 383 US 301, 314 (1966). There, South Carolina argued that the VRA violated the constitutional principle of equal statehood, violated the Due Process Clause by creating an "arbitrary and irrebuttable presumption of racial discrimination by South Carolina and her inhabitants in connection with her voter registration," and interfered with self-government in violation of the Guarantee Clause of Article IV. Brief for Plaintiff, at 13–15, 16, 24 South *Carolina* v. *Katzenbach*, 383 US 301 (1965) (No. 22), available at 1965 WL 130083. South Carolina also argued that the VRA was unconstitutional because the proposed remedies available under the statute lacked a sufficiently close relationship to proven racial discrimination. *Id.* at 30–33. And South Carolina claimed that the VRA essentially represented a legislative trial in violation of the prohibition on bills of attainder and the allocation of power to the courts in Article III. *Id.* at 36 and 37. But the US Supreme Court rejected these arguments. Chief Justice Warren wrote that "[t]he constitutional propriety of the Voting Rights Act of 1965 must be judged with reference to the historical experience which it reflects." Katzenbach, 383 US at 308.

[159] *Id.* at 314.

the constitutional prohibition of racial discrimination in voting."[160] Under that standard, the Court found that the VRA was a legitimate response to the problem of discrimination, particularly given the ineffectiveness of case-by-case litigation.[161] Limiting the remedies to a select number of jurisdictions based on a coverage formula was a permissible way for Congress to deal with this problem.[162] And the Court concluded that each of the specified metrics in the VRA and the mandated solutions were rational and appropriate.[163]

Since *Katzenbach*, the Supreme Court has also handed down the *Shelby County v. Holder* case.[164] This landmark decision struck down part of the VRA coverage formula.[165] Nevertheless, this decision did not invalidate the *concept* of a coverage formula – it merely said that the *specific* coverage formula used in the VRA was invalid as it relied on decades-old data to judge states decades later.[166]

In order to satisfy constitutional scrutiny, any coverage formula as applied to police departments would need to prove under *Katzenbach* that Congress is using rational means to enforce constitutional limitations on police conduct. Conversely, courts could also turn to a standard from a different case, *Boerne* v. *Flores*, and require that any coverage formula applied to police departments demonstrate "congruence and proportionality between the injury to be prevented or remedied and the means adopted to that end."[167] A federal coverage formula for local police departments is likely to satisfy either of these two standards.

A federal coverage formula for local police departments could be narrowly directed at unconstitutional conduct by local police departments. The remedies could be closely tied to the correction of these problems. Unlike the VRA, which burdened entire states, thereby raising questions of unequal state sovereignty, this proposal could target individual police departments. This would suggest that as a regulatory tool, coverage formulas for individual police departments are even more rational (or congruent and proportional) than the VRA.[168] Thus, federal coverage formulas may provide a radical, but constitutionally

[160] *Id.* at 324. [161] *Id.* at 328. [162] *Id.* [163] *Id.* at 322–328.

[164] 113 S. Ct. 2612 (2013). [165] *Id.* at 2630. [166] *Id.* at 2625–2627.

[167] 521 US 507, 520 (1997).

[168] This also should not raise commandeering concerns as it merely imposes federal requirements on existing state activity other than requiring states to get involved in regulating private parties on behalf of the state. This should fall within the *Condon* and *Baker* exemptions.

permissible, way for the federal government to take on a more proactive role in regulating local police departments.

Conclusion

When protests engulfed Ferguson, Missouri, in August 2014, many advocates hoped that it would usher in a new era in police oversight. Much like after the vicious beating of Rodney King on the side of a California highway over eleven years earlier, the Michael Brown shooting galvanized widespread support for police reform. The deaths of Tamir Rice, Walter Scott, Eric Garner, and an estimated 1,134 other individuals at the hands of police officers in 2015 have added to the calls for reform.[169] The events surrounding Rodney King inspired Congress to pass one of the most important statutes in the history of American policing law – § 14141. Because of § 14141, the DOJ has been quietly overhauling American police departments throughout the country over the last two decades. This statute has shown how forceful, external regulation can stimulate reform in local police departments. Because of these § 14141 cases, policymakers now have a clear blueprint for future police regulations. While there have been some definite bumps in the road, the DOJ today appears to have developed a package of reforms that brings about at least temporary reform. In major American cities like Los Angeles, Washington, DC, Cincinnati, Pittsburgh, and Detroit, the DOJ has appeared to make a meaningful difference in local police departments through mandating the implementation of this core package of reforms. Today, the challenge in addressing police misconduct is not about figuring out what works. Thanks to § 14141, we know what kind of procedural changes work.

The challenge is now figuring out how to get the thousands of police departments across the country to buy into these reforms – reforms that admittedly can be time and resource intensive. Section 14141 will likely be insufficient to inspire widespread reform. The DOJ simply lacks the resources and necessary information to use this statute aggressively. The reforms discussed in this chapter may well represent

[169] Jon Swaine, Oliver Laughland, Jamiles Lartley, & Ciara McCarthy, *Young Black Men Kileld by US Police at Highest Rate in Year of 1,134 Deaths*, The Guardian, December 31, 2015, *available at* www.theguardian.com/us-news/2015/dec/31/the-counted-police-killings-2015-young-black-men.

the next frontier in police regulation. Ferguson may become this generation's Rodney King – an opportunity for policymakers to rethink the way the federal government oversees local policing. Each represents a valuable step in improving the oversight and regulation of local police behavior. This sort of increased federal oversight of police departments may not, in and of itself, represent the ultimate answer to police misconduct. But it may be as close as we can ever get.

Appendix A

Investigations by the DOJ

Agency Name	Opened	Closed	Reopened	State
Torrance Police Department	May 1, 1995	September 14, 1998		CA
Adelanto Police Department	June 16, 1995	September 14, 1998		CA
Steubenville Police Department	July 31, 1995	March 3, 2005		OH
Pittsburgh Police Department	April 11, 1996	June 16, 2005		PA
New Orleans Police Department	April 15, 1996	March 23, 2004	May 14, 2010	LA
New Jersey State Police	April 15, 1996	October 26, 2009		NJ
Illinois State Police	April 15, 1996	September 27, 2002		IL
Montgomery County Police Department	June 1, 1996	February 1, 2005		MD
Los Angeles Police Department	July 31, 1996	May 16, 2013		CA
Beverly Hills Police Department	August 12, 1996	November 14, 2000		CA
New York City Police Department (Eastern District)	August 21, 1997	December 23, 2004		NY
Buffalo Police Department	December 9, 1997	July 9, 2008		NY
Columbus Police Department	March 13, 1998	May 14, 2004		OH
Eastpointe Police Department	March 20, 1998	January 12, 2005		MI

Agency Name	Opened	Closed	Reopened	State
District of Columbia Metropolitan Police Department	January 31, 1999	February 10, 2012		
New York City Police Department (Southern District)	March 17, 1999	March 31, 2005		NY
Charleston Police Department	March 31, 1999	November 12, 2003		WV
Riverside Police Department	June 29, 1999	March 26, 2007		CA
Prince George's County Police Department	July 1, 1999	January 13, 2009		MD
Cleveland Division of Police	October 1, 1999	March 15, 2005	March 14, 2013	OH
Mount Prospect Police Department	April 5, 2000	December 28, 2006		IL
Highland Park Police Department	May 18, 2000	December 7, 2004		IL
Tulsa Police Department	February 8, 2001	July 21, 2008		OK
Cincinnati Police Department	May 7, 2001	April 12, 2007		OH
Detroit Police Department	May 29, 2001	March 2, 2016		MI
Schenectady Police Department	April 4, 2002	January 9, 2013		NY
Portland Police Department	May 6, 2002	June 27, 2005		ME
Miami Police Department	May 31, 2002	May 19, 2006	October 11, 2011	FL
Providence Police Department	December 11, 2002	March 26, 2008		RI
Villa Rica Police Department	January 27, 2003	December 23, 2006		GA
Alabaster Police Department	March 4, 2003	September 7, 2005		AL

Agency Name	Opened	Closed	Reopened	State
Bakersfield Police Department	June 24, 2003	January 25, 2008		CA
Virgin Islands Police Department	February 13, 2004			VI
Beacon Police Department	August 3, 2004			NY
Warren Police Department	November 29, 2004			OH
Easton Police Department	October 14, 2005	July 1, 2015		PA
Orange County Sheriff's Office	January 10, 2007	April 4, 2013		FL
Austin Police Department	May 25, 2007	May 27, 2011		TX
Yonkers Police Department	July 24, 2007			NY
Puerto Rico Police Department	April 30, 2008			PR
Harvey Police Department	September 5, 2008	January 24, 2012		IL
Lorain Police Department	November 20, 2008	May 22, 2012		OH
Escambia County Sheriff's Office	December 30, 2008	October 14, 2012		FL
Maricopa County Sheriff's Department	March 10, 2009			AZ
Inglewood Police Department	March 11, 2009	October 1, 2015		CA
Suffolk County Police Department	September 9, 2009			NY
East Haven Police Department	September 30, 2009			CT
Alamance County Sheriff's Department	June 2, 2010			NC
Seattle Police Department	March 31, 2011			WA

Agency Name	Opened	Closed	Reopened	State
Newark Police Department	May 9, 2011			NJ
Portland Police Department	June 7, 2011			OR
Los Angeles County Sheriff's Department (Antelope Valley)	August 19, 2011			CA
Meridian Police Department	November 29, 2011			MS
Missoula Police Department	April 25, 2012	May 11, 2015		MT
University of Montana Office of Public Safety	April 25, 2012	July 1, 2015		MT
Albuquerque Police Department	November 27, 2012			NM
Ferguson Police Department	September 4, 2014			MO
Evangeline Parish Sheriff's Department	April 21, 2015			LA
Ville Platte Police Department	April 21, 2015			LA
Baltimore Police Department	May 8, 2015			MD
Chicago Police Department	December 7, 2015			IL

Appendix B

Negotiated Settlements Between DOJ and Police Agencies

Agency	Agreement Date	Close Date
Pittsburgh Police Department	April 16, 1997	June 16, 2005
Steubenville Police Department	September 3, 1997	March 3, 2005
New Jersey State Police	December 29, 1999	October 26, 2009
District of Columbia Metropolitan Police Department	June 13, 2001	February 10, 2012
Los Angeles Police Department	June 15, 2001	May 16, 2013
Highland Park Police Department	July 11, 2001	December 7, 2004
Cincinnati Police Department	April 12, 2002	April 12, 2007
Columbus Police Department	September 4, 2002	May 14, 2004
Buffalo Police Department	September 19, 2002	July 8, 2008
Mount Prospect Police Department	January 22, 2003	December 28, 2006
Detroit Police Department (1)	June 12, 2003	March 2, 2016
Detroit Police Department (2)	July 18, 2003	December 23, 2006
Villa Rica Police Department	December 23, 2003	December 23, 2006
Prince George's County Police Department (1)	January 22, 2004	January 13, 2009
Cleveland Division of Police	February 11, 2004	March 15, 2005
Prince George's County Police Department (2)	March 11, 2004	March 12, 2007
Virgin Islands Police Department	March 23, 2009	
Easton Police Department	September 8, 2010	July 1, 2015
Orange County Sheriff's Office	September 16, 2010	April 4, 2013
Beacon Police Department	December 23, 2010	
Warren Police Department	January 26, 2012	
Seattle Police Department	September 21, 2012	
East Haven Police Department	December 21, 2012	
New Orleans Police Department	January 11, 2013	
Missoula Police Department	May 15, 2013	May 11, 2015

Agency	Agreement Date	Close Date
Puerto Rico Police Department	July 17, 2013	
Suffolk County Police Department	January 1, 2014	
University of Montana Police Department	June 10, 2014	July 10, 2015
Portland Police Department	August 29, 2014	
Albuquerque Police Department	November 14, 2014	
Los Angeles County Sheriff's Department (Antelope Valley)	April 29, 2015	
Cleveland Police Department	May 26, 2015	
Meridian Police Department	June 19, 2015	

Note: Departments with two settlements listed agreed to separate consent decrees, with generally one governing the entire police force and another governing another specific area like jail conditions.

Appendix C

Change in Property Crime Rates in Targeted Jurisdictions Relative to National Average, 1994–2014*

Jurisdiction	Change in Property Crime Rates During Intervention (%)	National Chance in Property Crime Rates (%)	Difference (%)
Pittsburgh	+5.18	−22.90	+28.80
Steubenville	+4.52	−22.90	+27.43
Washington, DC	−19.77	−20.98	+1.21
Los Angeles	−37.24	−24.53	−12.71
Cincinnati	−12.15	−10.43	−1.72
Columbus	−10.04	−3.94	−6.10
Buffalo	+3.71	−12.12	+15.83
Detroit	−28.81	−28.49	−0.32
Villa Rica	−25.69	−7.82	−17.86
Prince George's County	−33.93	−15.31	−18.62
Cleveland	+12.23	−4.45	+16.68
Easton	−18.43	−14.64	−3.79
Beacon	−18.20	−14.64	−3.56
Warren	−21.16	−10.65	−10.52
Seattle	+19.15	−10.65	+29.79
East Haven	−13.48	−10.65	−2.84
Missoula	−8.25	−9.20	+0.95
New Orleans	+12.18	−9.20	+21.38
Portland	+7.61	−4.93	+12.53
Albuquerque	−0.44	−4.93	+4.49
Puerto Rico	−8.77	−9.20	+0.43
Average Change in Property Crime Rates			**3.88**

Note: This table does not include data for Mount Prospect, Highland Park, or the Virgin Islands. These agencies did not report crime data to the FBI during these time periods. Steubenville did not report data during the year immediately before federal intervention. In its place, I substituted the next available year. Additionally, this table does not include crime data from the Orange County Sheriff's Department in Florida, because it is not considered the primary law enforcement agency for most of that county's residents. Finally, although the New Jersey State Police underwent federal intervention in the past, this table does not include crime data for the entire state of New Jersey, as the state police are not the primary law enforcement unit for New Jersey residents.

* This table calculates the change in property crime rates by measuring the difference in crime rates in the year before federal intervention to the property crime rates in the year when federal intervention ended. For completed cases, this includes the entire period of federal intervention. For ongoing cases, I used the most recently available crime data from 2014.

Appendix D

Change in Violent Crime Rates in Targeted Jurisdictions Relative to National Average, 1994–2014*

Jurisdiction	Change in Violent Crime Rates During Intervention (%)	National Change in Violent Crime Rates During Same Time (%)	Difference (%)
Pittsburgh	+27.21	−26.33	+53.54
Steubenville	−52.11	−7.04	−45.07
Washington, DC	−21.85	−23.61	+1.76
Los Angeles	−68.67	−27.36	−41.31
Cincinnati	−10.40	−6.48	−3.92
Columbus	−9.33	−8.19	−1.14
Buffalo	+8.67	−9.10	+17.77
Detroit	−4.06	−26.07	+22.01
Villa Rica	−50.63	−3.05	−47.57
Prince George's County	−23.16	−9.23	−13.94
Cleveland	+5.83	−1.43	+7.25
Easton	−43.23	−17.46	−25.77
Beacon	−41.02	−15.37	−25.64
Warren	−28.13	−5.58	−22.55
Seattle	+1.75	−5.58	+7.33
East Haven	+38.46	−5.58	+44.04
Missoula	−2.33	−5.53	+3.20
New Orleans	+19.47	−5.53	+25.00
Portland	−2.07	−0.65	−1.42
Albuquerque	+13.92	−0.65	+14.58
Puerto Rico	−13.73	−5.53	−8.20
Average Change in Violent Crime Rates			**−1.91**

Note: This table does not include data for Steubenville, Mount Prospect, Highland Park, or the Virgin Islands. These agencies did not report crime data to the FBI during these time periods. Steubenville did not report data during the year immediately before federal intervention. In its place, I substituted the next available year. Additionally, this table does not include crime data from the Orange County Sheriff's Department in Florida, because it is not considered the primary law enforcement agency for most of that county's residents. Finally, although the New Jersey State Police underwent federal intervention in the past, this table does not include crime data for the entire state of New Jersey, as the state police are not the primary law enforcement unit for New Jersey residents.

* This table calculates the change in violent crime rates by measuring the difference in crime rates in the year before federal intervention to the violent crime rates in the year when federal intervention ended. For completed cases, this includes the entire period of federal intervention. For ongoing cases, I used the most recently available crime data from 2014.

INDEX